Sport Sociology

Second edition

Active Learning in Sport – titles in the series

Critical Thinking for Sports Students	ISBN 978 1 84445 457 0
Coaching Science	ISBN 978 1 84445 165 4
Personal Training	ISBN 978 1 84445 163 0
Research Methods in Sport	ISBN 978 1 84445 261 3
Sport and Exercise Science	ISBN 978 1 84445 187 6
Sport in the UK	ISBN 978 1 84445 383 2
Sport Management	ISBN 978 1 84445 263 7
Sport Sociology (2nd edition)	ISBN 978 1 84445 464 8
Sport Studies	ISBN 978 1 84445 186 9

To order, please contact our distributor: BEBC Distribution, Albion Close, Parkstone, Poole, BH12 3LL. Telephone: 0845 230 9000, email: **learningmatters@bebc.co.uk**. You can find more information on each of these titles and our other learning resources at **www.learningmatters.co.uk**.

Sport Sociology

Second edition

Edited by
Peter Craig and Paul Beedie

LearningMatters

First published in 2008 by Learning Matters Ltd
Reprinted in 2008
Second edition published in 2010

British Library Cataloguing in Publication Data
A CIP record for this book is available from the British Library
ISBN: 978 1 84445 464 8
This book is also available in the following ebook formats:
Adobe ebook   ISBN: 978 1 84445 727 4
EPUB ebook   ISBN: 978 1 84445 726 7
Kindle ebook   ISBN: 978 0 85725 004 9
The right of Peter Craig, Paul Beedie, Gordon Mellor, Ping Wu and Amanda Jones
to be identified as the authors of this Work has been asserted by them in
accordance with the Copyright, Designs and Patents Act 1988.
Cover design by Toucan Design
Text design by Toucan Design
Project Management by Swales & Willis Ltd
Typeset by Kelly Winter
Printed and bound in Great Britain by TJ International Ltd, Padstow, Cornwall
Learning Matters Ltd
33 Southernhay East
Exeter EX1 1NX
Tel: 01392 215560
Email: info@learningmatters.co.uk
www.learningmatters.co.uk

FSC
Mixed Sources
Product group from well-managed
forests and other controlled sources
Cert no. SGS-COC-2482
www.fsc.org
© 1996 Forest Stewardship Council

Contents

Part One

On your marks: understanding sport and modern society

Chapter 1
An introduction to sport sociology

Peter Craig

Our passion

There are few nations where sport is such an important part of the national culture as it is in the UK. Sport unites us. In offices and factories, shops and homes, Monday morning conversation invariably revolves around the great sporting contests of the weekend. Whether it's the one-on-one drama of Wimbledon fortnight or the mass participation of the London Marathon, title races in national team games – football, rugby or cricket – or the bravery of individuals in world-title boxing bouts, all are analysed, argued over and admired . . . we are a nation of players as well as supporters. Around 20 million people – half of all the adults in the UK – take part in sporting activities each week. A total of 420,000 people are also employed directly or indirectly in sport. And, in London alone, sport generates £4.7 billion each year.

(www.london2012.com)

Introduction

When the British government announced support for a bid to host the 2012 Olympic Games, its rationale for doing so drew on a number of complex social, cultural, economic and political considerations. When some time later the announcement of the winning bid was screened live on television, millions around the world watched and those in the UK waited in nervous expectation. Whatever the political motivations behind the decision to support the bid, when the name London was read out as the winner, the nation collectively rejoiced and celebrated. In those few moments of euphoria it was clear to all that sport matters and that while we might not always agree about it, its national and international importance means that it is much 'more than a game'.

The hosting of sports events that have a global importance such as the Olympics or the football World Cup is now widely expected to bring significant benefits. The named city, and by implication the host country, enjoy an enhanced international profile. The global media coverage of the Olympics provides an unparalleled opportunity for the host city (and country) to showcase its culture to the rest of the world. The economy is boosted by tourism and other business opportunities, and there are real opportunities to address home-grown economic and social necessities, such as urban regeneration.

Possibly even more significantly, the emphasis that the London 2012 Organising Committee of the Olympic Games (LOCOG) and the Government (DCMS, 2008a) are placing on the 'legacy' of the Games evidences a commitment that the 2012 Games should bring a series of social and cultural benefits that will extend way beyond the actual period of the Games, a process also recently repeated by Rio de Janeiro in its winning bid for the 2016 Games. The Games and the process of preparing athletes and facilities provide a fertile arena for the development of disabled sport and sports programmes designed to promote social cohesion and integration (DCMS, 2008a). Schools can develop project work based on Olympic issues. Moreover, the enhanced profile that sport enjoys can be utilised to address key lifestyle issues such as diet and regular exercise, and thereby contribute to national agendas of health and wellbeing (Coe, 2009).

But the importance of the Olympics or the World Cup or sport more generally reaches out far beyond the boundaries of any nation and far beyond the timeframe of any specific sporting event. Sport today is one of the most important points of global interconnection – between nations and their governments, national and international sports organisations, for example, the British Olympic Committee, the International Olympic Committee, the Football Association, Fédération Internationale de Football Association (FIFA), and between the billions of people from around the world who love to play and watch sport.

Consider the following statements:

We see it as our mission to contribute towards building a better future for the world by using the power and popularity of football. This mission gives meaning and direction to each and every activity that FIFA is involved in – football being an integrated part of our society.

(www.fifa.com/aboutfifa/federation/mission.html)

A Games for the youth of the world
London 2012 Organising Committee for the Olympic Games and Paralympic Games Chair Sebastian Coe has confirmed its vision 'to stage inspirational Games that capture the imagination of young people around the world and leave a lasting legacy'.

(www.london2012.com/en/ourvision/)

If the claims and commitments made in these statements are serious and acted on, then sport really does matter, socially, economically and culturally. Once we realise this, it is also clear that there is a need to develop an informed and critical understanding of sport and its connections to these complex processes and claims. This is the task of sport sociology and it requires us to enter into a series of debates about the interconnections between sport, modern society and how that society is itself changing in quite radical ways. Sport may be a commonplace part of our lives and our social world, but its everyday familiarity begs a number of questions with regard to the part played by sport in the production and reproduction of our modern world, and how that world is itself being transformed.

In order to develop these sorts of insights we need to examine the importance of the institutional structures that characterise all modern societies and explore how sport is linked to them. How we socially experience and understand sport is not a simple process and can be based on complex interplay between the objective, biographical and subjective dimensions of everyday life (Sugden and Tomlinson, 2002; Giulianotti, 2004; Jarvie, 2006). Our understanding of sport, sports organisations and sporting behaviour therefore needs to move beyond a reliance on our everyday experiences of doing it, reading about it or watching it.

One requirement needed for this to happen is the development of an understanding of how sport has been influenced and patterned by social structures and processes that may at first glance be seen to have relatively little to do with sport. While we might not always be aware of them, our experience of sport – whether it be as an active participant, spectator, administrator, fan or just a casual armchair viewer – is nonetheless fundamentally interconnected to the social structures of our modern society. These structures act in ways that both enable and constrain, disadvantage and advantage, people in sport. The world we live in is subject to powerful and sometimes disturbing processes of change. The task before us is therefore to create an understanding of how sport has been structured by modernity and also to look critically at these processes of change and what they might mean for the future of sport.

As you will discover, the immense significance of sport within today's world has produced a wide-ranging, diverse and at times challenging body of sociological research and analysis. In undertaking this journey into this exciting and challenging field, you should have a clear sense of where we intend to go and why we want to take you there.

Aims

The aims of this book are fourfold:

1   Through a detailed analysis of sporting examples, to develop your awareness and critical understanding of the complex and dynamic interrelationship between sport and society.
    As a demonstration of this the Olympic Games will be used as a recurrent sporting theme as it is both a high-profile reference point and a contemporary area of significant importance for the UK.
2   To develop a sociological analysis of sport that demonstrates that sport is much more than a game.
    Sport today has a significant role in shaping how a society operates. The values that most of us would see as characterising sport are not merely a reflection of the world of sport; they are also the same ones that influence the structure of society more generally. Thus, sport and society have a symbiotic relationship that can bring benefits and detriments to both.
3   To engage you with a critical introduction to a series of sociological themes and issues that are fundamental to an understanding of the social and cultural construction of sport.
    These are:
    - *the institutional and organisational structure of modern society;*
    - *the interconnections between the social and cultural structure of society and the everyday actions and intentions of people;*
    - *the importance of power relations connected to these structures and how they act in ways that both enable and constrain, and provide opportunities for some and disadvantages for others;*
    - *the importance of the media and consumerism;*
    - *the importance of globalisation and the processes of social and cultural change that it brings.*

4 To develop your critical understanding of the various sociological theories and concepts that have been applied to sport.

While we will always attempt to develop your understanding of these sociological concepts and theories through grounded sporting examples, your critical assessment will not be successful unless you actively spend time reading some of the recommended additional texts and, through discussion with your tutors and peers, think about and apply these concepts and theories for yourself.

Structure

To help organise your introduction to the sociology of sport the book has four sections.

Part 1 *On your marks:* understanding sport and modern society

Chapter 1 An introduction to sport sociology

Chapter 2 Sport and modernity: an introduction to the sociology of sport
In this chapter we will examine the structure of modern society and its impact on the formation of modern sport. The chapter also introduces you to the ways in which sociology seeks to analyse and understand sport in the context of a world that is undergoing rapid change.

Chapter 3 Sport, modernity and the Olympics: a case study of the London Olympiads
In this chapter we will ground some of the major sociological themes identified in the preceding chapter by exploring an extended case study of the London Olympiads.

Chapter 4 Introduction to sociological theories of sport in modern society
This chapter will provide a brief overview of the major sociological theories and concepts that will be explored at greater length and detail in the subsequent chapters of the book.

Part 2 *Getting set:* key debates in the sociological analysis of modern sport

Chapter 5 Sport's organisation and governance
This chapter provides an examination of the organisational structure of modern sport and the influence of the processes of rationalisation and bureaucratic control on the experience and structure of modern sport.

Chapter 6 Sport, physical education and socialisation
In this chapter we introduce structuralist and functionalist theories of sport, and explore how sport and physical education are connected to the processes of socialisation.

Chapter 7 Class and gender differentiation in sport
Here we continue to explore how social and economic structures impact sport. Through the application of Marxist sociological theory we examine how capitalism underpins some of the most influential structures of power and control within sport. The specific issue that this will lead us into examining is social class. From this the chapter then turns to explore how gender and sport interact to produce complex patterns of social differentiation.

Chapter 8 Sport and diversity: issues of race, ethnicity and disability
This chapter extends some of the sociological themes of power and control established in the previous chapter by exploring how culture and cultural practices are connected to the experience of race, ethnicity and disability in sport.

Part 3 *Go:* analysing contemporary issues and themes – the changing world of sport

Chapter 9 Sport and consumer society
Sport today has moved far beyond its modest recreational and amateur beginnings: it has become big business. This chapter explores the major elements of this transformation and how sport is now intimately connected to the complex benefits and problems of consumer culture.

Chapter 10 Sport and the media
In our contemporary world sport and the media have become completely intertwined. In this chapter we examine this relationship and identify how sport, the media and popular culture influence each other, and what this might mean for the future of sport.

Chapter 11 Sport in a global world
In this chapter we turn our attention to how the processes of globalisation are transforming the modern world and examine how sport and, more specifically, global sports events such as the Olympics and the World Cup are linked to these processes.

Part 4 *New games:* emergent and transformative forms of sport?

Chapter 12 Sport and the body
Our society today evidences a whole range of concerns around the body. Whether it be in terms of health and wellbeing or as a way of representing our sense of identity, the body has never had a more prominent place in our society. In this chapter we examine how the body is socially and culturally constructed and the role that sport plays in establishing dominant images of the body.

Chapter 13 Sport and adventure
The age we live in has become heavily influenced by concepts of risk. Many young people are now seeking new ways of expressing themselves in sport through their development of new and sometimes quite radical sporting activities. In recognising both these trends this chapter examines the link between sport, risk and adventure.

Chapter 14 Sport and community
There are two aims to this chapter. First, it introduces a number of concepts and theories to help explain the relationship between sport and community. Second, it provides a context for exploring further many of the themes raised elsewhere in the book. In the process, we focus on aspects of government policy and, in particular, return to the question of the aims and intended legacy of the 2012 Olympics.

Our world and the world of sport is a dynamic and changing one full of potential successes and problems. We hope that this text will stimulate you to develop your sociological imagination in ways that will help you understand more deeply these interconnected worlds and the potential that sport has to be a positive influence within them.

The second edition

In preparing a second edition, we have developed the text in a number of ways. In particular, we have provided *a new chapter* (Chapter 14) on sport and community. We have also provided a *new feature* – 'Research focus' – designed to highlight key research contributions. In each one we focus on a specific text or researcher. We hope this feature will act as an invitation to readers to explore the field of sport sociology research directly for themselves. To facilitate this, we have provided *additional references* to the literature of the field.

We would like to thank the peer reviewers and the many users (both lecturers and students) whose constructive feedback has guided us in the preparation of this new edition.

Research Focus

Sport worlds: a sociological perspective

As the sub-discipline of sport sociology has grown over the past three decades, numerous texts have been published to provide students with an introduction to this exciting field of enquiry. Our text reflects one of the most recent and contemporary contributions. Although its roots can be traced back to the 1960s, it was the 1980s that saw the publication of a number of texts that were to firmly establish the field. Within British sport sociology one of the most influential texts was *Sport, Power and Culture* by John Hargreaves (1986b). This book's influence was that it introduced a number of vital debates about power and culture and how these have shaped access to, and the experience of, sport. By the 1990s the field had become so well established and diverse that a number of texts were increasingly being published with the aim of providing an introduction to the field as well as detailed commentaries on the complex theoretical and conceptual debates that had and were continuing to emerge.

One of the most important British sport sociology texts to be published during this time was by Jarvie and Maguire (1994). As they correctly recognised, sport sociology had become deeply fragmented on theoretical and conceptual lines. Among others the impact of a feminist analysis of sport had opened up a number of pivotal debates that are still vital to sport sociology. The strength of their contribution was its attempt to transcend these divisions. Although extensive use was made of texts such as this, for many undergraduate students who were encountering the discipline for the first time, these substantive but also rather dense explorations of theory could create a disengagement with the field rather than the hoped for engagement. Since that time the 'field' has moved on significantly and today the libraries of many universities, colleges and schools (through the A level PE) have a wide range of texts introducing students to sport sociology. This short commentary is merely a snapshot of this diverse literature: there is no claim that this brief overview of this field is comprehensive.

As evidenced by Jarvie and Maguire's (1994) text it is probably fair to suggest that initially British sport sociology resisted the production of generalised introductory texts because of concerns regarding the depth of sociological analysis. One outcome was that the introductory level texts being used were often written by American authors and focused on American sports and issues. There can be little doubt, if for no other reason than it is now in its 11th edition, that one of the most influential of these has been Jay Coakley's text *Sports in Society: Issues and Controversies*. Not surprisingly, for Coakley, the task was to introduce American students to sport sociology through a range of sociological research and debates developed though a discussion of contemporary sports examples. More recently, as the text has developed and matured (especially in its most recent co-authored version), this American perspective has been expanded to present *a 'global view of the sociology of sport'*.

Within British sport sociology, the last decade has seen a number of significant contributions. Given their established importance within this field it is probably again not surprising that Grant Jarvie and Joe Maguire have continued to have a significant and valuable presence. In the multi-authored text *Sport Worlds: A sociological perspective* (Maguire, Jarvie, Mansfield and Bradley, 2002), the aim is to demonstrate how sport is an endemic and immensely important part of modern life. From a sociological perspective their intention is to demonstrate how sport sociology critically examines *the role, function and meaning of sport in the lives of people and the societies they form* (pxviii). Of particular significance is their exploration of how sport sociologists have detailed how sport's norms and values are inherently allied to the exercise of power, processes of socialisation and the complex ways this creates, *possibilities, for people's involvement and success in sport as performers, officials, spectators, workers or consumers* (Maguire et al. 2002, pxviii).

Jarvie's (2006) recent entry into the field, *Sport, Culture and Society: an introduction*, has further extended this exploration by critically considering how sport, sometimes in rather naïve and idealistic ways, is socially, culturally and politically connected to the building of society, culture and communities.

Further Reading

British introductory texts

Jones and Armour (2000) *Sociology of Sport: Theory and Practice*. Harlow: Longman.

Jarvie, G (2006) *Sport, Culture and Society: An Introduction*. London: Routledge.

American introductory texts

Yiannakis, A and Melnick, M (2001) (eds) *Contemporary Issues in the Sociology of Sport*. Champaign IL: Human Kinetics.

Nixon, H and Frey, J (1996) *A Sociology of Sport*. Belmont: Wadsworth Pub. Co.

Coakley, J (2006) *Sports in Society: Issues and Controversies*. Boston, London: McGraw-Hill.

Readers

Coakley, J and Dunning, E (2000) (eds) *Handbook of Sports Studies*. London: Sage.

Tomlinson, A (2007) *The Sport Studies Reader*. London, New York: Routledge.

Maguire, J and Young, K (2002) (eds) *Theory, Sport and Society*. Vol 1, London: JAI Press.

Sport sociology – advanced/critical perspectives:

Sugden, J and Tomlinson, A (2002) (eds) *Power Games: A Critical Sociology of Sport*. London: Routledge.

Giulianotti, R (2004) (ed) *Sport and Modern Social Theorists*. Basingstoke: Palgrave.

Giulianotti, R (2005) *Sport: A Critical Sociology*. Cambridge: Polity Press.

Chapter 2
Sport and modernity: an introduction to the sociology of sport

Peter Craig

Minds are of three kinds: one is capable of thinking for itself; another is able to understand the thinking of others; and a third can neither think for itself nor understand the thinkings of others. The first is of the highest excellence, the second is excellent, and the third is worthless.

(*Niccolò Machiavelli*, The Prince)

This chapter provides you with an introduction to the ways in which sociology seeks to analyse and understand sport in the context of a world that is undergoing rapid change. To achieve this, the discussion that follows is designed to:

- introduce you to sociology and explain how it can play an important role in the understanding of sport in contemporary British society;
- encourage your development of a 'sociological imagination';
- introduce you to a number of sociological concepts that will aid your understanding of the social processes that have had a pivotal role in the formation of modern British society;
- develop your understanding of how these processes have deeply influenced the character of modern sport.

Learning Objectives

On completing this chapter you should be able to:

- give sociological explanations of the following terms: society; social reproduction; modernity; division of labour; bureaucracy;
- identify and explain the primary institutional characteristics of modernity;
- explain with clear and appropriate sport examples why sport must be understood as the product of modern society;
- describe and give a brief explanation of the five characteristics of modern sport identified in the discussion of Guttmann's (1978) analysis of modern sport;
- explain how the Olympic Movement and Olympism provide good examples of these five characteristics.

Introduction

Almost everybody reading this book will have an active working knowledge of sport. Indeed, in our increasingly globalised world, it can be fairly convincingly argued that sport is one of the common elements of people's lives across the globe. In whatever country we might choose to look at, people are born into a world where a wide variety of sports that are played competitively or recreationally within the nations of the world are well-known and understood. It doesn't matter if you live in London, New York, Madrid, Beijing or Jakarta: if we want to play a game of football or badminton, people don't have to think too hard about it – they know what to do, where to go and how to play. What's also clear is that success in sport, particularly in global sports events such the Olympic Games, brings with it a high status and, more often than not, financial rewards.

In common with our other everyday routines and behaviours, on the surface sport seems relatively simple. However, once we take a closer look, we begin to see that it is actually very complex. So, if you sit and think for a moment about sport you can quickly begin to understand why sociologists have over the last few decades started to take a very keen and active interest in 'sport'.

Reflection Point 2.1

Here are some issues and questions that might help you think about this.

1. To an important extent all sports are defined by their rules and fields of play, but can you explain why they developed as they did?
2. Do sports have an important social purpose or are they just simple, relatively unimportant recreational activities?
3. Other than the basic biological and sexual differences between men and women, can you explain why your gender has such an important impact on your experience of sport?
4. All sports are controlled by a complex structure of national and international governing bodies, but other organisations such as the media and large transnational sport companies (such as Nike) also have a huge influence. What are the roles of these different organisations, and who has the most power to affect the way we play and how we think about sport?

Learning Activity 2.1

Thinking about sport in everyday life

As one of Britain's most important sociologists Anthony Giddens (2001, p2) has observed, the ability to develop a sociological understanding of the world around us requires us to *'think ourselves away' from the familiar routines of our daily lives in order to look at them anew.* So if we adopt a sociological perspective, what might we begin to observe if we consider the mundane act of wearing sports clothes and shoes?

The first thing we might observe is that many people now wear sport shoes when they are not playing sport. Indeed, if you go into any of the big sports retailers and ask them about who they sell sport shoes (and a vast array of other sportswear) to, they will quickly tell you that between 70 per cent and 80 per cent of the shoes they sell are primarily being bought as fashion items. Sportswear therefore possesses a symbolic value. Brand names and looks are often seen as far more important than the functional purpose of the clothes or the shoes. For some people, brands reflect their choices about lifestyle and a sense of individuality. To be an effective consumer requires us to spend a significant amount of time developing knowledge and understanding of products, styles and brands.

The second thing we might notice is that an individual's choice of sportswear often indicates membership of different social groups. In recent years there has been a very significant trend for people to wear replica team kits to demonstrate their allegiance to a particular sports team, even though they may not live anywhere near where the team plays. The most obvious example of this is the wearing of the team strips of premiership football teams, but there is also evidence from other sports, such as basketball, which do not have such a direct and powerful presence in the sporting life of the country. Others find that the wearing of the national team strip (while football is again probably the best illustration, other sports such as rugby and cricket also provide significant examples) provides one of the few opportunities for them to express a common bond with, and allegiance to, the other members of their nation. In an evermore globalised world, sport provides one of the few opportunities for people to celebrate having a distinctive national identity. This is particularly true if their national team is playing in a major championship.

The third thing we might observe is that the ability to wear sports clothes and shoes only happens because of a complex chain of economic and social relationships. Most of the sports clothes and shoes that we wear are not produced in this country; they are produced in countries where the price of labour is cheaper and often exploitative. While we might consider the conditions of work in these factories to be problematic, the workers themselves rely on these wages and the countries benefit by having access to international trade. Designs and brands are controlled by hugely influential transnational business corporations such as Nike, Adidas and Reebok. Sports clothes and shoes are transported from these countries by

●●● ▶

Learning Activity 2.1 continued

large shipping firms. They are sold to us by chains of retailers from supermarkets to sports stores and Internet sources. In order to buy them we need money. For most of us, access to money or credit is dependent on our being involved in paid employment and having bank accounts.

A fourth observation might be that, as we travel around the world on holidays or for work, many people seem to be adopting similar habits and patterns of consumption relating to sportswear. Around the world, young people in particular are beginning to dress alike and sportswear is one of the most common elements of this. If this trend is as powerful as some suggest, we are then faced with two questions. Are cultural traditions around the world beginning to merge into one globalised consumer culture? What role does sport play in these processes?

None of these reflections have touched upon sport in the way that most people tend to think about it or experience it – as a fairly simple, enjoyable and exciting physical and competitive set of activities. What it does show is that sport is deeply connected to the world that we live in and to the processes of change that are impacting and transforming that world.

- Go into a large sports store and walk around, taking note of how the store sells its sports clothes and shoes. Talk to some of the staff about the technical benefits of one shoe over another and see if they have the knowledge to help a dedicated sports person make a well-informed choice.
- Think about how you wear sports clothes. Do you recognise any of the above observations as providing an explanation for your behaviour? Are there other explanations that you think should be included in these reflections?

Understanding the social and cultural production of sport

Definition: culture
Sociologists use the term 'culture' to refer to the patterns of human activity and their symbolic meaning that can be seen to characterise a specific society or group within that society.

Reflection Point 2.2

If we look at contemporary British 'culture' we will probably quickly conclude that sport is an important part of the culture. In other words, it is something that many people in the society share and value. In addition, we would also probably conclude that the most 'important' sport within British culture is football. We would 'know' this from the evidence that on a daily basis there is a significant amount of 'cultural' activity all focused on football in terms of the amount of people who play it, watch it, read about it and talk about it. However, within British society not everybody would see football as 'their' game. It could be argued from looking at their 'cultural' activities and habits, that people from a middle-class background seem to prefer rugby over football, or that more women play netball than football. Equally, if you went to the USA and were talking about 'football', most people would assume you were talking about American football rather than soccer. From this we can conclude that different cultures produce different ways of understanding, or evaluating, human activities such as sport.

As your reflections on the above issues and questions plus the learning activity should have made clear, the ways in which a society is organised and structured have a profound impact on sport. Moreover, as you should now also recognise, none of the processes and structures impacting on the social and cultural production of sport are simple and unchanging. Indeed, as your own experience of life probably demonstrates, these processes and structures are becoming ever more complex and problematic. We all now live in a world that is 'information rich' (especially through the huge flow of information brought about by the Internet), but our ability to make sense of this information is often very limited. Yet, making sense of the changing, often exciting and inspiring, but also sometimes troubling and problematic world of sport is exactly the task that lies before us. An understanding of how these processes, structures and changes are socially produced is the major concern of sociology. It is also probably worth recognising at this stage that the journey into a sociological understanding of sport this book will take you on may provide some personal but very worthwhile challenges. As Giddens (1989, p17) states:

Sociological findings both disturb and contribute to our common-sense beliefs about ourselves and others . . . sociological findings do not always contradict common-sense views. Common-sense ideas often provide sources of insight about social behaviour. What needs emphasizing, however, is that the sociologist must be prepared to ask about any of our beliefs about ourselves – no matter how cherished.

As these observations suggest, sociology cannot be just a routine process of acquiring knowledge. Many sociologists therefore stress that the development of the ability to think sociologically requires the development and cultivation of powers of the imagination.

Reflection Point 2.3

The idea of the sociological imagination was first developed by the sociologist C Wright Mills (1970). As we noted in the above learning activity, the development of a sociological imagination requires you to place yourself outside the familiar and commonplace routines and practices that you normally do in sport and to look at them with a new, more inquiring and questioning mind. As we have noted already, this might well be a rather disturbing process and require you to regard cherished beliefs with a more critical attitude.

Sociology: some key terms

Sociology, like all of the sciences, has developed its own very specific range of theories and concepts. It is therefore very important that you begin to engage with these ideas and develop a familiarity with them.

Definition: sociology
Sociology is the study of human social life, groups and societies. It is a dazzling and compelling enterprise, having as its subject matter our own behaviour as social beings.

(Giddens, 2001, p2)

As we can see from this definition, the concept of society is fundamental to sociology.

Definition: society
A society is a system of structured social relationships connecting people together according to a shared culture.

(Giddens, 2001, p669)

While the societies that people live within are very real, it should be clear from this quote that from a sociological perspective the term society needs to be regarded as an *abstract concept* in that what it is referring to is something that does not have a fixed or unchanging form.

Reflection Point 2.4

Although modern society has become globally familiar, you should remember that even today there are many different types of society. Societies and the types of sport that they played are not and have not always been the same. Although to a large degree these earlier forms of social organisation have disappeared their legacy can still be seen and experienced through our sporting traditions and beliefs. For instance, many of our ideas about sport in terms of fortitude, honour and fair play plus the exclusion of women from sporting activities can be traced to ideas about sport that first developed in ancient Greece.

As our initial discussion demonstrates, the language used by sociologists to describe and analyse 'society' often draws on words such as 'structure', 'impact', 'influence', and the way we use these words can convey a perception that societies are autonomous entities that somehow act on their own behalf. These terms can also create a perception that, because our lives are clearly structured by the social and cultural environment, this somehow means that this structure completely determines our behaviour. While this is a use of language that is relatively easy to fall into, it is nonetheless a mistake. An important starting point in thinking about sport is to recognise that though all sports are highly patterned and structured sets of activities, the outcome and the meaning generated by the sport may often be highly uncertain (and this is often one of its main attractions).

The rules, codes, regulation and fixed environments of sport mean that sport and our sporting behaviour have very consistent regularities. While our sporting activities have transformed, and continue to transform, the physical environment (e.g. through the creation of physical structures such as sport stadia), stating that sport has a recognisable social structure does not mean that sport has the same character as a physical structure, whose existence is independent of human actions. Sport does not exist other than through its active production and reproduction through people's everyday actions.

Reflection Point 2.5

In thinking about this complex process you should consider how sport as you experience it is created by a whole range of different people doing diverse and often intricate arrays of behaviour. Some examples are: learning the physical skills required by the sport; obeying rules; playing in organised sports leagues; supporting local and national teams; watching sport on TV and reading about it in our daily newspapers. Without our reproduction of this complex array of actions, sport as we know and understand it would cease to exist.

Sporting example

Cricket has a number of ritualised actions that most players unconsciously adhere to as they are an inherent and accepted part of 'playing the game'. Some of the most familiar of these are wearing cricket whites, walking to the crease and accepting the umpire's decisions without argument.

The same processes that we observe in the social and cultural production of sport are also true for our society. It is people who produce and reproduce society and sport in all its diverse forms, through their everyday routines and actions repeated in very consistent ways over significant periods of time. The structured social relationships, which we develop through these processes, are themselves powerful constituents of what we perceive as the commonplace realities of social life. However, it is important to stress that no matter how enduring this reality might seem at a particular time and in a particular place, this reality is socially and culturally constructed (Berger and Luckmann, 1966).

Definition: social reproduction
Social reproduction refers to the concept that over time social groups, such as those constructed around social class and gender, act in ways that help reproduce the social and cultural structures that characterise the specific society.

Although we have only sketched out some of these important sociological ideas, they should help you identify two important starting points. On the one hand, it is important to recognise that people are 'born into' a society and, as they grow and learn to be a member of that society, the social structures and the cultural norms of the society have significant influence on the way people live and interact. Clearly, sport is one of these social structures. On the other hand, people do not merely play sport because they have been socialised into doing so. However powerful and influential the social structure might appear to be, people engaged in sport are conscious and reflexive individuals who can and do make choices about the sports they take part in and they can attach quite different meanings to their sporting experiences.

Although it might seem a rather daunting prospect, it should now be evident to you that our journey into the sociological analysis of sport requires you to develop a critical understanding of a fairly extensive body of sociological theories and concepts. The aim is to engage you with these theories and concepts in ways that permit you to examine and analyse the relationship between the power of social structures to pattern how we behave and ways that people act as conscious agents purposefully directing the course of their lives.

There are some important points you need to remember from this opening discussion.

- Within any society there are recognisable regularities and patterns in how people behave. Sport is an excellent example of this.
- It is these regularities to which the concept of social structure refers. The term social institution is often used to denote these specific structural regularities. In this sense, sport can be termed a social institution (other typical social institutions are family, industry, government, the military establishment, the church, etc.).
- What we perceive to be the relatively fixed and enduring reality of sport (and society) is, in fact, a social and cultural construction.
- Significant development or transformation of any of the underlying social conditions, such as those caused by new technologies (e.g. computer technology), can have a profound impact on the overall structure of the society.
- Individuals and groups may be born into a society with a well-established social structure that will be a significant influence on the way they live their lives, but they are nonetheless conscious and reflexive agents who can, and often do, have a dramatic effect on the way the social structure operates.

Sport and the formation and structure of 'modern society'

The way in which sport has come to be organised and structured is fundamentally a product of the modern world. When sociologists use the term 'modern' they are using it to denote a specific conceptualisation of our contemporary social world and not the more common everyday usage meaning 'most recent' or 'up to date'. To understand modern sport, we must therefore start with an understanding of the nature of modern society and how its specific social structure has helped form sport as we recognise it today. In a general sense, one of the major tasks undertaken by sociology has been to identify and explain the character and development of modern society. One of the most important concepts that you need to become familiar with, and which is often used interchangeably with the term modern society, is *modernity*.

Definition: modernity

. . . the institutions and modes of behaviour established first of all in post-feudal Europe, but which in the twentieth century increasingly have become world-historical in their impact. Modernity can be understood as roughly equivalent to the 'industrialised world', so long as it be recognised that industrialism is not its only institutional dimension.

(Giddens, 1991, pp14–15)

A term designed to encapsulate the distinctiveness, complexity and dynamism of social processes unleashed during the eighteenth and nineteenth centuries, which mark a distinctive break from traditional ways of living.

(Bilton, Bonnett, Jones, Skinner, Stanworth and Webster, 1996, p18)

As an outcome of these social processes, a widespread belief grew up that the process of modernisation reflected a powerful and dramatic break with the past. One of the most important tenets of this new era, that was to have a powerful impact on the development of sport, was a commitment to the idea that rational control and organisation would create a world where humans could begin to actively control, direct and improve the conditions of human existence (Bilton et al., 1996, p18). Linked to this perspective Giddens (1990) argues that modernity has four defining institutional formations that have had a fundamental impact on all aspects of life within modernity:

- industrialisation;
- capitalism;
- state control of everyday life;
- military power and the institutionalised control of violence.

From a sociological perspective, industrialisation refers to the process whereby complex systems of organised production have been developed. As this system increased in scale and sophistication (especially through its application of science and technology), it transformed our physical and social environment. Work for the vast majority became dominated by the regularities of the working week and the highly rationalised and controlled conditions of industrial labour. Although many experienced this work as depersonalising, alienating and exploitative, the mass production it created of a whole new array of affordable goods brought opportunities of increased standards of living and the possibility of new and exciting lifestyles based on consumption.

Definition: mass consumption

Mass consumption refers to the process whereby the consumption of a vast array of manufactured products and services becomes an accepted, expected and necessary part of everyday life for the majority of the population. Some common examples relating to the consumption of sport are equipment and clothing, programmes on television, DVDs and sports services (e.g. coaching, physiotherapy).

The issue of consumer culture is now a major theme within the sociology of sport and we will examine this in Chapter 9.

Capitalism is an economic system in which most of the ownership of capital wealth is privately owned and invested by those who own it to create profit. To work effectively, capitalism requires relatively free product and labour markets. For some social theorists such as Karl Marx, capitalism is the primary source of the economic inequalities and class divisions that dominate many aspects of modern life. Understood in this way capitalism is much more than just an economic system – it is actually the defining characteristic of the whole social system. The influence of capitalism on the formation of modern sport has been a major theme of a number of influential sport sociologists such as John Hargreaves. We will examine this work and its analysis of the economic, social and cultural divisions created by capitalism in Chapter 7.

Particularly through the course of the twentieth century, the power and scope of the state to control the conditions of everyday life was established at an unprecedented level. Today, a taken-for-granted fact of modern life is that we live in a nation-state that has an elected system of government that operates at both national and local levels, a judiciary and police force, armed forces, a health service, a system of education – and a collection of semi-official bodies such as UK Sport and Sport England that can assert a great deal of influence on sports policy. In Chapter 5 we will examine this issue in more depth as we consider the complex structure of sports governance and administration.

One of the most visible manifestations of the power of the modern state is its institutionalised control of violence. As is all too evident in our world today governments have the power to send significant numbers of its citizens to fight wars against other nations. On occasion, it will also grant its police force the right to use extreme forms of violence to protect its citizens. However, for the most part citizens are themselves prohibited from using violence and we often assess governments on how well they maintain a very low level of violence within our everyday world.

Sport provides a number of very interesting issues in respect to this. There are a number of sports where people can be actively aggressive and violent, albeit under highly controlled circumstances – boxing and rugby are two good examples. Equally, where violent conduct by those involved in sport, either as players or as fans, impacts the general public (football hooliganism is probably the best-known example), the government is very quick to step in and create legislation, systems of surveillance and punishment that are designed to re-establish the social order. Although we will not be looking at violence in sport as a specific theme, we will return to this issue in a number of chapters, most notably in Chapter 12 when we will examine sport and the body.

Other related and important characteristics of life in modernity that have had a defining impact on sport are:

- **Urbanisation** This is the process through which the majority of people ceased to live in the countryside and moved into the towns and cities. Because of the availability of facilities, coaching and systems of transport, most sport is played in an urban context.
- **Science and technological innovation** Science and technology has had a dramatic impact on most aspects of modern life and sport is constantly being changed by them. Modern sports equipment is often a complex technology designed to help us perform our sports more effectively and safely.
- **Distinctive modern forms of social stratification** Although we have already identified the important issue of social class, there are other important forms of social stratification that can be seen to impact on sport. These are gender, race, ethnicity, disability and age.
- **An interconnected system of nation-states allied to the promotion of national identity** As we have already evidenced in the opening chapter and the discussion of the London Olympiads, sport, especially in terms of competitions between national teams, is an important contemporary cultural, political marker of (national) boundaries, identities and markets (Boyle and Haynes, 2000, p164).

Within most societies the success or failure of the national sports teams provide a constant source for debates about the current state of the society.

- **Globalisation** Although a number of influential sociologists, such as Anthony Giddens (1991), have convincingly argued that globalisation has always been an inherent element of modernity, the last two decades have seen a massive global expansion and integration of commercially organised sport (Coakley and Donnelly, 2004, p330).
- **Mass media** The development and spread of modern sport across significant parts of the world pre-dates the technological development of electronic mass media forms, such as radio and television. Nonetheless, once these media technologies became widespread, the connections between the mass media and sport became so deeply intertwined that, as Rowe argues (2004b, pp1–4), they are now in effect 'indistinguishable' from each other.
- **Consumer culture** Debates about consumer culture and its impact on society have over the last few decades moved from being a relatively minor sociological issue to one of its most pressing. Recently, the advent of serious concerns regarding climate change has promoted an even more heightened level of interest in the processes of mass production and mass consumption. As Horne (2006) has recently detailed, sport is now a very significant part of global economic

activity and for many people it is an important and integral component of their lifestyle and patterns of consumption.

While it can be argued that *sport was and is universal, part of all human societies of which we have some record . . .* (Blake, 1996, p43), as we have identified above, the development of modern sport cannot be separated from the broader processes of modernity. Because of its historical relationship to pagan religious festivals, violence as an element of public entertainment and amusement, social disorder and drunkenness, it is not surprising that the emergence of the modern era brought with it pressures to develop new, more civilised (Elias and Dunning, 1986), ordered and rationalised forms of social existence and organisation (Rojek, 2000). Holt's (1989) study of sport and the British evidences from the mid-Victorian period onwards that sport became an issue of political and moral concern. The social and cultural impact of British modernity on sport (Blake, 1996, p45) was not only important for the British, but through the impact of its global empire and its influence on organisations such as the International Olympic Committee, it was to influence sport profoundly throughout the modern world.

These brief comments have highlighted that modern societies and modern sport are not the outcome of a single evolutionary process, but the complex interaction of a number of different economic, political, social and cultural processes and national histories. While most people who are involved with sport are unlikely to think about it in this way, there is no doubt that modernity has a profound influence on the way we experience sport today.

Learning Activity 2.2

While we will be developing our sociological exploration of these issues in more depth in later chapters, now is a good time to start putting your sociological imagination to work. One of the assumptions made in the above discussion is that your sporting habits, how you perceive and understand sport and your aspirations have all in some way been shaped by the social processes we have been discussing.

Based on the above discussion of sport and modernity, together with your current knowledge and experience of sport, take 20 minutes to:

1. identify how the processes discussed above are evidenced in your own experience of how sport is played and organised;
2. identify any problems within sport that may be directly linked to any of these processes.

The organisational structure of modern sport

As you might now recognise, the *organisational* nature of modern society is one of the most crucial characteristics impacting on sport. Indeed, as Giddens (1991) forcefully argues, modernity is not just about the development of organisations; it is also about the process of organisation and its regularised control over human behaviour. Guttmann (1978) in his influential examination of sport's transformation into its modern forms identifies several characteristics of modernisation that are fundamental to the emergence and social organisation of modern sport. These are:

- – secularisation;
- – equality of opportunity (to compete and in the conditions of competition);
- – specialization of roles;
- – rationalization process;
- – bureaucratic organization;
- – quantification;
- – the quest for records.

(Guttmann, 1978, p16)

While all of these have had a significant impact on the nature of modern sport, it is the initial five that have a specific relevance to this chapter's examination of the impact that modernity has had on both the structure and character of modern society, and on modern sport more specifically.

Secularisation

Secularisation refers to an historical process through which religious ideas begin to lose their power and influence. Theorists such as Ernest Gellner (1974) have argued that secularisation does not suggest that religious beliefs are no longer important to a great number of people, but that for many they have been replaced by other forms of knowledge such as those produced by science. As Guttmann (1978) details, prior to modernity many sporting forms were embedded in religious or quasi-religious festivals and rituals (a good example of this is the ancient Olympics in Greece). For Guttmann (1978), the primary characteristics of modern sports are, as we shall discuss in more detail below, that they are rationalised, open to scientific and quantifiable evaluation and, most importantly of all, are pursued by individuals 'for their own sake' and not for any defining spiritual or mystical purposes.

While the process of secularisation has undoubtedly had a profound impact on modern society, and that this is reflected in sport is evident, there are a number of significant problems with an uncritical acceptance of this perspective. As numerous influential sociologists (Berger, 1973; Gellner, 1974, 1992; Bauman, 2001) have identified, religion retains for many a powerful defining reality. The process of secularisation has become increasingly contested as the utopian promises of rationalised modernity have failed to be delivered. Moreover, as sport sociologists such as Blake (1996) also point out, the modern history of sport in most countries shows clear connections to religion. For example, in England many of the Christian churches had an important role in the spread of team games (which they saw as an antidote to excessive drinking and gambling). Even up to the present day, in Ireland the Gaelic Athletic Association organises its clubs based on the parish boundaries of Catholic churches. Possibly even more interesting is the view that, for many, sport itself has become a form of religion (Jarvie, 2006). Sports stars are now worshipped, people pray for their teams and around the world sports stadia have become the new cathedrals of worship.

Equality of opportunity

For Guttmann, as sport became progressively modernised it created for many an increased level of opportunity to compete and take part in sport. As numerous histories of sport (Holt, 1989; Struna, 2000; Guttmann, 2000) demonstrate, in pre-modern times and in the early modern period, sport was often exclusive, with only members of certain social groups within the society having the right to take part. For instance, in Britain during the nineteenth century many amateur sports such as athletics and tennis had rules that were quite clearly designed to prevent members of the working classes applying for membership of clubs. Throughout the nineteenth century and up to the latter part of the twentieth century, women faced many restrictions on their ability to compete in sports. With regard to race, it was not until the latter part of the twentieth century that the last vestiges of racial inequality and segregation in sport were formally challenged through the introduction by the British government of laws prohibiting racial discrimination. As a result of these legal requirements, all sports organisations in the UK must have policies that are intended to address the problems of racial inequality and prejudice.

However, according to Guttmann's analysis, progressive modernisation has continued to erode these restrictions and inequalities. In support of this view, a brief trip to the International Olympic Committee (IOC) website (**www.olympic.org/uk/index_uk.asp**) will make abundantly clear that, in organisational terms at least, today the situation has clearly changed. In most sports and in most parts of the world, athletes from any background (whether this is based on nationality, race, social class, gender, sexuality or disability) are actively being encouraged to take part. That accepted, it is also abundantly clear that the ideals of the inclusivity and equity of sport remain for many just that, an ideal, rather than a reality. We shall return to some of the important sociological debates surrounding the inequalities that impact on sport in Chapters 7 and 8.

Specialisation of roles

Two hugely influential social theorists who were responsible for some of the most important analyses of the impact of modernity on the nature and structure of society were Karl Marx and Max Weber. Although there will be a more detailed overview of their work in the latter part of this chapter, it is important to note that one of the characteristics of modern society that both philosophers stress is how the complexity of modern society requires an ever increasing division of labour and specialisation of roles.

Definition: division of labour

A social process related to processes of rationalisation that leads to a progressive and inevitable specialisation of roles. This specialisation leads to boundaries between roles that can restrict the opportunities to move between roles.

Guttmann's (1978) analysis also details how, as sport modernised, it was inevitable that the processes that rationalised other parts of social life into ever increasing levels of role specialisation also began to deeply influence the organisational and playing characteristics of many modern sports. Although there still exist some sports that require an athlete to be multi-skilled across a number of distinct sporting disciplines (e.g. decathlon, octathlon, modern pentathlon, the all-rounder in cricket), for the most part sport has become dominated by a highly segmented range of roles whose names we all recognise. For instance, in football there are goalkeepers, right backs, centre backs, midfield players, strikers, coaches, managers, chairmen, fans, stewards, and so on.

Rationalisation process

Blake (1996, p77) stresses that it is the link between the processes of rationalisation and modernisation of sport that lies at the heart of Guttmann's argument, which claims that:

> *Modern societies have designed new sports, or redesigned existing ones, along rational lines, with both the rule-bound sports themselves and the preparation of them susceptible to rational organisation. Rationalisation is present at almost every level of sport . . . Training for sports is increasingly rationalised, seen as 'sports science', with sub-areas of diet, physiology and medicine and psychology, contributing to the preparation of both athlete and coach . . .*

This concept is closely associated with the work of Max Weber who suggested that rationalisation was a process where beliefs, social institutions (such as sport) and individual actors (players, officials, administrators) all become more logical, orderly, and to some degree predictable and controllable. While the complexity of the modern world, and high level sport specifically, is highly reliant on this process, it is equally evident that it is a process that is also often resisted. The downside of the process is that other aspects of life that many people hold very dear begin to receive less attention or are deemed to be unimportant. The sensual, creative, spiritual and traditional aspects of social life can all decline. As will be discussed in the next section, the significance of the process lies in how it has determined the organisational structure of modern sport.

However, how far the process of rationalisation actually determines our experience of sport is open to some debate. Indeed, there is ample evidence that for many the significance of sport in their lives stems not from the nature of its structure or its rules and regulations, but from its unpredictability, sensuality, vitality and the often irrational passions it produces.

Bureaucratic organisation

Of all the characteristics of modern sport identified by Guttmann, bureaucratic organisation is without doubt the most important. Modern sports are organised and run by a complex array of interconnecting bureaucratic structures. From the IOC to the international federations, from the national Sports Councils to the national governing bodies, and onward into the regional organisations and locally organised clubs and their committees, sport operates within a bewildering set of bureaucratic structures and regulations.

Definition: bureaucracy

A form of organisational structure that is operated by officials who work within a hierarchical structure of authority. The purpose of the bureaucracy and those who work within it is to make sure that the organisation effectively achieves its aims and goals.

Sports bureaucracies determine all the formal aspects of the sport, from the size of the playing field to the types of surface to the numbers of players, the rules and any fines or penalties that may be imposed for an infringement of these rules. Because of the global nature of modern sport, the organisational structure has to operate on a local, national and international level. Without this level of complex organisation and control, sport as we know it today could not exist. However, sports bureaucracies are not always completely benign. As the work of numerous sport sociologists such as John Hoberman (1984), and John Sugden and Alan Tomlinson (2002) clearly evidences, these sports bureaucracies can be self-interested, unrepresentative and, in some cases, corrupt (Simpson and Jennings, 1992; Jennings, 1996). Relatively few of them have clear democratic processes or external systems of oversight and accountability. The outcome is that those in charge can surround themselves with carefully chosen supporters who are not necessarily there on merit. As Blake correctly summarises, *Bureaucratisation without democratic representation is dangerous and not in the interests of performers or public* (1996, p81).

Although Guttmann's view of sport's modernisation is overly rationalistic and prone to some rather naïve views about the nature of progress, it helps us make important connections to the view that the economic and rationalised spheres of modern life are its defining characteristics. This perspective is important because it draws attention to the fact that within modern society and sport, control and power were firmly located in those who owned and controlled the economic and industrial spheres of life. The outcome of these processes was that the culture of modern sport and its modes of organisation emphasised a number of characteristics that came to dominate how we understand sport. Typifying these are sport's rational control, rules, order and moral purpose.

Learning Activity 2.3

The IOC and the philosophy of Olympism

Olympism is a philosophy of life, exalting and combining in a balanced whole the qualities of body, will and mind. Blending sport with culture and education, Olympism seeks to create a way of life based on the joy found in effort, the educational value of good example and respect for universal fundamental ethical principles.

(Olympic Charter: Fundamental principles, paragraph 2)

This task requires you to use the Olympic Movement as a practical case study on which to base your applied understanding of the sociological issues and concepts we have introduced in the preceding sections.

Learning Activity 2.3 continued

The first part of the task requires access to a computer with web connection. Using the main websites for the Olympic Movement (**www.olympic.org/uk/ index_uk.asp**) and those for the London 2012 Games (**www.london2012.com**), explore the sites and become familiar with the wide range of information and issues that they present.

Once you have familiarised yourself with the sites, we want you to undertake a more reflective sociological examination of them. If, as we hope, we have sparked your 'sociological imagination', you might discover that as you do the first part of the task you are already identifying a wide range of issues that might be of interest to a sport sociologist. However, in case we haven't, the second part of the task has a specific requirement linked to the discussion we have just undertaken regarding the nature of modern sport. This part of the task requires you to see if these sites provide evidence to support Guttmann's conceptualisation of modern sport (hopefully, you can remember that these were: secularisation; equality of opportunity (to compete and in the conditions of competition); specialisation of roles; rationalisation process; bureaucratic organisation; quantification; the quest for records).

Some questions to guide your investigations:

1. Do the IOC's or London 2012's discussions of the concept of Olympism demonstrate the process of secularisation? What points do you think are most important?
2. Do the IOC Missions and the 2012 website make clear statements about the importance of equality? Can you identify some clear policies being put forward that demonstrate this commitment?
3. How do the IOC and the structure of the 2012 Organising Committee demonstrate the specialisation of roles?
4. Using the issue of drugs cheats, can you identify how the IOC is rationalising the process of protecting sport from this sort of abuse?
5. Is the IOC a bureaucratic structure? If so, can you write out a map of its organisational structure? Looking at the 2012 site, can you map out the planning structure for the organisation and the delivery of the London Games?
6. Based on the IOC site, can you identify an emphasis on results and records?

Do you think that this might be a contradiction in terms of some of the core values of Olympism and the philosophy of the Games?

Some additional issues you might explore:

1. How does sport help people (and groups) differentiate themselves from each other? Is sport an important social arena for the development of a sense of national identity?
2. Could the IOC and the Games exist without the support of commercial sponsors and the media?
3. Why would large global companies want to provide the London Games with millions of pounds of sponsorship?

Research Focus

Roche, M (2000) *Mega-events and Modernity: Olympics and Expos in the Growth of Global Culture*. London: Routledge.

Though there is a substantive body of sociological, historical and political literature examining the Olympics, within the field of British sport sociology, there is little doubt that Roche's (2000) study of mega-events and modernity still rates as one of the most important and comprehensive contemporary analyses of the Olympics. For Roche, without modernity the development and growth of mega-events such as the Olympics would never have happened. These essentially modern mega-events can be defined as *large-scale cultural (including commercial and sporting) events which have a dramatic character, mass popular appeal and international significance* (Roche, 2000, p1). This text not only provides an ambitious and wide-ranging sociological analysis of the Olympics, it is also a project that provides a richly detailed and informative exploration of the social, cultural and political development of the Olympics, from the end of the nineteenth century to the contemporary period. In far more detail than has been possible to indicate in this chapter, Roche's work shows how the Olympics, as one of the '"great shows" of modern society', has been profoundly shaped by the institutional characteristics of modernity and how in turn the Olympics has itself played a crucial role in the global spread of these same institutions. As he correctly suggests in his preface (2000, pxi): *To understand something of their (mega-events) origins, nature and development in modernity is to throw light on phenomena and processes within modernity which continue to influence us even when the lights of any particular event have been switched off . . .*

To achieve these aims the book is organised into three sections. In the first, Roche establishes some of the major sociological perspectives and themes informing his analysis. In doing so, he identifies the basic sociological questions that explain why we need to analyse these mega-events. Like many contemporary sport sociologists (including the authors of this text) Roche's analysis recognises the need to critically analyse how modern social structures have shaped the Olympics while at the same time paying close attention to the fact that the Olympics are also events constructed, encountered and experienced through the actions of individual athletes, officials, spectators, politicians, business and media employees. For Roche, it is therefore a sociological necessity that a multi-dimensional analysis is developed that works at three interconnected levels. As already stated, requires our sociological interest in the 'macro-level' and specifically in how the structure of modern societies change and how these changes are reflected in the characteristics of specific historical periods.

The 'intermediate level' is the arena for a critical sociological analysis of contextual dimensions of 'every day reality'. It is at this level that power relations pattern opportunities and processes of consumption. The final level requires us to mine into the 'micro-level' as this is the location of experience and meaning. People are conscious agents who reflexively experience the Olympics and from this develop memories that directly shape identity.

In the second section of the book, Roche charts in impressive detail how mega-events intersect with and are aligned to the institutionalised power structures of the modern world. The initial chapter within this section explores how the Olympics promote the cultural power of nations alongside the extension of national political and economic interests allied to the growth of capitalism and international trade. This is followed by an analysis of how the Olympics (and other mega-events) have played and continue to play a vital role in the development and international spread of modern forms of citizenship, popular culture and consumerism. In the final chapter in this section, Roche explains how modernity's development through the course of the twentieth century inevitably leads to the need for ever greater levels of international co-operation and the emergence of transnational and supra-national systems of sporting (and other forms of) governance that we associate with organisations like the IOC and FIFA.

In the last section of the book, Roche usefully turns his attention to the growth of global culture and the role played by the Olympics within this complex process. Like other social theorists (Giddens, 1990, 2002) for Roche, one of the defining characteristics of modernity has always been its globalising character. In exploring these processes and echoing the work of Bale (1994, 2003) and his sport geography, Roche details how through the Olympiads' tour around the major cities of the world they became a major conduit for the global flows of people, ideas, finance, technology and consumer culture. The Olympics not only bring the host city and its nation to the attention of the rest of the world they also bring the rest of the world with their cultures to the city. Moreover, as media technology developed through the latter half of the twentieth century through live television broadcasts into the TV screens in people's living rooms, the Olympics quickly became a global experience fracturing the meaning of time and space. Sport and the Olympics became synonymous with the expanding reach of globalisation and the penetration of globalised forms of culture into all the nations of the world. By the late twentieth century the Olympics had an unparallel capacity to impact the governance of nation-states and their views on citizenship and equality. To enable a candidate city to be considered for the award of a Games demanded that the nation be open to global public scrutiny of its processes of governance and its approach to the 'human rights' of its citizens. One of the possibly ironic outcomes of this process was that the power of the Olympics became itself somewhat corrupting with various members of the IOC being accused of taking bribes in return for their vote in favour of a particular candidate city. Following on from the ground-breaking work of investigative reporters (Simpson and Jennings, 1992; Jennings, 1996), Roche explains how the IOC could not insulate itself from critical outside scrutiny by the world's media. This sort of media scrutiny meant if the IOC could demand that a nation be accountable for weak, ineffective and corrupt governance then the same demands for reform could be made of the IOC. Although proud of its independence and autonomy, the reality was that by the 1980s and 1990s the cost of the Games completely relied on media finance and so there was little choice for the IOC other than to start a process of reform.

As this brief overview demonstrates, Roche's contribution to a sociological understanding of the relationship between modernity, sport and the Olympics has been significant. It is a very creditable and significant contribution to the field of sport sociology that deserves the attention of students. As he modestly notes in his conclusion to the text (Roche, 2000, p235): *To understand mega-events better is thus to understand something more broadly about the nature and fate of human agency and social structure, and of continuity and change, in modernity . . . In this book I have aimed to make a preliminary contribution to the agenda of research and analysis that this implies.*

Learning Activity 2.4

Review of learning objectives
Before you move on to the following chapters, spend some time carefully reviewing what you have learned from this discussion of sport and modern society.

Review tasks
1. Write out a short definition of the following key sociological concepts: sociology; modern society; modernity; social reproduction; division of labour.
2. Based on your reading of the discussion of Alan Guttmann's analysis of modern sport, provide a clear statement on how the following processes are embedded in the way we socially organise modern sport: secularisation; equality of opportunity (to compete and in the conditions of competition); specialisation of roles; rationalisation process; bureaucratic organisation.
3. Give a brief explanation of the primary institutional characteristics of modernity identified by Giddens and why they are relevant to a sociological analysis of sport.

Chapter Review

As we hope this introduction has highlighted and the subsequent chapters will more comprehensively detail, sociology has now established a very important interest in the world of sport. Modern sport is socially constructed. In its modern form, sport also has a dual structure. On the one hand, it promotes ideals such as freedom, equality, diversity, experimentation and escapism. On the other, it is also based on control, discipline, and the passive acceptance of authority, tradition and constraint. Thinking about sport sociologically shows that whatever your level of involvement, it is important to realise that sport is a significant part of the modern world. As that modern world has developed, its institutional structures and cultural traditions have deeply influenced how sport developed and evolved. Sport is an integral part of modernity and modernity is an integral part of sport. Hence, our examination of sport reaches far beyond the confines of sport itself and will, we hope, provide you with a rich and exciting arena for the development of your sociological imagination and an understanding of our contemporary world.

Finally, as a way of guiding your sociological development, the chapter has also introduced a number of important sociological ideas or premises that underpin many of the sport sociology debates that will be explored in the subsequent chapters. However, because we have only given you a brief introduction to them, you should not as yet expect to fully understand them or their application to sport. Read the following premises carefully and then, as you address some of the more challenging debates in the next chapters, return to them to act as a useful starting point for your further work.

Premise 1 All human experience is socially influenced. Because this is the case, as Giddens (1989, p11) suggests, an understanding of the subtle, yet complex and profound ways in which our lives reflect the context of our social experiences is basic to the sociological outlook. As this chapter explained, one of the main tasks of sport sociology is to describe and explain these differing contexts and how they impact on the experience of sport.

Premise 2 The world we live in is not simple, but complex and subject to dramatic change. Living in this world demands that we 'learn' to behave appropriately in a variety of social contexts and also adapt to new forms of knowledge.

Premise 3 To some degree, everybody seeks to understand the world they live in. The success or failure of this process depends on knowledge. This includes having access to it and the ability to put this knowledge into action. Understood in this way, knowledge is an important component of how power operates.

Premise 4 In attempting to construct an objective and systematic understanding of the modern social world, sociologists are forced to develop theoretical models.

Further Reading

For a general introduction to sociology read:

Chapter 1: Introduction, in Bilton, et al. (2002) *Introductory Sociology*. 4th edition. London: Macmillan.

Alternatively, read:

Chapter 1: What is sociology? in Giddens, A (2006) *Sociology*. 5th edition. London: Polity Press.

To extend your understanding of the impact of modernity on the social construction of sport read:

Guttmann, A (2004) Rules of the game, in Tomlinson, A (ed*) The Sports Studies Reader*. London: Routledge.

Struna, NL (2000) Social history and sport, in Coakley, J and Dunning, E (eds) *Handbook of Sports Studies*. London: Sage.

Chapter 2: Sport, history and social change, in Jarvie, G (2006) *Sport, Culture and Society: An Introduction*. London: Routledge.

Chapter 3
Sport, modernity and the Olympics: a case study of the London Olympiads

Gordon T Mellor

In this chapter we will ground some of the major sociological themes identified in the discussion of sport and modern society by exploring an extended case study of the London Olympiads. In identifying social and cultural reproduction, the dimensions of modernity, the influence of sports bureaucracy and the role of politics, this chapter aims to set the scene for a more detailed discussion of the importance of sport in contemporary British society by using the Olympic Games as a starting point. What follows is the story of the modern Olympics, but told with a focus on the London Games of 1908, 1948 and 2012. The narrative is inevitably partial, but this chapter can be used like a road map for the rest of the book: the issues raised will signpost some of the important sociological debates that the text will require you to engage with.

Learning Objectives

On completing this chapter you should be able to:

- understand the Olympics as a modern social narrative;
- understand how a critical evaluation of the Olympics illuminates key themes within the sociological analysis of modern sport;
- detail how these themes have developed over time as illustrated by the London Olympic Games;
- outline through Olympic-based examples the social and cultural meanings attached to modern sport.

Introduction

The overarching ambition of the book is to encourage a *sociological* understanding of sport in modern society. The Olympic Games is a convenient and high-profile starting point for such a critique, but the themes we develop here are more broadly applicable to the relationship between sport and society. We endeavour to show that sport has a significant role in shaping how our society operates, but that the values that guide such a construction are a reflection of those that influence society more generally. Thus, sport and society have a symbiotic relationship that brings benefits and detriments to both. It is not our purpose to be judgemental about what these benefits or detriments are, but rather to raise awareness by knowledge and understanding that these exist. We also contend that, as members of the society we are describing, we are all responsible for the way things are, but also have the potential to shape the future. Understanding and illumination are crucial, and we begin with the story of the London Olympics.

London 1908: the Games of the IV Olympiad

Historical circumstance

The founder of the modern Olympics was Pierre de Coubertin. His desire to revive the Games stemmed from his conviction that sport was the springboard for moral development and that a large international sports competition would help promote peaceful co-existence among the nations of the world. To organise and promote the games, de Coubertin campaigned for the formation of the International Olympic Committee (IOC). The first of the modern Olympics took place in Athens in 1896.

Stepping up to the mark in November 1906, London formally accepted the IOC's invitation to host the fourth Olympic Games, to be held in 1908. De Coubertin had intended the 1908 Olympiad to have been in Rome, a city that he felt was replete with the symbolism of antiquity that had inspired the Games. It would indeed have been an Italian affair but for the 1906 eruption of Mount Vesuvius and the resulting financial hardship experienced in Italy. Negotiations with the British had begun during the interim Games in Athens in 1906 after the Italian authorities had announced their withdrawal.

Known as the Intercalated Games, the 1906 event highlighted the emerging political dimension of the Olympics. Even at this early stage in the development of the modern Olympics, national interests (and rivalries) were evident. What is clear is that sport in general and the modern Olympic Games in particular were already established as a tool of social reproduction within industrial societies.

It is evident that de Coubertin's modern Olympic Games is essentially a celebration of modernity. The global spread of modernity was already strongly developed even in the late nineteeth century and the sense that the world and everyday life was becoming increasingly globalised was already well established.

Early developments

The Athens Games of 1906, only recently acknowledged as a Games 'proper', had been an attempt to revive the modern Games after the very limited success of Paris in 1900 and the debacle of St Louis in 1904. It signalled the high point of Greek aspirations to have the Games held permanently in Athens, the city the Greeks believed to be the spiritual home of the modern Olympic Movement. De Coubertin, holding on to his original concept for the modern Games, consistently stood against a permanent site. However, always the pragmatist, he recognised that if they were to continue, the Games needed a success to rival the inauguration in 1896: expectations had increased, yet the experience had fallen well short of them. The Greeks would certainly provide a successful Games, even if their motivation was somewhat at odds with his own. The idea accepted by the Olympic bureaucracy, the IOC, was that an Athens Games would be held midway through every four-year cycle or Olympiad. In the event, this was the only 'intercalated' or interim Games ever held and, despite being out of sequence with the other Games, its status as a full Olympics is undoubted.

Organisation

With less than two years in which to prepare for the 1908 Games, Lord Desborough, the first Chairman of the British Olympic Association, harnessed the expertise in sports organisations born out of the tradition of the Victorian codified games. A stadium with a capacity of something in the region of 70,000 people was built at Shepherd's Bush in West London. The running track was one-third of a mile in length and surrounded by a concrete cycle track, while in the centre was a 100m (330ft) swimming pool. Existing facilities and venues were used for other events, such as tennis at the All England Club at Wimbledon and rowing at Henley-on-Thames. Sailing was held at Ryde on the Isle of Wight and on the River Clyde in Scotland. It is to be noted that prominent sports such as these had (and arguably still have) a strong class orientation. While being linked with an international trade fair running in London, the Games were not subsumed in, nor overawed by, an event being held concurrently. However, the proximity of commercial interests is noteworthy.

International issues

The London Games began on 27 April 1908 and lasted until 31 October, although the main competitions were held during July. For the first time individual entry was not permitted; the Games were truly an international sporting competition – competition between nations, where the nation had become elevated over the individual competitor. Despite fulfilling part of de Coubertin's concept in mobilising and empowering nations through sport, national competition in the Olympic context was immediately fraught. In the opening parade at the new White City stadium, the United States and Swedish flags were not flown with the flags of the other competing nations. What was an administrative bungle became an international incident.

The prominence of the 'sportsman' as a national representative was immediately apparent and international tensions were inevitably imported into Olympic sport. The American shot-putter Ralph Rose was the bearer of the US standard. However, being of Irish descent and angered by the British government's refusal to grant Irish independence, he refused to 'dip' the flag in salute as he passed King Edward VII and Queen Alexandra. This insult set the tone for the conduct of both the British and US athletes and officials throughout.

Other international issues surfaced. The Finnish team objected to having to march behind the flag of Tsarist Russia, as they considered Russia to be an aggressor towards their homeland. In turn the Russians refused to recognise Finland as an independent nation, with the result that the Finns marched into the stadium with no flag at all.

Sporting cultures

It was, however, the tension between the host nation and the United States that was to result in an incident that was ultimately to lead to an important change in Olympic protocol. The US team were, as they had been since the Paris Games, pre-eminent in the sprinting events. However, Britain put up a Scottish sprinter, Lt Wyndham Halswelle, who had taken second place in the 400m and third in the 800m at the Intercalated Games in Athens two years previously. Having set the fastest time in qualifying, Halswelle faced three American sprinters in the final – Taylor, Robbins and Carpenter. The British feared that the Americans would run as a team and that underhand tactics would be used against the flying Scot.

Track athletics in the US was at the time rather less formalised with regard to conduct during races, with pushing (boring), jostling and blocking acceptable practices. Under the auspices of the Amateur Athletic Association in Britain, such behaviour was deemed to be unsporting. The 400m was not run in lanes at this time and a clash of both athletes and athletic cultures was almost inevitable. Since 1900 all track umpires and organising officials were provided by the host nation, although in Athens in 1896 some of this expertise was invited from Britain and France. Thus, in the London Games, with their heightened tensions and overt national rivalries, all British officialdom was certainly perceived to be partial and indeed was very likely to be so.

The 400m final on 23 July saw the competitors warned about foul play prior to the race. An extra precaution saw trackside officials placed at 20m intervals in order to ensure no jostling or blocking was attempted. Clearly, the pre-race tensions and rivalries were not lost on the media of the day. The enhanced profile of this clash not only raised the audience's anticipation (the excitement of entertainment), but also elevated the competitors' social standing (emergent celebrities). The race lived up to expectations with the American Carpenter blocking Halswelle as he attempted to take the lead. It was reported by *The Times* that the Scot was forced from a position close to the inside bend to within inches of being forced off the outside of the track in the space of 20 yards. An official called foul and a judge broke the tape before any of the runners could cross the finish line. 'No race' was called and, amid confusion and protests, Carpenter was disqualified.

The race was re-run two days later with the lanes demarcated by cord to ensure there was no contact between the sprinters. However, the American athletes would not compete without their disqualified team-mate and Halswelle himself did not wish to run without the US competitors. After considerable debate, he bowed to pressure and ran the race alone, taking the gold medal. With the American press calling the British 'bad losers' and *The Times* maintaining 'the race was run in England, where tactics of this kind are contrary alike to the rules that govern sport and to our notions of what is fair play, the committee had no option but to punish the offender', the friction was set to continue.

The American sprinter Taylor, who was forcibly removed from the track during the furore over the disqualification of Carpenter in the first running of the 400m final, later became the first black athlete to win a gold medal at a modern Games, running as part of a victorious relay team.

The furore over the 400m final is a fine example of how the differing 'cultures' of sport – the British and the North American in this instance – led to conflict. Despite the globalising tendencies evident in modernity and manifest in the Games, little could mollify the deeply held convictions that each nation had been wronged by the other.

Though it can be claimed that sport has a number of values that transcend national and cultural differences, social reproduction tends to work on a far more local level and re-affirms commonplace beliefs and realities consistent with national concerns. The IOC, the bureaucracy with overarching responsibility here, recognised and acted on the core of the dispute. While supporting the British hosts in this particular context, they enacted profound protocol changes for future Games.

Amateurism

This was a key component of the Victorian/Edwardian British sporting ideal. This is not to say that amateur status went uncontested – soccer (Association Football), rugby football and cricket all struggled to resolve the debate between the amateur and professional.

The amateur ethic was, of course, far more than an innocent tag indicating a love of the sport or game: it illustrated a middle-class aspiration. Furthermore, it was a mark of demarcation, a tool in the social divisions within the British class system. The amateur ethic was closely allied to British ideals of sportsmanship, fair play and gentlemanly conduct.

Further conflict

Perhaps the abiding image of the 1908 Games in London, and one that well illustrates how powerful cultures of sport are, is that of Dorando Pietri, the Italian marathon runner, in a state of collapse, being half-dragged, half-carried over the finish line by the clerk of the course. Having entered the stadium in the lead, Pietri fell twice in the closing straight; both times he was helped to his feet by officials. The Italian was pronounced victor and the Italian flag was raised. However, this was followed by a protest from the American team whose runner Hayes had come in a strong second place. The IOC panel upheld the protest and the Irish-American Hayes was presented with the gold medal.

Such was the outpouring of sympathy for gallant Pietri that Queen Alexandra presented him with a gold cup in honour of his courage, while the animosity towards the Americans reached new heights. De Coubertin's sympathies were with the British who were apparently concerned with the spirit of sportsmanship, while the Americans focused on victory.

Standardisation

The marathon had been run over a distance of approximately 25 miles (40km) at the previous Games, but due to a quirk of geography and British deference to the Royal Family, it became 26 miles and 385 yards in 1908. This was the precise distance from below the royal nursery windows at Windsor Castle to the stadium at the White City. This became the internationally recognised distance for the marathon in 1924.

Sports bureaucracy and resolution

The Americans led numerous protests about official bias, the rigging of heats, starting irregularities, illegal coaching, rule breaking and unfair judging. Such was the disquiet about the allegations that the British Olympic Association and the IOC produced a booklet entitled 'Replies to Criticism of the Olympic Games'. However, the positive legacy of these disputes was that by the following Games in 1912, all judges were drawn from a pool supplied by the competing nations, and that control of events and rules governing competition were placed in the hands of newly established international governing bodies.

Codification

The internationalisation of sporting governance was, of course, only a further step in the process that is referred to as codification (the rationalisation of competition), whereby competition becomes possible through a mutually beneficial recognition of recorded rules, conditions and dimensions of the sports, together with an agreed, although often unspoken, 'way of playing'. It was codification that took the athletic games of the English public school into the realm of what we call modern sports, enabled fair and entertaining competition, and ultimately implanted these sports in the consciousness of the British and then the civilised world. We return to this process and its significance in Chapter 5.

1908: a retrospective

Despite the considerable animosity between some competing nations and the tangible damage to British sporting self-esteem and international standing, the 1908 Games were successful. London became the best British performance, before or since, if overall position on the medal table is such a measure. Beyond the domestic scene, however, further measures of the growing significance of sport can be seen: 22 countries were represented; 1999 male competitors attended; 36 women athletes and competitors took part. The London Games established the modern Olympics in a way that the previous Games had not: they were organisationally competent; they were popular and well attended by the public; they brought into focus some serious issues that needed to be confronted by the IOC; and they forged the template for international sport that would serve for the foreseeable future.

The British sporting establishment, just over a decade before, had doubted the wisdom of an idea promoted by a French aristocrat for an international sporting competition under the name of an ancient Greek religious festival. Having been represented at each of the four previous modern Games – Athens 1896, Paris 1900, St Louis 1904 and Athens 1906 – the British had engaged with the Olympic concept and contributed substantially to ensuring that it continued. The legacy of the public school games that had given birth to the codified sports that de Coubertin had used to shape his idea had been added to in practical terms. The IV Olympics in London in 1908, for all its shortcomings, stood as the Games that showed beyond doubt that great things lay ahead for this modern sporting phenomenon.

Summer Games venues

1896 Athens; 1900 Paris; 1904 St Louis; 1906 Athens; **1908 London**; 1912 Stockholm; 1920 Antwerp; 1924 Paris; 1928 Amsterdam; 1932 Los Angeles; 1936 Berlin; **1948 London**; 1952 Helsinki; 1956 Melbourne; 1960 Rome; 1964 Tokyo; 1968 Mexico City; 1972 Munich; 1976 Montreal; 1980 Moscow; 1984 Los Angeles; 1988 Seoul; 1992 Barcelona; 1996 Atlanta; 2000 Sydney; 2004 Athens; 2008 Beijing; **2012 London**.

> ### Learning Activity 3.1
>
> Identify the important differences that led Britain and the United States into dispute over the 1908 Olympic competition. How do these illustrate the cultures of sport and how did the Olympic bureaucracy act to minimise the risk of similar disputes occurring again?

London 1948: the Games of the XIV Olympiad

Historical circumstance

In the grips of Britain's post-war austerity, the XIV Games returned to London. With no Olympics having been staged since 1936, there was a real possibility that they would not be resurrected at all. There had been some protest both prior to and at the time of the Games in Berlin that had been so successfully yet predictably used by the Nazis. It was nonetheless with the benefit of hindsight that the Olympic world looked back with a mixture of shame and horror to the overtly fascist Nazi agenda of Berlin 1936. The Second World War had seen civilisations break new ground in industrial warfare with the large-scale bombing of civilian targets, the Holocaust and ultimately the atomic bomb. The association of the Games with Hitler's Nazi propaganda in Berlin could well have resulted in the modern Olympics being consigned to history.

World events

Tokyo was to have hosted the XII Games but the Sino-Japanese war caused them to be transferred to Helsinki. When the Russians invaded Finland, however, all plans to hold an Olympics in 1940 were cancelled. Just months before Europe plunged into the second major conflict of the century, the IOC awarded the XIII Games to London, to be held in 1944. In the event, this was also an impossibility, and with Japan and the United States entering the conflict, de Coubertin's dream appeared to have died. Indeed, it may have done so had not Avery Brundage (from the United States and future IOC President) been so committed to maintaining it.

Organisation

After a postal ballot of IOC members in 1946, the then President, Sigfrid Edstrom, awarded the Games to London, some of which was still in ruins after the Blitz. In the context of the times, with Britain still rationing both food and clothing, this would not be an extravagant celebration. The £600,000 budget was tight and few new facilities could be built. Male competitors were accommodated in military barracks and female competitors housed in colleges and schools. A temporary running track was put down in Wembley stadium, rowing returned to Henley, sailing was held at Torbay in Devon, shooting took place at Bisley and swimming at Aldershot. Although Germany and Japan were not invited to attend, 4099 competitors from 59 nations made the 1948 Games the largest yet staged.

Naïve idealism

The success of the 1948 Games was a triumph for Western populist naïvety: the belief that sport was above politics. The English-speaking world – the victors of the Second World War – articulated considerable distaste for the overt politicisation of international sport and particularly the 1936 Olympics in Berlin.

In many ways, this was a rehearsal for what was to come during the Cold War, when Soviet use of sport to promote and demonstrate political superiority was resisted and belittled. The modern Olympic Games (as all sport) is inherently political in constitution. Its very existence was, and its continuation is, a political statement in itself.

Personalities

The 1948 Olympics are remembered for two remarkable athletes: the Czech distance runner, Emile Zatopek, and the Dutch jumper and sprinter, Fanny Blankers-Koen.

Emile Zatopek, 'the metronome'

Although not untutored, Zatopek came almost intuitively to a training regime that would become validated by later physiological and sports science research. Showing an application to athletic training that bordered on the obsessive, the Czech trained for pace in addition to distance. He knew he could run middle and longer distances steadily, so he focused on speed and strength. Repeated extended sprinting interspersed with a rolling or running recovery, together with work on breathing control, helped to condition Zatopek in a manner that was well ahead of his time. Winning the 10,000m by three-quarters of a lap, he narrowly failed to take Gold in the 5,000m.

Fanny Blankers-Koen, 'the flying housewife'

A remarkable talent, Blankers-Koen was denied the ability to defend her world high and long jump records by the restriction of women track and field athletes to three individual events. The restrictions placed upon her capacity to enter all the events she was capable of doing well in is indicative of the male-dominated sporting world of the time. Winning four gold medals, she equalled the mark set by Jesse Owens in 1936, by taking the 100m, 200m, the 80m hurdles and the 4x100m relay. Consistent with the media appreciation of women athletes of the time, the media reports focused not on her precocious abilities but rather on the fact that she was a 30-year-old housewife and mother of two. Rarely have such profound athletic achievements been so trivialised.

The Olympic ideal

While Britain's international standing was certainly high, her days of Empire and global influence were almost over. The first Games after the Second World War are remembered not for aggressive nationalistic jingoism or victory-fuelled celebration, but for the rebirth of something that would prove far more enduring despite its intangibility; the Olympic ideal. During the Second World War, Western civilisation had descended to the depths of human depravity, yet the Olympics, in the form of the London Games, was one of the first international events to rise out of the ashes, not quite phoenix-like but certainly in the belief that youthful endeavour in sports could offer more than conflict and misery.

Sporting cultures

Post-war Britain was less obsessed with amateurism than had been the case in the early years of the twentieth century. This is not to say that the issue had played itself out completely – this would take another 30 years or more. However, the more egalitarian realities of post-war Britain did much to erode the worth of, or indeed the need for, idealist amateurism.

The British model of sport around which de Coubertin had constructed the modern Games had been replaced by the North American one. The cultural dominance that the United States exerted upon the West, and ultimately the entire globe, ensured that ways of playing altered – gentlemanly conduct and fair play were of less concern, while personal endeavour, responsibility and winning became paramount.

1948: a retrospective

With the benefit of hindsight, it is possible to see how important the London Games of 1948 were for the Olympic Movement and beyond: a bowed but unbroken host nation that needed to renegotiate its place in the order of nations; a Western Europe that would have to unite in order to regenerate; and a world facing a distinctly new power struggle between the USA and the Communist regimes of the Eastern bloc. If de Coubertin's inception of the modern Olympics in 1896 had been the result of a coalescence of ideas, then 1948 was the result of a coalescence of national and geopolitical need. What was all the more remarkable was that from the jaws of irrelevance, Edstrom and Brundage had seized the moment and resurrected the modern Olympics. Speaking of the London Games, Zatopek said: 'After all those dark days of the war, the bombing, the killing, the starvation, the revival of the Olympics was as if the sun had come out.'

Learning Activity 3.2

Select three famous Olympic athletes (you might like to choose historical figures like Zatopek and Blankers-Koen or more recent examples such as Carl Lewis, Steve Redgrave, Paula Radcliffe). Briefly summarise the sporting characteristics that they share and those that are different. Then consider the following:

- How important is it for the Olympic Movement to have world-famous sporting personalities taking part?
- What do you conclude about the social importance of sport having examined their sporting characteristics?

London 2012: the Games of the XXX Olympiad

Historical circumstance

At the 2005 Congress in Singapore when IOC President Jacques Rogges announced that the Games would return to London, national euphoria and enthusiasm was tinged with both reticence and self-doubt. Britain has a fine Olympic heritage: it was the nineteenth-century British model of sport that de Coubertin had taken as the template upon which to build the international festival; Britain has been represented at every modern Games both summer and winter; London in 1908 and again in 1948 was of particular importance for the Olympic Movement, and the success of both Olympics established the Games at times when their continuation was clearly questionable.

London's credentials

- Britain's passion for sport.
- Commitment to the Olympics – attended every modern Games.
- Hosted the 1908 and 1948 Games.
- Cultural diversity – 300 languages, 200 nationalities.
- London is one of the world's most vibrant cities.
- Huge range of accommodation to suit all tastes and pockets.
- Britain's historic record of being able to deliver.
- Britain's security credentials.
- Combination of iconic and new venues.
- Comprehensive transport system.
- Internationally accessible Games (European rail links, budget airlines, multiple airports).

Requirements

The growth of the modern Games has amplified the contributions of nationalism and commerce to the event, but has also opened up a range of new dimensions. Two very obvious examples are the increasing participation by female athletes and the emergence of the Paralympics as a way of showcasing sport through disability. Gender and disability are two social dimensions that have enjoyed elevated acknowledgement and empowerment as the twentieth century has progressed. Here is evidence that more broadly based social concerns over access and equality are being mirrored in sport.

To be awarded the 2012 Games required more than an impressive Olympic tradition. Success in this regard was due to an opportune coalition between some very effective players, led by the then prime minister, Tony Blair, the former Mayor of London, Ken Livingstone, and the Chairman of the London Organising Committee, Lord Coe. As a track athlete, Sebastian Coe had won the 1500m gold and the 800m silver medal at the 1980 Olympics in Moscow, and then repeated the performance at the 1984 Los Angeles Games.

The Olympic brand

It is claimed by many (the IOC, national governments, host cities, big business, broadcast media) that the Olympic brand has no negative connotations, but rather an association with such words as competitive, peaceful, multi-cultural, honourable and dynamic. But what about performance-enhancing drug use, commercialisation, overt media control, political 'hijacking' and jingoistic nationalism?

A rational project

The demands in hosting the modern Olympics have changed markedly since London's last experience. Today, in recognition of the massive financial responsibility involved in staging them and in keeping with the notion of accountability to those who pay, a legacy is required. The Games have become a vehicle through which cities regenerate housing, transport and commercial infrastructure. An equally important aspect of legacy is the cultural one: the Olympics aspire to reach well beyond sport alone.

The intended consequences of hosting the 2012 Games in a domestic context are to have sport's profile raised on the broader political and social agenda, recognising its importance in helping cultural integration. Understanding the increasingly secular and fragmented nature of modern society, politicians see sport as a rational means of working towards social cohesion and integration. With this increased use of sport to achieve political objectives (which, of course, is nothing new), the 2012 Games have become a tool in the development of a modernist liberal/centre-left agenda. While increased funding is an undoubted benefit for those interested in, or involved with sport, it is also the case that 'there is no such thing as a free lunch': sport has both to deliver the broader objectives and conform to the intended stereotype.

More practically, the 2012 benefits for governing bodies are increased 'mass' participation at grass-roots level; the development of talent identification systems; the development of high-performance models; and influence and a profile for these bureaucracies. In terms of sporting benefits, there will doubtless be an improved sports infrastructure together with increased funding for elite sport that, alongside the advantages of competing in one's home country, ought to lead to improved results for the British teams.

A legacy for the 2012 London Games

It is said that there is no direct translation from the French to English of 'legacy' (Sadd, 2009) and that the closest approximation is probably the notion of 'heritage'. Nonetheless, de Coubertin was driven by the need for the Olympics to deliver tangible change and hope on a scale far beyond the sporting arena (Smith, 2004). International Olympics Committees have taken this as a given and wrestled with the nature if not the content of such delivery. Whilst it is often poorly identified, frequently assumed, and always hedged about with the pragmatics of both national and international demands, at the very core of the Olympic endeavour is an aspiration that is currently articulated through the notion of legacy.

The London 2012 Tracking Research (DCMS, 2008b) reported that about a third of the British population had considered the notion of Olympic and Paralympic legacy and what it might deliver; unsurprisingly this figure showed a regional bias with the South East reporting higher rates than elsewhere. Social class was also a determinant in this. Unsurprisingly, London was recognised as the primary location for the delivery of legacy. Considerable support was shown for the provision of improved sporting facilities and venues, while providing opportunities for young people was also a frequently articulated desire. Interestingly, new housing and cultural participation (both significant dimensions earlier in the preparation cycle), registered as less important. In a characteristic show of scepticism, the public of 2008 believed that while the 2012 Olympics would be delivered appropriately and that competition facilities would be built, far fewer were convinced that the cultural, environmental or social legacy would meet the promises made.

Included in the original Legacy Action Plan document (2008) were the long-term benefits that the government believed they could achieve through London hosting the Olympic and Paralympic Games in 2012. The plan made five promises to set the scale for the ambition:

1. To make the UK a world-leading sporting nation;
2. To transform the heart of East London;
3. To inspire a generation of young people;
4. To make the Olympic Park a blueprint for sustainable living;
5. To demonstrate the UK is a creative, inclusive and welcoming place to live in, visit and for business.

The 2008 tracking research explored public awareness of the government's aims, by means of 'simplified versions of the government's legacy aims for the 2012 Olympic and Paralympic Games'.

- Improving on Team GB's medal performance.
- Creating more jobs.
- Building major new sports venues and parks in London.
- Improving public transport in London.
- Building new homes in East London.
- Increasing take-up in sports.
- Encouraging young people to benefit from playing an active part in their communities.
- Developing a UK-wide programme of cultural events called the 'Cultural Olympiad' in the run-up to 2012.
- Showing the rest of the world that the UK is a great place to visit.
- More opportunities for British business.
- Setting an example of how new business developments can be environmentally-friendly.
- Setting an example of how communities can reduce their carbon footprint.

Thus the UK government's legacy aims, ranging from job creation to carbon neutral communities, from moving up the Olympic medal table to demonstrating that the UK is a great place to visit, illustrate where the social legacy intersects with the sporting legacy.

Living the dream

Hosting a world celebration such as a modern Olympic Games is without doubt a risk for any city and the nation that it represents. Failure to deliver anything other than a truly excellent Games would mean a loss of face that would be a national disgrace.

However, the benefits of success are also enormous: for a short time London will be the focus of the entire world's media. Britain will project its own cultural message, define its own aspirations, perform on its own stage (or in its own sports stadium). The 'feel good' factor in terms of domestic political gain is well understood, while the extensive regeneration and smartening up of some of London should have an enduring effect.

Although there is something of the 'celebrate now and pay later' mentality involved (going well beyond sport itself), Britain is deeply committed to the Olympic ideal. Whatever the risks, the costs and the work ahead, the potential gains, both national and political, are tantalising.

London 2012 estimates

- More than 200 nations.
- 10,500 athletes.
- 6,000 coaches and officials.
- 2,000 judges and referees.
- 5,000 Olympic family members (e.g. IOC members).
- 20,000 media representatives.
- 7,000 official sponsor representatives.
- Over nine million tickets will be sold, equivalent to around 500,000 spectators per day.
- 4,000 athletes and 2,500 officials in the Paralympic Games.

The Games move on

With preparations for London now well advanced, the planning focus has moved towards the 2016 Games of the XXXI Olympiad. The award of the Olympic and Paralympic Games to Rio de Janeiro was announced at the 13th Olympic Congress held in Copenhagen, in October 2009. It will be the first Games held in Brazil and the second held in Latin America, after Mexico City 1968. It is a clear articulation of IOC President Jacques Rogge's ambition of providing the opportunity of hosting the Games to as many of the Olympic family as possible. While going outside the 'club' of rich and developed nations is certainly a risk, his aspirations are entirely in keeping with the Olympic ethos.

Learning Activity 3.3

The London Olympics of 2012 will be the 'biggest and best ever'. Prepare a mini-presentation that is a critical evaluation of this statement. Useful websites are:

- **www.olympic.org** The start for comprehensive links into the Olympic Movement.
- **www.london2012.org** The focus on London with details of the bid, the plans and the progress.
- **www.perseus.tufts.edu/olympics** Useful history, particularly on the ancient Games.
- **www.nbcsports.com/olympics** Insights into the 'Americanisation' of the Olympics with video clips and a commentary of commercial expediency.

Important social themes in the representation of the modern Olympics

The influence of the ancient Games

Many claims have been made, not least by de Coubertin himself, that the modern Games were a revival of those ancient festivities at Olympia in Greece. The ancient Games were, however, a religious festival in honour of Zeus. The Hellenic religion would seem very alien to a modern eye, being predicated on the notion that the gods had a physical manifestation and walked among humans, interfering in people's lives as they saw fit. While many of the ancient contests bear a similarity with those we recognise as athletic sports, the meanings and values attached to them are likely to be so distinct from those that we share, that it is questionable if we can call the ancient Games a sporting celebration in anything but the broadest sense.

While much was made of the supposed amateur status of the ancient competitors, it remains the case that neither the notion of amateur nor professional would have been explicable to them. These terms have only become meaningful to us through the concerns of the British (and subsequently European) middle and upper classes in the late eighteenth and nineteenth centuries.

Using the symbolism of the ancient Games was beneficial for de Coubertin in establishing his modern Olympics, and we still willingly engage in this project. However, to claim that we are involved in the same endeavour as were the ancient Greeks is dubious at best.

Cultural currency

De Coubertin was not the first to use the name 'Olympics' in relation to a festival of athletic activities. Robert Dover's Olympiks held in the Cotswolds between 1612 and 1850 featured physical contests; the Liverpool Olympics (1862–1867) was a modern athletic festival; and the Much

Wenlock Olympian Games (1850–1895) founded by Dr William Penny Brookes, so influential in relation to de Coubertin's ideas, are merely the British examples of this phenomenon.

Fascination with the lost cultures of ancient Greece had been evident in Britain since at least the 1500s. There were rumours of a great festival where the Greeks showed their physical prowess in contests watched over by their gods. Much of the substance of these tales came from the Latin texts of Pindar.

Olympism: the ethical basis of the modern Games

Pierre Frédy, Baron de Coubertin, was a French aristocrat who hoped through pedagogy to invigorate the youth of his country. He was something of an historian and an anglophile influenced by the ideas of Thomas Arnold, the headmaster of Rugby School. The notion of athletic games as formulated in the English public schools in the mid-nineteenth century appealed to de Coubertin, as did the code of the amateur sportsman. On seeing a dramatic re-enactment of the ancient Olympics on a visit to an American university, he brought the ideas together with the aspirations of the aforementioned Penny Brookes, and created the concept of what we now recognise as the modern Olympic Games.

De Coubertin, together with Carl Diem, were responsible for articulating a philosophy relating to the Games. This has become known as 'Olympism' and is a collection of quite complex ideas that underpin the greater claims of the modern Olympic Movement. Formulated around equity, friendship, freedom and peace, they articulate the belief that the Olympics is much more than a mere sports festival.

Politics and the modern Games

There is no sanctity in sport and the inevitable demands of conflicting national interests have bedevilled the Games to a far greater extent than de Coubertin envisioned. Making political statements on a world stage is too good an opportunity to miss for those with a grievance. As such, the IOC has had to deal with politically motivated posturing, boycotts and terrorism at the Games themselves, while beyond these confines it has had to initiate exclusions in order to reflect opinion well beyond sport. The conflicting demands faced in such circumstances are well illustrated by the IOC response to the terrorist outrage at the Munich Games in 1972. Castigated by many for undue haste in restarting the Games after 11 Israeli athletes and coaches were taken hostage and killed together with some of the terrorists, the IOC had sought to continue only after a consensus had been sought among competing nations.

The problems and demands of staging a successful Olympics

The demands of success have been considerable for the greatest cultural festival of modern times. The seemingly endless desire for sports both traditional and novel to become part of the Olympic family has resulted in a phenomenon that is now recognised as gigantism, where the Games become too large to be affordable to stage, to manage and to maintain the necessary media interest. Abandoning the amateur code was also painful and protracted, but to maintain the focus as the premier festival for elite sportsmen and women in the modern world, it was a necessity to allow professionalism into the Games. Likewise, sponsorship of the Games, teams and athletes is a reality, overturning many of the long- and dearly-held maxims of the Olympic ideal.

Such is the cachet of an Olympic medal that the ethics of sport are constantly challenged through cheating and performance-enhancing drug use. That this appears to be a feature of all elite sports, both within and beyond the Olympics, does not lessen the profound difficulties faced by the Games' authorities and sports governing bodies in this regard.

Women

The journey made by women throughout the development of the modern Games is one that illustrates both the strengths and the weaknesses of organised sports. Initially denied access to the Games (attributed to de Coubertin's reservations about the suitability of competitive sports for women), pressure and the tide of the times resulted in a strictly limited and somewhat begrudging inclusion of women in tennis, golf and yachting at the Paris Games in 1900. Women's swimming events were introduced in 1912 and athletics in 1928. The programme of events for women is now extensive, although it still has some way to go before it matches that available to men. The notion that sport was a genre created by men for men has been successfully challenged by sporting women throughout the twentieth century; this is reflected in the composition of the modern Olympics in the early years of the new century.

The Paralympics

A small sports competition for British war veterans with spinal injuries was held at Stoke Mandeville Hospital on the day that the 1948 Games opened in London. This put in place a train of events that has culminated in what we now know as the Paralympic Games. Dr Ludwig Guttmann who arranged the modest beginnings believed in the benefits that sport could bring to all (Scruton 1998). This sentiment whilst quite novel at the time, sits very comfortably with contemporary sensibilities. Guttmann's games were joined four years later by similarly injured athletes from the Netherlands, and an international movement began. Following the Olympic template, games for athletes with disability were first held in Rome in 1960. Under the banner of the Paralympics, the movement came of age in Toronto in 1976.

The Paralympics are sports events for athletes from six designated disability groups. Emphasising athletic achievements rather than the disability, the event is truly elite in nature. Participants in the Paralympic Games have increased from 400 athletes from 23 countries in Rome in 1960 to 3,800 athletes from 136 countries in Athens in 2004. The Paralympic Games are held in the same year as the Olympic Games. Since 1988's Seoul Paralympic Games, they have taken place at the same venues as the Olympics. In June 2001, an agreement was made between the IOC and the International Paralympic Committee (IPC) enshrining this practice. After 2012, the city chosen to host the Olympic Games will also host the Paralympics.

Since the Second World War, sporting bureaucracies have reacted to the growing awareness of and inclusion in Western societies of those with disability by making efforts to include them. The IOC, after some initial reservations, has moved to bring the IPC into the Olympic family. The ultimate merger of the Olympics with the Paralympics is still some way off.

Learning Activity 3.4

Who was Pierre de Coubertin? Write an entry for an imaginary book of 'Significant Sporting People'.

In this account you will need to locate factual information about the man; indicate something of his motivations and the source(s) of his inspiration and key influences; make some comment on the importance of his legacy for the social formation of modern sport.

Research Focus

The modern Olympic Games have been much written about. The vast majority of this literature has been populist, descriptive and non-reflective and, while this can be interesting, has no place here. In fairness the Games are a difficult subject matter, at once too close, too familiar and too contemporary to be the subject of dispassionate analysis, while demanding just that through their complexity, social influence and relevance. In the academic realm there is work to be admired however. In a British context the work of Jim Parry has been influential, as has the output of Mike McNamee. With regards to the Paralympic Games Ian Brittain is important. The work of Andy Miah has challenged many contemporary ideas. Vasilis Girginov has published widely on the Games, while Beatriz Garcia is unsurpassed in her consideration of the ceremonial aspects of the modern festival. Dipping into the recent past we might cite Hoberman as being critically insightful and Guttman as being highly informed.

For the undergraduate student, however, one of the most consistent and influential theorists remains the American academic, John Apostal Lucas (1927-). While his work is rooted in the mid-to-late twentieth century manifestation of the Games, his work has an insight and vigour that makes it highly accessible. Now retired, Professor Lucas was a long serving academic at Pennsylvania State University in the United States. He came very close to being an Olympic athlete in his youth, being a fine distance runner. His academic work focused upon the history and philosophy of the modern Olympics, looking beyond the structure and operation of the Games themselves and examining the Olympic Movement. Ultimately he stepped into conjecture suggesting how the Olympic ideal might adapt as the Games move into the future.

Lucas, JA (1964) 'Coubertin's Philosophy of Pedagogical Sport'. *Journal of Health, Physical Education and Recreation*, 35 (7), pp26–27.

Lucas, JA (1976) 'Victorian "Muscular Christianity": Prologue to the Olympic Games Philosophy'. *Olympic Review* (99/100), pp49–52.

Lucas, JA (1979) *Penn State at the Olympic Games: (1904 to 1976)*. Pennsylvania: Pennsylvania State University.

Lucas, JA (1980) *The Modern Olympic Games*. London: Th. Yoseloff.

Lucas, JA (1981) 'The Genesis of the Modern Olympic Games', in Segrave, J and Chun, D (eds) *Olympism*. Champaign IL: Human Kinetics, pp22–32.

Lucas, JA (1987) *Baron Pierre de Coubertin and the Formative Years of the Modern International Olympic Movement 1883–1896*. Ann Arbor Mich.: Univ. Microfilm International.

Lucas, JA (1992) *Future of the Olympic Games*. Champaign IL: Human Kinetics.

Lucas, JA (1994) 'USOC President Douglas MacArthur and his Olympic Movement 1927–1928', in, Barney, RK and Meier, KV (eds) *Critical Reflections on Olympic Ideology*. Ontario: International Centre for Olympic Studies, pp67–69.

Lucas, JA (2009) *John Apostal Lucas: Teacher, Sport Historian, and One Who Lived His Life Earnestly. A Collection of Articles and Essays with an Autobiographical Sketch*. Lemont Berlin: Eifrig Publishing.

Lucas articulates, in a manner more compelling than other Olympic commentators, de Coubertin's belief in the importance of sport education. Lucas demands a reach that always stretches beyond that currently embraced by the 'ideal', whereby the need for an 'instinctive and unfailing fair play in life as in sport' becomes central (Lucas 2009, p265). Situating Olympism in the context of an ethic for all humankind, in much the way that de Coubertin did, Lucas proposes both a future and a possible demise for the Games. In the utopian frame he promotes the Olympics from a sporting festival to a secular philosophy for life – capable of all that De Coubertin dreamed for it; while he warns that future Games will fail, despite any excellences in planning, staging and conducting them, unless the competitors engage with the ideal of fair play in deed and spirit. It is clear they will function as commercial and nationalistic celebrations, but they will not be Olympic Games. To Lucas, these are and remain much more.

The canon of work undertaken by Lucas is informed by the context of the United States' involvement in the Games. In engagement and in boycott, in triumph and in adversity, Lucas decries the politicisation of the Olympics. Furthermore, from the home of capitalism and the free-market, the notion of the amateur in sports and athletics is promoted and developed. In a very similar way, although without the class connotations of the traditional British concept, the importance of amateur participation out of love and in a free spirit is central. His work effectively confronts the professionalisation of the Games and signposts what he sees as the dangers inherent in the promotion of commercialisation in the Olympic context.

Learning Activity 3.5

Review of learning objectives

Now that you have worked through the chapter, you will understand the Olympics in terms of a modern social narrative. In order to ensure that you have met the learning outcomes of the chapter, you should now write a short paragraph on each of the following topics, making sure that you clearly relate your work back to specifics in the chapter:

●●●▶

Learning Activity 3.5 continued

1. How does a critical evaluation of the Olympics illuminate the sociological analysis of modern sport?
2. Based on your understanding of the London Olympic Games of 1908, 1948 and 2012, detail how the social themes inherent in the Olympics have developed and changed over time.
3. Using Olympic-based examples, identify the social and cultural meanings attached to modern sport.

Chapter Review

The modern Olympics has emerged from a complex synthesis of historical circumstances, idealism and the use of sport as a vehicle for economic investment, cultural education and social development. The political dimension of Olympic sport was already visible in 1908 with the evident Anglo-American tensions. As the twentieth century progressed, new challenges to the established order of sport also became ever more prominent. Three of the most significant were the emergence of powerful social agendas reflecting political and social demands for greater equality based on race, gender and (dis)ability.

The outcome of these social dynamics can be seen in the planning for the 2012 Games and the structural changes to sport, such as the emergence of equity and the diversity of policies within the governing bodies of sport. London has established a pre-eminent Olympic tradition that helped propel the city towards winning the 2012 bidding process. The Olympics has become an important sporting event that embraces a host of meanings and agendas that this book sets out to illuminate.

In particular, we will show how sport is an outcome of the modern age (it embraces value systems concerned with competition, discipline and productivity, for example); how sport is structured and organised in specific ways (that facilitate international sporting events, for example); how sport reflects stratification in society (certain sports have a clear class bias among participants, for example, while sport more generally favours male propensity over female); how sport is a vehicle for social development (physical education in schools, for example, and recreational activities that may include engaging risk as in adventure sports); how sport has a role to play in shaping and maintaining our most obvious source of identity – the body. Moreover, it is the pictures, words and other images prevalent in the media that set the agenda of the idealised human body (here, the athletic body is the ideal to aspire towards). Finally, we will address the area of sport and commodification, and discuss how sport has become more like a business, with participants and spectators engaged in a series of exchange systems.

Further Reading

There are many excellent books on the Olympics. One of the best to extend your understanding of the Olympic Movement is:

Guttmann, A (2002) *The Olympics: A History of the Modern Games.* Urbana: University of Illinois Press.

To review further the London Olympiads, you are advised to read the following:

Holt, R (1989) *Sport and the British: A Modern History.* Oxford: Oxford University Press.

For a more sociologically focused analysis read:

Toohey, K and Veal, AJ (2000) *The Olympic Games: A Social Science Perspective.* Oxford: Oxford University Press.

Young, DC (1996) *The Modern Olympics: A Struggle for Revival.* Baltimore: Johns Hopkins University Press.

If you want to further enhance your academic understanding of the Games, some of the best sources of information are in academic journals which can be accessed through your college or public library, for example:

Brown, G (2000) 'Emerging issues in Olympic sponsorship: implications for host cities', *Sport Management Review,* 3(1): 71–92.

Guttmann, A (2003) 'Sport, politics and the engaged historian', *Journal of Contemporary History,* 38(3): 363–75.

Hong, F (1998) 'The Olympic movement in China: ideals, realities and ambitions', *Culture, Sport and Society,* 1(1): 149–68.

Loland, S (1995) 'Coubertin's ideology of Olympism from the perspective of the history of ideas', *Olympika: The International Journal of Olympic Studies,* 4: 49–78.

Murray, B (1992) 'Berlin in 1936: old and new work on the Nazi Olympics', *The International Journal of the History of Sport,* 9(1): 29–49.

Scruton, J (1998) *Stoke Mandeville: Road to the Paralympics.* Peterhouse Press. Aylesbury.

Chapter 4
Introduction to sociological theories of sport in modern society

Paul Beedie

The modern world is a complicated place to grow up in. Sport is an important component of this world in lots of ways, many of which (for example, how the media promotes sport, how we consume sport and how we invest physical capital in our bodies) will be explored in much more depth in later chapters. This chapter has a number of specific aims. The first is concerned with understanding the importance of theory within the sociological analysis of sport. The second is to provide you with an explanation of theory and its usefulness. The third is to set out the main points of the major sociological theories that inform the subsequent chapters. The fourth is to provide some guidance on how sociological theories and concepts might be usefully applied to an understanding of sport.

Sociology, that is the scientific investigation of human behaviour, emerged as recognisable from a genesis that can be traced back to the work of Auguste Compte (1789–1857). A brief introduction to Compte and other key historical thinkers in sociology is given below because an understanding of how this academic discipline emerged sheds light on how the key theoretical positions outlined in this chapter have developed over time. However, it is important to remember that sport is a social phenomenon – that is, it has a history that predates us and which determines 'what sport is' in a social sense. In other words the social order that exists in the present is a product of the past reproduced and/or challenged in the present in ways that will determine the forms it will take in the future. It is Berger and Luckmann (1966), two German sociologists, who produced arguably the seminal text of their era to explain this. Titled *The Social Construction of Reality* this book argues that: *Man's humanity and his sociality are inextricably intertwined. Homo sapiens is always, and in the same measure, homo socius* (1966, p51). The book argues that all social activity operates in a framework of social order that exists as a construction outside the biological and empirical world: in short that social order is a 'human product'. They go on to argue that we are all subject to processes of 'habituation' in our interactions with the social order and this plays a significant role in the reproduction of the social order. Thus, according to Berger and Luckman's view of the world we can see that sociology is concerned with this social order and how it is constructed.

Although many of the key theorists from sociology were not concerned specifically with sport, they were/are concerned with how society is ordered (or structured) and how we contribute to this social order (through our agency). The key idea here is that sport is a part of this construction, that is, it is human organisation and human activity that give sport its meanings. Because sport is a social construction its status, values, purpose and forms are not fixed, rather they can best be thought of as fluid – staying broadly the same (because humans are 'habituated' through processes of socialisation) yet retaining a dynamic that simultaneously accommodates and resists change. Social theory, then, is a way of understanding this complex situation. The adaptation of a particular theory or theoretical position, as we shall see below, is determined by what aspect of sport in society a person wants to understand.

To pursue this idea, that theoretical ideas can help us understand the complexity of the social world, leads us to the concept of the 'sociological imagination' first developed by C Wright Mills (1959). Mills suggests: *The sociological imagination enables its possessor to understand the larger historical scene in terms of its meaning for the inner life and the external career of a variety of individuals* (original reprinted in Hamilton and Thompson, 2002, p 317). Mills is suggesting that by reflecting upon and thinking about our experiences in the social order we can better understand ourselves and the circumstances, views and values of others. Ultimately these insights will affect the person we become as we 'career' through life. Social theory is a useful framework for this ongoing reflection because it raises our awareness of what Mills calls 'public issues' and thus our capacity to both understand and effect change within the social world.

Learning Objectives

On completing this chapter you should be able to:

- provide a brief outline explaining what sociological theory is;
- explain the role of sociological theories within the analysis of sport in modern society;
- explain the major characteristics of the dominant sociological theories;
- summarise how they can be applied to an understanding of modern sport;
- detail how sociological theories address the issue of agency and structure;
- explain why all theoretical analyses of sport are limited by their own specific focus.

Introduction: what is theory?

Social theory is an explanation of a relationship or relationships in the real world. Houlihan (2003, p12) suggests that theory is *the best currently accepted explanation of the available evidence of a relationship or a natural phenomenon.* Miles (2001, p1) goes further than this when he suggests: *effective social theory is capable of having a real impact on how we perceive our own individual place in that world and how our own experiences actively reflect broader processes of social change.*

Sociology and the emergence of key theories

The origins of the academic discipline of sociology are generally attributed to ideas first articulated by Auguste Compte (1798–1857) (Giddens, 2006; Bilton et al., 2002). All the founders of sociology were concerned with the changes transforming society and each has had a major contribution to the theoretical positions outlined below. Compte was essentially a 'functionalist' who believed that by establishing universal 'laws' leaders of society could advance towards more enlightened policies. Emile Durkheim (1858–1917) developed these ideas, but distanced his position from the political dimension advocated by Compte. Durkheim's significant contributions concerned a recognition of the effects of industrialisation in the modern world, and in particular the development of the division of labour – the emergence of specialised jobs – and the problems of the rapidity of change impacting social wellbeing and creating what he called 'anomie' – a purposelessness created by the new social order. While industrialisation featured prominently in the thinking of Karl Marx (1818–1883), his emphasis upon economic conditions meant a departure from a functionalist explanation of society to an explanation predicated on a stratified society of unequally distributed resources resulting from a materialist conception of history. Marx was concerned with the emergence of capitalism and his thinking was foundational for conflict theory.

Max Weber (1864–1920) was influenced by Marx, but developed his own broad-ranging analysis of social conditions, and in particular the study of bureaucracy – the structuring of organisations (government departments, schools and business corporations for example) in ways that simultaneously create rational efficiencies of production while also empowering 'experts' (e.g. managers, specialist operatives such as teachers) whose position is advanced by the circumstances of their work. These theorists, together with others such as Talcott Parsons (1902–1979) – whose empirical studies significantly promoted the authority of functionalism as the dominant theoretical framework for sociology in the first half of the twentieth century – were broadly concerned with the 'structure' of society. The other half of the structure-agency equation was not completely ignored however, particularly in America where an approach to what became 'symbolic interactionism' was pioneered by George Herbert Mead (1863–1931). Mead was concerned with the way language and symbols contribute to shaping human behaviour and his work led to the interactionist theories developed by people such as Erving Goffman (1922–1982).

Inevitably, because of the complexity of the social world and the rapidity of change characteristic of modernity, social theories themselves become a part of this social dynamic. Social theorists of the nineteenth century have set out a template that has an 'anchor' in the social realities of the times when they were writing but that, as social conditions have evolved, have necessitated critical interrogation leading to the emergence of 'new' theoretical ideas and positions. This process is ongoing precisely because social change is ongoing. The overarching ambition of social theory remains to provide the best explanation it can for how and why this social complexity remains and to explore which people (or groups of people) are catalysts of change and what benefits (or otherwise) accrue and for whom. Sport sociologists take the positions advocated by mainstream sociologists and develop theoretical and empirical investigations within these scientific parameters. The aim is to understand sport in society.

Why do we need theory?

Theory is important, then, because although we are all educated and may feel we know about how the real world operates because of the way we interact with people in different places on a day-to-day basis, we rarely, if ever, see the complete picture. Many of us, if not all, intuitively 'theorise' all the time. This is because in order to participate in the social world of everyday life we have to understand our place in that world. Inevitably, our understanding of that place is determined by the social circumstances of our arrival into and subsequent growing up in that world. We intuitively understand difference and otherness as in boy–girl, white–black, rich–poor because it is part of our empirical experience of the world. 'Theorising' in this respect is the reflective process by which we position ourselves in the world – that is, to be located and with a sense of identity. The theory outlined in this chapter helps us extend our knowledge and understanding into the realm of insight. That is, as people (agents) we operate within structural constraints but, by developing a sociological imagination that extends our theorising potential beyond the intuitive into scientific investigation, we can use theory to understand much more about the social world – it helps us to see a more complete picture, although for any one person that picture will still contain socially and culturally determined limitations. There are a number of reasons for this.

First, there are all sorts of power relationships and structural constraints which for most of us are invisible and yet which have major impacts upon our social activities. The idea of the 'hidden curriculum' in schools illustrates this point well. Pupils attend lessons in maths, English, PE, geography and others to gain specific subject knowledge, but by doing so they are 'learning' other things, such as boys are segregated from girls at certain times; the teacher is a figure of authority; to be in a certain place at a certain time; 'work' can be monotonous, but dedication to a task will bring its own rewards; personal organisation (books, kit, lunch) is required; passing exams leads to better employment opportunities; academic knowledge is valued as 'superior' to vocational expertise, and so forth. In sport more specifically, to be ignorant of the latest exploits of the top football teams or the winners of Olympic medals risks being socially sidelined as out of touch with the *zeitgeist*.

Power relationships and structural constraints in schools have been extensively investigated because schools are important social institutions that everyone experiences, continuously, throughout a formative time in their lives – childhood and youth (see, for example, Abercrombie and Warde, 1998; Walford, 1998; Willis, 1998). Of physical education (PE) in schools, Penney (2000, p 59) reminds us that: *education is not neutral nor value free and nor, more specifically are any of our curricula or teaching in PE*. It is the hidden curriculum that selects agendas, interests and values to legitimise. Penney argues the case for greater equity in schools (and PE in particular) where equity is: . . . *giving value to and celebrating social and cultural differences of individuals and in society* (Penney, 2000, p60) but in doing so acknowledges the reality of inequality. Existing inequalities privilege certain people (or groups) and marginalise others. To understand the 'hidden' components of school curricula is an insight that not everyone can achieve, but theory – in this case critical theory (see below) – can help us. The case of the formulation of and agendas within PE is an important concern for sport sociologists because of the common ground of physical activity in PE and sport.

Second, society is not a fixed social circumstance, but rather it is dynamic and evolutionary. As it is generally accepted that the pace of life and therefore the rate of change is speeding up, it becomes even more important to have theoretical 'tools' to help understand these changes.

Third, the application of social theory to understanding sport offers an additional perspective that needs to be acknowledged alongside other scientific investigations of sport. Physiologists can explain with increasing confidence athletic achievement in relation to the body as a 'machine' with its physical development potential for enhanced performance through training regimes, technological support and strict adherence to nutrition controls. Psychologists also reside predominantly in a positivist paradigm with its espousal of universal laws of mental and emotional attributes. It is no coincidence that elite athletic performance (in athletics or in premiership rugby and football or in county cricket) is supported by 'experts' in these areas – biomechanists, nutritionists, technical coaches with specialist remits (such as goalkeeping coach in football, the separation of batting and bowling coaching in cricket, kicking coaches in rugby, etc.). This is entirely consistent with the insights provided by sociologists such as Durkheim and Weber about how the modern world has adapted to an industrialised setting of rationality, and yet this view of sport is unbalanced without the insights provided by social theory, especially the social theories that have developed the ideas of sociology's founders, and particularly the ideas of critical theory and feminism. Thus to accept that sport can be understood through scientific investigation of the body and the mind is to miss the obvious point that we all live and operate everyday in a social environment. Sport sociology acknowledges that any person's involvement in sport is potentially enhanced and constrained by the social circumstances of his/her social circumstances. One extremely important role of social theory is therefore to identify the structuring dimensions of our lives and the (usually invisible) agendas commensurate with those structures and agendas that determine who does what sport, where and with whom. These, and similar questions that can be asked, are explored below in the more detailed outlines of the main sociological theories in use today.

Theory can therefore:

- provide a framework for asking questions about the social world;
- provide a 'toolbox' of concepts and ideas for understanding the social world (e.g. 'capital');
- help us predict and explain what is happening in the world;
- help us make informed decisions and choices.

This chapter, indeed this book, is in tune with Giulianotti's (2004) position that, although there are clear theoretical positions or 'schools' (such as the Frankfurt school) which contemporary theorists tend to gravitate towards, there is much to be gained from an: *abandonment of sectional division . . . to embrace theoretical diversity among communities of sport scholars within the social sciences (2004, p1)*. This book will advance examples of all the theoretical positions outlined below because all have something to offer our understanding of sport.

There is, however, some resistance to the idea of theory, and there are a number of reasons for this. In particular, there is the idea that theory is the preserve of academics who write in ways that are inaccessible to the general population. Related to this is the question that, as the world is changing so rapidly, how can theoretical frameworks developed many years ago be relevant today? With reference to sport, this chapter is a response to such criticisms and will show that theories are themselves sets of ideas that contain a certain fluidity (and can thus respond to social dynamics), and where rigidity becomes an issue other theories emerge to accommodate more recent social conditions. It will also endorse the position championed by Miles (2001, p2) who advocates social theory that operates from grounded contexts in the 'real' world and in doing so reminds us that social reality is indeed a social and cultural construction:

> Broad patterns of social change have actively altered our everyday experiences of social life. Social change is not remote in any sense of the word. It actively impinges on who and what we are. It manifests itself in how we relate to each other as human beings and in how we construct our individual and social identities. Social change is the very stuff of social life. We are indeed the actors in the play of social change.

Social theory therefore has an important role to play in understanding the modern world. It has many applications from the everyday common-sense understanding of why we do things in certain ways (for the individual) to the more specifically applied possibilities of social policy development (for the government). This leads the discussion back to the creative tensions in sociology between structure and agency – the institutional constraints of daily life (structure) set against the empowerment of individuals to behave in a manner of their own choosing (agency).

Social theory and its usefulness in the study of sport

There are two broadly defined groups of theory. Those that align themselves with a structural view of society (sometimes known as macro theories) can be subdivided into functionalist and conflict theory. Theories that draw upon an individualist perspective (sometimes known as micro theories) can be subdivided into interactionist, critical and feminist theory. It is broadly correct to say that structural theories such as functionalism and conflict theory have been foundational in the emergence of sociology in the social sciences – as such these theories have, because of the ways of thinking they have created, in turn led to more sophisticated theoretical ideas which exist because they attempt to offer a response to the criticisms and limitations of what came before. Thus, for example, conflict theory or Marxism evolves into neo-Marxism which is best positioned under the umbrella of critical theory (see below). Many of the variations of critical theory can be thought of as post-structuralist, that is 'going beyond' the theoretical limitations of the original structuralist theories.

The original theories still have a role to play in understanding the social world. Loy and Booth (2002, p8), for example, put the case for re-examining: *the functionalist perspective within the sociology of sport, as its principles and assumptions continually reappear.* As other chapters in this book will show, sport is still used as a social tool (or function) in the generation of social cohesion; many initiatives in community sport development today are testament to this. Moreover, the economic basis of conflict theory is still evident today in the relationship between sport and commercial interests: evidence of the ongoing exploration of the commercial possibilities created by sport is provided by the pay-to-view Internet-only access to a screened version of the England–Ukraine men's football match, a European Championship qualifier, on 10 October 2009 – the first such screening of a full England football international.

What has developed over time is that the theoretical boundaries that hitherto compartmentalised the different theories have become eroded so that, as in the case of critical theory for example, theories have become more sophisticated in the respect that they better reflect the real world, but also more fragmented and complex as they critique and cross reference other positions. In some cases, in feminist theory for example, a whole new branch of theory has evolved as a response to the recognition of the disproportionate power wielded by men in society in general, and most certainly in sport in particular. Indeed the concept of power – what it is, who has it and how it is used – has always been central to sociological analysis. One of the reasons why social theory has become more sophisticated is an increasing realisation that the original structure–agency debate has a complexity that needs to be unraveled. One of the most important attempts to do this was developed by Anthony Giddens (1984) and became known as 'structuration theory'. The position that Giddens adopts is that power relations become a starting point for understanding social organisation. He argues that all of us possess some power to potentially transform our lives – we can, to a greater or lesser extent depending on circumstances, manipulate the social environment. Power, like all resources that impact the social world, is unequally distributed so that at any one time there are people, or groups of people, who have more power than others but power is contained in the institutional structures of the social world that we have created. Therefore, even subordinate groups have some power to offset the power of dominant groups. Thus Giddens has developed a kind of interactionist position that moves the structure–agency debate forward by acknowledging we are both created by and in turn help create the social world we inhabit.

It becomes obvious that 'capturing' the breadth and complexity of the theoretical frameworks informing sport sociology today is a very difficult task. It is more important to understand what sort of questions each theoretical position can help us answer. The following sections, then, remain true to the differentiation of social theory into the groups and positions that the literature generally ascribes to each. When reading on in this chapter, do not lose sight of the fact that any social theory is but a 'best fit' that may, in different combinations, be used, discarded, developed and re-evaluated over time – the prefix 'neo' or 'post' is a clue here. In general structural approaches are concerned with processes of socialisation and stratification.

These two central ideas are developed in Chapters 6, 7 and 8. Socialisation is concerned with how we learn to play our role in the social drama of everyday life. A good example here is that sport is important because being physically active and fit means our contribution to society can be positive – so traditionally boys play football and girls play netball, except that this is changing because, despite structural 'guidance' about gender-specific games, these ideas can be and are challenged (girls' football is one of the fastest-growing sports). Stratification is concerned with the 'strata' or layers in society that create social boundaries; here, the chapters concerned with class, gender, race, ethnicity and (dis)ability extend the discussion. Age is a good example of how society is stratified – we attend school between the years of 5–18, we can vote and drink alcohol aged 18, we retire at 65. All these conventions create social groups, which disguises the heterogeneous characteristics of people who might, for example, choose to go on working into their 80s. Nevertheless, structures such as these underpin both functionalism and conflict theory.

Functionalist theory

Definition: functionalist theory
A sociological perspective that emphasises the need to identify and study the function of a social practice or institution and from this to determine the contribution which the practice or institution makes to the effective running of the society as a whole.

Functionalism is a theoretical perspective that is based on the premise that social events can best be understood in terms of the 'function' that they perform, that is, the contribution they make to the continuation of society. In this view, society is seen as a number of interrelated parts that share common values and thereby transcend the differences between people – the whole is greater than the individual. Functionalists see society as corporate, that is, a body, with 'bodily parts' that need to operate together to make society continue. Functionalism assumes that there are scientific truths about how the body works and these, when understood, can be set down as 'laws'.

This is a useful theoretical perspective as it enables us to see sport as a social institution that is a reflection of society as a whole. This institution can then be compared to and understood in relation to other 'bodily parts' in society. Sport is studied in relation to the contribution that it makes to the bodily system as a whole, for example, a physically fit population can form a productive workforce in the economy. Research that informs this theoretical position explores sport participation and its positive outcomes for society (e.g. improved health and wellbeing through sport tackling obesity).

There are, however, problems with this theoretical position. General criticisms point out that functionalism lacks the capacity to adapt over time as social circumstances evolve. Additionally, it overemphasises consensus while 'hiding' potential conflicts and it ignores agency. Regarding sport, functionalism assumes that all social groups benefit equally from sports and it does not recognise that sports are social constructions that privilege or disadvantage certain groups over others. Lastly, it overemphasises the positive consequences of sport for society (Bilton et al., 2002).

Functionalist theory will help us understand:

- the promotion, development and growth of organised sport;
- how sport plays a vital part in the processes of socialisation;
- the increase in sport participation opportunities;
- the increasing amounts of supervision and control of athletes;
- the importance of compulsory physical education and coaching education programmes;
- the success of elite programmes.

Conflict theory

Definition: conflict theory
A sociological perspective that emphasises that modern society is characterised by social
divisions that are based on an unequal distribution of economic, social and cultural resources
and this inevitably leads to a conflict of interests between those who benefit from this distribution
and those who do not.

Conflict theory has emerged from the theoretical framework set out by Karl Marx and is often, therefore, known as 'Marxism', with its more recent developments (Marx was writing in the nineteenth century) often referred to as 'neo-Marxism' (Giddens, 2001).

Conflict theory recognises that resources in society are finite and not equitably distributed. When resources are scarce, groups struggle to gain access to and control of these. Here, the emphasis is upon socio-economic and political relationships. In particular, conflict theory unites resources and power, arguing that, when resources are scarce, those groups who have access to them acquire a form of power (economic, political and social) over those groups who do not.

Learning Activity 4.1

Once you have grasped the basic theoretical ideas encompassed by conflict theory, think through how this might apply to sport.

- Who are the groups/people who control sport?
- Think about club chairpersons, managers, chief executives, TV moguls, coaches . . . do these all have equal power?
- Think about how many professional footballers become coaches and why?
- Are the powerful people in sport black? White? Male? Female?
- How many sports clubs are actually run by the fans?

Conflict theorists study sports in terms of how they promote economic exploitation and capitalist expansion. Research to support this theoretical position is therefore concerned with how sports operate to perpetuate the power and privilege of elite groups in society. There are limitations to this theoretical position. By using economy as the baseline, there is an assumption that all social life is economically determined. Similarly, the emphasis upon wealth-specific resources ignores the importance of other structuring dimensions of society such as gender, race, ethnicity and age, which appear to be important to the world of sport in particular. Lastly, this theory ignores the possibilities that participating in sport can be a personally and socially empowering experience.

Conflict theory will help us understand:

- the significance of class inequality and how it might be reduced or even eliminated through sport;
- how athletes and spectators are used for the profit and personal gain of the economic elite;
- that, by emphasising play and recreation above commercial spectator sports, participation may be more 'productive' for the individual.

So, although far from being a theoretical panacea, structural theories do give us some conceptual 'tools' to work with so that we can make sense of sport in society. Functionalism introduces the idea of the body and how sport can make a contribution to this corporeal operation of society. Conflict theory draws our attention to notions of economy, resources and power – the concept of 'capital' is particularly useful to understand sport because it can take a number of transferable forms such as 'physical' (investment in the body), 'economic' (sport and money), 'social' (who one knows) and 'cultural' (what one knows about sport) capital.

Interactionist theory

Definition: interactionist theory
A sociological perspective that usually emphasises the need to interpret social behaviour by examining everyday social actions so that our perceptions of social reality can be demonstrated as constructed out of the complex interactions between individuals and the social world they inhabit.

Whereas functionalism and conflict theory are concerned with the structures of society, interactionist theory focuses on the individual. The base assumptions here are that society is created and maintained by social interaction: we are all actors on a stage who generate meaning through what we do, where we do it and who we do it with. Interactionism draws upon the micro-social investigations of Erving Goffman (see, for example, *The Presentation of Self in Everyday Life*, 1959). Goffman developed a number of useful concepts that theorise social activity at the level of the individual. These include the metaphor of 'stage' (the place where social activity happens), 'front and back regions' (the locations where we are either on social display or resting), 'actors', 'scripts', 'directors' (encompassing the 'performance of everyday life' – we act out a script, drawing on negotiated or common language that may have been 'written' by people who have been there before us) and 'face' (the negotiation of social encounters in ways that enable both parties to retain their social decorum).

Interactionists who are interested in sport use interpretive and qualitative research methods that endeavour to present the views of the people being investigated. The interest here is to uncover the social processes associated with becoming involved and staying involved in sports, and in particular how people negotiate a sense of identity through sport. An additional concern for this theoretical position is the creation of subcultures, that is, how they emerge and how a person becomes 'in' or 'out' of such a socially defined group. This theoretical approach can help us understand a number of different relationships, for example, between Olympic sport achievement and ideas of nationalism and patriotism. Equally, it can be useful in illuminating how a skateboarding subculture operates where inclusion and exclusion might be much more than one's ability to follow a dress code.

While providing a useful alternative theoretical position to structuralist theories, interactionism can be criticised for overemphasising the individual and failing to recognise adequately the role that differences in power have to play, particularly with regard to structural inequalities. More generally, the social world becomes relative so that nothing can be wholly false or wholly true. Lastly, interactionism does not adequately address social change.

Interactionist theory will help us understand that:

- sports might need to change to match the perspectives and identities of those who play them (e.g. touch rugby, mixed junior football, special schools athletic events such as the 300m);
- sports organisations need to become more democratic, less autocratic and less hierarchically organised (e.g. the 'real' Manchester United FC after the US-driven Glazer take-over of that club);
- identity formation processes that normalise pain, injury and substance use in sport need to change.

Critical theory

Definition: critical theory
A series of sociological perspectives that emphasise the complex interrelationships between modern social structures and institutions, the impact of systematic power inequalities, culture and social groups.

Critical theory is not a single theory but, even more so than structural theories and interactionism, one that embraces a whole raft of theoretical ideas. For some theorists, for example, feminism is under the umbrella of critical theory, but such is its importance to the understanding of sport (because of the gendered aspect of sport participation) that it is considered separately here. Critical theory uses ideas from other theoretical strands, for example, it is interested in power and the distribution of resources in the same way that Marxism is – and thus might be thought of as neo-Marxism, but it is essentially concerned with more than economics. In their book *Power Games* (2002), John Sugden and Alan Tomlinson develop ideas from Gidden's structuration theory and other sources such as hegemony theory to advance the case for the centrality of power in understanding contemporary sport. They suggest (2002, p6): . . . *it is people, either individually or collectively, and not systems, that wield, challenge, seek or reaffirm power. They act, of course, within the context of institutional structures, but those structures are themselves contingent upon ongoing and embodied power relations.* Sugden and Tomlinson adopt a critical theory position because they argue that power is actually integral to the process of resistance. Critical theory, then, rejects the view that sports history – and the great significant others that populate that history – can in itself account for the way sport is organised today; it is rather more nuanced and 'messy' than this. Critical theorists, then, go beyond the Marxist position that class is the only constituent of social organisation (although economic resources are still important, hence 'neo-Marxism') to integrate ideas of politics and cultural flows and forces (Hargreaves, JE, 1986b; Sugden and Tomlinson, 2002). Although critical theory can be thought of as a series of theories, one really important component of this position is that the power struggles that are ongoing in everyday life are empowering; so, to engage in a process of resistance changes who we are and how we contribute to the social world we inhabit.

Critical theory thus has an ambition to get 'under the surface' of the social world to uncover the assumptions, values, positions and ideas that form our culture, that is, how culture is produced and reproduced. It is concerned with power relations, that is, how these operate in cultural production and reproduction, and it is concerned with ideological struggles. Ideologies are literally the organisation of ideas into 'systems' that determine a way of thinking about the world. To this way of thinking sports are social constructions that change as power relations change and as narratives and discourses change – that is, the stories, pictures, news items and advertising images through which we construct our understanding of the world. This constantly moving social 'landscape' can be illustrated in sport by the example of marathon running; originally the preserve of elite male athletes, running a marathon has now become an important sporting aspiration (socially and physically) for a much greater range of 'ordinary' people (old and young, male and female, casual joggers and club runners).

Critical theory's key insight, beyond the obvious point that 'sport' is too diverse to include as a single 'function' of society, is that sports are much more than a reflection of society. Instead, sports are about people and places – or 'sites' – where there are ongoing struggles over the organisation and meaning of sports. Coakley (2003) suggests that sport is not a straightforward reflection of society but rather may be thought of as broadly similar to the social site of 'family'. People in families are in constant negotiation about how their lives should be organised as children argue and resist the structuring propensity of their parents and sibling rivalry operates to create a family dynamic that will be located somewhere on a continuum between functional and dysfunctional, but for all of us is a site for raising questions about how families should be organised: . . . *all social relationships are grounded in political struggles about how social life should be defined and organised* (Coakley, 2003, p 48). An example called 'Drawing Lines' is set out by Jeff Howe (2003). He discusses in a narrative form the artistic merits of skateboarding. The group he was involved with skate for pleasure at a wasteland they have taken 'ownership' of and where they have built their own topography of jumps, ramps and runs. The group skate for the intrinsic aesthetics of participation as a form of 'deep play' and actively resist subscribing to commercial pressures within skateboarding to 'further' their sporting careers by accepting sponsorship and by taking part in competitions – they take pride in resisting the structuring propensity of sporting interests that some skateboarders have subscribed to. This group is an example of resistance to the mainstream, a position predicated on an ambition to remain true to skateboarding as a form of self-expression.

Academics who are interested in research using critical theory are interested in the narratives and images people use to give meaning to their sport. They are also interested in how dominant narratives, images and power relations can be disrupted to promote progressive changes. The limitations of this approach can be seen in the complexity and diversity of theoretical ideas encompassed. For example, there are no clear guidelines for identifying and assessing forms of resistance and strategies for producing transformation. Similarly, there are no unified strategies for dealing with social problems, conflicts and injustice. Lastly, the emphasis upon resistance ignores instances when dominant norms are good, for example, as in the Olympic social legacy of urban regeneration.

Critical theory will help us understand that:

- sport can be a way of challenging and transforming exploitive and oppressive practices;
- sports are diverse and provide a range of participation opportunities across all social groups;
- the ideological implications of sport can be challenged and redefined;
- people are more empowered than they think to make these changes, and alternative positions of power and of ideas can be promoted by fanzines, blogs and enlightened journalism.

Feminist theory

Definition: feminist theory
A sociological perspective that emphasises the centrality of gender in analyzing the social world, and particularly the uniqueness of the experience of women.

(Giddens, 2001, p689)

Feminist theory takes several different forms. According to Storey (1993) these four forms are: 'radical' (in which women resist an oppressive male patriarchy); 'Marxist' (which explores women's domination that results from capital's dominance over labour); ' liberal' (which considers domination to be a function not of patriarchy or capitalism but of embedded in law or 'expressed in the exclusion of women from particular areas of life' (Storey, 1993, p125) and 'dual systems' (which bring together elements of radical and Marxist feminist positions). Two of the key feminist theorists to take up the investigative focus of sport are Jennifer Hargreaves (1982, 1986, 1987, 1994, 2000, 2004) and Susan Birrell (2000). Feminist theories applied to sport began as a critique of existing theoretical ideas that did not, it was suggested, take women's issues seriously. Thus, as with much critical theory, it has evolved as a refinement/advancement of existing theory. Birrell (2000) reminds us that this has been an ongoing development and has moved the feminist position forward from the beginning of a perspective that might be described simplistically as 'women in sport' to the more advanced integration of liberal feminism to sport analysis. Liberal feminists take the view that women have much in common with men but have come to live different lives because of: *different opportunities and different expectations, because society erects barriers that restrict their equal participation in society* (Birrell, 2000, p64). More recently, and particularly through the work of Jennifer Hargreaves (2004), feminist theory has become even more complex as it has moved into the realm of the post-modern. The advancement here is into the realm of 'third wave feminists' that move beyond the modernist structural constraints (of patriarchy or capitalism for example) so that women can define what sports they do 'on their own terms' (Hargreaves, JA, 2004, pp194–195) not just in relation to sports set up and developed by men. Most importantly, as we see through the emergence of women's football, rugby and cricket for example (England's women's football internationals are televised now, predominantly by the BBC), these important sporting developments are redefining gender roles and meanings leading to what Hargreaves identifies as 'cultural shifts and political changes'. One recent example illustrates the increasing profile of female athletes: Wendy Bedeau of Queen's Park Cricket Club, Bedford, an England cricketer, received an award from the International Cricket Council for outstanding service to cricket for her work bridging 'racial, religious and gender divides' (*Beds On Sunday*, 2009, p72).

Feminism, then, is particularly relevant to understanding sport because sports are generally gendered activities grounded primarily in the values and experiences of men with power and influence (Bilton et al., 2002). Research using feminist theory is interested in how sports reproduce gendered ideas and practices related to physicality, sexuality and the body. Of particular interest here is how sports are involved in the production of ideas about masculinity and femininity. For example, more people are now participating in running and jogging, and therefore consume, that is, buy and wear, a range of footwear, shorts, leggings and tops to do so. A visit to a sports shop will demonstrate how this equipment and clothing reinforce ideas of masculinity and femininity. Typically, female running shoes are in pink and pastel colours, while men's items are in dark and 'strong' colours; women's clothing offers more choice in terms of quantity and emphasises 'clinging' designs that accentuate female bodily curves whereas men's clothing is loose and 'free-flowing'. Feminist theory, therefore, is especially useful to understand sport because gender is such an important structuring dimension of the organisation of sports today.

Learning Activity 4.2

Buy one or more magazines focused on sport. Look carefully through the text and critically examine its displays of physical activity, clothing and footwear. Pay particular attention to colours, shapes and visual displays, such as pictures of athletes and presentation generally (such as advertisements and the models used).

Using ideas drawn from feminist theory, try to explain the ways that men and women are portrayed differently in sport.

Once you have undertaken this brief piece of research, take some time to talk over your findings with some of your peers. Were your findings broadly similar?

What do you conclude? Should the differences we see in sport across the gender divide be explained as merely a reflection of biological differences? Or are there other, more socially focused, explanations available?

There are limitations to feminist theories; for example, as with other forms of critical theory, there is a lack of clear guidelines for assessing forms of resistance. Similarly, feminism does not give enough attention to the relationship between gender and other categories of experience. Lastly, feminist theories often lead to victimising and over-generalisation or over-compensation.

Feminist theory will help us understand:

- that sport can become a site to challenge aspects of society that systematically privilege men over women;
- how to expose and transform oppressive forms of sexism and homophobia in sports;
- how sports can empower women to promote notions of partnership and competition with others.

Research Focus

Erving Goffman (1922–1982) was born in Canada and only came to academia later in his working life. He gained his PhD from the University of Chicago in 1953 and the observational studies that he developed in his subsequent academic career owe much to the traditions of this 'school' of sociology. But he was always his own person and there is a richness to his interactionist analysis that is wide-ranging and has proved historically enduring. Birrel and Donnelly (2004, pp51–52) summarise his importance as follows: *Most researchers see Goffman as a generator of sensitising concepts and insightful interactionist principles rather than a social theorist. The significance of his sociology lies in his powers of observation and his ability to capture social life in particularly appropriate terms, such as 'impression management', 'role distance' and 'face-work'. Goffman's legacy is such that his work is not so much cited as taken for granted as a sort of sociological common sense.* Goffman's concerns for quotidian life have a resonance for sport studies because when we are 'doing sport' we are undertaking a social activity in almost all settings. This is true even when the sport is an individual one such as road racing – as evidenced by television coverage of such British classics as the Great North Run and the London Marathon – when the race itself, but also the training, is commonly a festival of human interaction in a sporting setting: if Goffman had been a runner he would have had an orgy of notetaking at these events. Instead we are left with his legacy though the interactionist analysis and narrative accounts of academics indebted through his legacy.

Goffman's articulation of the drama metaphor, first set out in his first book *The Presentation of Self in Everyday Life* (1959) has been discussed in the section above. In order to illustrate the richness of his theoretical contribution I will now briefly outline his thoughts on 'face engagements'. Goffman suggests that when two or more people are present they contribute to an 'encounter' or face engagement. Mutual proximity necessitates interaction which is commonly verbal but *there are still other kinds of encounters where no word is spoken* (Goffman, 1997, p29); these are 'significant acts' and include 'gestures' and 'moves'. Moreover, a 'multi-focused' gathering becomes a 'participation unit' which may include 'bystanders' in the encounter. Goffman goes on to differentiate between 'unfocused interaction' where we do not engage in an encounter (and are merely 'checking out' the place, possibly as a bystander) and 'focused interaction' which is a sustained social engagement of conversation or game. In developing the micro-sociology of the latter form he goes on to explore the importance of the eyes in making or sustaining or ending or deflecting the encounter, which is typically initiated by an 'opening move' from one person and ended with a 'clearance' that is mutually agreed and simultaneously enacted: . . . *mutual glances ordinarily must be withheld if an encounter is to be avoided, for eye contact opens one up for face engagement* (Goffman, 1997, p31).

This brief summary of just one of Goffman's conceptual developments can be applied to any social encounter, including sport. The framework of face engagement recognises the complexity of social negotiation and draws our attention to social interaction as a way of gaining insight into how sport participation operates as a social endeavour. But equally one can see the limitations of a diminished 'complete picture' as the focus of the encounter precludes integration of other social factors such as those promoted by structural theories. Nevertheless Goffman's work is constantly revisited because of the insights it continues to provide. Birrel and Donnelly (2004) illustrate one of these in relation to feminist theory and sporting participation. They suggest (2004, p 60) that early attempts to explain women's low rates of involvement in sport focused on 'role conflict', the suggestion being that notions of 'athlete' and 'feminine' were thought of as counterintuitive. However, the application of Goffman's dramaturgical metaphor and his notions of 'role segregation', 'multiple selves' and 'role distancing' might empower would-be female athletes to recognise that deployment of role distancing techniques could solve the problem of different role expectations which become place and time specific when viewed from this perspective.

Learning Activity 4.3

Review of learning objectives

Before you move on to the next section of the book, you should spend some time carefully reviewing what you have learned from this discussion of sociological theory and its application to the study of sport in modern society. Based on your understanding of the chapter and the undertaking of the learning tasks, answer the following questions:

1. What are the main purposes of a social theory?
2. What are the four theoretical perspectives highlighted by the above discussion?
3. Can you briefly describe the main characteristics of each perspective?
4. Which of the perspectives emphasise the need to address the ways individual agency and the social structure interact in the social construction of sport?
5. Can you explain why all theoretical analyses of sport are limited by their own specific focus?

If you found any of the answers to the above review questions difficult, there are a number of ways to increase your confidence within this complex terrain of theories and concepts. The first is to use the questions to focus your re-reading of the relevant sections of the chapter. The second is to proceed to the next section of the book where you will find that each of these perspectives will be re-examined through a more detailed and applied discussion of sport.

Chapter Review

No one theoretical position offers a straightforward way of understanding sport. Instead, each has a series of strengths and weaknesses. The key here is to recognise these and to apply them with one's investigative hat on so that certain theoretical positions and/or certain conceptual ideas are used when they are useful to the ambition of explaining sport in society. What one is trying to understand will be determined by one's interest so that, for example, when an academic gets a research grant to investigate a certain aspect of sport s/he needs to use theoretical ideas that most closely match his/her research question. For example, research on behalf of Sport England to establish the health benefits of regular sport participation is likely to use a functionalist approach, whereas an investigation of how identity construction through sport (or not) operates among British Pakistani populations is more likely to use an interactionist perspective. Appropriate research designs will follow from the theoretical ideas that best inform the question, that is, what one wants to find out about sport.

Further Reading

There are a number of excellent introductions to sociology that cover all the main theoretical positions and illustrate these with examples, such as:

Bilton, T, Bonnett, K, Jones, P and Lawson T (2002) *Introductory Sociology*. 4th edition. Basingstoke: Palgrave-Macmillan.

Giddens, A (2006) *Sociology*. 5th edition. Cambridge: Polity Press.

Within sport sociology there are numerous texts that provide a more extended overview of the importance of sociological theories. Two highly recommended ones are:

Chapter 2: Using social theories: how can they help us study sports in society, in Coakley, J (2003) *Sports in Society: Issues and Controversies*. 8th edition. New York: McGraw-Hill.

Chapter 1: Sport, theory and the problem of values, in Jarvie, G (2006) *Sport, Culture and Society: An Introduction*. London: Routledge.

Giulianotti, R (ed) (2004) *Sport and Modern Social Theorists*. Basingstoke: Palgrave-Macmillan.

Part Two

Getting set:
key debates in
the sociological
analysis of
modern sport

Chapter 5
Sport's organisation and governance

Peter Craig and Gordon T Mellor

This chapter examines the organisational structure and ongoing development of modern sport. The chapter will further extend your understanding of some of the important social processes that have helped structure modern sport introduced in Chapter 2. Here we will be concerned with developing your understanding of the ways in which modern forms of sport have become rationalised and bureaucratically controlled; the complex nature of sport's organisational structure and governance; and how ongoing political, social and economic changes are continuing to transform sport's organisational structure and its processes of governance. When considering sport's social role and its modes of organisation, we need to recognise the importance of developing a sociological perspective.

As the issues discussed in the chapter will demonstrate, the policies and strategies adopted by the various elements of sport's organisational network are not always adequately integrated and sometimes focused on conflicting interests. Collectively, however, they have a far-reaching impact on the contemporary structure and future of sport. While the focus of the discussion is orientated towards sport in a British context, where the analysis can usefully extend into wider political, economic, social and cultural contexts, the mode of sports organisation and governance within international sport will also be considered.

Learning Objectives

On completing this chapter you should be able to:

- give examples of the historical development of modern sport's codification and organisation;
- detail the major components of the sports organisational structure in Britain;
- identify and explain the six areas of government intervention in sport identified by Houlihan (1997);
- explain the work of sport quangos within the development of British sport;
- outline some of the major influences that are influencing the changes that are impacting the organisation and governance of sport in Britain.

Introduction

One of the most persistent issues that sociology has sought to understand is how the way in which we organise our social institutions dovetails with the requirements of social control. Underpinning this is a desire to identify the processes that give our society its structure and sense of order (Eitzen, 2000). As you should remember from your reading of Chapter 4, for some sociologists (Durkheim and Parsons are two good examples), the ordering of our complex modern world is evident in the way the social institutions (such as sport) are structured and organised. Because most of us tend to believe that we should attempt to act in the 'best interests' of our society, we mostly accept, albeit sometimes reluctantly (e.g. the paying of taxes or the acceptance of an umpire's decision), the requirements of British legal order and its bureaucratic controls.

It is a normal state of affairs and a sign of a healthy society when most of us are reasonably content to accept some level of social control of our lives. Other social theorists, most notably Marx, reject this analysis and suggest that the maintenance of social order emerges out of the ways that those who have economic wealth and power control the social system so that it always acts in their 'best interests' and not in the interests of everyone. More recently, a growing body of influential social theorists (Giddens, 1990; Featherstone, 1991) have argued that social processes, such as globalisation, the feminist critique of male power, the mass migration of peoples and cultures, and the rise of consumer society, have meant that many of our traditional assumptions about the order of the modern world need to be radically revisited. The point to be drawn from this work is that there is a need to question how best to organise, control and manage our social world and the world of sport, which is now such an important part of it.

One of the most important contemporary social theorists who has set out to examine how these changes have impacted on modes of social organisation within our contemporary world is Castells (1996, 1997, 1998). For Castells, society and its modes of organisation are shaped by its system of values and institutions. Power within the society (to maintain the existing social order or to effect change) is determined by the structural capacity to impose one's will, and politics is the process of determining where power lies and governs its exercise.

Definition: power
Power has many sources but can be understood as the ability of individuals, or members of a group, to achieve aims and further the interests they hold.

(Giddens, 2001, p696)

However, power and politics (which is closely associated with the use of power to achieve specific social aims) need to be understood as being historically and culturally specific. They are deeply affected by social changes in traditions and conventions, new media and computing technologies, and the globalisation of economic systems. Castells' thesis revolves around the effect of these changes and the rise of what he terms 'the network society' (Castells, 1996). The network as a mode of organising our social world was primarily driven by economic activity, but it is now extending its logic to other domains and organisations such as those that characterise sport. As we will examine later, in sport the network is made up of international, national and local sport organisations, governments, transnational corporations and other social institutions that have little option but to work collectively in strategic alliances. Because of this, the ways in which we understand the processes of governance and the uses of power and social control need to be redefined.

The emergence and codification of modern sport

While the process of development or evolution in modern sport was undoubtedly underway before the start of the nineteenth century, it was Victorian modernity that saw the development of modern organised and codified sports. The very tenor of the modern times facilitated the growth of the 'new' sports. The increasingly industrial, urban, organised and outward-looking world power of Victorian Britain was built on rationality and, unsurprisingly, its recreations and entertainments reflected this (Blake, 1996).

At this time athletic games (as opposed to the older 'field sports' such as hunting, etc.) were made up in the main by the football sports that were to become soccer and the codes of rugby-football; a modernised cricket that had left behind the excesses of the eighteenth-century versions of the game; and the family of athletic activities that we would now include under the title of track and field. Such was the growing power of these sporting forms that in an almost unquestioned process, the belief in the moral virtues and social benefits apparently attainable from such manly sports became ingrained in the structure of modern British society.

The public schools had channelled and then promoted codified games, in the first instance to manage the boys who were in their charge. So extensive were the benefits both for the schools and the boys themselves, that these 'proto' sports were almost guaranteed a wider success. By 1864, the Clarendon Commission that was set up to examine and report on the major public schools, commended them for instilling in the boys *their love of healthy sports and exercise*. Conforming as the sports did to an understanding of 'muscular Christianity', and with the boys from the schools going on to university, the army and navy, into the civil service, into business and the professions at home, as well as serving throughout the Empire, the Victorian model of modern athletic sports was popularised both quickly and effectively.

Of course, some sportive games had undergone organisation prior to this period, but the motivation here was somewhat different. The 'aristocratic' sports, such as horse racing, cricket and golf, were governed by well-established and exclusive clubs. Here we see control and ownership as the prime concerns in activities that were considered to be the province of the upper classes. Because racing and cricket were vehicles for gambling, and with the wealthy willing to wager large sums, there was a need to assure that the outcomes were fair.

A further impulse that facilitated the growth, organisation and standardisation of sports was, of course, commercialisation. The growing middle classes were entrepreneurially capitalistic, and it became evident that there were money-making opportunities inherent in the provision, organisation and promotion of the increasingly popular sports.

What you need to note from this was that the organisation, bureaucratic control and codification of modern sport was never a simple developmental social process. It was and remains a complex process in which agreed rules, a participation ethic, established authority, clear identity and popular support combined to produce an activity that conforms to the dominant ideology. Through the processes inherent in its modernisation, sports were both a product of modern society and an essential institution in the reproduction of the modern social order across the classes and generations.

The organisation of modern sport: some historical landmarks

The impulse to formalise and organise the activities swept through British society in the mid to late nineteenth century in a wave: the Football Association in 1863; the Amateur Athletic Club in 1866; the Bicycle Union in 1866; the Amateur Swimming Association in 1869. The 'handling' game became organised under the Rugby Football Union in 1871.

Major Wingfield published and subsequently marketed the rules of lawn tennis in 1874 (he also sold the equipment). There followed the Hockey Association in 1876 and the Amateur Rowing Association in 1882. Governing bodies were set up to regulate and organise play, venue, duration, players, spectators and commercial aspects.

Some major competitions pre-date this drive for formalisation, but organising or governing bodies were essential to controlled and regular fixtures. Henley Regatta was begun in 1839, the Oxford and Cambridge Boat Race in 1849, the Amateur, Professional and Open Golf Championships were set up in 1858–1861, the FA Cup in 1871. County Cricket began in 1873, the All England Croquet Club (Wimbledon) in 1877, England versus Australia Test Matches in the 1880s, while the Football League was started in 1885. These sports had joined the 'rational recreations' and were justified on many counts.

It was in keeping with the spirit of the time that the athletic sports began to become another recreational option for many men regardless of class; if they were good enough to shape the public schoolboy, why not the rest of society? In an age dominated by 'self-improvement', the sports were codified in order to facilitate competition and this enabled, perhaps even demanded, popular access (Holt, 1989; Birley, 1993). By the start of the twentieth century, sport became more and more part of British popular culture and a modern imagination. These new forms of sport opened up increased levels of participation and fanship based on the 'facts' that sports were now regarded as:

- godly and moral (through 'muscular Christianity');
- 'healthy' through their promotion of physical exercise;
- socially important as they 'taught' important virtues such as discipline, courage, selflessness, self-reliance, aspiration to excellence, and so forth;
- economically important;
- a widely admired part of British cultural life that was starting to be emulated by many countries around an increasingly interconnected world.

Conforming to the world-view of Victorian modernity, organised sport captured the imagination of the modern age. It was this template, forged in the mid to late nineteenth century that set the course that British, and indeed world, sport followed well into the twentieth century. As has been articulated earlier in this book, the founder of the modern Olympic Games, Pierre de Coubertin, used it to fashion what was to become the largest, most impressive and influential cultural festival that the modern world has seen. Until the 1960s and 1970s, the aspirations, expectations and concerns of the Olympics were discernibly recognisable as those appropriated from how Victorian modernity shaped and defined the organisation of modern sport.

One of the defining legacies of this process was that most sports were run as independent, self-directing bureaucratic organisations that had little or no direct connection to the broader processes of democratic organisation, governance and public accountability that underpinned most of the other significant aspects of British society. It was not until the 1950s and 1960s, and only after a number of disturbing sporting failures, that public concerns about the lack of any co-ordinated national structure for the development of sport became a matter of political concern. One important outcome of this concern was the formation of the national Sports Council. The initial development of the Council in 1965 largely kept it within the control of the government. This was altered in 1971 when it was decided to insulate the Council from political control (Henry, 1993). Although this meant that the Council had a significant degree of political autonomy, because the government remained in control of its funding, how far this independence extended has remained open to question (Henry, 1993). By the mid-1970s, the Council had become an integral element of the organisational structure of sport in Britain and, under its 'Sport for All' banner, was supporting a vast variety of participant sports.

Definition: QUANGO

This term stands for quasi-autonomous non-governmental organisation.

The government sets up a 'quango' when it is clear that, while it is in the national interest that it promotes certain activities (e.g. sport, the arts) at the same time it does not want to have the direct responsibility for its organisation and administration: e.g. CCPR (Central Council for Physical Recreation).

As Houlihan (1997, p61) details, government intervention in sport tends to be a reaction to specific social problems. These governmental concerns about sport generally fall into six main policy concerns, to which we now turn.

The protection of the interests of powerful social groups

A good example of how powerful social groups were protected was the introduction of laws protecting landowners from unauthorised use of their land for various sporting and recreational purposes. A succession of game acts safeguarded landed hunting and shooting interests in the eighteenth, nineteenth and early twentieth centuries – this is a continuation of a long-established appropriation of animals of the chase by the elite. In a different guise, restriction of access to land for non-hunting purposes, such as recreational walking, picnicking and the like, led to the mass trespass on Kinder Scout in the Peak District in 1932. The more recent 'Right to Roam' legislation illustrates a modern hegemony in a different light: access to all non-proscribed and non-cultivated areas has now been permitted, despite opposition from land-owning interests, farming and indeed conservation bodies. As the recent banning of hunting with dogs highlights, the traditionally powerful sections of British society are no longer able to use governmental controls to guarantee their own interests in the face of the 'democratic' might of the massed population.

Health promotion and benefits

These are often targeted at low income (lower class) families and as a result of the problems associated with industrialisation and urbanisation. From early in the process of popularisation, the health benefits of sports and exercise have been claimed. Often contrasted with poor diet, housing and access to medical care, the locus of responsibility sits firmly with the 'individual'. This is seen clearly in recent initiatives on obesity.

Social integration

An example of this was how the doctrines of 'muscular Christianity' and 'self-improvement' were used to instil discipline within the urban working classes in British cities (the education acts of 1870 and 1902) (Houlihan, 1997, p62, or Hargreaves, JE, 1986b). Furthermore, there is a wider dimension in play here, where the recognition of, and involvement in, common activities enables and promotes social cohesion. However, 'Integration' at this level may remain entirely tokenistic, with sections of British society playing the same sports, but doing so separately: municipal tennis (working class) and club tennis (middle class); Asian soccer teams and leagues.

Military preparedness

The introduction of physical training in elementary schools across Britain (classes often instructed by ex-army, non-commissioned officers) came as a response to the perceived poor performance of the British Army during the Crimean War of 1853–56. In fact, poor nutrition, illness and disease were far more detrimental to the war effort than was the physical preparedness of the soldiers who embarked for the Crimea. Archibald Maclaren (1818–94) was charged with introducing a system of physical training for the military and this was subsequently introduced into elementary schools for working-class children. The middle- and upper-class boys in the public school system had an extensive games culture already established by this time. Collectively, these became the antecedents of our system of physical education that is now a compulsory element of the national curriculum (see Chapter 6).

Promotion of international prestige and nationalism

While the popular appeal of sport always meant that it has had close associations with expressions of nationalism and patriotic sentiments (Edensor, 2002), the celebration of, and investment of public money in, elite athletes and national teams was, until relatively recently, distinctly limited. Today, massive public celebrations of sporting victories – an open-top bus tour for the England Rugby Union World Cup winning team in 2003 and the Ashes-winning England cricket team of 2005 – are well established. Though almost unheard of until the 1970s, today we expectantly look forward to the announcement of the government's New Year Honours List to see which of our successful sports stars will receive national awards. In recent times, some of the more notable ones have been Dame Kelly Holmes, Jonny Wilkinson, MBE and Paula Radcliffe, MBE.

Sport and economic regeneration

Although we will discuss this issue in a more detailed way in Chapter 9, it is important to recognise that the economic significance of sport is such that no government can easily ignore it. The London

Olympic Games in 2012 and the Glasgow Commonwealth Games in 2014 are subject to the expectation that major sports festivals will provide tangible economic regeneration and leave a beneficial and lasting legacy. Indeed, in the British context the Manchester Commonwealth Games in 2002 proved a considerable success in this respect.

Time, however, does not stand still and, as Giddens (1990) notes, one of the defining characteristics of the modern world is its restlessness and constant change. Over the past few decades there have been a number of major political, economic, social, cultural and organisational changes that have dramatically altered some of the fundamental elements of modern society (Henry and Theodoraki, 2000). Some examples that you will be familiar with from your own lives and sporting experiences are globalisation; the seemingly endless growth of mass consumption; and the diverse ways that computer-mediated technologies have become an integral element of everyday life. While these changes have created a great deal of debate within sociology (Giddens, 1990; Featherstone, 1991) and within sport sociology (Andrews, 2000; Giulianotti, 2005), the focus here is not to explore these often dense and highly abstract arguments, but to examine how the changes have impacted (and are continuing to impact) the organisational structure of sport in contemporary Britain.

The structure and organisation of British sport

Not surprisingly, given the processes identified above, within the UK the 'governance' and organisation of sport is full of complex and at times confusing relationships. Governance in sport can be broadly understood as *consisting of self-organising interorganisational frameworks* (Jarvie, 2006, p154). In this next section we will briefly map out some of the major structural characteristics of the network of sport governance impacting British sport. As the diagram below shows, when we take a national governing body of sport (NGB) as a starting point, a variety of private, public, political and commercial organisations can influence how the NGB organises and controls its specific sport. There are a number of important points to note from this diagram. All sports in Britain are organised and controlled through a complex web of national, international and supranational interests. There is the wide range of governmental organisations that, while exerting a powerful influence on sports policy, have no direct responsibility for the actual organisation of sport. Indirectly linked to these, we can identify three other organisational groupings (media companies, commercial transnational sport companies and event management agencies) that can have an important commercial influence on sport, but whose businesses are not directly linked to sport. An example here is how companies such as Walkers Crisps – whose products have almost no connection with the 'playing of sport' – sponsor sports teams and use sport celebrities like Gary Lineker to promote and sell crisps. The deepening influence of commercial and media companies on all aspects of modern sport will be discussed more fully in Chapters 9 and 10. Lastly, what is presented only reflects some parts of the network; the choice of the NGBs as the starting point is just one of a multitude of possibilities.

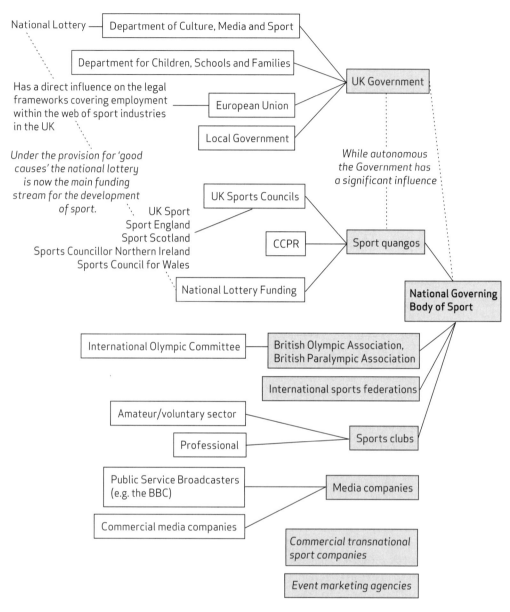

Figure 5.1: The organisational network of British sport

Sport and central government: Department for Culture, Media and Sport

The following statement by Tessa Jowell (then Secretary of State for Culture, Media and Sport) captures the British Government's commitment to the development of sport:

My ambition for sport in the UK is to start a 20-year process of re-establishing this country as a powerhouse in the sporting world (from 'Game Plan: a strategy for delivering the Government's sport and physical activity objectives').

At present, the Government has a number of strategic aims for the development of sport and these are supported by significant levels of investment of public money. According to the Government's own assessments, by 2006 £2 billion of public and National Lottery money had been invested in sport. This investment includes £459 million for a variety of school sports; £62 million in the development of grass-roots football, plus community and education initiatives through the Football Foundation.

The recognition of the importance of success in international sports competitions has also meant that each year approximately £60 million is being awarded under the World Class Programme, which has developed even more national significance due to the 2012 London Olympics. A significant reason that enabled the United Kingdom to win the right to host the 2012 Olympic and Paralympic Games was the guarantee that the costs of the Games were underwritten by the government. The production of the Games is not, however, the direct responsibility of the government but of specific organisations such as the London Organising Committee for the Olympic Games (LOCOG). Currently, the estimated costs have risen from an initial estimate of £6 billion, to an estimated £12 billion. Much of this massive expenditure is expected to come from the National Lottery and from community and business taxes in London and the Home Counties.

The cost means that the decision to bid for the Games is inevitably a politically contentious one. As Roche (2000) outlines, there is a range of arguments, some supporting the Games because of the benefits that such 'mega events' bring and others stressing the negative effects that such enterprises can incur. As with all political decisions, the government faces a complicated task of weighing the interests of those groups that will directly benefit from the hosting of the Games against the interests of other groups that lose out because of them.

In recent years worries about the health of the UK population, and especially that of young people, has led to an increased focus on the levels of exercise (or lack of it) that the country's increasingly sedentary population is engaged in. Sport England's Active People Survey conducted in 2005 produced the following findings:

- 21 per cent of the adult population (8.5 million people) take part regularly in sport and active recreation. Regular participation in sport and recreation is defined as taking part, on at least three days a week, in moderate-intensity sport and active recreation (at least 12 days in the last four weeks) for at least 30 minutes continuously in any one session.
- Regionally, regular participation ranged from a high of 22.6 per cent in the South East to a low of 19.3 per cent in the West Midlands.

- Walking is the most popular recreational activity for people in England. Over eight million adults aged 16 and over (20 per cent) did a recreational walk for at least 30 minutes in the last four weeks. 5.6 million people (13.8 per cent) swim at least once a month, while 4.2 million people (10.5 per cent) go to the gym.
- Over 2.7 million people put some voluntary time into sport – with an estimated 1.8 million hours unpaid support every week of the year. This equates to over 54,000 full-time equivalent jobs.
- 4.7 per cent of the adult population (1.9 million) contribute at least one hour a week to sport volunteering.
- 25.1 per cent of the adult population (10.2 million) are members of a club where they take part in sport – an increase from 17 per cent in 2002.
- Regular participation in sport and active recreation varies across different socio-demographic groups – for example, male participation is 23.7 per cent and female participation is 18.3 per cent.

Other research (Sport England, 2005) suggests that many of those surveyed recognised that there were health benefits associated with physical activity and that 71 per cent of those researched stated that they would like to do more sport and active recreation, but do not normally get round to it. However, some of the findings painted a more worrying picture, in that as many as 21 per cent of women spend more time doing their hair than exercising and around 41 per cent spend more time in the shower or bath than they do taking exercise. As for the men surveyed, 31 per cent spend more time playing computer games than undertaking sport or active recreation.

Learning Activity 5.1

Find out more about the government's support for sport by going to the DCMS website (**www.culture.gov.uk**). Once there, follow the links to 'What we do for sport', select three of the following categories and carefully examine what is presented:

- Sport England;
- UK Sport;
- equality in sport;
- community sport;
- funding sources for talented athletes;
- professional sport;
- sports facilities;
- world-class competitors.

Based on what you have found out and the issues identified in the above discussion, carefully answer the following question.

If the government had to limit its expenditure on sport, should it prioritise the promotion of exercise and a healthy lifestyle or the development of elite athletes who can compete effectively in world sport?

Local government and the provision of sport

In terms of the provision of many of our sport facilities, it is local government policy and strategy rather than those of central government that are vital for the promotion of sport (Henry, 1993). However, as a recent report from the Audit Commission (2006) in association with Sport England identifies, the quality and accessibility of local public sports and recreation facilities may not match the public's current expectations on health and fitness or offer the best value for money. The report suggests that across England the strategic planning of provision is underdeveloped. Owing to local political considerations, local councils are often focused on maintaining an historic pattern of sports and recreation service provision and rarely form strategic partnerships with other councils, private leisure providers, sport organisations or other cross-sector partners such as health and education departments, to improve and develop facilities.

UK Sport quangos

UK Sport

Established by Royal Charter in 1996, UK Sport is responsible for managing and distributing public investment in sport and is the statutory distributor of the sports funds raised by the National Lottery. In this role it is accountable to Parliament through the DCMS. Its stated mission is to *work in partnership to lead sport in the UK to world-class success* and its principal goal is to direct investment in sport that will underpin the development of world-class sporting performances by UK athletes (**www.uksport.gov.uk**).

The Central Council for Physical Training and Recreation (CCPR)

As the independent voice of UK sport, the CCPR is the umbrella organisation for the national governing and representative bodies of sport and recreation in the UK. Its general role is to act on behalf of its members to promote, protect and develop the interests of sport and physical recreation at all levels. This means that it is one of Britain's sports lobbying agencies, providing support and services to those who participate in and administer sport and recreation. Unlike UK Sport, it is completely independent of any form of government control and has no responsibility for allocating funds (**www.ccpr.org.uk/**).

While UK Sport and the CCPR act as umbrella organisations many of the major responsibilities for the development of sport have been devolved to the regional sports councils. This enables these sports councils to set their own priorities in terms of the development of sport within England, Scotland, Wales and Northern Ireland. Although it is not the purpose of this discussion to provide a detailed examination of the similarities and differences that exist between of each of these devolved bodies, a short overview of their principal aims is useful in order to highlight how the impact of political devolution in the UK is impacting on the governance of sport.

Learning Activity 5.2

Go to your local council and find out about the range of sporting facilities they provide. In addition, see what you can find out about their plans for sport and how they view the importance of sport for your community. You will also be able to find this information online.

From what you can find out consider the following:

- Does their plan for the development of sport include working with other interested agencies?
- Do they identify specific target groups within their development plan? If so, who are they and how is this targeting of resources explained and justified?

Sport England

The role of Sport England is to promote and invest in community sport within England.

Its aim is to encourage people of all ages to start, stay and succeed in sport at every level and make England the most active and successful sporting nation. Sport England has nine Regional Sports Boards (RSBs), each made up of appointed experts from areas such as business, local government, sport, health and education. The RSBs provide the strategic lead for sport in their regions and distribute investment for grass-roots sport (**www.sportengland.org**). Sport England has the stated aim to create opportunities for people to start sport, to enable them to stay in sport and to succeed. It provides the strategic lead for sport in England and is responsible for delivering the government's sporting objectives. Since 1994, it has invested some £2 billion in sport in England.

At a time when the eyes of the nation will soon be firmly fixed on preparing for the 2012 Olympics, it is hardly surprising that one of Sport England's strategic concerns is the importance of developing elite, successful athletes. To justify this there is often an assumption that there are clear benefits for a society to be derived from having world-class sports performers that represent it in international competition. These elite athletes can act as role models for the young, help foster national pride and aid the external validation of the nation's global status. As the sporting successes of countries such as Australia indicate, if adequate levels of resources are channelled from the support of mass participation into the development and support of elite performance, all of the above aims have the potential to be attained.

Once identified, sportsmen and women who have the potential to succeed at the highest levels of world sport need to be carefully nurtured. This is the role of the English Institute of Sport, which is at the forefront of the transformation of sport development in England: *The English Institute of Sport seeks to operate on world pace, to excel in a rapidly evolving, constantly challenging environment. Its task to provide world class services to athletes supported by world class performance programmes, requires breadth of vision and clarity of purpose* (**www.eis2win.co.uk**).

Sport Scotland

Sport Scotland is directly responsible to the Scottish Parliament for the delivery of the Scottish government's national strategy for sport and the investment of Scottish Executive and National Lottery funds. The major aims of Scotland's national strategy for sport are:

- a country where sport is available to all;
- a country where sporting talent is recognised and nurtured; and
- a country achieving and sustaining world-class performance in sport.

To achieve these aims, it has set four national priorities for the development of sport in Scotland that aim to deliver well-trained coaches, administrators and athletes; strong national sports organisations; quality sporting facilities throughout Scotland; and the provision of clear organisational structures designed to establish the pathways needed to achieve all its aims (**www.sportscotland.org.uk**). The major goals for the development of sport are laid out in *Sport 21 – 2003–2007: The National Strategy for Sport*. *Sport 21* produces a vision of sport in Scotland (that is in some ways quite distinctive from that proposed for England by Sport England) that emphasises widespread community involvement in sport (rather than the development of elite sport) through its overarching goal to get 60 per cent of Scots taking part in sport at least once a week by 2020.

Sports Council for Wales

The Sports Council for Wales is the national organisation responsible for developing and promoting sport and active lifestyles within Wales. It is directly responsible to the Welsh Assembly Government for the distribution of the National Lottery funds for sport. It also acts as the main adviser to the Welsh Assembly Government on sporting matters. One of its primary objectives is to help the delivery of the Assembly's vision for a physically active and sporting nation. In its implementation of these policy objectives, its main focus has been to increase the frequency of participation; persuade those who are currently sedentary to become more active; and to encourage people, young and old, to develop a portfolio of activities through which to achieve healthy levels of activity (**www.sports-council-wales.org.uk**).

Sport Northern Ireland

Given the historical problems of community division in Northern Ireland and the potential of sport to act as a catalyst for community integration, it is unsurprising to see that inclusivity is one of the principal aims of SportNI (**www.sportni.net**). As it notes in its corporate plan, its vision is *through sport, to contribute to an inclusive, creative, competent, informed and physically active community* (SportNI, 2007, p6). Underpinning this it has established ten values that govern the way in which Sport Northern Ireland operates: belief in sport; social inclusion; new targeting of social need; partnership; consultation; sustainable development; respecting difference; innovation; valuing people; public service.

SportNI is responsible to the Department of Culture, Arts and Leisure (DCAL) which is a governmental department within the Northern Ireland Assembly. From a sociological perspective, the relationship between the two is one of the most interesting within all sections of sport governance in the UK. They have directly set out a social agenda that includes the concept of cultural capital, which has recently become a significant analytical concept within sport sociology (Giulianotti, 2005; Jarvie, 2006).

DCAL, in conjunction with SportNI, are committed to the development of policies and resources that will *protect, nurture and grow our cultural capital for today and tomorrow* (SportNI, 2007, p10). For DCAL and SportNI, the cultural capital of sport is manifested in three ways:

- People – the creators and consumers of cultural capital, including sportswomen and sportsmen.
- Infrastructure – the physical spaces within which culture is created and enjoyed, including sports grounds.
- Products and services – cultural output, including sporting success.

Learning Activity 5.3

Go online and visit the websites of all the home nation sports quangos. Your task is to find out how they are planning for the 2012 Olympics. What are their strategies and their priorities? Do you note any significant differences between the four councils and, if so, how might you explain these differences?

International sport federations

International Federations (IFs) are international non-governmental organisations recognised by the International Olympic Committee (IOC) and their national members as administering their sport (or in some cases sports) at world level. While they have independence and autonomy from other global sports organisations in respect of the administration of their sports, the reality is that these external bodies can and do have a major influence on the way in which sport is organised nationally. International sports federations seeking IOC recognition must ensure that their statutes, practice and activities conform with the Olympic Charter.

The IFs have the responsibility and duty to manage and monitor the everyday running of the world's various sports disciplines. This includes the practical supervision of the development of athletes practising these sports at every level; the sport's promotion and development; the everyday administration of their sports and guarantee of the regular organisation of competitions as well as respect for the rules of fair play. The IFs also formulate proposals addressed to the IOC concerning the Olympic Charter and the Olympic Movement in general. These include the organising and holding of the Olympic Games, such as expressing opinions concerning the candidatures for organising the Olympic Games, particularly the technical capabilities of the candidate cities. IFs also collaborate in the preparation of the Olympic Congresses and participate in the activities of the IOC commissions.

Recognised IFs whose sports appear on the Olympic programme have the status of International Olympic Federations. As such, they participate in annual meetings of the IOC Executive Board with the International Olympic Summer Federations and with their winter Games counterparts. In order to discuss common problems and decide on their events calendars, the summer Olympic federations, the winter Olympic federations and the recognised federations have formed associations: the Association of Summer Olympic International Federations (ASOIF), the Association of International Olympic Winter Sports Federations (AIOWF), the Association of IOC Recognised International Sports Federations (ARISF) and the General Association of International Sports Federations (GAISF), which also includes other sports federations.

The International Olympic Committee

The Olympic Movement encompasses organisations, athletes and other persons who agree to be guided by the Olympic Charter. The Olympic Movement groups together all those who agree to be guided by the Olympic Charter and who recognise the authority of the IOC, namely, the IFs of sports on the programme of the Olympic Games; the National Olympic Committees (NOCs), the Organising Committees of the Olympic Games (OCOGs), athletes, judges and referees, associations and clubs, as well as all the organisations and institutions recognised by the IOC.

The IOC is the supreme authority of the Olympic Movement. It is an international non-governmental, non-profit organisation and the creator of the Olympic Movement.

The IOC exists to serve as an umbrella organisation of the Olympic Movement. It owns all rights to the Olympic symbols, flag, motto, anthem and Olympic Games. Its primary responsibility is to supervise the organisation of the summer and winter Olympics.

The purpose of IOC Commissions is actively to contribute to promoting the ideals of the Olympic spirit (Olympism) in their specific domains. In order to study certain subjects and make recommendations to the Executive Board, the President of the IOC sets up specialised commissions. Some of these include IOC members, representatives of the International Olympic Sports Federations and the National Olympic Committees, athletes, technical experts, advisers and sports specialists.

There are currently 203 NOCs and they cover all five continents. The NOCs propagate the fundamental principles of Olympism at a national level within the framework of sports activity. The NOCs come together at least once every two years in the form of the Association of National Olympic Committees (ANOC) to exchange information and experiences in order to consolidate their role within the Olympic Movement. ANOC also makes recommendations to the IOC regarding the use of funds derived from the television rights intended for the NOCs. These recommendations focus on the implementation of the Olympic programmes. The 203 NOCs are split among five continental associations, which have a powerful influence on the selection of sites for the summer and winter Olympiads:

- Africa: ANOCA (Association of National Olympic Committees of Africa)
- America: PASO (Pan American Sports Organization)
- Asia: OCA (Olympic Council of Asia)

- Europe: EOC (European Olympic Committees)
- Oceania: ONOC (Oceania National Olympic Committees)

British Olympic Association

The BOA was formed at a meeting at the House of Commons on 24 May 1905. The Association then included representatives of the following sports: fencing, life-saving, cycling, skating, rowing, athletics, rugby, football and archery. All these sports had governing bodies or clubs at the time. Great Britain is one of only five countries that have never failed to be represented at the Olympic Games since 1896, Australia, France, Greece and Switzerland being the others (**www.olympics.org.uk**).

Reflection Point 5.1

Developing the network of British sport

Although the discussion presented in this section of the chapter has concentrated on providing a brief overview of the major elements, relationships and principal policies and responsibilities of the various segments of the network, a number of points of concern are emerging. In terms of the effective control and development of sport in Britain (and more especially internationally), the network is too large, too complex and too full of competing interests to be easily managed, transformed and made publicly accountable. On this last point, as Sugden (2002) has argued through his analysis of how this global and national network operates within the context of professional football, this does not mean that a serious and sustained attempt should not be made to reform the way in which sport, especially international sport, is governed and controlled. Over the next few years changes are almost inevitable and this begs the question as to whether these changes will be driven by powerful commercial interests, national governments seeking to maximise the social and health benefits of sport, or other as yet unforeseen combinations of political, social, economic and cultural forces.

As for how Britain will address the challenges posed by the social changes it now faces in terms of the powerful equity and diversity agendas that are now impacting on all sport organisations (see Chapter 8), the framework for the organisation and development of sport being developed in Northern Ireland offers some interesting signposts. While Northern Ireland has a number of characteristics that make its circumstances very different from those of the other areas of the UK, if UK sports organisations are to meet their own targets for social inclusion, they will need to make a sustained critical evaluation of their current planning. If some of the problems of social exclusion and alienation that have until recently been a characteristic of life in Northern Ireland are to be avoided, sports organisations will need to make significant efforts to explore how their organisational processes can address the problems of social need and the development of effective partnerships, based on consultation, that are committed to sustainable developments that respect our growing cultural diversity.

Social change and the organisational structure of contemporary British sport

The politics that shape the agendas of the government and therefore how politicians might desire to influence the governance of sport have, over the past few decades, changed in a number of important ways. International relations have changed dramatically with the fall of communism and the ending of the Cold War. International sport is no longer subject to the cynical control of governments and their desire to promote their own ideologies (Hargreaves, JE, 2002). In addition, processes of globalisation (see Chapter 11) allied to technological changes, have led to the freer movement of people, greater levels of international connections based on globalised capital, an international system of production and the global flow of information. Today, international sport all too clearly shows the irony of the global age, in which countries and their sports teams are becoming ever more interdependent, while at the same time evidencing the growth of nationalism with rival nations' competing wealth and status.

Definition: nationalism

A set of political beliefs, cultural practices and symbols that are designed to create a strong identification with a specific national community.

In recent decades some profound changes have taken place within the politics of most Western societies and specifically within British politics. Since the election of Margaret Thatcher's Conservative Government in 1979, there has been a significant shift away from the politics and social organisation of state-welfarism towards those of liberal individualism (Henry, 1993). Whether these changes represent a fundamental shift in the structure of modern society remains a matter of intense sociological debate (Henry and Theodoraki, 2000). What is undeniable is that these changes are real and are having a dramatic impact on all aspects of the sporting network identified above.

This noted, as Henry and Theodoraki (2000) stress, it is also inevitable that there has been, and will continue to be, significant variations in how the various sectors of the British sport network respond to these changes. As processes of political devolution take hold within Britain, it is likely that governmental structures that are in place for each of the four home countries, will continue to drive further development of their own separate agendas for sport. What this will mean for the governing bodies of sport whose responsibilities (nationally and internationally) cover all of the UK (e.g. UK Sport, the British Olympic Association and the British Paralympic Association) or whose organisational structures are a federated union of the specific sport's home nation associations (e.g. British Athletic Federation), only time will tell.

Research Focus

The work of Barry Houlihan

For political scientists such as Houlihan (2003, p47) the development of *a comprehensive understanding of the social significance of sport in contemporary society* requires a number of analytical approaches that 'encompass not just the politics *of* sport but also politics *in* sport.' For almost two decades Houlihan's body of work (1991, 1997, 2000; Houlihan and White, 2002; Green and Houlihan, 2005; Houlihan and Green, 2006) has attempted to explore these internal and external political processes within sport. In doing so he has not only provided a detailed critique of these analytical approaches but also supported their analysis with an extensive set of empirical evidence demonstrating the changing economic and social importance of sport and how this in turn has influenced and been influenced by the state, its bureaucratic structures and its political/policy interests.

One of the clear and unambiguous outcomes of this work is the absolute rejection of the idea that sport can be separated from the concerns of governments and annexed off into non-politicised parts of civil society. In one of the most comprehensive studies yet undertaken Houlihan (1997) draws on a range of international comparative studies to highlight how many governments around the world now regard sports as a resource that they are able to co-opt (willingly or otherwise) into the delivery of important public policy initiatives that range from health and lifestyle management, juvenile justice programmes, community cohesion projects and recreational to elite sport development programmes.

Though some of the political motives behind this increasing involvement with the world of sport are often complex and shifting they nonetheless indicate that within a number of government departments sport is being linked to the assessment of the social and cultural wellbeing of communities and the nation (Houlihan and White, 2002). Within the UK this political significance and the fact that the sport councils and the national governing bodies of sport can now rely on a fairly consistent and extensive form of funding (due to the impact of the National Lottery), means that UK sport development within the twenty-first century can be regarded as an area of *successful innovation and service development* albeit that the party political nature of UK politics and economic instability mean that this development is also framed by *an environment of policy instability and uncertainty* (Houlihan and White, 2002, p206). His two recent co-authored texts further elaborate and develop these themes through their detailed examination of the growth and current status of UK sport development (Houlihan and White, 2002) and elite sport development (Green and Houlihan, 2005).

For sport, the plus side of these policy arrangements has been a significant increase in funding and there seems to be some cause for optimism in that sport development is now regarded as a mainstream activity/policy instrument integral to a diverse range of governmental policy fields. However, as Houlihan and White (2002) argue this also means that sport faces some important challenges. Sport in the UK, especially elite sport, needs the financial investment of governments but this investment inevitably brings with it a loss of autonomy. Once sport organisations become dependent on government funding it means that they also have to adapt to the reality of having to deal with the variability of governments, political parties and their changing policy priorities. Strains on the public finances mean that public scrutiny and accountability also inevitably follow. Houlihan and White

(2005) therefore suggest that the reliance on government funding by elite sport means that more complex organisational arrangements are emerging that are increasing the separation of elite athletes and their funding from other areas of the sport and its governance. The outcome of this is increasing fragmentation and a widening of bureaucratic controls. By its very nature elite sport is a very expensive enterprise and the costs of supporting elite athletes can be seen as running counter to public welfare interests as funds get diverted to supporting the few rather than helping the sporting development of the many. For Houlihan and White (2002) this process sets up political tensions within sports as they seek to resolve the competing and very different interests of 'grass-roots' and elite athletes.

In some of his recent work, Houlihan (Houlihan and Green, 2006) has turned his attention to the analysis and understanding of policy change in school sport and PE. This work suggests that the increased emphasis on the pursuit of elite international sporting achievement has inevitably meant that the education system (within England and Wales), and its capacity to contribute to elite sporting success, especially in the context of the 2012 London Olympics, has become the subject of considerable debate. Research by Houlihan and Green (2006) indicates that school sport is now a highly contested policy area subject to pressure from competing sectoral interests. The fairly recent implementation of the specialist sports college initiative seems to represent a compromise between these competing interests, though the extent to which this policy has achieved its aims remains somewhat questionable.

The breadth and empirical depth of Houlihan's contribution to a sociological understanding of the political interests impacting sport, its organisational structure and processes of governance has been and remains one of the most important within the field of sport sociology.

Learning Activity 5.4

Review of learning objectives

Through reading the chapter and doing the various learning tasks, you ought to be able to answer the following:

1. When did the codification of games change them into the modern sports that we take part in today?
2. What were the social dimensions of Victorian modernity that drove governing bodies to be established?
3. Identify and briefly explain the major components of the organisational network that impacts on the ways national governing bodies of sport organise and control their specific sports.
4. Sport is a very important element of British public life. How is this reflected in terms of the government's involvement with sport?
5. What is the role of the Department for Culture, Media and Sport within the governance of sport in Britain?
6. Identify some of the major similarities and differences that exist between the home nation sport councils.

•••▶

> ## Learning Activity 5.4 continued
>
> 7. The levels of investment (financial and social) in sport mean that there has to be some form of public accountability. Do you think these arrangements are adequate?
> 8. What are the organisations with specific responsibility for elite performers, and what are their aims?
> 9. Detail how the British Olympic Association is structured and explain its role in the organisation of the 2012 London Games.

Chapter Review

This chapter has overviewed the creation of codified sports and their associated forms of national and international organisation. It has also examined how the organisation of sport has become an important arena of governmental interest. This has become even more complex with the devolved control of sport to the governmental structures of the home nations. We have argued that it is important to understand that sport organisations and the governance of British sport operate within an historically complex, dynamic and changing network. How this network operates is also subject to three very different sets of pressures: national political concerns and issues that are often subject to democratic accountability; the concerns and issues of international sports federations which have significantly reduced levels of public accountability; and the commercial pressures that transnational corporations and media companies can exert through their huge financial investments in sport. The complex relationships between the sporting organisations within the network and their competition to achieve their own aims and objectives, while protecting the vested interests of their sport(s), mean that the sociological analysis of sport needs to start with the clear recognition that sport is not governed by a single set of codes, organisational structures or strategies.

Further Reading

For an excellent historical overview of the development of modern sport in Britain read:
Holt, R (1989) *Sport and the British: A Modern History*. Oxford: Clarendon Press.

For a recent assessment of the impact of political and governmental interests on sport read:
Houlihan, B (2000) Politics and sport, in Coakley, J and Dunning, E (eds*) Handbook of Sports Studies*. London: Sage.

To further extend your understanding of the concept of social control read:
Eitzen, DS (2000) Social control and sport, in Coakley, J and Dunning, E (eds) *Handbook of Sports Studies*. London: Sage.

To develop your understanding of the policies and strategies of the UK sports quangos, it is best to visit their websites and read their strategy documents, all of which are easily downloadable.

Chapter 6
Sport, physical education and socialisation

Peter Craig and Gordon T Mellor

This chapter looks at the dimensions of sport and physical education in terms of their role in socialisation. It will now be clear to readers that a dynamic society both creates, and is created by the activities of the social institutions. These social institutions promote the norms and values of the overarching society. By reviewing how sociologists explain sport and physical education as working components of the social process, it is hoped that the important role that social theories play in our understanding of society will be made clear. In terms of physical education, it will be seen that the development of our contemporary model arose from diverse roots and the differing motivations that existed in the mid-nineteenth century; how women battled for a physical education of their own, and how the social concerns of the twentieth century have shaped what we currently teach in our schools.

Learning Objectives

On completing this chapter you should be able to:
- explain through clear sport and physical education examples what is meant by:
  - social institution;
  - primary and secondary socialisation;
  - social norms and values;
  - how you yourself have experienced processes of socialisation;
  - functionalist social theory;
  - functional prerequisites;
  - interactionist perspectives of socialisation;
  - gender socialisation;
- provide a context for the development of physical education in our schools and justify its current place in the national curriculum;
- demonstrate a good understanding of how, in a dynamic and changing world, sport helps society adapt.

Introduction

When we think about sport, why some people take part and others don't, why some succeed and others don't, we are often confronted by two very different sets of questions and possible explanations. Is our involvement and behaviour in sport governed by what we have learned, or is it determined by the physical and psychological capacities that we were born with? This is known as the 'nature–nurture' debate.

Nature (socio-biology)	Nurture (sociology)
Our capacity for sporting action is inborn.	Our capacity for sporting action is learned
Competition, between humans or between humans and the circumstances of their physical world, is a natural condition of life.	The natural condition of modern life is that it is socially and culturally constructed. All aspects of sport and its meaning, such as the meaning of competition, are learned and taught.
Human instincts and needs have shaped sport.	Sport is learned and is part of the culture of the society. As societies and their cultures change, so do how we take part in and understand sport.
Much of how we behave in sport is 'pre-programmed' (e.g. fight or flight instincts).	Sporting behaviours have to be learned and this socialisation process starts as soon as a child is born.

To some degree this debate lies at the heart of all sociology. Even if sport sociologists disagree about how they understand the way the modern world is structured or to what extent these structures determine our sporting behaviour, they all agree that the modern world provides a powerful influence on how we understand our lives and the possibilities they hold. As we look around our world, it is also obvious that the diverse ways in which different countries and cultures condition that understanding is a vital part of how children grow up. Because of its importance within our modern world, an understanding of the roles played by sport and physical education in this process has been an important area of interest.

Sport, physical education and socialisation

When a child is born, s/he has no social or cultural knowledge. Children need to become productive and confident members of their society. They have to learn how to be part of this world. More specifically, they have to learn its culture and traditions.

Definition: socialisation

The ongoing process whereby individuals learn and/or are taught to conform to the existing system of norms and values.

Definition: sport socialisation

A process that, through an individual's involvement in sport, teaches and reinforces knowledge, values and norms that are essential to participate in social life.

One important approach to understand modern society is to see it as a complex and dynamic 'social system'. As we discussed in Chapter 2, our everyday experience of our social world suggests that it has a fairly consistent structure (such as its various component parts: families, schools, sport, etc.) that endures over many generations. Within the family, various members can recount sporting events whose memory becomes part of the shared identity of the family. In this way, many families develop a long-lasting relationship with a particular sport. The same is also true for our experience of schools. As we walk into many schools, we can see on the walls pictures of the school teams going back many generations, that celebrate the school's sporting traditions and successes. No doubt, when you were in school you became aware of these traditions and that often these meant that certain sports were given status within the school while others were not.

Every society is characterised by a set of relatively stable and interrelated social structures that give the particular society its unique character. Some examples of these, which you should already be familiar with, are how families are organised; its forms of government; its economy and system of production; the education system; and sport. The term that sociologists have developed to describe these social structures is 'social institution'. Social institutions can be regarded as *the cement of social life. They provide the basic living arrangements that human beings work out in their interaction with one another and by means of which continuity is achieved across the generations* (Giddens, 1989, p381).

Definition: social institutions

Social practices that are regularly and continuously repeated, legitimised and maintained by social norms.

As this definition details, one of the most important roles performed by a social institution is the maintenance of patterns of behaviour. In sociology these are called social norms.

Definition: social norms

Forms of behaviour that are usually accepted as correct and 'proper' by the majority of the members of a society.

Learning Activity 6.1

Based on your experiences of sport as part of the PE curriculum and/or as part of a team, make a list of five 'social norms' that would be considered to be accepted and proper behaviour in sport. Then, by thinking back over your experience of sport, see if you can identify how you became socialised into perceiving sport as having these norms of behaviour. Use the following column headings.

Sporting social norm	When, where and from whom did you first learn that this behaviour was part of 'playing' sport?

Reflection Point 6.1

Sporting beliefs and our assumptions about everyday life

Please make sure you attempt the above exercise before reading this!
Some examples you have identified may be directly related to the playing of sport: a serious sports person must make sacrifices and be dedicated; dedicated sportsmen and women always seek competition in order to test their abilities; athletes accept risk and pain as a possible consequence of their sport. Others may be to do with the social side of sport: sport helps people to make friends; sport helps people develop self-confidence; getting fit for sport helps you keep healthy. Yet others may be linked to the realisation that sport seems to mirror some of the divisions we also can see in our society in that different social classes, males or females and racial groups play different sports. Clearly, all these observations can be challenged as being stereotypes, but they are nonetheless reflective of the common everyday experience of sport in Britain. Of course, the other interesting questions that sociologists are very interested in are where, when and through whom you learned these beliefs about sport. The fact is that once we have learned them these beliefs become largely part of our unconscious interpretation of the world – that is, until we are asked to do an exercise like this or we see something that disturbs our set of comfortable assumptions.

Competing sociological perspectives of sport and socialisation

As we explained in Chapter 4, sociology has developed a number of competing perspectives in respect of how we interpret sport and the structure of the modern world. These equally apply to how we interpret the role of socialisation. Some start with a system orientation in that they look first and foremost at the structure of the social system and how the society 'reproduces' itself over time and across different generations; some have developed a more critical examination of the structure of modern society; while others are concerned to emphasise how the individual reflexively engages with these social structures.

Learning review

Consider the following statements and match the correct theoretical perspectives that were outlined in Chapter 4.

Statement	Theoretical perspective
Sport is created by people who are consciously acting on their own behalf, yet the historical social structure of sport also constrains them.	
Sporting norms and values inform us how to behave. Sportsmen and sportswomen do not decide what these formal and informal rules are and are aware that if they break them they will be punished.	
All humans who take part in sport are conscious and reflexive agents who decide what they will do or not do. They are not just passive recipients of culture.	
Sport is an important part of our culture as it helps create a social structure that patterns how we behave and interact with others.	
Sport is part of our culture and was designed and shaped by powerful members of the society in order to protect their dominant position. Processes of socialisation are important elements of this process.	•••▶

Statement	Theoretical perspective
Sporting norms and values are created through a process of negotiation and agreement.	
Socialisation into the norms and values of sport provides an important way for the individual members of modern society to bond together.	

The study of socialisation in sport sociology has been heavily influenced by structural-functional perspectives (Nixon and Frey, 1996; Loy and Booth, 2000). While this theoretical perspective has been somewhat sidelined due to a series of serious criticisms regarding its failure to adequately account for processes of change and the distribution of power within society, it can be argued that the study of socialising processes in sport and society remain important. It is therefore important for sociologists to extend their analysis to understand how individuals act within the social and cultural constraints of their own personal circumstances and the prevailing social structures.

Within sociology the functionalist perspective sets out to define the role and importance of social institutions and to detail how these institutions interact in such a way as to ensure the continuation of the society. What this permits sport sociologists to understand is the social function that sport plays within the maintenance of contemporary British society. As Giddens (1989, p696) notes: *To study the function of a social practice or institution is to analyse the contribution which the practice or institution makes to the continuation of the society as a whole.* It is clear that sport can be regarded as a (modern) social institution with a number of definable social norms that to some degree are maintained across successive generations. When sociologists such as Luschen (1981) developed a functional analysis of sport, one of their primary concerns was to identify how sport is not only a product of that social world, but also how it helps reproduce it. For Luschen (1981, p209) the modern system of sport reflects *a fundamental structural pattern of human and social existence.*

While the basics of functionalism can be identified as originating in the late nineteenth century from the work of Durkheim, in the twentieth century this tradition has become most clearly associated with the work of Talcott Parsons who suggested that all societies need to achieve four specific outcomes in order to survive. He termed these as the functional prerequisites or functional imperatives (Craib, 1984).

- **Pattern maintenance** – all societies must develop effective cultural processes that help maintain and reproduce the existing social order across succeeding generations.
- **Integration** – all societies, but especially complex modern societies, must create social systems that can deal with deviance, maintain the existing social order and discipline people into working effectively within the social system. Because of the nature of modern society, these systems must be highly organised and bureaucratic.

- **Goal attainment** – all societies must develop effective political and educational systems that enable the society and a majority of its members to achieve their goals. In much of the modern world, belief in the equality of opportunity and a sense of what one's goals in life are, become tied to complex concerns about lifestyle and identity.
- **Adaptation** – all societies face changing circumstances. In order to survive they must adapt/evolve. This means that social institutions such as sport must also adapt to the changing needs of the society.

For sport sociologists such as Loy and Booth (2000), the enduring and highly successful development of sport within modern society can be explained in part by the fact that the functional imperatives of modern society are inherent in most sports. Sports' systems of rules both define the 'goals' of the sport and also provide a means through which individuals can attain these goals. The structure of sporting competitions such as the FA Cup is an excellent example of this, and the ways in which sporting successes and failures become ingrained in the public's consciousness (often via the media), act to reinforce and reproduce existing cultural understandings of sport. Sport's bureaucratic structure and those charged with making sure that the rules are understood and obeyed (club officials, referees, etc.) are examples of how sport assists social integration: those who do not conform are routinely identified and punished and those who do conform are rewarded. Our constant desire for higher levels of achievement that we see in our public celebration of world records, the winning of Olympic medals and at major championships requires constant adaptation of coaching and training methods so that teams and individual athletes remain competitive.

Learning Activity 6.2

The problems posed by the introduction of new performance-enhancing drugs means that our sporting institutions such as the Sports Council have to constantly adapt to control how new drugs and their misuse can be controlled.

Find out more about how sport in the UK is doing this by visiting the following website: **www.uksport.gov.uk/pages/drug_free_sport/**

Within each society the collective combination of roles, norms, values and institutional characteristics is distinctive. In general terms, this is what sociologists are referring to when they use the term 'culture'. For example, while we might say that British society has deep concerns over the use of drugs in sport, what we are actually saying is that the majority of people in the society share this concern and that their views are part of our sporting culture and the institutionalised framework that we have developed to organise and regulate our sport.

Case study: sport, competition and co-operation

Two of the characteristics of modern sport that most children come to understand as essential are competition and co-operation. Yet being successfully socialised into this recognition does not by itself mean that everybody agrees what these concepts actually mean. Both can be understood in a variety of ways that not only influence how we understand sport, but also how we understand the nature of the social world.

Competition:

- is a process through which success is measured;
- sets the rules for distributing rewards and influences relationships between people;
- is usually understood as a zero-sum process that means that only some can win and this will be at the expense of those who lose. At its most extreme, for some this means that 'winning isn't everything, it's the only thing'.

Sport also has a non-competitive reward structure that emphasises **co-operation**.

- In team sports co-operation is a process through which success is measured by the collective achievements of a group of people working together to reach a particular goal.
- Although in individual and team sports individual standards of performance can be used to measure success, at the same time there is a recognition that without the essential co-operation of others the sport is not possible.

Sport also emphasises the need for groups to co-operate within the competitive context of sport (and modern life).

- Sport relies on inter-group co-operation to create competitions and leagues.

At the heart of the process is the assumption that all players and teams will play within the rules.

- Intra-group co-operation within sports teams requires that individual players repress their own needs to those of the team and its attempts to win.

Learning Activity 6.3

Take a few moments either to discuss with a peer and/or note your thoughts on the following questions:

1. Is the competitive nature of sport a good or a bad thing?
2. Is sport merely an extension of the way the world works or is it a separate and distinctive area of life where different rules apply?
3. When you play sport, do you think it is better to play well and lose, or play badly and win?
4. Would you cheat if you thought that:
   – the other team was cheating?
   – it could help you win the game?
5. Thinking back, can you remember when and where you learned to think about sport in these ways?

As we will examine in much more detail over the subsequent chapters, many sport sociologists accept that while functionalism has usefully identified how sport can be understood as an important social phenomenon within the structure of modern society, it has a number of significant limitations that reduce its ability to explain the social and cultural construction of sport. Of particular concern is the tendency within this perspective to view socialisation as unproblematic and that the values systems into which we are socialised are not contested or conflictual. Moreover, functionalism's emphasis on how the social world shapes the individual overlooks how individuals and groups reflexively monitor their lives. In response to this, many sociologists have now adopted more critical and interactionist perspectives of the socialisation processes. In the chapters that follow these perspectives will be examined in more detail.

From the preceding discussion it should be clear that processes of socialisation are essential for all societies. There are, however, a number of additional questions that we need to consider. In particular, we need to explore more closely how socialisation within sport is part of our everyday life and some of the important outcomes of the process.

Entering the world of sport

The way we become socialised into sport is significantly influenced by three factors:

- *a person's abilities and characteristics;*
- *the influence of significant others, including parents, siblings, teachers and peers;*
- *the availability of opportunities to play and experience success in sports.*

(Coakley, 2003, p100)

It is the second of these factors that we will primarily address in the remainder of this chapter.

One of the primary social institutions responsible for young people taking up sport, and then sustaining their involvement in it, is the family. In general, families have a significant social responsibility for the reinforcement of the existing patterns of social stratification and status, and the reproduction of the normative structures of order and control that characterise the society. The family is a major site of play, recreation and leisure, and deeply influences children's socialisation into sport and the types of leisure that they will experience.

Although all this may to some degree seem fairly obvious, we must also stress that the family, often founded on inherited blood ties, is itself a social construction. Social change has, and continues to have, a major impact on the structure of families in Britain.

Today, it is wrong to assume that what people call their family refers to what sociologists term the 'nuclear family'. The conventional nuclear family of a married male and female couple with a number of dependent children is no longer the dominant family setting. Unmarried couples, single-parent families, reconstituted families (divorced and remarried), and gay and lesbian family units all make up a complex and diverse set of family settings for the rearing of children. To this can also be added the often profound influences that different cultural groupings can have on family roles. These points noted, in recent years relatively little attention has been paid by sport sociologists with regard to how this diversity of family units impacts on how children become engaged with sport.

The research that has been done documents a fairly consistent set of family influences on how children engage with sport. They are:

- emotional support and encouragement (how to deal with success and failure);
- encouragement, monitoring and facilitation of participation (setting up contact with clubs and coaches, driving to training and competitions, etc.). A number of sociological studies have concluded that individuals who achieve in sport had often begun their participation by ages 5–6 and only rarely did they begin later than age 10;
- financial support (payment of fees and for equipment, etc.);
- regulation and control of interactions with others (how to be a 'team member');
- that parents, older siblings and members of the extended family often serve as role models and provide clear ideas about sporting aspirations, status and values.

Children often draw on family experience to base their judgements about the perceived importance/appropriateness of particular sports;

- that parents who have participated in sport are more likely to encourage their children into sport than those who do not;
- that families are often a primary source of sport knowledge, values and engagement with exercise regimes;
- that the family is a major focal point for the consumption of media sport;
- that although we will not examine these in any detail at this point, there is ample evidence that the family also has a profound impact on how social class, gender, race and ethnicity impact on

the child's perceptions of themselves and what they consider to be appropriate sporting choices. The social class, racial and ethnic characteristics of the family are all important determinants in the social reproduction of class, racial and ethnic divisions within sport.

The family is also an important site of gender socialisation. As Jennifer Hargreaves (1994) has explained, socialisation into sport has been viewed as a social learning process through which significant others in the family context teach, demonstrate and reinforce gender roles and behaviours. While the socialisation of gender roles through sport appears to be highly consistent within most modern societies for males, the same is not true for females (Greendorfer, 1981). Greendorfer suggests that female socialisation into sport is a volatile, inconsistent, selective and extremely complex process which needs more research. The outcome of these processes means that from an early age boys are encouraged to explore the environment and be active in physical activity, whereas girls are more restricted and protected from the environment.

Differing participation patterns become ingrained even before children go to school.

Within sport, girls and boys show quite different preferences, with girls tending to participate in far fewer numbers. Surveys also suggest that many parents rate a daughter's talent for sport substantially lower than a son's. They also provide sons with more opportunities to participate in sport activities than they provide daughters.

Once they are in school, teachers rate boys higher in sport ability than girls, although they do not rate the genders differently for mathematical and reading abilities. Boys perceive a greater importance to their parents that they do well in sports than girls perceive.

Sport, physical education and the national curriculum: processes of secondary socialisation

Physical education

Historically often known as physical training, what we now refer to as physical education (PE) has become a core component of the curriculum in British education. The aims of PE are frequently addressed through participation at a practical level rather than studying the discipline itself. As will be seen in the following section, PE has developed from specific roots to meet specific perceived needs – some national, some social, others individual. Our modern understanding of physical education is orientated to provide pupils with the capabilities (skills), knowledge and values that will enable them to create and maintain an active, healthy lifestyle into and throughout adulthood. Schools have also been tasked in some instances to address obesity among pupils.

Sports, often still referred to as 'games' in an educational setting, are a key component of physical education. However, the discipline is much broader and contemporarily, at least, its aims go much further. It uses sporting activities and opportunities to promote physical fitness, to develop motor ability, to provide practical experience of teamwork and/or individual motivation, and, of course, competition. It also provides a route into sport, into the world of athletic games.

From the preceding study it should be clear that in our modern world the process of becoming a sports person or athlete is deeply intertwined with the process of becoming an adult. One of the most important social institutions that is tasked with this process is our system of education. Within our schools, extracurricular sport and PE have often been seen as the essential educational link between these two processes. For over a century, sport in schools has been associated with teaching children a range of socially beneficial values, such as sportsmanship, fair play, morality and a work ethic to name but a few of the most obvious. In the last few decades, extracurricular sport and the physical curriculum have also become associated with a number of social goals in terms of developing social integration and the acceptance of cultural diversity; the reduction of educational dropout and the promotion of educational aspirations; increasing access to all levels of education for the poor and minority groups (Rees and Miracle, 2000).

The next section of the chapter will detail how the British education system has been essential to the way in which sport has become deeply ingrained in our culture.

While families are one of the primary institutions of socialisation into sport, for the vast majority of British children it is school, PE and the playing of extracurricular sport that are vital to the process.

Case Study

Health and activity has become a central aspect of the debate and an article by Nick Triggle, a health reporter for BBC News, captures a very contemporary concern:

Fears over child fitness levels

Sedentary lifestyles are making children less fit – even among those who are not obese, a study suggests. Essex University staged fitness tests on 600 10-year-olds a decade apart in an area with low levels of obesity. They found significant falls in fitness levels, concluding the average 10-year-old in 1998 could beat 95 per cent of youngsters in 2008 in running tests. The researchers said the focus on obesity was obscuring the health risks of wider declines in fitness levels. Children are routinely weighed and measured in schools in England as part of the government's drive to tackle rising obesity rates, but there is no equivalent for fitness.

The Essex team of sports experts chose to focus on Chelmsford, an affluent town with traditionally low levels of obesity, to illustrate how being a normal weight did not necessarily equate to having good fitness. In 1998, they carried out 20m shuttle run tests – commonly known as the bleep test – on 303 children from six schools. In 2008, the tests were repeated on a similar number of 10-year-olds, the Archives of Disease in Childhood reported. While obesity levels had hardly changed, there was a significant shift in fitness which was "large and worrying". Researchers said similar if not worse findings would be expected in areas with high levels of obesity.

Lead researcher Dr Gavin Sandercock said: "The measurement of obesity alone may not be sufficient to keep an eye on children's future health. We need some form of monitoring of fitness. We have a generation of children who are spending more and more time in front of a screen, whether it is a TV or a computer. Schools are now trying to do more, but it is the lack of unstructured activity outside that is the problem." Professor Alan Maryon-Davis, president of the Faculty of Public Health, said: "We have been concerned about the sedentary lifestyles of children for some time. But the focus on obesity is right at the moment because it is more directly linked to chronic conditions such as diabetes and heart disease." A Department of Health spokesman said promoting physical activity remained a "top priority" and a key part of the obesity drive.

Story from BBC News: http://news.bbc.co.uk/go/pr/fr/-/1/hi/health/8425161.stm

Sport and physical education in Britain

As we established in the previous chapter, modern sports can be considered as a group of socially constructed activities that are rationalised, codified, rule-bound and bureaucratic. In the British context, these activities took their modern form in the nineteenth century and predominantly through the workings of the English public schools. The rationale that underpinned the development of these sports also saw the promotion of physical education throughout elementary education (the state education of the day).

The constituents of modern sport

If the context was the society of newly industrialised and urbanised Britain, and the vehicle was the public school, then the components that infused games with their central values were amateurism, the gentleman and the muscular Christian. These projected an emerging and powerful morality that reflected the aspirations and concerns of the middle classes. The result of this mix was what we now recognise as sport. For the Victorians, ideas about competition and 'survival of the fittest' (justified by using the work of Darwin in a social context) all became unquestioned characteristics of sport. The expectations regarding how the different genders were to engage with these sporting characteristics were profoundly different. Gender socialisation for males worked through a powerful set of public and private social institutions such as the family, the school, the church, the military, the civil service, business and, of course, sport and athletic games. For women, access to these public institutions (including sport) was far more limited and hence the processes of socialisation were more often than not directed at the reproduction of the family and domestic spheres of life.

Social status in Britain in the nineteenth century was founded on 'old wealth' and the traditional aristocratic power that accompanied it, bolstered by 'new wealth' and the entrepreneurial and organisational energy of the middle classes. Their growing influence as the administrators and managers of the industrial project and the increasingly powerful Empire, enabled them to assert a moral, social and political ideology that quickly extended into physical education and sport.

The school

Public school education and the authority that it asserted was a development that coincided with the growth of middle-class influence. While a number of public schools had been in existence for many years prior to the industrial period (Winchester being the oldest, founded in 1382), they had not catered specifically for the male children of the increasingly wealthy middle class. Defined as places for the education of the sons of gentlemen, public schools such as Charterhouse, Eton, Harrow, Rugby, Shrewsbury, Westminster and Winchester became established as the benchmark for the public school system that survives even today.

The duration of the schooling was important to the processes of socialisation that the boys experienced. Being boarding establishments, the boys were away from home for most of their formative years. The schools thus became the 'families' to which the boys showed loyalty and affection throughout their lives. School life was certainly hard and, in some respects, brutal, but the boys had autonomy unlike any experienced during home tutoring or day schooling, which were the alternatives available at the time. Outside the formal delivery of the classics, which formed a large part of the curriculum of the day, authority in the public schools was largely devolved to the boys themselves. The schools imposed an acceptance of social order based on seniority and social rank. Senior boys ruled in accordance with the school's traditions, organised the domestic lives of the pupils, adjudicated in disputes and dispensed punishment. As younger boys became seniors in turn, so they took on the governance of the 'inner' school. Critically, the boys organised their games and amusements.

While the games were no more civilised than those seen elsewhere in British society at the time, boys undertook cricket, rowing and football – often despite the disapproval of headmasters and masters alike. The established autonomy that the boys enjoyed made it very difficult, however, for the censorious to effect much change. Games became tolerated and endured by school authorities, but were certainly not encouraged, at least in these early years. The critical aspect was that the boys, or at least most of the boys, loved the games. Indeed, it might be asserted that they became obsessed with game playing.

The schools were, however, ripe for reform, as was British society as a whole. Part of the Victorian character was a strong desire to improve on what had gone before. Thomas Arnold, as headmaster of Rugby from 1828 to 1841, in instructing his prefects, said: *You should feel like officers in the army or navy where want of moral courage would, indeed, be thought cowardice* (Armytage, 1955). Here he betrays both a desire to inculcate his understanding of morality, but also the need to do so through the authority of the boys themselves. He also wrote: *What we must look for here is, First, religious and moral principles; Secondly, gentlemanly conduct; Thirdly, intellectual ability* (Arnold, 1869).

By the middle of the century the role that the public schools played in an increasingly self-confident, and indeed self-aware, Britain was well recognised. The Earl of Clarendon, as chairman for the Royal Commission on Public Schools in 1864, was able to report that:

The bodily training which gives health and activity to the frame is imparted at English schools, not by gymnastic exercises which are employed for that end on the continent – exercises which

are undoubtedly very valuable and which we would be glad to see introduced more widely in
England – but by athletic games which, whilst they serve this purpose well, serve other purposes
besides . . . the cricket and football fields . . . are not merely places of exercise or amusement;
they help to form some of the most valuable social qualities and manly virtues, and they hold,
like the classroom and the boarding house, a distinct and important part in Public School
education.

(Report of the Royal Commission on Public Schools, 1864)

The social dissemination of athleticism

The network of athletic games (sports) spread from the public schools to grammar schools, to
universities and beyond. The military embraced the new 'sport' for the officers while maintaining
'drill' for the other ranks. The civil service accommodated sports and then promoted the genre. It
can be seen in the foregoing that the games in the English public school illustrate pattern
maintenance, integration, goal attainment and adaptation. They established social norms and
promoted values in a very effective manner.

Schools and the exporting of sport to the Empire

Games had become important in the schools because they were considered to be an aid to
discipline; they helped to keep order, they were thought to channel violence, they were considered
healthy forms of exercise. In a wider context, however, as the Clarendon Commission had reported,
the English people were indebted to the schools for the qualities they instilled: *for their* (the boys')
capacity to govern others and control themselves, their aptitude for combining freedom with order, their
public spirit, their vigour and manliness of character, their strong but not slavish respect for public
opinion, their love of healthy sports and exercise (Report of the Royal Commission on Public Schools,
1864).

The dimensions of courage, loyalty, bravery, discipline and honour deemed to be inherent in the
athletic games became central to British imperialist ambitions: sport, militarism and the public
school ethos were fused in popular literature, poetry, art and song. This is well illustrated in Thomas
Newbolt's poem 'Vitai Lampada', written in 1897:

There's a breathless hush in the Close to-night.
Ten to make and the match to win.
A bumping pitch and a blinding light,
An hour to play and the last man in.
And it's not for the sake of a ribbonned coat
Or the selfish hope of a season's fame,
But his Captain's hand on his shoulder smote
"Play up! play up! and play the game!"
The sand of the desert is sodden red,
Red with the wreck of the square that broke;
The Gatling's jammed and the Colonel dead,

And the regiment blind with dust and smoke.
The river of death has brimmed his banks
And England's far, and Honour a name,
But the voice of a schoolboy rallies the ranks:
"Play up! play up! and play the game!"
This is the word that year by year,
While in her place the School is set,
Everyone of her sons must hear,
And none that hears it dare forget.
This they all with a joyful mind,
Bear through life like a torch in flame
And falling, fling to the host behind –
"Play up! play up! and play the game!"

Learning Activity 6.4

Write a short paragraph answering the following questions:

1. What are the themes that underpin the poem?
2. Why did the public schools become such an important part of the boys' lives?
3. What are the characteristics thought to be learned from athletic games?

Reflection Point 6.2

Consider your own experience in PE and identify how it differs from the English public school approach in the late nineteenth century. Apply some of the sociological theories identified earlier on to the experience of the public schoolboys and to your experience. What does this tell you?

The notion of 'fair play' and 'sportsmanship' result from the amateur code and class system of the nineteenth century. It might be argued that amateurism was the driving 'morality' that in a secular sense matched what muscular Christianity was contributing in a religious one to athletic practice. Played in the public schools, the codified games that became the sports we recognise today were the vehicles that carried these values.

The reinforcing of social position and role is central to the process of socialisation. It is clear that the expectations of officers and other ranks (soldiers and seamen), and practices used in military training reflect this process in action. Public and elementary schools were equally important in this dynamic. As we have seen, the athletic games that we now consider our sports were developed in the elite education system and played an important part in the lives of the boys who undertook their schooling in that system during the nineteenth century. Physical training, or what we now know as physical education, is rather more than the playing of these athletic games, however, and it is to its introduction and development that we now turn.

Outside the public schools there was no comprehensive system of education in Britain. Provision was patchy: many societies were set up with the aim of providing affordable education to the children of working people. Much of the effort was organised through the church, with some parishes providing schools while others failed to see that it was their responsibility. Very little attention was paid to the physical in the fragmented and inconsistent elementary school system of the time, but it had been noted that in many settings physical training was the least of the concerns for the poverty-stricken and half-starved children who occasionally attended.

Compulsory elementary education was eventually provided as a result of the 1876 and 1880 Education Acts. Initially, physical training was taken care of by retired army non-commissioned officers, who instructed the pupils in the rudiments of drill. There is little evidence that this teaching was informed by the work of Archibald Maclaren, or any of the insights from the Swedish or German systems of gymnastics. The instructors were paid on the basis of six old pence a day (2.5 pence in today's decimal currency) with the addition of a penny per mile marching money. McIntosh (1957, p194) states that it was hoped that the exercises *would be sufficient to teach boys habits of sharp obedience, smartness and cleanliness*. This approach was the only officially sanctioned form of physical education in the elementary schools until 1890.

Physical education, sport and women

The contested area of games, sport and physical activity was just one area of life where changes were occurring for women. 'Modern' Britain would provide a platform upon which the status of women would be challenged. Two powerful cultural forces clashed with regard to the involvement of women in physical activity and sport. The Victorian stereotype of the 'female', with much stress on bodily weakness, medical vulnerability, emotional 'nature' and social limitations, was countered by the values of the culture of games, health through physical activity and fair play.

In this era, appropriate gender socialisation and their processes of reinforcement were seen to be an essential component of a stable and well-ordered society, albeit that it was an order created by men and designed to benefit them. While this can be considered a powerful example of how socialisation reinforces 'pattern maintenance' and processes of 'social integration', as will be illustrated, the capacity for adaptation is equally powerful, and in the area of female emancipation (in its broadest sense), physical education, games and sports became an important site of contestation.

The 'male' ideology of athletic games was adopted by a new breed of female educationalists: what was good for sons and brothers was good for daughters and sisters. In a 'me too' feminism, girls and young women of the upper and middle classes became enamoured with games and sport, just as their brothers and fathers had done.

To the Victorian male the spectre of women undertaking competitive athletic games was difficult to accept. Men developed stamina, perseverance, teamwork and competitiveness through their sports and then used those qualities during their work, when they were 'recreated' once again through their sports.

Thus, work and sport were mutually re-enforcing. In the context of the middle-class female, this was seen to be quite alien. The widely held notion that 'man does, woman is' illustrated well one of the major difficulties that men faced with women taking up sports. Man believed he was active and woman passive; man was culture (civilisation), woman was nature; man would aspire, woman would accept.

By the close of the century it had become established, at least in liberal and progressive circles, that fitness and femininity were not opposed; they were both required to create 'healthy, moral, middle-class families'. By blending games, hitherto the province of boys, with a carefully graded set of exercises to promote suppleness, balance and agility, many of the medical profession's reservations about female physical activity were overcome. Educated young women were forging a different life for themselves, given the obvious constraints of the times. These women expected more freedom and often linked educational, political and professional aspirations with the right to use their own bodies as they wished, be it to play lawn tennis or ride their bicycles.

Despite the obvious emancipatory aspects that these upper- and middle-class young women were bringing to the lives of late Victorian women, it often reaffirmed the established stereotype. Despite new opportunities in education, and physical education in particular, these privileged women became boxed into the confines of physical activity within the environs of the girls' public school, the family garden and the private club.

Class distinctions

Women's sport had struck a balance between physical emancipation and social respectability. In the late Victorian period there was a redefinition of the female body that allowed a more active physical life, but the distinction between the capacities and character of men and women was rigidly maintained. Female sport in this period was predominantly the preoccupation of privately educated young women. Working-class girls undertook little in the way of recreational exercise.

The year 1878 saw the London School Board introduce therapeutic gymnastics into girls' elementary education. By 1885, over 700 teachers had been trained to supervise simple remedial exercises for girls. By the end of the nineteenth century, gym classes for girls were being encouraged in cities such as Liverpool as part of the national drive for efficiency. Games or sport was rarely included for the working-class girls, however: 'games for the classes, gym for the masses' was the mantra.

During the First World War, young women working in munitions factories were encouraged to take part in games and it was found that they had little experience, or understanding, of team games or indeed any form of exercise for pleasure.

Learning Activity 6.5

Think back over your experience of PE and write a short reflection on the following questions:

1. What differences can you identify between the PE experiences of boy and girl pupils in schools?
2. How is this manifested in the curriculum?
3. How might some of the issues discussed above explain your own experience?

Twentieth-century changes

By early in the twentieth century, while some games were included, the majority of the programme was based on the Swedish system of gymnastic exercises. Physical training was considered to be beneficial in two distinct areas: positive physical, health and maturational effects; positive educational effects focused on mental wellbeing, alertness, memory, learning, self-control, self-restraint, fostering a public spirit, etc.

Kirk (2003) correctly identifies that physical education, like sport, is a highly contested social construction. He sees the evolving of educational gymnastics in British schools as a positive, though much resisted process. For the first half of the twentieth century women had dominated the PE profession. By the 1950s men were entering the profession and the balance shifted away from educational and creative gymnastics towards physical education programmes built on sports, athletic games and fitness training regimes. Kirk concludes that by the 1960s the male influence had prevailed and become dominant.

The evidence presented in the preceding historical discussion demonstrates a number of important points. The first is that sports did not just drift into the educational setting. They were included because of the way they aided the process of socialisation into the demands of modern life. Sociological analysis of school sport and physical education, while supporting some of these assumptions, also clearly shows that there is a need for a more critical understanding of the process.

Sport, physical education and socialisation: some closing questions

The view that sport builds character has been extensively examined both here and elsewhere (Rees and Miracle, 2000). Contemporary thinking suggests that there appears to be no significant difference between the moral attitude and the adherence to positive social values, between groups who play and who do not play sport. Indeed, some research (Bredemeier et al., 1987) suggests that the longer young people are involved in contact team sports the lower the level of moral reasoning. This may be due to students becoming aware of 'game play' – the 'winning is not everything, it's the only thing!' It is obvious that sport is not always played fully within the constraints of the rules and that to some degree the bending of the rules to the advantage of the team is either encouraged or expected. Football provides many examples of this from the 'professional foul' to the vehement claiming of the ball when it has gone out of play, even when it is patently obvious that your team was responsible for the ball going out. As Hughes and Coakley (1991) note, sport, rather than socialising people into appropriate forms of moral behaviour, can often be seen as a special area of life where the 'normal' rules and codes of moral conduct are suspended.

The claim that sports are a vehicle through which positive moral character can be developed nonetheless persists, despite some clear indication to the contrary and with little empirical evidence to support it. From the inception of athletic games and sports in the English public school, to the development and inclusion of physical education in our national curriculum, part of the rationale has been the importance of building character in our young people. While frequently stated overtly, but far more regularly tacitly assumed, the belief in the moral benefits accrued through sports and games is clearly something that we need to be very careful about.

As Coakley (2003, p124) has recognised: *Efforts to understand what happens to people when they play sports have been sidetracked by the popular belief that sports build character. This belief is grounded in the oversimplified conception of sports, sports experiences and socialization.*

Research Focus

Professor David Kirk is at the forefront of an academic, research-based renaissance of interest in physical education. Spanning the discipline from teacher education for physical education, interventions through models based practice, the social construction of physical education and pupils' experiences of school and community sport, he has provided considerable insight into why the discipline is important in an educational setting, how we ought to approach it in practice and what methods we need to utilise in evaluating its utility.

Recognising that the physical education curriculum is the enabling structure that permits pupils to develop and engage in a wide range of physical activities, Kirk has focused on how best results are achieved. Promoting the development of a wide range of skills, the ability to use strategies and a free imagination to perform successfully, the pupil's experience is foremost in his thinking. By developing a reflective approach to their own performances, pupils effectively situate physical education in the context of their wider studies. Kirk sees this as vital if the value of healthy, active lifestyles, and lifelong physical activity is to be fully realised.

Currently Professor Kirk is the Alexander Chair in Physical Education and Sport and the Director of the Institute for Sport and Physical Activity Research in the School of Physical Education & Sport Sciences in the Faculty of Education & Sport at the University of Bedfordshire. He is a past Pro-Vice-Chancellor (Research) and Professor of Physical Education and Youth Sport at Leeds Metropolitan University, where he was also Dean of the Carnegie Faculty of Sport and Education from 2005 to 2008. He holds an Honorary Chair in Human Movement Studies at the University of Queensland in Australia. He has edited the journal *Physical Education and Sport Pedagogy* and was European Editor of the *Journal of Curriculum Studies*. The International Olympic Committee awarded him President's Prize in 2001 for his research in physical and sport education.

A much published academic, his work includes:

Kirk, D (1988) *Physical Education and Curriculum Study: A Critical Introduction.* London: Croom Helm.

Kirk, D (1992) *Defining Physical Education: The Social Construction of a School Subject in Postwar Britain.* London: Falmer.

Kirk, D (1998) *Schooling Bodies: School Practice and Public Discourse, 1880–1950.* London: Leicester University Press.

Kirk, D (2002) *A-level Physical Education: The Reflective Performer.* Champaign, IL: Human Kinetics.

Kirk, D (2003) *Senior Physical Education*. Champaign, IL: Human Kinetics.

Kirk, D and Bailey, R (eds) (2008) *The Routledge Physical Education Reader*. London: Routledge.

Kirk, D (2010) *Physical Education Futures*. Abingdon, Oxon: Routledge.

This body of work, together with other contemporary scholarship on physical education, illustrates a sophistication unseen in the influential works of an earlier era. Developing out of an examination of the nature and values of the discipline, a critical evaluation of the assumptions and epistemology arises that situates physical education as part of the educational canon. While following the postmodern orientation of focusing on the individual, be they teacher or pupil, and the specific, be it intervention or experiential, the context remains one of the meta-narratives. The social reality of education in general, and physical education in particular, is and remains its perceived purpose: how it contributes to the bigger picture. Being a social construct of a particular type, physical education has been recruited to combat multiple political issues such as declining activity levels in young people, the obesity epidemic, and the perceived decline in sports performance at an elite or national level.

Learning Activity 6.6

Review of learning objectives

Having worked through this chapter, you should now take some time to carefully answer the following questions:

1. Why are processes of socialisation so important to an understanding of sport's social importance?
2. When we learn about sport through being part of a family, would a sport sociologist describe this as an example of primary or secondary socialisation?
3. Can you identify at least three examples of the character-building processes that are normatively associated with sport?
4. How do functionalist and interactionist perspectives of sport and socialisation differ? Have the gender differences within sport evident in the late nineteenth and early twentieth centuries significantly changed?

Chapter Review

Sport is a social institution, one that is made up of a series of legally and formally constituted organisations (sporting, local, regional, national, international). It is used extensively to confirm elements of modern identity (gender, racial; local/regional; national/cultural). More than this, it is a concept that even today is invested with norms and values whose origins lie in the social and cultural conditions of nineteenth-century Britain. Since this time, sport and physical education have played an important role in the processes of socialisation and have acted in influential ways shaping how people have engaged with society. While involvement with sport has largely remained a voluntary activity, the significance of physical education as a powerful educational and socialising medium has been recognised, with it becoming a compulsory element of the national curriculum. Explained primarily by a functionalist theoretical approach, socialisation through sport and physical education has been considered and illustrated. A sociological counterpoint of the interactionist perspective has also been included and used to demonstrate the importance of creating a sociological analysis of sport that effectively explains how conscious individuals reflexively engage with sport.

Processes of gender socialisation were also discussed and highlighted as a major issue within both sport and physical education. The gender divisions that can still be observed in sport and physical education have well-established roots within the moral framework of Victorian society. These values have, however, not gone unchallenged within sport and physical education. Indeed, though often overshadowed by the prominence of males in sport, historically the roles that women have played in the development of physical education have been a vital part of its success and development. While this can be seen as an example of the struggle for female emancipation, it also helps to demonstrate that one of the characteristics of modern society has been its capacity to accommodate internal pressures for change (in this case by women), while also attempting to produce and maintain social stability. As we shall see in the next chapter, not all sport sociologists have followed this line of analysis and they have set out to argue that, at its heart, modern society produced a social system that privileged some while marginalising and repressing others. In directly challenging some of the assumptions within the functionalist perspective, they argue that change is not evolutionary but occurs through confrontation and conflict. As we shall see, sport was, and is, deeply embedded in these processes.

Further Reading

To extend your understanding of the functionalist analysis of sport read:
Loy, J and Booth, D (2000) Functionalism, sport and society, in Coakley, J and Dunning, E (eds) *Handbook of Sports Studies*. London: Sage.

To explore further how sport is linked to socialisation processes (primarily from an American perspective) read:
Chapter 4: Sports and socialisation, in Coakley, J (2003) *Sports in Society: Issues and Controversies.* 8th edition. New York: McGraw-Hill.

To examine how sport can be argued to be connected to processes of social control read:
Eitzen, DS (2000) Social control and sport, in Coakley, J and Dunning, E (eds) *Handbook of Sports Studies*. London: Sage.

To extend your understanding of the historical and sociological issues impacting the development of physical education read:

Birley, D (1993) *Sport and the Making of Britain.* Manchester: Manchester University Press.

Kirk, D (1998) *Schooling Bodies: School Practice and Public Discourse, 1880–1950.* London: Leicester University Press.

Kirk, D (2003) Sport, physical education and schools, in Houlihan B (ed) *Sport and Society: A Student Introduction.* London: Sage.

Kirk, D and Bailey, R (eds) (2008) *The Routledge Physical Education Reader.* London: Routledge.

Chapter 7
Class and gender differentiation in sport

Peter Craig and Paul Beedie

In this chapter we will introduce you to the important sociological concepts of social stratification, differentiation, power and inequality. Specifically, we will explore how these concepts help our understanding of how social class and gender impact on the experience of sport in the modern world. In undertaking this brief overview, it is not our intention to engage you with a detailed exploration of the complex array of theories on class and gender differentiation, rather the chapter will introduce you to a number of important sociological ideas that will help you begin the process of critically thinking about the ways these two important areas of social differentiation impact on the experience and structure of modern sport.

Learning Objectives

On completing this chapter you should be able to:

- give sociological explanations of the following terms: social stratification; social class; inequality; gender; ideology; hegemony; patriarchy;
- describe how these terms can be applied to the analysis of modern sport;
- detail how functionalist, conflict and neo-Marxist theories provide distinctive insights into the influence of social class and participation in sport;
- explain the main sociological premises underpinning a feminist analysis of sport;
- outline how social differentiation is related to the distribution of power relations within a variety of sporting contexts.

Introduction

If you take even a few moments to look carefully at people passing by on any street in any town in Britain, you will quickly spot differences. Judged by their behaviour and the style of their clothes, some will appear to be more or less the same as you, others may appear more wealthy and others less well off. Look again, and think about what you are observing with a 'sociological imagination' and you will see commonality and distinct differences based on gender, race, ethnicity and age. A major question that sociology poses is whether these differences can be understood as socially produced. Sociologists are generally in agreement that the modern world has developed complex mechanisms of social differentiation.

The analysis of inequality has always been a central interest of sport sociologists. As Coakley (2003, p326) correctly notes, this interest is partly sparked by the fact that *People like to think that sports transcend issues of money, power and economic inequalities.* At the heart of many of our most cherished ideas about sports lies our belief that sport is open to everyone and that the sports field is one where people, no matter what their social class, gender, race, ethnicity, age, sexuality or disability, compete fairly and the outcomes are mostly determined by those who have the most talent, skill, strength and fitness. However, even a cursory glance at sport shows this to be, at best, a rather naïve viewpoint.

Reflection Point 7.1

Consider equestrian sports. Horse racing seems at one level to be fairly egalitarian, at least when it comes to attending the race meetings and enjoying a 'flutter'. But when you look a little more deeply, you will see numerous class and gender divisions. The working classes are heavily involved, but as 'sports workers', not as owners. They are the stable hands, and a few are jockeys, and all make their living out of the sport. While this may be also true for the 'trainers', it is usually not the case for the actual owners of the horses, most of whom are independently wealthy and enjoy their often very costly involvement in the sport as part of their leisure. Look again and you will also see that while there are a lot of female stable hands and grooms, there are relatively few who are jockeys and even fewer who are trainers and owners.

If we look at another equestrian sport – show jumping – then we see a completely different set of divisions. Young women have a much greater presence and many of the elite performers are women. Riders often own their horses directly or have ones that are sponsored by companies. In terms of social class, there is little evidence that the working classes are significantly involved or even interested in the sport. Middle classes therefore can be seen to have a powerful and dominating influence on the sport. Given this reality, what do you think the experience of a young working-class girl would be if she decided that she would like to join a pony club? You might also like to think about examples such as this once you have completed the section on gender and sport in order to consider the ways that class and gender intersect in creating processes of social differentiation within sport.

Learning Activity 7.1

This activity is about exploring popular culture and the everyday representations of sport, social class and gender.

Over a number of days collect one of the most popular tabloid newspapers (e.g. the *Sun* or the *Mirror*) and one of the most popular 'broadsheets' (e.g. *The Times*, the *Guardian*

●●● ▶

> ### Learning Activity 7.1 continued
>
> or the *Telegraph*). Make a careful list of what sports are discussed in which newspapers and then group these by 1. class divisions and 2. gender representation.
>
> What do you conclude from your findings?
>
> After completing this task, make sure you retain the newspapers as you will use them in a later activity.

Sport, modern society and the problem of social stratification

As you should recall from the opening chapter, the modern age has been deeply patterned by a number of distinctive processes. Industrial capitalism itself has created new and distinctive patterns of inequality and differentiation. The term that sociologists have developed to describe these is 'social stratification'.

Definition: social stratification

The way in which all societies develop unequal layers (or strata) based on income, wealth, status and power. In the modern age, these have led to distinctive systems of differentiation based on social class, gender, age, race, ethnicity, religion, disability and sexuality.

Sport and social class

The social and cultural formation and reproduction of social class today is fundamentally a reflection of the way modern society has structured its economy around capitalism and industrialism.

Definition: social class

A term widely used in sociology to identify specific groups of people through economic considerations that emphasise groups' differences on the grounds of wealth, income and status.

As Sugden and Tomlinson's (2000) discussion of sport, social class and status details, within sport there are multiple and easily identifiable markers of the relationship between sport and social class. Sports such as boxing always draw from those social groups who are at the bottom end of the social order. The same is also true for sport for those who are higher up the social order or who are privileged to belong to the small elite at the top. They state (2000, p309):

> *For instance, in the context of British society, involvement in a polo match in the grounds of Windsor Castle, participation in Henley's boating regatta or a trip to the grouse moors of Scotland*

can be clear signals of high social status. Similarly playing golf [and] attending Twickenham for a rugby international . . . all convey messages about the social location of the participants.

Wilson (2002) and Engstom (2008) both provide empirical data to support the social trends outlined by Sugden and Tomlinson (2000). Wilson's study is based on data collected from working class and middle and upper class people in America and Engstom's longitudinal study followed the sporting careers of Swedish school children from randomly selected schools as they grew from adolescence to middle age. Both authors draw upon theoretical ideas developed by Pierre Bourdieu. Wilson is particularly concerned with economic and cultural capital and his theoretical framework recognises class stratification as it occurs in sport through an alignment between the working classes and 'prole' (short for proletarian) sports. Wilson argues that sport is a key social indicator because his data demonstrates that those people richest in cultural capital are the least likely to be involved in 'prole' sports such as stock car racing. Wilson's data also shows support for the previously recognised conclusion that the higher a person's social class, the more likely that person is to be involved in sport generally. Thus Wilson finds support for Bourdieu's theory of distinction in which Bourdieu argues from a structuralist perspective that a socially generated 'habitus' – that is patterns of behaviour that shape everyday actions and which though learnt in the social context of our upbringing operate subconsciously – leads us towards certain social interactions and life choices that are class specific. Engstrom's (2008) study draws similar conclusions. The empirical investigation he draws data from is a somewhat rare methodology – an extensive longitudinal study (spanning 38 years) which charts the sport and physical activity careers of a sample of people from adolescence to middle age. Engstrom concludes (2008, p339): *There is no doubt that a middle-aged individual's level of exercise is very closely linked to that person's social position and, accordingly, to his or her educational capital.* Both Wilson and Engstrom therefore acknowledge that sport and class are linked.

Class, then, has a number of characteristics that in turn contribute to who does what sport, where and with whom. Class is not based on division by religion or legal provision and is therefore a social construction. Because it is more than an 'accident of birth', it is possible to move up or down a class. Economic conditions provide the commonest criteria by which classes are distinguished. However, because class divisions exist over generations (generating a form of class habitus), there are more complex indirect indicators – including education (as indicated above), location, culture and social capital – that shape and reinforce these divisions and their commensurate ramifications for sport. A number of social theories, including functionalism, conflict theory, neo-Marxism and feminism, help us to understand how issues of class and gender are part of sport in modern society.

Functionalist perspectives of sport and social class

In the twentieth century the major proponent of a functionalist perspective (see Chapter 4) was Talcott Parsons (Bilton et al., 2002). While Parsons agreed with Marx that class was fundamentally the product of the economic system, unlike Marx he argued that the hierarchical divisions between social classes were a necessity. All societies need to create a system that allocates people to different social positions and then produces appropriate incentives to encourage them to perform the duties required by those positions. Although in principle this perspective takes the view that modern society is essentially meritocratic (i.e. the best get to the top), this also suggests that inequality is a necessity as it creates the incentive for work. The explanation for class position is often directed at the individual and their talents, and how they actively develop and nurture those talents. In simple terms, society needs to provide social outcomes that demonstrate that hard work is 'worth it' and that everyone can be successful. The belief is that even children born into poor working-class families can succeed, as modern education systems should give all children the opportunity to recognise and develop their productive potential.

As Sugden and Tomlinson (2000, pp312–313) have detailed, much of the early sociology literature that took an interest in sport was American and adopted aspects of the functionalist perspective in the attempt to explain how sport 'worked' within society.

This analysis included explanations for the linkages between different social classes and various sports, how sport reflected the inherent structures of the modern social system, and whether sport could act as a vehicle for social mobility. Sugden and Tomlinson (2000) also highlight that this type of sociological scholarship has been heavily criticised for being uncritical, rather naïve and unrealistic in its understanding of the inherent and deeply ingrained inequalities and disadvantages that social class creates.

Reflection Point 7.2

The Sutton Report on Social Mobility 2007, a long-term study, drew a number of important conclusions. Taking all the report's results together suggests that the sharp decline in intergenerational mobility that occurred between the 1958 and 1970 cohorts has not continued for more recent generations of children. However, at the same time, mobility levels have not reversed or started to improve, and remain very low. The fall in intergenerational mobility between the 1958 and 1970 cohorts appears to have been an 'episode'. Social mobility worsened and took a steep change downwards, leaving the UK close to the bottom of the intergenerational league table of mobility. Parental background continues to exert a significant influence on the academic progress of recent generations of children.

Stark inequalities are emerging for today's children in early cognitive test scores – mirroring the gaps that existed and widened with age for children born 30 years previously. Inequalities in degree acquisition meanwhile persist across different income groups, with those from high income groups still over four times as likely to graduate as those from low income groups (Blandon and Machen, 2007).

Conflict theory, sport and social class

Probably the most important aspect of Marx's work is that, as Elias (1977 cited in Rigaur, 2000, p28) notes: *Marx was undoubtedly the first person who succeeded in creating a comprehensive and coherent theoretical model of human society and its development based on the perspective of the less powerful and the poorer groups of people.*

The focus of Marx's work cannot be separated from the context of his social world. His was a time of deep social and political unrest, allied to a rapidly expanding system of industrial capitalism and its ingrained political and economic differences and contradictions. These were most acutely felt in the growing rivalries and conflicts between the old elites (the aristocracy), the emerging elite (the bourgeoisie/middle classes) and the working classes (the proletariat). Nineteenth-century modernity laid the foundation of modern sport and therefore it is not surprising that sport came to reflect these same fractures.

The central elements of Marx's analysis focus on socio-economic and political relations, interdependencies and power imbalances: *Society does not consist of individuals but expresses the sum of relations and conditions in which these individuals stand by one another* (Marx, 1939, p41 cited in Rigaur, 2000, p30).

Sport is impacted by the realities of economic conditions, but is fundamentally part of the superstructure of capitalist society. A key function of the superstructure is the production, reproduction and circulation of ideologies. Cultural practices such as sport are fully integrated into these processes. As Brohm (1978, p117) states:

> *Thus the world economic hierarchy has direct consequences on a nation's level of competitiveness in sport. Today only the top nations can take on the organisation of major international competitions like the Olympics. This hierarchy naturally reasserts itself when it comes to choosing the country and city to organise the Olympic Games.*

Much has been made of the 'spiritual values' of the Games and their 'cultural legacy'. However, the motto that de Coubertin indelibly impressed on the Games – 'cistius, altius, fortius' (faster, higher, stronger) – is embedded in one of the central tenets of modernity; the belief in social progress grounded in the forming institutions of modernity (see Chapter 2). The emphasis on never-ending achievement mirrors and reciprocates the tenets of the global capitalist system and its ceaseless expansion. It also brings with it inevitable disappointment when these ideals are not maintained. Most recent world records now rely on ever more sophisticated systems of recording and measurement to detect and measure even the slightest improvement. Today, world records are ever harder to achieve and in many sports the outer limits of performance are now being approached. Indeed, many recent records have been tainted by the spectre of drug use as athletes and coaches are forced to seek ever more extreme measures to achieve the impossible. The financial rewards make it almost inevitable that some athletes will continue to make this 'rational' choice.

Today, the Olympics in particular, but also sport more generally, have to respond to a complex but familiar set of interconnected interests. These include nationalism, commercial interests such as sport companies, property and infrastructure development and media concerns. Therefore, Brohm's (1978) pronouncement that sport is 'alienating' and that it will disappear in a universal Communist society has proved to be false on a number of counts. The first is that to date nearly all of the societies that adopted forms of Communist governance and economic organisation chose to incorporate sport within their social system. Second, it is the Communist system that has almost completely disappeared while sport has continued to flourish. Indeed, sport has become one of the world's universalising systems.

The meaning and organisation of sports are heavily influenced by money and economic power. Class relations in most societies are based on an ideology (the systematic organisation of ideas) in which economic success is equated with individual ability, worth and character – competitive power and performance sports reinforce and reaffirm this ideology. The most powerful people in sport are white men who control the resources of major organisations that sponsor sports or present them in the media. Power resides in clubs and sports authorities, and the people who control these organisations, so that the reality is that athletes and spectators have little or no power in sports.

Social class and class relations influence who plays, who watches, who consumes information about sports and the kinds of information that are available. In general, as Wilson (2002) and Engstrom (2008) have shown, the higher a person's social class, the more likely they are to be involved in sport and the more influence (and power) they are likely to have over the forms that sport takes and the way(s) sport develops. Thought about in this way, it becomes clear that sport can become an important determinant of class-related lifestyles so that, for example, despite efforts to make rowing more egalitarian in its appeal across all classes, it remains a bastion of the upper-middle classes. This is certainly the case in Bedford, a town with a longstanding rowing tradition based on Victorian engineering of the River Ouse around the 'Embankment', where the grass-roots entry points to this sport are dominated by the town's fee-paying schools. Without a genuine opportunity for youngsters at state schools in Bedford to become involved in rowing, the clubs remain the preserve of the higher classes: rowing does not reflect the cosmopolitan diversity of social groups living in Bedford, but instead remains populated by those privileged educationally and who will, in turn, be more likely to be involved in the Henley Regatta (as participants or spectators) and other socially specific rowing events.

Neo-Marxist perspectives of sport and social class

One of the key critical positions on conflict theory recognises that it is overdependent on an assessment of class and its economic indicators at the expense of other social categories – the idea of economic determinism. The Marxist view of social class has often, mistakenly, been reduced to the recognition of two class groupings – the bourgeoisie and the proletariat. Class conflict is much easier to predict in the context of two groupings whose interests are so widely separated. The reality of the capitalist system is that there are at least four separate groupings, all of which Marx recognised to some degree. These are the bourgeoisie, the petite bourgeoisie, the proletariat and the lumpenproletariat. These more easily translate to a small and very wealthy upper class, the middle class, the working class and an underclass. All have their own separate interests and concerns, and all, to varying degrees of intensity, are interconnected and interdependent. The problem with 'allocating' class (and therefore how people recognise themselves and are recognised by others) is that the class labels are highly 'elastic'. There is a strong case that Marx's emphasis on economic power and the unequal distribution of resources was actually fairly close to that evidenced in the work of another major sociological theorist of social class and inequality, Max Weber.

Weber argued that all forms of inequality are based on some form of power. For Weber, a group that shares an identity and therefore acts in community (a recognisable collective) is better understood as a status group. People need more than abstract economic labels to form a common identity (this is why workers' unions have clearly demarcated lines of identification). In simple terms, what this means is that classes are composed of people with similar levels of income, skills and qualifications, and relatively similar ranges of life experiences and lifestyles. Clearly, sport could be directly relevant here. Bourdieu (1984) in his theory of Distinction applied a similar way of thinking. He argued that different classes accumulated and used 'capital' in a number of ways to 'position' themselves in a social context. Groups with the greatest 'cultural capital' were able to 'distinguish' themselves from other groups by establishing socially determined boundaries that operate with a degree of elasticity and permeability just as class/status boundaries do. The hub of Bourdieu's thesis is a structural explanation of forms of behaviour, including a propensity for sporting activity, commensurate with a class system. Bourdieu presented a lot of evidence to suggest that the middle class were the most likely to be involved with sports – but only those sports that were consistent with middle-class status.

The key idea here is that class and differing class interests exist, but they are much more diverse and fragmented than the original Marxist framework would suggest. Power has a number of forms and draws its capacities from a variety of different sources. Economic power is just one form of power, but it was and remains a very influential one. Neo-Marxist ideas accept this up to a point but recognise that other forms of power are apparent in class formation and the way people continue to construct representative social identities. Today, these are more loosely formed than in previous generations where class and other social categories were deepened so as to be very powerful determinants of social status and opportunity. Now, a 'plurality' of social groupings impact on the formation of identity, including nationality, race and ethnicity, regional and local groupings, gender, 'the lads', the team, the family, hunt protesters, Countryside Alliance, Greenpeace eco-warrior and many others. To be a group member requires some commitment to an acceptance of common styles, behaviours and attitudes – for Bourdieu this was cultural capital. Group membership(s) remain very important as they help to develop perceptions of self-worth and confirm status and, inevitably, sports have become an important focal point of these identities which might be thought of as a team or tribal affiliation.

Ideology

In order to more fully understand ideas of power implicit in the neo-Marxist position outlined above, it is necessary to explore 'ideology'.

Definition: ideology
Ideology is the shared ideas or beliefs which serve to justify the interests of dominant groups.
(Giddens, 2001, p691)

Ideologies are found in all societies in which there are systematic and ingrained inequalities between groups. So, the concept of ideology connects closely to that of power: *since ideological systems serve to legitimise the differential power which groups hold* (Giddens, 2001, p691).

Exploring ideology

Ideology is a crucial concept in the study of sport and contemporary (popular) culture. If Marx's critique of the power relations endemic in modern capitalist society is correct, then these same power relations must have patterned the structure of social life and how it continues to reproduce itself. In particular, our focus on sport must be directed not just at economic inequalities, but also at the 'structures of control and dominance' that direct us to act in particular ways. Neo-Marxist theorists stress that this structure has two component parts:

- class control based on ideology;
- class control based on culture.

Capitalist (class) ideology

Marx suggests that the ruling elite in a capitalist society controls the 'means of mental production'. What this means is that, without the material capacity to challenge the ruling 'intellectual force', subordinate classes are subjected to the ideas of the elite. In this way ideology operates in the interests of the powerful, but is invisible in everyday life by using processes of:

masking, distortion [and] concealment. Ideology is used here to indicate how some cultural texts and practices present distorted images of reality. They produce what is called 'false consciousness'. Such distortion, it is argued, works in the interests of the powerful against the interests of the powerless. Using this definition we might speak of capitalist ideology.

(Storey, 1993, p4)

Class ideology in sport as discourse

Within the sociological analysis of sport and popular culture, the concept of discourse has become a very important term. Its usefulness lies in how the way we talk and provide images that represent sport need to be understood as 'texts', that not only permeate all aspects of our everyday life, but also impose how we interpret these sporting texts. In this sense, discourse is related to the way that ideology helps produce and reproduce systems of power and control.

Definition: discourse
A discourse is a set of textual arrangements which organises and co-ordinates the actions, positions and identities of the people who produce it.

(Thwaites et al., 1994, p135)

In terms of our current interest, these textual arrangements often frame our understanding of class relations in sport.

Learning Activity 7.2

Look back over the newspapers you collected for learning task 7.1 and pay particular attention to any photographs that were published that involved sports people or sporting action shots.

Do you think that these show more than just the sport? Do they show some of the expected 'class characteristics' that may be associated with different sports? What sports are 'present' and what sports are 'absent'?

Comment: The way some newspapers make some sports visible to their readers and others don't can be a powerful way in which class discourse operates.

These discursive practices also frame how various sports organisations, communities and groups seek to represent their vision of sport. The IOC Sport for All Commission is an example. Its mission statement suggests a uniformity which, though it might be desirable, does not exist in practice because of the unequal distribution of material and other resources.

Sport for All is a movement promoting the Olympic ideal that sport is a human right for all individuals regardless of race, social class and sex. The movement encourages sports activities that can be exercised by people of all ages, both sexes, and different social and economic conditions.

(www.olympic.org/en/content/The-IOC/Commissions/Sport-for-All)

Sport and ideology: Barthes and mythologies

This particular use of the concept of ideology stems from the work of the French cultural theorist Roland Barthes (1973). Barthes argues that ideology works in subtle (in his terms, 'mythic') ways to fix the meanings of language and signs. For example, in all holiday brochures we see happy people 'having fun', looking healthy (slim and fit) and enjoying the sun (with allied images of beaches, swimming pools and palm trees). Some of the messages this presentation fixes in our minds are: a) that sun equals fun and happiness; b) that happy people go on holiday; c) that we will be slim and fit if we go on holiday, and so forth. For Barthes, this is a clear attempt to make universal and 'natural' what is actually partial and contested.

Ideology: neo-Marxist perspectives

In pointing out the reductionist problems of Marxist analyses, neo-Marxist analysis stresses how ideology becomes represented and is often hidden within everyday cultural practices and forms. Even everyday, commonplace cultural activities and practices such as sport (either engaged physically or just by watching it on TV) or taking part in PE, ultimately have an inherent set of meanings that inform how we should understand the world. Seen in this light, all these activities are, therefore, to some degree ideological in nature. In this sense, ideology is the most subtle and essential feature aiding the reproduction of modern society, for the very reason that it is largely hidden from view.

Hegemony

Connected to the discussion of ideology above is the concept of hegemony. Here the main theorists are Antonio Gramsci and Raymond Williams.

Definition: hegemony
Hegemony describes the social and cultural processes of domination of one class or gender over another.

While somewhat complex, the following quote elaborates why hegemony is such an important sociological concept:

> *It sees the relations of domination and subordination, in their forms as practical consciousness, as in effect a saturation of the whole process of living – not only of political and economic activity, nor only of manifest social activity, but of the whole substance of lived identities and relationships, to such a depth that the pressures and limits of what can ultimately be seen as a specific economic, political and cultural system seem to most of us the pressures and limits of simple experience and common sense. Hegemony is not then only the articulate upper level of 'ideology', nor are its forms of control only those ordinarily seen as 'manipulation' or 'indoctrination'. It is a whole body of practices and expectations, over the whole of living: our shaping perceptions of ourselves and our world.*
>
> (Williams, 1977, p110, cited in Clarke and Critcher, 1985, p228)

A number of key ideas about power, the distribution of resources and socially defined boundaries such as those of class relations are emerging in the discussion this far. It becomes clear that the modern world has become increasingly complex and a good example of this complexity is evident in the concept of hegemony. It is clear that a capitalist society has strata indicative of dominant groups and that these groups have ideological control over subordinate groups. It is not just the richest groups that are the most powerful in this respect; dominant groups maintain their position by securing the 'spontaneous consent' (Strinati, 1995, p165) of subordinate groups through the 'negotiated construction of a political and ideological consensus'. In simple terms, hegemony refers to the way discourse and ideology operate to position social groups, yet that 'positioning' is facilitated to a considerable degree (though never completely so) by the groups themselves, even when a subordinate group clearly has an inferior social status.

Cultural studies and the concept of hegemony

Hegemony has become a significant concept for the analysis of sport, leisure and popular culture in that it condenses a number of major themes stemming from neo-Marxist social theory, feminism and the analysis of race and ethnic relations regarding processes of cultural domination and conflict. It recognises conflict between cultural groups as a process that not only occurs at the level of political or economic relations, but also within the everyday lived practices of people (what Gramsci refers to as 'Civil Society'). These practices and their meaning are often ignored as part of this process because they are just that – commonplace and uncontroversial aspects of daily life.

Hegemony also recognises that the process of domination (i.e. the establishment and reproduction of hegemony) is never complete. Rather, it is always contested and resisted to some extent by those who inevitably find themselves marginalised and subordinate. This means that hegemony can change over time, as it is readjusted and renegotiated constantly. For Gramsci, modernity evidences two different modes of social control:

- coercive control, manifested through direct force or its threat (needed by a state when its degree of hegemonic leadership is low or fractured);
- consensual control, which arises when individuals voluntarily assimilate the worldview of the dominant group.

Sport and other arenas of popular culture are fundamental to the struggle for hegemony within modern societies.

Learning Activity 7.3

Over a few days (the weekend is probably best), take the opportunity to watch some news broadcasts on TV and pay particular attention to their discussion of sport.

From your observations, use the ideas of ideology, discourse and mythologies to show how certain messages are connected to sport participation. Arrange your notes so that you show how the 'natural' (e.g. that sport is healthy) is not a universal truism.

This task can be used in a variety of other contexts. You could listen to how people such as PE teachers, coaches or parents talk about sport.

Sport and gender divisions: feminist perspectives

The second significant element of stratification to inform this chapter is that of gender – the fulcrum of feminist theories (and other elements of critical theory). To state the obvious, males and females have different physical constitutions, which are essentially biological. However, most social theorists suggest that gender differences are only marginally biological; more important are the social and cultural environment in which we grow up. Nevertheless, it is biological characteristics that are most often used to 'explain' male dominance in sport.

Definition: sex

The anatomical and physiological differences that define male and female bodies.

(Giddens, 2001, p107)

Definition: gender

The psychological, social and cultural differences between males and females.

(Giddens, 2001, p107)

Feminist analysis of sport is not a unified field of sociological theory. Birrell (2000, p62) believes that feminist theory is a dynamic, continually evolving complex of theories or theoretical traditions that take as their point of departure the analysis of gender as a category of experience in society. Through the range of feminist perspectives, many of the differences of experience in sport are identified as quite distinct concerns about the nature of human (gendered) rights and needs. These include equality of opportunity, separatism, positive action, unnecessary divisions (e.g. biology) and capitalist power relations.

Definition: heterosexuality

Man and woman as the norm in sexual relationships. This is aligned with the assumption that a woman's sexual body will attract the man's 'gaze'.

(Hargreaves, JA, 1994)

As Jennifer Hargreaves (1994) suggests, women who play men's sports have constantly to negotiate their status in traditional cultural contexts of men's power and privilege, and in a general discourse of femininity, patriarchy and compulsory heterosexuality.

Definition: patriarchy

A system of power relations by which men dominate women. (History evidences that patriarchy is the most basic form of oppression within human society in that it emerges out of the essential physiological and psychological differences between the genders.)

Gender has emerged as an ideology sustained, in sport, by a male hegemony. Gender is crucial to how we think of ourselves and define ourselves in relation to others, and how we present ourselves in social settings. Gender ideology is based on a two-category classification system that assumes mutually exclusive categories of heterosexual male and heterosexual female; moreover, these are seen as opposites. This leaves no space for those who do not fit into these categories and it also leads to inequities about power and access to power. Society has therefore determined 'gender roles'; these are a set of characteristics, attitudes and behaviours defined as 'appropriate' to each gender. It follows that our 'gender orientation' is our degree of identification with those characteristics, attitudes and behaviours.

Such an ideology leads to a process of stereotyping so that females are seen as nurturing wives and mothers, organisers and, in sporting terms, spectators and cheerleaders. Males, conversely, are seen as breadwinners, leaders and, in sporting terms, players and even warriors. It follows that each stereotype has a set of characteristics which sees females as dependent, weak, emotional, non-rational, graceful, co-operative and fluid, while males are seen as independent, strong or powerful, assertive, rational, unemotional, competitive, instrumental and rough. These ideologically determined characteristics and behaviours are sustained by the processes of socialisation. However, because they are socially determined, they are neither inevitable nor unmodifiable – in other words, they are the outcomes of cultural discourse rather than personality traits.

Gender is not fixed in nature and therefore social institutions (such as sport) provide locations or 'sites' (physical and social) for the creation and maintenance of dominant definitions. In this critical theory way of thinking, sport becomes a battleground where gender stereotypes can be shaped and reaffirmed, or contested and challenged. Sports are often sites for celebrating traditional ideas about masculinity so that sports images and language commonly glorify a heroic manhood based on being a warrior.

Learning Activity 7.4

Undertake an Internet search for images and pictures of a specific sport – basketball would be an example – played by both males and females. What do the action shots tell us about gendered discourse in this sport?

Case Study
Female athletes and gold medals – Caster Semenaya

18-year-old female South African athlete Caster Semenaya won the gold medal in the Athletics World Championships in Berlin in August 2009. Her winning time of 1: 55: 45 was 2: 45 seconds faster than the fastest time in the year 2009. It was the size of the winning margin that provoked opinions and headlines, and it is an analysis of this response that illuminates the complexity of the gender and sport social territory. The concerns of commentators, analysts and media pundits might be summarised as: 1. 'no one had ever heard of her before these championships'; 2. 'no one can improve a personal best (PB) over as short a period of time as Caster' and 3. 'she does not look feminine, she has facial hair and unusually high levels of testosterone – even if tests prove she is not using illegal drugs'. This rapid and somewhat emotive response to Caster's victory was quickly translated into newspaper headlines, notably The Times (which produced headlines like ' Semenaya faces sex test before being able to claim her gold' and 'Woman who rocked athletics world is hermaphrodite') and the Guardian (from which: 'Gold medal athlete Caster Semenaya told to prove she is a woman' is illustrative). Interestingly, the criticism levelled at the 'fairness' of Caster's achievement came from other female athletes in the first instance (but was quickly fuelled by the media speculation that the event had generated). In a very level headed response to the media speculation Crocker and Davies (2009) made a systematic and scientifically grounded response to the three concerns outlined above. First they explained that it is not without precedent that young, relatively untrained athletes who have a physical propensity to running can make rapid progress. They point to the scientific advances in nutrition, running technologies, tactical racing awareness and training regimes that, when applied to a young person who already has ability, can account for rapid progress in an embryonic athletic career. Second, geneticists have shown that Caster has two 'X' and no 'Y' chromosomes in her genetic makeup and is therefore female. Crocker and Davies go on to explain that there are variations in the size and constitution of chromosomes – it's what makes us all different and accounts for the fact that some humans can run faster than others. They also dispense with the claims that the high levels of testosterone are indicative of 'maleness' by explaining that testosterone is found in males and females and the amounts can vary enormously in either sex. Typically, females have less testosterone than males and the hormone does affect various aspects of bodily development in both sexes, some of which – such as height – might be beneficial to athletic performance.

Lastly, Crocker and Davies (2009) have some interesting things to say about other gender controversies at major championships – and in particular the overlap between issues of gender in sport with those of sport politics, sport ethics and sport nationalism. As the following example shows, by using a critical theory perspective – that is to encompass multiple perspectives to explain a phenomenon by uncovering the socially defined layers that obscure the 'realities' of a situation – there is often a complexity to sport that can best be explained as an amalgam of competing interests. The 1936 Olympics were held in Berlin and the leading German female high jumper was a 17-year-old female called Gretel Bergmann. Gretel was Jewish and the Nazi organisers of the Olympics did not wish to upset Hitler. She was replaced by a man called Horst Raglan who changed his name to Dora and, after growing his hair long, competed successfully as a woman by having his genitals strapped up. He came fourth in the Berlin Olympics but two years later, still competing as a female, he broke the world record and was eventually exposed following a medical examination after his jumping competition. The initial swap with Bergmann was a result of perceptions of nationalism but the resultant cheating was clearly unethical.

The question of ethics and what is fair or unfair in competitive sport continues to occupy us as the profile of some sports grows, and thus our knowledge and awareness of the points of controversy. We have, in 2009, been challenged by ethical issues of 'diving' or 'going to ground too easily' (football), illegal drug enhanced performance (cycling) and the appropriateness of technologically enhanced performance (swimming costumes). The case of Caster Semenaya has been scrutinised in the same way as these others. While these public debates might be considered as a 'trial by media', we should not lose sight of the fact that we are all different as humans (and therefore some people are more naturally gifted at sport) but that this innate ability is nothing without the social context required to both discover and then develop this talent. Caster Semenaya was 'discovered late' because the social and political circumstances of her village upbringing were not conducive to developing her innate sporting ability in childhood. Thereafter, however, the resources required to quickly develop her into a world champion were *put in place. How many potential Caster Semenayas are there in a sporting world that, because of inequity of access to sporting opportunities, may never be discovered?*

When sports celebrate masculinity, female athletes are often defined as invaders. Girls and women in sport increasingly threaten the preservation of traditional ideas about gender – the film Bend it Like Beckham *is a good example of the way that the popularity of female football has been increased through a higher media profile. However, for every such stride forward there is resistance, such as the time Luton Town FC's manager Mike Newell used a perceived poor decision by a female assistant referee in a vital Championship game as an opportunity to assert the view that women have no place in 'serious' football. This is clear evidence of male sporting hegemony in action, and is nothing more than a recent example of a discourse that can be traced back to the nineteenth century when female participation in sport was extremely rare (e.g. exclusion from running middle- and long-distance athletic races such as the marathon until well into the twentieth century). The stereotypes do allow greater participation in certain forms of sport for females, particularly those such as gymnastics and dance that emphasise grace, fluidity and artistic interpretation. Conversely, females who want to participate in 'rough' power sports such as rugby, football and hockey are likely to be labelled 'tomboys'.*

One consequence of this gendered ideology in sport is a heightened awareness of homophobia – the irrational fear and/or intolerance of homosexuality. Because sport adheres for the most part to gender stereotypes and because it takes place in very public domains, it tends to emphasise compulsory heterosexuality, sometimes known as 'heterosexism'. Homophobia negatively affects all athletes, coaches and administrators regardless of their sexual orientation. Some hypothetical examples include a straight athlete avoiding joining a club with a reputation for being gay, regardless of the standard of coaching s/he might receive; a gay athlete hiding his/her sexual orientation to avoid ostracism; and a female coach dressing in a skirt and high heels at a sports match to appear more acceptably feminine. There are real difficulties for gay athletes who publicly 'come out' – that is, to make one's sexual orientation public knowledge – and therefore challenge or contest dominant ideologies: females risk losing social acceptance as do men, but males might also risk physical safety. Both genders risk putting commercial interests at stake (via sponsorship deals, for example), itself indicative of the way that commercial and business interests operate to sustain the gendered discourse in sports.

Reflection Point 7.3

Here is an example of the 'logic' of gender stereotyping in sport from mountaineering, a sport historically steeped in the celebration of maleness through bravery, judgement, physicality and endurance. Joe Simpson and Alison Hargreaves have been two of the pre-eminent British mountaineers of recent times. Simpson achieved far fewer significant groundbreaking ascents than Hargreaves, yet shot to fame in the mid-1980s when the story of his epic descent from Siule Grande in Peru was made public through his book *Touching the Void*.

The book and subsequent film documented how his climbing partner was forced to cut the rope, leaving Joe to 'die' in a huge crevasse on the glacier below. That he did not die, but was able to crawl to safety is now the stuff of mountaineering legend: he was the hero that overcame insurmountable odds to survive. Hargreaves had a different press. Following a successful career of mountaineering achievement, including the first female British oxygen-free ascent of Everest, she was tragically killed on K2 – the second highest mountain in the world – while descending (following a successful ascent) towards safety. When news of her death became public knowledge, it was the 'inappropriateness' of leaving her two children motherless that was the hub of the resultant reporting rather than her mountaineering achievements.

Feminist cultural studies and sport

Feminist theories in sport are essentially concerned with how ideologies of masculinity and male power are produced and reproduced through the participation in, and the spectating of, sports. This perspective aims to uncover how ideology and discourse operate to reinforce a male hegemony. The ambition here is to initiate change, particularly for females, to realign ideas about sport in the modern world. In order to achieve this, several related foci have been identified.

First, investigation has focused on popular culture, especially the media and how this is used to produce dominant conceptions of women and femininity. By identifying how stereotyped characteristics are represented within TV programmes, films, magazines, the Internet and other media outlets, awareness is raised and the potential for contested views developed. For example, Ellen MacArthur, the record-breaking solo round-the-world yachtswoman, was photographed with her manager (a man) on her successful return to Britain.

Second, investigation has focused on the body and body cultures as a site of gendered relations (see Chapter 12). Here, the ambition is to expose the hidden ways that we assimilate established ideas about male and female bodies. In a further example from adventure (see Chapter 13 for more detailed discussion), analysis of the front covers of the popular rock-climbing magazine *Climb* shows at least as many female climbers as males, but there are subtle differences, such as the steepness of the rock being climbed, the aggressiveness of the pose, the amount of bare skin that is visible and the prominence of the musculature on display.

Third, this perspective focuses on how women (and other groups who are repressed) can resist the processes of domination and subordination. There are many examples from sport to illustrate this focus, such as the emergence of Paula Radcliffe as a role model for female runners. Indeed, popular culture, and the media in particular, can be seen as a site where meanings are contested and dominant ideologies are disturbed. So, if an enlightened scriptwriter for *EastEnders* introduced a character who saw herself as an athlete, this could have a profound effect on popular consciousness. The question is, how likely is this to happen?

Learning Activity 7.5

In small groups, by drawing on the foci of feminist investigation into sport outlined above, list examples of the gendered dimensions of sport and PE. You might like to think about:

- the PE curriculum;
- films and literature;
- print media;
- TV;
- the Internet;
- sport activities and/or organisations.

Feminism has raised the profile of gendered discourse in sport and as such has led to changes. Sports participation by girls and women has increased dramatically since the early 1980s because of new sports opportunities, equal rights legislation, globally based women's rights movements, a raised profile of health and fitness issues and some increased media coverage of women's sport, such as the BBC's coverage of the 2007 Women's World Cup and the 2009 European Championships for football. However, there is still resistance to such developments and the future trajectory for women in sport is not necessarily clear. There are budget issues and resistance to government initiatives as well as a backlash among those who resent or feel threatened by 'strong women'. This is not just a position taken by men but, true to the principles of hegemony, there are many females who support the position that women should be submissive and unthreatening.

There are further reasons for caution in overstating the feminist case for sporting equality. These include a media that have the power to trivialise, or at least under-represent female sports; a continued emphasis on 'cosmetic' fitness for women, suggesting that it is more important to use fitness for aesthetic attraction rather than to build muscles for athletic achievement. Lastly, females are still significantly under-represented in positions of power in sports institutions. Among the reasons for this under-representation are the fact that women have fewer established connections and networks in sport; support systems for professional development for women have been scarce; sport organisations are not always sensitive to family responsibilities; and women may anticipate sexual harassment and more demanding standards than those used to judge men.

> ## Reflection Point 7.4
>
> Pierre de Coubertin, referring to women's participation in the Olympics, said: *It is indecent to expect that spectators should be exposed to the risk of seeing the female body being smashed before their eyes. No matter how toughened a sportswoman may be, her nerves rule her muscles; nature wanted it that way. She can't sustain the shock of competition.* De Coubertin's argument appears to be that men and women are complementary opposites and, so long as women are unlike men in the primary sexual characteristics and in reproductive function, they can never be absolutely alike (to men) in the highest psychic processes. Here, the implication is that reproductive function and biology impel men and women inevitably to think and act differently. Hence, if logical reasoning, violence and competition are the 'natural' conditions of human society, then men must always be dominant as women are by the necessity of biology tied to a more emotional (illogical) life.

Modernity and gender: issues of control and power

Foucault (1981), in trying to theorise the impact of modernity on the individual, identified three types of power:

- *institutional power:* which refers to gender, ethnic, social and religious forms of domination;
- *economic power:* which refers to the operation of the capitalist system;
- *subjective power:* which refers to personal struggles against the suppression of one's individual desires/potentials and passive submission to the pervasive social order.

These forms of power interplay in defining the realms of control exercised within the experience and practice of social groups and their sports. Within modern sport important elements of these dimensions of power are directed at men and women and their bodies, so the embodiment of sport becomes a major focus of attention. This also draws attention forcefully to the issue of agency. As Birrell (2000) points out, this has led to a number of feminist theorists arguing that the analysis of sport must proceed from a more 'synthetic' stance – that is, a synthesis of class, gender, race and ethnicity. However, this synthetic approach makes it difficult to identify which (if any) of these conditioning or structuring factors is the major determinant. Feminist theorising is complex, dynamic and unsettling (Birrell, 2000, pp61–62, cited in Hargreaves, JA, 2004).

Cultural Studies and the contribution of John Hargreaves and Jennifer Hargreaves

By the 1970s the sociology of sport was beginning to develop a more 'critical' perspective as it turned its attention towards concerns about inequality, power and how these were embedded in everyday cultural practices. As all the major reviews of the field broadly agree (Giulianotti, 2005; Sugden and Tomlinson, 2002; Hargreaves and McDonald, 2000), within British sport sociology, cultural studies has been one of the most influential of all the various and at times competing theoretical and research frameworks. Centre stage in this development lies the work of two authors: John Hargreaves and Jennifer Hargreaves.

Though he had sketched out many aspects of his argument in an earlier article (Hargreaves, JE, 1982), in a still highly influential analysis entitled *Sport, Power and Culture,* John Hargreaves (1986b) establishes how class power relations are not only manifested within politics but also in popular culture. At the heart of this analysis is the concept of hegemony and how it provides an illumination of *the nature of the contest and struggle over resources, the conditions whereby consent is secured by the dominant . . .* (Sugden and Tomlinson, 2002, p9). One of the strengths of the book is its use of a detailed social and cultural history of modern British sport and physical education to explain that it is not possible to separate the development of modern sport from the class struggles that were an endemic part of everyday life within the late nineteenth and early twentieth centuries. For Hargreaves, the sports culture that came to characterise late Victorian Britain is fundamentally locked into struggles for power and class domination. As Britain continued to modernise, industrialise and urbanise the growing middle classes (or in more formal sociological terms, the 'bourgeoisie') were actively seeking to differentiate themselves politically and culturally from the slowly emancipating working classes. The determining feature of this struggle for power is the ability of the 'bourgeois class' to mobilise capital and the ideological apparatus of the state for their own self interest. Some of the essential battlegrounds for this were: the ability of entrepreneurs to commercialise and commodify sport; to separate sport on the basis of amateurism and professionalism; to constrain and discipline the bodies of the working classes through the imposition of 'rational recreation' and latterly the adoption of physical education within the developing system of mass education.

The lasting contribution of this work was its establishment of a number of sociological perspectives that you should recognise as recurrent themes within many of the chapters in this text: a non-reductionistic view of class power; the centrality of class to the development of modern sport; the role of sport in normalising these class relations and processes of domination and subordination within the routine practices of everyday life allied to the recognition that 'hegemony' can never be complete and that sport also has the capacity to open up arenas of cultural resistance.

Some critics of Hargreaves's work (Giulianotti, 2005; Morgan, 1994) suggest that his analysis and his application of the term hegemony has a number of weaknesses. There are two main ones that will be noted here. The first is that Hargreaves overplays the power of class and hegemony and underplays individual agency and within-class divisions. There is little direct evidence that the middle classes ever had the capacity to act as a unified 'self-conscious' class. The elite groups in British society were (and are) highly divided by competing political and cultural aspirations. The diverse histories of sport and physical education evidence powerful divisions between competing perspectives; that sport should be an autonomous and freely chosen part of civil society and those who believe that sport has the capacity to harmonise society and create processes of social inclusion and greater equity (e.g. evidenced in policies such as 'Sport for All' or 'Every Child Matters'). The second is that this early body of work within cultural studies over-emphasises social divisions based on class and that this helps conceal other vital forms of power inequality in sport such as those associated with gender, sexuality, race, ethnicity and disability.

In one of the most important feminist contributions within British sport sociology, Jennifer Hargreaves (1994) in *Sporting Females* attempts to readdress this imbalance of an overly class-centric analysis while still grounding many aspects of the analysis within the concept of hegemony. Not surprisingly this work changes the focus from class to concerns with male domination in sport. Like her namesake she also draws heavily on a critical social history of sports development to support her analysis. In its broad ranging tour of the social, cultural history of sport stretching from the nineteenth century to the present day, the discussion provides a detailed commentary on how *the lived experiences of women in sports and the structural forces influencing participation . . . reveal the complex and paradoxical character of female sports* (Hargreaves and McDonald, 2000, p55).

The application of the concept hegemony within its feminist perspective opens up the overt and subtle ways that male dominance in sport systematically benefits men. This occurs through its ability to normalise and regulate the function of male power relations in sport to such an extent that the processes of male domination and women's subordination are seen as unproblematic and a 'natural condition' of sport and male physical prowess. One outcome of this hegemonic expression of power is that there is a need to recognise the role of women as well as men in the active day-to-day production and reproduction of gender discrimination and inequality. For Hargreaves, it is not only the activities and attitudes of men that create some of the gross gender inequalities in sport, it is also evident that *some women support, accommodate, or collude in existing patterns of discrimination in sports* . . . (Hargreaves, JA, 1994, p23). Hence, the development of liberating processes need not only address the relationships between men and women but those between women themselves.

There is no doubt that the works of both these theorists have provided highly significant contributions to the field of sport sociology. They have helped pave the way for a more systematic and culturally focused analysis of sport and power relations that has been and continues to be pivotal to a wide range of sport sociology both within the UK and internationally (Horne and Jary, 1987; Gruneau, 1983; Sage, 1990; Hall, 1996; Birrell, 2000).

Learning Activity 7.6

Review of learning objectives

Having worked through this chapter, you should now take some time to carefully answer the following:

1. Why does sociology suggest that all societies have systems of social stratification?
2. How is inequality in modern society explained and how does it impact on sport?
3. In their attempts to understand the impact of social class on sport, identify the major distinctions between a functionalist, conflict and neo-Marxist analysis. Which of these perspectives do you find explains your own experience of social class within sport?
4. Drawing on your understanding of the terms 'ideology', 'discourse' and 'hegemony', justify why it is important to consider sport's role within popular culture.
5. Name the principal positions within feminism and detail how they can be used to understand gender divisions within sport.

Chapter Review

Modern society is socially stratified and this stratification underpins forms of inequality that are evident in sport. The influence of social class on sport can be understood through Marxist concepts of economic inequalities and capitalist systems of production, neo-Marxist concepts of power and Weberian concepts of status systems. Disadvantage in sport due to class can be explained in both structural and cultural terms. The way that occupational class structure influences the life chances of the poor, the working class, and the middle and upper classes appears to be highly resilient. Feminist sociology challenges the assumption that class stratification is the primary basis of social inequality. Explanations about the gender differences within sport range from those focused on biology to those that stress the social and cultural construction of gender. The persistence of patriarchal power structures sustaining a male hegemony in society and within sport continue to significantly disadvantage women. Sporting bodies are moulded into highly persistent gendered patterns.

Further Reading

For a general sociological introduction to the processes of social stratification and the impact on social class read:

Chapters 6 and 7 of Bilton et al. (2002) *Introductory Sociology*. London: Macmillan.

For gender read:

Chapter 8: Gender relations, in Bilton et al. (2002).

For a detailed overview of sport and social class read:

Sugden, J and Tomlinson, A (2000) Theorizing sport, social class and status, in Coakley, J and Dunning, E (eds) *Handbook of Sports Studies*. London: Sage.

Chapter 15: Sport and social divisions, in Jarvie, G (2006) *Sport and Culture*. London: Routledge.

For a detailed overview of sport and gender from a feminist perspective read:

Birrell, S (2000) Feminist theories of sport, in Coakley, J and Dunning, E (eds) *Handbook of Sports Studies*. London: Sage.

Chapter 8
Sport and diversity: issues of race, ethnicity and disability

Peter Craig and Paul Beedie

In this chapter we will introduce you to the issue of cultural diversity and how it has influenced, and continues to influence in seemingly ever more direct ways, the social construction of sport. We will be specifically concerned to develop your understanding of how race, ethnicity and disability can be understood as social constructions, and why they have become vital concepts within the sociological study of sport. As with the previous chapter, one of the underpinning themes will be the issue of inequality and its impact on sporting experience.

Learning Objectives

On completing this chapter you should be able to:

- show an understanding of the problems, challenges and potentials that the increasing diversity of British society creates;
- identify some of the sociological problems involved in defining terms such as race, ethnicity and disability;
- demonstrate how race, ethnicity and disability need to be understood as social and cultural constructions that have produced inequalities of opportunity and experience within sport;
- identify how these processes have impacted on sport within your own everyday experience.

Introduction

As we established in the previous chapter, processes of social differentiation are a fundamental component of all societies. Modernity has produced its own distinctive systems of differentiation and inequality. Two of the main processes driving differentiation are those of capitalism and industrialisation. The rationality of capitalist economic relations has dominated how these processes have developed and had a dramatic and long-lasting influence on society and thus on participation in sport. Alongside gender and sexuality, the contemporary debates about mass migration and the increasing levels of ethnic diversity in Britain highlight race, ethnicity and disability.

The rise of the Paralympics, and disabled sport generally, demonstrate that the issue of equity in sport is also of paramount importance. Framing some of the central concerns of this chapter are the claims of politicians, community leaders and sport organisations that sport has an important role in addressing a range of social issues arising from inequality and social exclusion.

Thinking about diversity

One of the common terms used to reflect the changes we are experiencing in contemporary British society is that of diversity.

Reflection Point 8.1

The term 'diversity' is capable of many interpretations. In the context of equality in sport, it is often taken to mean that there is a need for sport organisations to recognise the differences in the values, attitudes, cultural perspective, beliefs, ethnic background, sexual orientation, ability or disability, skills, knowledge, age and life experiences of each individual in any group of people (**www.diversity.toolkit.org.uk**) taking part in sport. In this sense it should not be understood as the same as 'equal opportunities'. In sport the recognition and valuing of diversity puts a requirement on sport organisations to have policies and procedures that take the diverse needs and preferences of these groupings into account.

Sport is built on all those mechanisms and structures that the modern social world has designed to translate and transmit how it wishes to order itself. If our sport organisations (see Chapter 5), their policies, strategies and working practices are to successfully address the challenges posed by the increasing diversity of our social world, then it is likely that they will have to commit to a prolonged and critical assessment of their own structures and practices. This chapter will examine the changing social landscape of sport in Britain and aim to demonstrate that diversity is a significant issue for sport. However, as with any process of social change, there are advances, retreats and plateaus as *carceral* networks of power (Foucault, 1981) operate.

As well as the classic sociological writings of Marx and Weber, contemporary social theorists such as Anthony Giddens have placed the need to understand power at the heart of their work. For Giddens (1984), it is not enough to understand the sources of power (e.g. Marx's concerns with economic power). The ways in which power is used, negotiated and resisted are also vitally important considerations (Foucault, 1981). The way in which power permeates the cultural aspects of everyday life means that they are a vital expression of power relations. Popular cultural activities such as sport are not superficial pastimes of little or no sociological note. Rather, they are *the sites where this struggle for and against a culture of the powerful is engaged* (Hall, 1992, p239).

This emphasises that our sense of community and our identities are inevitably linked to the forms of culture we encounter. In an age where concerns over diversity and equity are an ever-present part of our (sporting) world, there is a need to explore how power and culture operate in ways that reproduce, resist or potentially transform the existing relations between groups.

Multiracial, multicultural Britain

Learning Activity 8.1

Before reading the following section, take a few moments to estimate what you consider to be the percentage of ethnic minority groups within British society. If there is time, also ask your friends and family to do the same estimate and see how close it is to your estimate and to the actual figures given below. If your estimates differ, why do you think this is?

The terms 'multiracial' and 'multicultural society' are relatively new, although the historical realities of Britain's past demonstrate that racial and ethnic differences have always been present (though not always remembered). The term 'multiculturalism' is usually used to identify how Britain is now a state characterised by cultural and ethnic diversity. For some of those advocating a policy of multiculturalism the main concern is to create a society in which all cultural and religious groups are treated equitably. At its most ideal this presents an image of a society in which no one culture is dominant. However, many use the term in a much less idealistic way and their intention is to describe how our society is changing to include an increasing number of minority immigrant cultures existing alongside (and within) indigenous British culture.

Part of the problem is a tendency to homogenise what is culturally diverse. There is a difference between society as multicultural and multiculturalism as policy. To describe British society today as multicultural is quite clearly just a statement of fact. The change has been rapid and its pace has been for many deeply disturbing.

Multiculturalism can be understood as generated by social and cultural interactions that are seen both as two-way (majority–minority) and as working differently for different groups. As a way of organising our society multiculturalism positions each cultural group as distinctive, and thus simple assimilation or integration processes do not proceed without significant resistance.

Assimilation is where the processes affecting the relationship between social groups are seen as one-way, and where the desired outcome for society as a whole is seen as involving least change in the ways of doing things of the majority of the country and its institutional policies.

Integration is where processes of social interaction are seen as two-way, and where members of the majority community as well as immigrants and ethnic minorities are required to make contributions; so the latter alone cannot be blamed for failing, or not trying, to integrate.

In the 1950s and 1960s the expanding British economy required the recruitment of labour from the former colonies that had been part of the Empire. This influx created a series of powerful dislocations that had significant political and cultural repercussions.

Despite the good intentions of politicians at local and national levels of government, throughout the UK and in Europe, processes of assimilation and integration rarely operate consistently, thus creating a gap between the rhetoric of politicians and the reality of the lived experience in communities. Among the many reasons for this is misunderstanding of the terms integration and assimilation. According to Bourne (2009) they are not the same in that assimilation assumes some kind of normalising experience of absorption of a minority culture by the majority culture whereas integration implies a co-existence between cultures in the same country. It is the latter scenario that is the common experience of ethnic minorities today in the UK, a circumstance partly created by relative poverty and lack of access to mainstream resources and partly by the cultural identities sustained by substantive differences between communities, particularly those generated by religion. Nevertheless, as we argue in the last chapter of this book, although this complex process of cultural identity ebbs and flows, there is evidence to support the view that the overall movement is forward towards a more enlightened multicultural society: for every national government decision that appears to antagonise this delicate situation – Bourne (2009, p7) cites *[France's] ill conceived ban on the hijab . . . represents a direct threat to the European tradition of human rights* – there are local community activists achieving advances in community cohesion through local projects. In Chapter 14 we discuss the work of the Rev. Jay MacLeod and his team in the Queen's Park area of Bedford in bringing together people from Muslim, Hindu and Christian faiths in community engagement. The key issue here is the role that sport can play as a mechanism of community bonding. Sport is like an international language that can create a shared environment for assimilation, thus going beyond integration.

Intolerance of cultural difference and racism remain a concern for many communities across Europe – something the EU Commission is very keen to tackle for its member states. Ian Henry (2005) was part of a research project to explore the role that sport might play as a vehicle for implementing policies for the promotion of: *intercultural understanding and mutual respect within and between communities, including legislation (on human rights, political rights, residency, nationality etc.), education and cultural policy* (Henry, 2005, p3).

Henry concludes that if governments are genuinely striving for transcultural or intercultural consensus, then sport has an important role to play in this social and cultural transformation.

Race and ethnicity become powerful markers of separation and distinction. These racial and ethnic distinctions were often used to mark out differences between the immigrant groups and mainstream 'white' British (Donald and Rattansi, 1992). These processes produced a series of inequalities based on education, (un)employment, sport and attitudes to physical activity, food culture and health. During this period, these minority racial and ethnic groups became largely confined to the inner-city areas of Britain's large metropolitan areas.

Some facts and figures relating to the racial and ethnic diversity of the UK

The results of the national census in 2001 (this is the most recent) estimated the size of the minority ethnic population to be 4.6 million or 7.9 per cent of the total population of the United Kingdom. Indians were the largest minority group, followed by Pakistanis, those of mixed ethnic backgrounds, Black Caribbeans, Black Africans and Bangladeshis. The remaining minority ethnic groups each accounted for less than 0.5 per cent, but together accounted for a further 1.4 per cent of the UK population.

In Great Britain the minority ethnic population grew from 3.0 million in 1991 to 4.6 million in 2001, a rise of 53 per cent. Half of the total minority ethnic population are Asians of Indian,

Pakistani, Bangladeshi or other Asian origin. A quarter of minority ethnic people described themselves as Black (Black Caribbean, Black African or Other Black). 15 per cent of the minority ethnic population described their ethnic group as Mixed. About one-third of this group is from White and Black Caribbean backgrounds.

Britain's ethnic minority population is predominantly a young one: while 20 per cent of the white British population is under 16, the figure rises to 38 per cent for those of Bangladeshi origin, 35 per cent for those of Pakistani origin and 50 per cent for those of mixed race. While children from ethnic minority groups make up 12 per cent of the total child population, they are disproportionately more likely to be poor. Rates of child poverty are particularly high among children of African (56 per cent), Pakistani (60 per cent) and Bangladeshi (72 per cent) origin, compared with a rate of 25 per cent for white children (**www.statistics.gov.uk**).

In common with many other liberal democracies, the UK is now in a process of producing legislative and policy frameworks that are designed to address the increasing diversity of its population. Typical of the government's commitment to a 'diversity mandate' is the promotion of ideas of equity regardless of race, religion, gender and (dis)ability, published on the UK Government's Home Office website (**www.homeoffice.gov.uk**).

Sociological theories of racial and ethnic inequality

Within sociology the term 'race' is a complex and often contradictory concept because of disagreements regarding its precise meaning (Giddens, 2001). Ethnicity is often the preferred term of sociologists as it avoids the fixed and dubious categorisations that are associated with race. In their use of the term, sociologists attempt to draw attention to a series of social and cultural practices that can be used to distinguish a particular group, community or nation from others.

Definition: race
Refers to a set of social relationships that permit individuals and groups to be assigned various capacities and competencies on the basis of a number of biologically identified features.

Definition: ethnicity
Refers to a socially and culturally defined social group based on their sharing of a common language, cultural values and traditions and religion.

As with the term 'race', references to ethnicity must also be treated with caution. Through the use of ethnic markers such as Asian or Islamic, it is all too easy to fall into a 'false ethnic universalism' (Fleming, 1994) which can lead to the damaging and dangerous processes of stereotyping.

Sociological concern with race and ethnicity and other social group categorisations (e.g. disability) focuses on how they are used to give meanings to certain experiences and to categorise others. The dominant meanings that are given to racial or ethnic groupings help to support a socio-economic and cultural hierarchy in which being perceived as white and Anglo-Saxon is generally rated more positively than being black and non Anglo-Saxon (Kidd, 2002).

Learning Activity 8.2

Personal reflection: think carefully how you might respond to the following questions:

- Why do you, or some people that you know, consider 'race' to be an important way of distinguishing different groups of people?
- What does race tell us about the nature of different human populations, their societies and cultures?
- Why do we hear comments in sport that place significant emphasis on the corporeality (the physical manifestations of bodies in terms of skin pigment, body hair, facial and skeletal characteristics) of 'race'?

Having thought about these questions, consider whether your views, or what you might be willing to say on these issues might change when you are in different groups. Why might this be?

Today, the presence of racially and ethnically distinct groups is increasing and racial categorisations are often habitually used to resolve the problems of social identification, that is, our sense of sameness and difference. Race is most often understood as being based on some sort of recognisable biological difference (skin colour, shape of eyes, etc.). Yet it only takes a brief reflection to realise that many of these racial categorisations are essentially meaningless. In sociological terms, the concept of race becomes reified by the processes of racialisation that are often hidden from view because of their institutionalisation.

Definition: reification
The treatment of a socially constructed category or phenomenon as if it exists as an independent or autonomous entity.

Definition: racism
A set of socially, culturally and politically constructed ideas/attitudes that deterministically associates (pre-judges) inherited biological differences with representations of physical, psychological, social and moral attributes.

Definition: institutional racism
The collective failure of an organisation to challenge the actions of its employees/members (e.g. professional actions, advice, etc.) where the employees' comments and/or actions are deemed to be manifestly (overtly or covertly) based on racist perceptions. In a school, for example, all

teachers have a responsibility to deal with incidents of racial prejudice, not just the head teacher and the board of governors.

Jarvie (2000, p334) suggests that there are contradictory characteristics in race and ethnic relationships. Summarising these views, he states that sport:

1. is inherently conservative and helps to consolidate patriotism, nationalism and racism;
2. has some inherent property that makes it a possible instrument of integration and harmonious race relations;
3. as a form of cultural politics has been central to the processes of colonialism and imperialism in different parts of the world;
4. has contributed to unique political struggles which have involved black and ethnic political mobilisation, and the struggle for equality of and for black peoples and other ethnic minority groups;
5. has produced stereotypes, prejudices and myths about ethnic minority groups which have contributed both to discrimination against and an under-representation of ethnic minority peoples within certain sports; and
6. is a vehicle for displays of black prowess, masculinity and forms of identity.

The social construction of race in sport

The ideological discourses that position race in sport as a significant classification of people tend to fall into four categories:

- the 'naming' of race;
- the assumed physical capacities of race;
- the economic conditions of race;
- the assumed mental capacities of race.

The first element of the discourse is the identification or naming of race. This makes race for the white athlete 'invisible', as it is *never* mentioned. Of course, the counterpoint is also true: by naming an athlete as 'black', the issue of race is placed as a central part of the presented explanation of their athletic ability. This ideological representation of athletes denoted by colour reinforces the more general representations of race that circulate within most Western societies. The perception of having a racialised identity is rarely seen as an issue for those who are white. However, for non-whites it is seen as an issue by both whites and non-whites. The use of these representations by sports journalists, editors and owners of the media is hardly surprising given that, in general, they are all white males. These ideas and images are discursively reproduced through a range of media. The discourses also suggest that white athletes have a greater mental capacity than black athletes, leading to a 'positioning' of black and white athletes often referred to as 'stacking'.

Explanations regarding why white soccer players tend to be found more often in central positions on the field still tend to emphasise that they have more organisational capabilities than black players. In this discourse, the over-representation of black athletes within boxing is due to the lower level of thinking/education necessary for success in boxing: in managing their professional affairs, it's recognised that someone else (the 'white' manager) has to do the thinking for the boxer. In terms of the dangerous nature of the sport, it's an obvious benefit if the person in the ring does not think too much beyond the objective of the contest.

Natural physicality and mental discourses are intertwined in the argument that short/powerful sport events require a different attitude from long-distance/endurance events. Sprinting events are assumed to require natural physical power allied to the ability to relax and not think too much. (Those who think too much become stressed and do not relax.) Long-distance runners are assumed to require a specific type of mental approach, such as planning a 'good' or 'strategic' race.

Case Study
Black footballers in the English football league

Football emerged as a team sport in the nineteenth century and, as discussed at several other junctures in this book, its organisation reflected the industrial and economic conditions of Victorian England. The game remained, however, almost exclusively white (players, managers, coaches and chairmen) well into the twentieth century; moreover, when more black people did become involved, inherent mechanisms of discrimination restricted this involvement in ways that retained power for those who already had it and restricted black involvement to the lowest rungs of football's hierarchy of power – that of the players.

Arthur Wharton was the 'first black footballer'. He played for Preston North End and Rotherham in the late 1880s. He originated from Ghana and demonstrated his athletic prowess as a sprinter (he once held the world record for the 100 yards) and a cricketer (he played for Yorkshire) as well as being a footballer. His grave remained unmarked until sport historians found it and contributed an appropriate plaque in 1997. Other black footballers were Andrew Watson, who played for the Edinburgh club Queens Park in the 1880s; Walter Tull, born in 1888 and who went on to gain a commission in the army in 1917; a South African called Albert Johannson who played at Leeds United in the 1970s and Clyde Best who played for West Ham United in the 1970s. Thus black participation in English football in the first 100 years or so of its formal history was so small as to be almost statistically insignificant.

However, as the twentieth century progressed there were signs of change. Three decades before he lost his commentator job for his infamous racist comment about the work ethic of the French footballer Marcel Desailly, Ron Atkinson had been instrumental in introducing black footballers to the West Bromwich Albion team that he managed in the 1970s. Of particular note were Laurie Cunningham, Cyrille Regis and Brendan Batson. Regis did well enough to make it into a full England squad, but English national footballers were exclusively white at this time. It was 1982 before a black footballer played for England – Viv Anderson played for the team managed by the late Bobby Robson – and another 12 years had to pass before England had a black captain – Paul Ince took the armband for the full international against the USA in 1994. Today 16 per cent of the registered club footballers in the Football League are black, but the figure is over 20 per cent if one just considers the Premier League. However, even allowing for the fact that not all footballers can become managers or coaches because there are far fewer jobs, these ratios are not reflected in the organising positions higher up the football hierarchy. Of the 92 clubs in the Football League, in 2010 there are only three black managers – Paul Ince at MK Dons, Keith Alexander at Macclesfield and Chris Hughton at Newcastle United. None of these teams are in the Premier League. This figure of 3 per cent black managers goes down to 1 per cent if one considers senior coaching staff who are black.

You might like to consider why this is. Is it racial stereotyping (black players are not seen as tactically intelligent)? Is it a lack of role models in coaching positions and assistant manager roles? Or is it because despite campaigns such as 'Sport Against Racism' (endorsed by the Football Association) there are still invisible lines of power operating in favour of a white hegemony in football?

There are further hurdles in place for marginal groups in society. Ethnic communities can often be found in socially and economically deprived areas of our cities – a place to escape from. The perception exists that more blacks than whites excel in sport because sport is 'the only way out' of the ghetto for blacks. Therefore, they are more ambitious in sport than white athletes. This way of thinking further reinforces the 'superiority' of the white, male, middle-class hegemony explained elsewhere in this book. Thus, although it could be argued that 'race' is a meaningless concept, this is not going to happen until there are significant changes to deeply entrenched views: 'race' still remains a significant part of the lived experience of many people in sport. Although there is no doubt that since the 1970s sport has proved a very successful route to fame and fortune for a significant number of black sportsmen and women, it also needs to be stressed that countless thousands have not achieved these levels of material wealth. For them, sport can still prove to conceal deep inequalities, racist beliefs, and to be a path to failure and disappointment (Jarvie, 2000, p336).

At an everyday level people habitually use terms such as 'Black', 'White' and 'Asian'. These terms are essentially meaningless in their ability to accurately define a specific racial group – our 'categorisation' is a cultural construction. The identification of someone as a 'black athlete' merely identifies someone with a particular tone of skin who is involved in athletic activity. It does not define by itself any potential athletic ability on the part of the individual. Skin colour has become attached (mostly by 'white people') to explanations of athletic ability. We never hear people offering a 'racial' explanation for the dominance of white people in sports such as skiing, ice hockey or golf.

Sport and ethnicity

The social construction of ethnicity has three defining characteristics:

- perceptions by other members of the society or by members of other societies/nations that a defined group of people are different (external identification);
- perceptions by the members of the same group that they are different from these 'others';
- perceptions by those within the ethnic group that their lifestyle should habitually adopt a range of distinct activities (these can include religion, dress codes, food, music and sport) that actively help to reinforce their sense of having a distinct ethnic identity.

When ethnic groups seek to represent themselves actively, or have identity thrust upon them by dominant cultural groups, the label is no longer neutral but it becomes a marker of difference and in some cases rivalry, marginalisation and oppression. Ethnicity is therefore about identity and sets of cultural activities and behaviours. Once established, ethnic identities become a socially recognisable system of group classifications. Sometimes the label of ethnic identity (as with those concerned with race) is essentially meaningless as it collapses a multitude of ethnicities into one category such as the term 'Asian'.

In sport, ethnic identification can be used to stereotypically ascribe patterns of behaviour (real and mythic) and their meaning. These stereotypes may have a special function when used by dominant groups. Dominant groups need to stereotype subordinate groups because of the risks associated with the possible loss of power and privilege to the subordinate groups. Dominant groups manipulate the public's perceptions of threat to reinforce their own positions of privilege and power. Racial and ethnic markers such as dress codes provide easy ideological markers for the threatening 'alien' (immigrant/invader). The dominant group becomes the protector of nation, tradition and cultural identity.

The social and cultural construction of ethnic identity means that it is not permanently 'fixed' but open to change. Ethnicity is therefore reflexively monitored and socially organised. Ethnic communities' use of sport and other physical recreation activities can validate membership of an ethnic community, and how this ascribes opportunities and social status is often deeply embedded in the power structures of the society. Sport can do more than ascribe status within an ethnic community; it can also build bridges across to 'other' social groups. The multi-faceted identity of British boxer Amir Khan is an example. In a poll conducted for the BBC in 2005, the overwhelming majority of Muslims – 89 per cent – said they feel proud when British teams do well in international competitions, a similar figure to the national population (http://news.bbc.co.uk/1/hi/uk/4137990.stm).

Case Study
Amir Khan: British-born boxer of Pakistani descent

Amir Khan was born on 8 December 1986 in Bolton. His father suggests that his hyperactive son, who went through a conventional education in the state system, was 'a born fighter'. He first came to fame in the 2004 Athens Olympics when he won a silver medal in the lightweight division, aged 17. He lost the final to a much older and more experienced Cuban (Mario Kinderlan, whom AK beat in 2005 in his last fight as an amateur). His 14 fights as a professional have all been won, 11 by KO decisions. He is an avid supporter of Bolton Wanderers FC and often uses the training facilities at the Reebok stadium. He is part of an athletic extended family that includes his first cousin, Sajid Mahmood the England cricketer, and his brother, the boxer Haroon Khan, together with a second cousin, Wadhah Saleh, who is a world champion in karate, aged 14. AK's high profile has been used to support a range of causes linked to issues of race, religion and ethnicity. He has travelled to Pakistan to help earthquake victims, and has also made a series of TV programmes for Channel Four called Amir Khan's Angry Young Men in which he promotes boxing, faith and family values as a focus for young men distracted into anti-social behaviour.

The changing context of race and ethnicity in sport

The political and social context of the diversity mandate and the requirements of the Race Relations (Amendment) Act 2000 mean that all public authorities in the UK, including all of those concerned with sport, are now subject to a series of antidiscrimination provisions and their implementation (www.uksport.gov.uk).

While the legal context may have changed, there are still widespread concerns that although many sport organisations maintain that they have an 'open door' policy, this has not necessarily changed the traditional levels of participation and involvement in sport. Research shows that many sports have low participation levels by women and girls, ethnic minority groups, disabled people and, in some cases, young people, and these groups are therefore under-represented (www.uksport.gov.uk).

It is unlikely that many sporting clubs have actively sought a membership base outside of their usual population groups. Keogh (2002) argues that the approach of many clubs neglects the benefits of a more diverse membership that include a greater range of sports, more financial income, an understanding of other cultures and greater participation.

So, why have ethnic minority groups and the disabled been overlooked by sporting organisations for so long? Keogh (2002) identifies a number of possible explanations.

- If clubs are doing well and have a strong membership base, they may not see the need to diversify further.

- Developing new networks, programmes and procedures may be seen as too difficult, too expensive or too time-consuming for already over-stretched volunteers/staff.
- A lack of knowledge about the benefits associated with diversification.
- A lack of knowledge about the needs and backgrounds of specific cultural groups.
- A lack of knowledge about where to source assistance and support.
- A lack of awareness about available support options.
- Unwillingness to become culturally inclusive.

It is evident that implementing the new diversity standard may well prove to be a significant challenge for most sports. UK Sport suggests that concerns regarding sports' failure to address diversity adequately and the requirements of the Race Relations Act (2000) will require all UK sport organisations to spend a considerable amount of time focusing on policy formulation and implementation to improve equality. Authorities such as UK Sport and Sport England can offer a leadership role here, for example, by disseminating good practice and facilitating grant applications.

If sport is to deal with the challenges of ethnicity effectively, then it needs to critically assess the challenges posed by the problems of racism and cultural discrimination. Sport has allowed racism and other forms of discrimination to become structurally embedded through its history into the institutions of sport and thereby to inform or shape the views of those individuals who participate in sport.

Sport and disability

The questions of the definition of disability and how persons with disabilities perceive themselves are knotty and complex. It is no accident that these questions are emerging at the same time as the status of persons with disabilities in society is changing dramatically.

Definition: impairment
Any loss of normal psychological or anatomical structure, or function.

Definition: disability
Any restriction or lack (resulting from an impairment) of ability to perform an activity in the manner or within the range considered normal for a human being.

Definition: handicap
A disadvantage for a given individual, resulting from an impairment or disability, that limits or prevents the fulfilment of a role that is normal, depending on age, sex, social and cultural factors, for that individual.

These definitions reflect the idea that disability is a social construct. Most people believe they know what is and is not a disability. If you imagine 'the disabled' at one end of a spectrum and people who are physically and mentally capable at the other, the distinction appears to be clear. However, there is considerable middle ground in this construct, and it is in the middle that the scheme falls apart. What distinguishes a socially 'invisible' impairment, such as the need for corrective eyeglasses, from a less acceptable one, such as the need for a corrective hearing aid or for a walking frame? Functionally, there may be little difference. Socially, some impairments create great disadvantage or social stigma for the individual, while others do not. Some are considered disabilities and some are not.

A disability implies a problem or a disadvantage that requires compensatory or ameliorative action. The concept does not seek to specify whether the problem is located in the individual or in the environment, nor does it attempt to identify the rationale for measures that are taken in reaction to the perceived disadvantage. Nonetheless, such policies represent an official belief that a disability constitutes a disadvantageous circumstance that obliges a public or a private agency to offer some type of response (Hahn, 1984, p294).

UK Sport, as a listed public authority, is required by the Disability Discrimination Regulations 2005 to produce a Disability Equality Scheme (UK Sport, 2009). The Disability Discrimination Acts 1995 and 2005 requires such bodies to have due regard to:

- promote equality of opportunity between disabled people;
- eliminate discrimination that is unlawful;
- eliminate harassment of disabled people that is related to the disability;
- promote positive attitudes towards disabled people;
- encourage participation by disabled people in public life;
- take into account disabled people's disabilities, even where that involves treating people more favourably.

A critical reading of this scheme suggests support for dominance of the medical model of discourse emphasising the differences between able-bodied and disabled people. This is explained briefly below but in more detail in the 'Research focus' section near the end of this chapter.

The idea of dependency has been used socially to produce and reproduce disability as a problem. This has implications for sport as Brittain (2004) shows. Drawing on his research at the Sydney Paralympic Games 2000, he sets out the two theoretical positions of disability. In the 'medical model' doctors, consultants and health experts combine to sustain discourses about the body and mind that are grounded in scientific knowledge and perpetuate the view that *the problems that face people with disabilities are the result of their physical and/or mental impairments and are independent of the wider socio-cultural, physical and political environments* (Brittain, 2004, p430). This model of disability in the individual is dominant in modern-day Western societies. Conversely, the 'social model' positions disability as a social construction: disabled people can only make a limited contribution to society and this lack of 'worth' contributes to this group's marginalisation. It is argued that, because this view is subordinate to the medical model, it is necessary to change people's attitudes to disability. However, making physical changes to the environment (such as wheelchair access to buildings) will change the life experiences of disabled people, but is unlikely in itself to change the values deeply embedded in a society essentially supportive of the medical model. The Disability Discrimination Act of 1995 aimed to achieve equal access to public places for all, but only reinforced the recognition of disabled people as a distinct social group. The ambition of pressure groups who lobby on behalf of disabled groups is, therefore, to advance understanding and change attitudes. Sport has the potential to become a vehicle for such social advancement and the Paralympics is an example of a raised profile for disabled sport. Brittain's detailed research shows that both able-bodied and disabled people appear to support a medical model of disability that essentially means that disability becomes a dominant identity feature through perceptions and self-image. Tanni Grey-Thompson (see the case study on p151) resisted attending her local special school while growing up in Cardiff because she didn't want to be set apart from mainstream society. Here is evidence of some resistance to the predominant able-bodied hegemony.

Some of the common social and cultural factors that mitigate against disabled people in sport are:

- poor motivation and confidence;
- negative school experiences;
- lack of support from family and friends;
- lack of information about opportunities;
- lack of disability-friendly facilities;
- transport problems;
- lack of time, money and other resources;
- poor access.

Disability sport, rather like the concept of physical and mental impairment, exists on a continuum without clear boundaries. For purposes of discussion here it is useful, however, to think about access to sport generally (e.g. physical education in schools) at one end and elite performance (e.g. the Paralympics) at the other. Across the continuum there has been a gradual evolution such that the place of disabled groups in society has moved towards a more equitable circumstance. For example, following the 1944 Education Act pupils with disabilities were assigned to medically defined categories (such as 'handicapped' or 'educationally subnormal') and segregated to special schools without consideration of their abilities. The 1981 Education Act recognised that special educational needs (SEN) covered a range of conditions that, for the most part, were not best served by segregation and therefore endorsed reintegration into mainstream education. In physical education this helped all but the most severely physically disabled, a situation extended by the introduction of the Physical Education National Curriculum (PENC) in 1992 which established the entitlement of all pupils to a 'broad and balanced curriculum' (Thomas, 2004). In practice, however, although some progress has been made, Sport England has identified that 53 per cent of primary aged disabled children and 41 per cent of 11–16-year-old disabled children spend less than one hour a week doing PE and that only 20 per cent of disabled pupils spend two hours per week in PE lessons compared to 33 per cent of the overall school population. Additionally, only 40 per cent of disabled school children undertook extra-curricular sport compared to 79 per cent of the general school population (Thomas, 2004).

The Paralympics

The Paralympic Games are a multi-sport event for athletes with physical, mental and sensorial disabilities. The name fuses the Greek *para*, meaning 'beside' or 'alongside', with the word 'olympic'. Paralympic has shifted its meaning since the 1950s when the term was first coined to indicate a union of 'paraplegic' and 'olympic'. The history of disabled sporting competition can be traced to Ludwig Guttmann who, in 1948, organised the Stoke Mandeville Games for war veterans with spinal injuries. Interest from countries such as Holland expanded the idea and in 1960 the ninth Annual Stoke Mandeville Games took place in Rome. Because these Games paralleled the Olympic Games, the event is considered to be the first Paralympic Games. Winter Paralympics followed in Ornskoldsvik, Sweden, in 1976, and since 1988 the summer Paralympics have been held in conjunction with the Olympic Games in the same host city. Today, any city bidding to host the Games has to include the Paralympics in its bid and both Games are now run by a single organising committee. Just as the format of the two events has come together, so too have cheating issues emerged. Whereas in mainstream sport these commonly involve performance-enhancing drugs, in the Paralympics 'scandals' often arise as teams enter individuals to inappropriate categories – for example, in Sydney 2000 non-disabled athletes were entered in the Spanish basketball team. The six recognised categories for competition are amputee; cerebral palsy; intellectual disability; wheelchair; vision impaired and 'les autres' – a category to sweep up disabilities that don't obviously fit elsewhere. These categories are under constant review.

A pattern of first recognising disabled needs and second an evolution of these needs into 'the mainstream' is therefore identifiable in physical education. This sequence has parallel developments in sport more generally and has been particularly evident since the 1990s when, via the Sports Council publication *Sport for people with disabilities* in 1993, a climate of integration between the National Disability Sport Organisations (NDSOs) and mainstream National Governing Bodies (NGBs) was established. Initially, this integration failed to make progress, but in 1998 an English Federation of Disability Sports (EFDS) was established with a mission of sporting inclusion for disabled groups via better choices for sport, professional services and improved disability sport structures. Thus, progress has been made, but as Thomas (2004) shows, able-bodied administrators working for mainstream NGBs and those working with elite disabled athletes have often (for different reasons) slowed down the integration of disabled sport into mainstream participation.

Case Study

Tanni Grey-Thompson: Paralympian wheelchair athlete

Born on 26 July 1969 with spina bifida, Tanni Grey-Thompson's disability made her more determined to succeed in the world, hence her resistance to attending a special school for the physically handicapped. She recognised that this appeared to diminish drive and ambition rather than increase commitment to succeed. Her first competition was 100m at the Welsh National Games in 1984.

Racing over a range of distances from track sprints to road marathons, Tanni Grey-Thompson has accumulated 16 Paralympic medals (including 11 golds). She has held 30 world records and won the London marathon six times between 1997 and 2002. TG-T was voted BBC Wales Sports Personality of the Year in 1992, 2000 and 2004; she was made a Dame in 2005. Married, with one daughter, she retired from athletics following appearances in the Paralympic World Cup in Manchester, May 2007. The accolades that followed from significant others in sport (e.g. Richard Caborn, Minister for Sport, and Mike Brace, President of the British Paralympic Association) emphasise her 'track record', her longevity, her dedication to sport and her ambassadorial role for disabled sport.

Research Focus

Sport and disability

Ian Brittain is a sport sociologist who has a specialist research interest in disability and sport. His PhD thesis was titled 'Perspectives of elite athletes with disabilities: problems and possibilities' and it is the publication of this study (Brittain, 2004) that is cited in this chapter. His methodology was qualitative as he was particularly interested in the perspectives of the disabled athletes he interviewed. The findings of this study will be discussed below – as they help explain the dominance of the medical model in our understanding of disabled sport. Ian has worked as a Disability Sports Research Officer with the Greater Warwickshire Sports Partnership – where he wrote a four-year development strategy for disability sport – and more recently as a researcher and lecturer at the University of Bedfordshire. His investigations of disability sport are far ranging and include critical investigations of physical education and sport in relation to people with disabilities in schools. It is his paper published in the *Journal of Sport and Social Issues* (Brittain, 2004) that is arguably his most important recent publication.

In this key paper he argues that, despite the possibilities that exist for many 'alternative' constructions for the assimilation of disabled groups into mainstream society, the power of the medical model is so dominant that, even though there have been some significant developments in recent times, the social positioning of 'disability' as 'otherness' or difference – with all that this implies for perceptions of such people – is likely to remain for the foreseeable future. Indeed he shows that disability is shaped and our understanding of this sustained by the 'cognitive authority' of the medical profession. This authority, he argues, operates well beyond medical institutions such as hospitals to include government bureaucracies, insurance companies, courts, schools, charities, rehabilitative organisations and employer bodies (2004, p430). This discursive reinforcement of a particular view of disability could, he argues, be changed if there is a political will to enact effective public policy to remove environmental barriers, but that for this to have a significant impact there would need to be a more fundamental change in underlying attitudes and . . . *levels of understanding that are key to changing the situation for people with disabilities* (2004, p431). This ambition became a focus of his investigation, and thus his methodology of in-depth semi-structured interviews with elite Paralympians, which was particularly concerned with: . . . *perceptions of disability within British society [and how these] affect social interactions in relation to people with disabilities and the role these perceptions play in the formation of the self-perceptions of people with disabilities* (2004, pp431–432).

This research project provided detailed evidence to support a number of key indicators about the relationship between mainstream sport and disabled sport. There is, for example, a widely held perception that physical activity, especially if it is strenuous, is not appropriate for people with disabilities. Similarly, he found that there is a socially imposed feeling of worthlessness (among people with disabilities) as a reaction to physical difference (by the able-bodied). A combination of these two can lead to a magnification of sensitivity to stereotyping, and especially so in sport where the context is . . . *likely to exacerbate the visibility of the very physical differences that lead to these feelings and perceptions in the first place* (2004, p440). Of particular note from the findings he explores are differences between those people that are born disabled and those who become disabled as the result of an accident at some later point in their lives. One finding is that disability is far from being groupable in some homogenous way; another is that prejudice and lack of understanding and empathy can exist between people with different disabilities, and a third – and perhaps most prescient because it connects to Gramsci's work on hegemony theory – is that many disabled people and their carers unthinkingly accept the medical model and strive for individual rather than environmental change. Something similar happens with the media coverage of disabled sport which has undoubtedly increased in recent times but, because sports programmes are defined by people with little or no knowledge of what it is like to be disabled, provide the type of coverage that simply reinforces the 'integration' of disabled sport (that is its existence alongside mainstream sport) – in support of the medical model – rather than the assimilation of disabled sport to create a different sporting world in support of the social model. Ian Brittain's research shows just how difficult (and complex) the process of social (and sporting) change can be.

Learning Activity 8.3

Review of learning objectives

To aid your assessment of whether you have achieved the learning outcomes that we stated at the beginning of the chapter, please do the following activities:

1. Write a short paragraph detailing the differences between the concepts of race and ethnicity.

2. Reflect on your own experience of sport. Do you think that some sports are dominated by one specific race or ethnic group? Why do you think this is? How might a sport sociologist seek to explain it?

3. Take part in the following group workshop activity exploring the social experience of race and ethnicity.

●●●▶

Learning Activity 8.3 continued

The purpose of the activity is to explore the position of certain racial and ethnic groups in the 'race' to sporting success. You will need to revisit the key points from this chapter, but you may also want to refer to other chapters, particularly those that deal with the processes of socialisation and stratification. You will need to work in small groups in the first instance but to feed back into general discussion at certain times in the activity. Each group should nominate a different spokesperson at each feedback point. It will be useful to use a teaching space that has the capacity to 'cluster' tables so that each group can operate its own discussion.

Group brainstorming stage In your group write down on a piece of paper the characteristics of growing up in Britain that appear to determine 'success' in life.

Class feedback 1 Feed back your findings by each group taking it in turns to summarise your discussion. Listen carefully to all the feedback and add to your own group list if other groups have come up with ideas that you have not considered.

Group work Each group now needs to organise the list of characteristics that determine success into a table. The exact form of this table may well vary from group to group, but it needs to have at least three columns: 1 = Characteristics of success, 2 = White, 3 = Non-white/Ethnic. Your group will write short notes to 'fill in' the table you have created that relate to your understanding of the relationship between the characteristics of success and each column, headed 'White' and 'Non-white'. For example, if 'geographic location' is a characteristic of success, you might want to note that ethnic communities are often found in poorer parts of towns and cities. The task is to produce one table per group but with notes that are a contribution from all group members.

Class feedback 2 Each group, in turn, explains their findings which at this stage are concerned with opportunities to be successful in life generally.

Group work This stage is a return to group discussion to establish the extent to which the generalised findings above might be applied specifically to sport.

Class feedback 3 The intention here is for each group to summarise in turn the outcomes of their discussions about the application of these success characteristics to involvement with sport for white and non-white people. There might be some discussion at this point about the type of sport that different ethnic groups may be involved with and the form of this involvement, that is, as participant or spectator. At this stage the ensuing general class discussion might expand to include other elements of social stratification such as gender, age and disability. The final stage of the exercise is to draw up a set of conclusions about racial and ethnic groups, and their involvement in sport in Britain today.

4. Show your understanding of the social construction of disability within sport. Based on your reading of this section of the chapter, write two short paragraphs describing the medical model of disability and why so many sport sociologists think it needs to be challenged.

Chapter Review

The discussion of race, ethnicity and (dis)ability should have indicated to you the importance of cultural diversity within sport today. Each is representative of the way that sport is part of a social landscape characterised by an unequal distribution of resources and therefore power. As has been demonstrated elsewhere in this book, sport in Britain today is a product of the socio-cultural, economic and historical circumstances that preceded it. The sociological analyses presented suggest that dominant groups (mainly drawn from those who are white European, educated, middle class and male), often use sport as a way of retaining a dominant perspective that reflects their hegemonic power. Thus, any groups that are not able-bodied or white European or male often have to struggle to change the established order of things. While drawing heavily on this perspective, the chapter has also attempted to document processes of change. As we enter the twenty-first century, there is within sport an organisational evolution through which athletes belonging to these often disadvantaged groups (NB we accept that the use of the term 'group' within this discussion assumes a homogeneity within such categories that almost certainly does not exist) are gaining improved integration and equity within their chosen sports.

However, a closer examination reveals the overall picture to be more complex. Just as the growth in women's sport participation is not reflected by a comparable change in the number of female sports administrators, so too with race and ethnicity – e.g. despite the significant profile attained by the British Muslim boxer Amir Khan, boxing remains in the control of a minority of non-Muslim, white males. Moreover, although the achievements of elite disabled athletes such as Tanni Grey-Thompson are to be applauded, they are achieved through an extraordinary dedication to rigorous training as a professional sportsperson, similar to sports preparation by elite able-bodied athletes. The Paralympics have clearly raised the profile of disabled sport, but have done so in a context that celebrates competition and reinforces an understanding of sport as reflecting a value system privileging the able-bodied. Thus, the Paralympics is an adjunct to the main event. Paradoxically, while striving for the assimilation of diverse groups into mainstream sports, by failing to address the commensurate inequalities in the distribution of resources, the required standards will be harder to achieve for those groups for whom access to sport is already an issue. Racial and ethnic groups and the disabled therefore have to make disproportionate efforts and have all manner of additional costs and hurdles to clear before genuine equality in sport can be achieved.

The sociological analysis of race, ethnicity and disability can therefore be seen to raise a number of important issues about sport in Britain. Although problematic to define, it is clear that these categories are social constructions that account for different patterns of sport participation. Sport in Britain is still 'measured' in relation to a white, male middle-class understanding of those sports and their participants that is 'mainstream'. Thus, although great strides have been made in changing the sporting landscape to accommodate diversity, there is a gap between the rhetoric and the reality for the peripheral groups discussed here that reflects the power of the sporting hegemony evidenced by this chapter.

Further Reading

To extend your understanding of sport, race and ethnicity read:

Jarvie, G (2000) Sport, racism and ethnicity, in Coakley, J and Dunning, E (eds) *Handbook of Sports Studies*. London: Sage.

To explore real-life accounts of disability in sport start by reading:

Andrew, J (2003) *Life and Limb: A True Story of Tragedy and Survival Against the Odds*. London: Portrait.

The drama lies in the tragedy that led Jamie Andrew to lose his lower arms and legs, but the interest lies in the way 'abled' becomes 'disabled', and the social inclusion and exclusion this circumstance creates.

Because issues of diversity are such an active area of change within sport today, some of the best additional reading is available through websites:

www.sportdevelopment.org.uk/html/ethnicity2000 A downloadable PDF file is available here which shows the published results of the 1999–2000 national survey of sport in ethnic communities.

www.efds.net This is the English Federation of Disability Sport. Good links to the BBC (who have gained awards for their TV and journalistic coverage of disability sport) and Sport England (a major conduit for funding).

www.londonsportsforum.org.uk This charitable body has an ambition to increase disability sport and recreation participation in greater London by one per cent each year.

www.fdso.co.uk The Federation of Disability Sports Organisations based in Wakefield is a benevolent organisation run by volunteers that aims to increase disability sport and recreation opportunities in Yorkshire and Humberside.

www.sportengland.org/sport_england_the_magazine__annual_review_2005 This document is a contextual report demonstrating advances in sport in the community and healthy lifestyles.

Part Three

Go: analysing contemporary issues and themes – the changing world of sport

Chapter 9
Sport and consumer society

Peter Craig

I Shop, Therefore I Am.
(Benson, 2000)

This is the first of three chapters that will examine some of the ways that sport and modern society have been impacted and transformed by the rise of mass consumption, the mass media and an increasingly interconnected global world. This chapter provides you with an introduction to the ways in which sociology seeks to analyse and understand the ways that the rise of consumer society and its inherent processes of commodification and consumption have played an integral and increasingly significant part in the construction of sport. Therefore this chapter aims to:

- introduce you to how sociology has sought to explain the rise of the consumer society;
- detail how the media have been crucial to the integration of sport within this process;
- introduce you to a number of sociological theories and concepts that will extend your understanding of consumer society and the associated processes of consumption and commodification;
- develop your understanding of how important the consumption of sport is to British society and particularly the British economy.

Learning Objectives

On completing this chapter you should be able to:

- give sociological explanations of 'consumer society', 'commodification' and 'media sport';
- detail how modern sport has been impacted by the processes of consumption and commodification;
- detail the diverse ways in which sport is a vital element of the British economy;
- provide an informed discussion regarding how the development of the mass media has transformed sport.

Introduction

Over the past few decades sociology has developed a considerable interest in the process of consumption. Central to this development has been an awareness of two interconnected processes.

First, the period since the late 1950s has seen a vast increase in mass consumption that has not only impacted the UK but, as the massive changes currently occurring in China and India indicate, is global in its scope and reach. Second, this development has occurred concurrently with what appears to be a weakening of some of the organisational modes of modernity, especially those focused on the processes of production. During the twentieth century the growing affluence of the working class (Goldthorpe et al., 1968–1969) helped the establishment of mass markets based on consumer products that were largely undifferentiated by nation, class, gender or race (Smart, 2003). Partly as a result of these processes, the power of modern social structures (we have already explored some of the major arguments here through our examination of class, gender, race and ethnicity) to significantly influence our identity (i.e. how we and others think about who we are) has diminished. In his examination of these issues Bauman (2000) argues that our contemporary world, its structures and cultural relations have become much more pluralised and flexible, or, as he puts it, 'fluid'.

Because of its significance within these transforming processes, a number of influential social theorists (Bauman, 1998, 2000; Smart, 2003, 2005) contend that consumption needs to be a central concern of the sociological analysis of contemporary life. As Bocock observes, we need to recognise that although *Consumption appears to be rooted in the satisfaction of purely natural, biological or physical needs . . . there is nothing natural about the ways in which millions of people now shop for consumer goods* (1992, p121). Other theorists take this even further and have suggested that consumption is not only an important dimension of modern life, it is a defining element of it that could be argued is driving our very history (Miller, 1995a, p50). A history that, if the proponents of climate change are correct, will be increasingly unsustainable (Giddens, 2009).

Not surprisingly, given the multitude of ways that sport is connected to the processes of consumption, a number of sport sociologists, such as John Horne (2006, p1), have argued that a sociological understanding of sport in the twenty-first century must begin to systematically locate its analysis within *consumer culture, consumer society and consumption.*

Towards a sociological understanding of sport and consumption

Living, playing and consuming in modernity

The modern age has created a number of interconnections between sport, the media and advertising that have helped to create the impression that the pivotal social and personal experience of the modern age is to be a consumer. Within this ideology, shopping and consumption lie at the very heart of modern life. Because of this, the processes and meaning of consumption have become an important topic for sociological investigation.

By the late nineteenth and early twentieth centuries the growing significance of consumption on modern life had attracted the interest of a number of social theorists. The work of Simmel (Bocock,

1992) did much to sociologically establish how the rise of a new, essentially modern urban culture was linked to new patterns of consumption. The complexities of modern city life also gave rise to concerns about identity. As mass production makes consumer products more widely available and economically affordable, problems of status and distinction become more problematic for the higher social status groups. For Veblen (1953), the expanding group of wealthy individuals (the new middle class) whose wealth stemmed from their entrepreneurial success (rather than being inherited and connected to the land-based wealth of the aristocracy) faced a specific set of problems. To help establish their social status they engaged in a process of 'conspicuous consumption' designed to demonstrate not only their wealth, 'good taste' and 'good background' (Bocock, 1992, p128), but also the cultural advantages and social power of their class. During this time, their impact on sport was quite profound as they sought to establish domains of sport and sporting behaviour that reflected their bourgeois credentials (Hargreaves, 1986b).

When we get to the latter half of the twentieth century, Marxist and neo-Marxist sociologists (Marcuse 1964; Adorno and Horkheimer, 1977) refocus attention on the realities of working-class life within capitalist society. Their main concern was to emphasise the hidden costs of the inequalities of power within the capitalist class system. The more recent work of Bourdieu has once again drawn attention to the intersection of social class and processes of distinction (Bourdieu, 1984).

Theoretical approaches to sport and consumption

In drawing on the work of these influential theorists, Horne (2006, p7) identifies a number of useful categories that can help us to understand the many-faceted debates that the sociological analysis of consumption has developed. These are:

- the production of consumption approach;
- the modes of consumption approach;
- the pleasures of consumption approach.

Although each has developed a sophisticated and detailed body of academic debate and analysis to support it, the limited space of this book means that it will only be possible to examine the principal debates generated within each approach.

The production of consumption approach

This approach is typified by the work of a number of critical social theorists who draw on a Marxist critique of capitalist society. Although they emphasise the significance of class relations, one of their main concerns is to stress how ever more aspects of culture became commodified (Horne, 2006, p7).

Definition: commodification

The process by which goods and services (aspects of our social and cultural world, such as sport) that were previously outside the control of capitalist interests, systems of mass production and market forces are drawn into their webs of control, production and distribution.

Clarke and Critcher (1985), in drawing on the ideas of Adorno and Horkheimer (1977), argue that the interests of capital permeate all aspects of life, albeit that for the most part they remain mostly invisible. The process has two interconnected dimensions. First, what people do in their leisure, recreation and sport becomes co-opted by entrepreneurs into processes designed to create profits. Second, leisure (of which sport is a major component) no longer represents an escape from the boring and routinised world of work. Rather, it is either just an extension of it, in that it is merely a preparation for the inevitable return to work, or an essentially unsatisfying process that is *inevitably short-lived, lacking in challenge and therefore ultimately disappointing* (Horne, 2006, p7). Consumption is no longer a process of material consumption driven by the requirements of real human needs. The power of advertising and the media saturates our perceptions of need until we can no longer determine 'true and false needs' (Marcuse, 1964).

The rather depressing outcome of this argument is that, driven by the interests of capitalism, the processes of commodification have created a consumer culture that dominates all of our lives. It controls and dominates our involvement with work, and it controls and dominates what we do outside of work. Even in areas such as our involvement with sport, which we perceive to be freely chosen and self-directed, the processes of commodification have saturated all aspects of it. Our lives are inescapably caught up in visible and hidden webs of production, consumption and commodification.

Reflection Point 9.1

Thinking about consumption in sport – the hidden costs

When we consume various sports products, do we actually take any time to consider how they were made or do we merely focus on our desire for the product? Consider the following: in 1995 a Christian Aid report on Nike and Reebok found that the mostly female workers involved in the production of the shoes were paid less than 10 pence an hour and worked ten-and-a-half hour days for six days a week. The outcome was massive profits for the sport shoe companies who could charge £50 and upwards for shoes that had only incurred labour costs of £1.

Although this perspective offers a powerful critique, there are a number of problems with this approach. It establishes a fairly deterministic analysis of the processes of consumption and commodification that leaves little or no alternative ways of understanding how individuals or groups interpret or challenge these processes. In terms of how we consume sport, it largely ignores how we can act creatively and actively to engage critically with and transform the way we consume. Hence, although aspects of this approach are plausible, overall, it does not adequately account for the complex ways that we reflexively reproduce the social world.

The modes of consumption approach

The focus of this approach is to engage with the concerns highlighted in the above observation. One of its main intentions is to illuminate how consumers see and understand their consumption not as a process of alienation and exploitation, but as a *means of personal empowerment, subversion or resistance, that is . . . mediated by active consumers/audiences* (Horne, 2006, p8). Although one way of expressing the adequacy and power of our 'social knowledge' is to make it 'visible' through consumption, there are a number of significant tensions within the process. The knowledge that we bring to how we consume in sport is deeply influenced by our membership of class, racial, ethnic and gender groupings. If we consider an activity closely, but not directly, connected with sport – the consumption of alcohol – we can quickly identify that there are potentially many different forms of meaning that can be applied to the how, why, what and where we decide to drink.

Within sport and popular culture consumption is not, therefore, only about an unreflexive use of finished products (Fiske, 1989). Class, gender, race and ethnicity all transform both what we consume in sport and the meanings we attach to the process. As the processes of liberalisation have eroded the divisions that used to exist between these social categories, the use of consumer products has begun to lose its distinctiveness as the process has been democratised (Warde, 2002). From this sociological perspective, consumption in the twenty-first century, therefore, needs to be understood as an exploration of meaning within which people have the capacity to challenge old forms of social identity (based on assumptions about social class, gender, community and nation, etc.) and to seek the development of new lifestyles and forms of identity. Skateboarding, snowboarding and surfing cultures are all interesting and fairly recent examples of these innovative forms of consumer culture in sport in terms of how they integrate new sports (which themselves are often a challenge to the old assumptions about sport) with music, clothes, hairstyles, magazines, the Internet and lifestyle aspirations.

The pleasure of consumption approach

This approach emphasises that consumption is also a process that is sensual and connected to the satisfaction of a range of pleasures and desires. It is not something that is merely done as a physical act; it is also a complex and shifting abstract process.

Moreover, as we struggle with the demands of modern life and develop a lifestyle that reflects our desires and aspirations, consumption is no longer an option. It is a necessity that in profound ways defines what our sense of being is. For social theorists such as Baudrillard (1998) this means that we need to begin to think about consumption as an uncertain and dynamic social act.

One reason for this is that *The technology of everyday life in advanced societies has reached a point where essential improvements are hard to envisage* (Sulkunen, 1997, p5). The key word here is essential. Until recently (i.e. the advent of concerns over the efficiency of products in terms of their carbon footprint), the technological baseline for most of our necessary everyday technologies (transport, housing, food production and distribution, entertainment) has been well established with little room for any further substantive improvements or changes. The concern has therefore shifted to how we use these products.

The act of consumption and the meaning put on the process by the person engaging in it (and others who might comment on it – parents and friends, for example) becomes assigned through the process of doing it (Baudrillard, 1998). The meaning, therefore, is not fixed. Consider the simple act of buying a pair of football boots. The first thing we realise is that there is a wide range of boots, different styles, brands and prices. Thus (returning to a point made earlier), for Baudrillard, sociologists cannot critique the process by trying to assign 'true' or 'false' need. Consumption is ultimately a highly individualised act based on perceptions of need and/or desire and their satisfaction.

This accepted, because value becomes attached to goods and behaviours, they are also inevitably expressions of power and capital, albeit that in this case the capital is often symbolic rather than economic (Bourdieu, 1984, 1986). Consumption generally and in sport more specifically is not just our accumulation of goods (e.g. iPods, Nike trainers and club membership fees), it plays an important role in defining our level of social prestige. What is also vitally important is our knowledge about these goods, how to use them appropriately and how to discriminate (the 'good' and the fashionable from the 'bad' and the unfashionable) within the complex array of consumer choice that confronts us. Moreover, while it doubtlessly brings feelings of satisfaction and pleasure, there is a price to pay for our consumer behaviour.

This success of our consumption is necessarily dependent on whether or not others affirm and reassure us that our choices were appropriate and valued. Even if they are, these affirmations and achievements can only be temporary, as the symbolic value of our choices inevitably fade and become outdated and unfashionable. For Baudrillard (1998), the world of the consumer is one that is also inherently neurotic. Consumers are under the constant threat of change and the disappointment of unvalidated consumer choices. However, while Baudrillard is clearly raising an important point, some serious questions can be directed at this perspective. When we act as consumers of sport, are all our behaviours and the meanings we assign to them as transitory, depthless and dislocated as he suggests?

In summary, these sociological approaches detail that sport consumption needs to be understood as much more than the selection, purchase and use of sports products.

These are obviously real factors, but we must also sociologically take into consideration how consumption in sport is about the seeking of identity and lifestyle, and a process that is creative, imaginative and pleasurable.

Sport and the birth of modern consumer culture

You might recall from the opening chapters that the nineteenth-century development of modern sport occurred at a point of time when a number of other social changes were also occurring that were to have a massive influence on sport. One of these was that cities had established themselves as the dominant public spaces of modern life. Within these cities new forms of 'democratic space' or 'sites' began to emerge where the meaning of group and individual life in the modern era could be debated.

One of these was the mass media in the form of newspapers. Once newspapers became widely available, many of those in power became concerned over the 'freedom of the press' and its ability to engage large numbers of the working class in political debates. As Goldlust (1987) identifies, newspapers were essential to the construction of class consciousness in the nineteenth century. In Britain, the last remaining controls over the press were removed by the 1850s. The freedom of expression that this created, allied to the increasing levels of suffrage (the right to vote), helped to lay out the familiar landscape of British politics.

Newspapers, however, also quickly became dependent on advertising as a major source of revenue. By the end of the nineteenth century newspapers had not only become a significant consumer commodity in their own right, but they were also the main vehicle for the selling of an ever-expanding range of consumer items. By the 1880s newspapers had developed a significant interest in sport and specialist sports journalists and writers had become a well-established feature of British popular culture.

While the material for their vivid descriptions of sporting action was dependent on the quickly expanding world of professional and semi-professional sports teams, through their reporting they also helped to fuel its development and the massive rise in fans and spectators. The growth of 'spectator sport' at sports grounds and the vicarious enjoyment of games through newspaper reports created new understandings of sport – sport as a commodity and sport as entertainment for the rapidly expanding urbanised masses.

Learning Activity 9.1

Based on your experience of sports stadia, read the following quote from John Goldlust's (1987) book and see if you can identify the different ways that sport stadia act as an important site of sport consumption:

The successful growth of spectator sport was premised on a set of well established entrepreneurial principles that applied throughout the 'entertainment' industry. As determined by the organisers, a price, or a range of prices was fixed, the payment of which entitled any member of the public to be admitted to a venue in which the performance or event would take place. The venue, be it a . . . cinema or stadium, was physically constructed in a manner that limited the potential audience to a finite number of paying customers who, from variably privileged vantage points – depending on the price they were prepared to pay – could experience that performance or event.

(Goldlust, 1987, pp73–74)

An important element of this new modern urban space was consumption (Miller, 1995b). To cater for the needs of the urban masses, new forms of consumer retailing came into being. Cities and towns all developed new types of shops and new shopping areas where people could easily assess their rapidly expanding ranges of consumer items (Bocock,1992). In these spaces, increasing numbers of the British population could not only access the goods they needed for everyday life, but also engage with the processes of consumption creatively focused on the establishment of social difference and distinction (Bourdieu, 1984). While it certainly did not happen immediately, over the course of the twentieth century the ability to make consumer choices (to buy or not to buy) helped to create an impression of a new sense of freedom, albeit, for the most part, dependent (though not entirely) on the ability to pay. For the vast majority the ability to consume was dependent on gaining employment within the modern world's industrialised systems of production. Ironically, this was a world characterised not by freedom, but by limited opportunity, frustration, boredom and routine.

As an exciting antidote to this world of work, leisure and recreational activities such as sport quickly became an integral and important part of this consumer market (Clarke and Critcher, 1985). The emergence of the governing bodies of sport discussed in Chapter 5 not only reflected a desire to create more rationalised and regulated forms of sport, but also a more rationalised and regulated *market* for sport as an important commodity within modern urban consumer culture. By the end of the nineteenth century, many of the major football clubs had been formed and were playing in national competitions. The FA Cup Final was attracting more than 50,000 spectators. As a market this offered entrepreneurs a wide range of possibilities. Fans needed transport to and from the matches; they needed food and drink; for those who could not get to the matches reports in magazines and newspapers were an essential part of being connected to the game and the team; scarves and other symbols denoting team allegiance could be sold (the familiar replica shirts worn by fans today did not exist at this time).

Like all markets, once established, growth and diversification was a necessity for those wishing to make a profit. The outcome of these processes was that by the 1930s sport had developed into a distinct and successful sector of the British economy. Rowe (2004b, p21) has identified its main characteristics:

- sporting clubs and associations formed by subscribing members;
- competitions with attractive prize money;
- a labour market to handle the transfer and valuation of professional and semi-professional 'sport-workers';
- state funds donated to the development of sport;
- sportswear and fan merchandise manufactured and sold;
- newspapers, magazines, newsreels, films, radio (and, later, television) programmes devoted to sport.

However, the way that this sport market grew is not a story of uncontested growth and development; the legacy of this development has a far-reaching social and economic significance that extends far beyond sport itself.

Economic significance of sport in the UK

According to most of the available statistical evidence, UK sport-related economic activity has continued to increase year on year. It has been estimated that in 1985 expenditure was in excess of

£3.3 billion and that by 2003 this had increased to £13.5 billion (based on current prices). Taking inflation into account, this represents a real increase of 107 per cent over the period (Sport England, 2007). In the same period (1985 to 2003) it has also been estimated that the UK economy grew by 59 per cent in real terms. When compared the figures highlight a number of important facts. The first is that the UK's sport economy is a large and vital element of our economy. The second demonstrates just how attractive the sports market is to potential investors as the growth of the sport economy easily outstripped that of the UK economy as a whole. The third is that by 2003, across its diverse sectors sport was generating economic value greater than the combined output of radio and TV, music and the visual and performing arts, video, film and photography, designer fashion, and arts and antiques sectors.

Consumer expenditure

According to the Department for Culture, Media and Sport (DCMS, **www.culture.gov.uk**) in 2003 consumer expenditure on sport in England was estimated to be £13,969 million. There was a 30 per cent increase in consumer spending on sports equipment during the period 2000–2003 (these figures are based on constant prices – i.e. price increases over and above any increase due to inflation). In England in 2003 the estimated breakdown of consumer expenditure on sport was: subscriptions and fees, 21 per cent; clothing and footwear, 21 per cent; sport gambling, 18 per cent; TV, 10 per cent; sports equipment, 7 per cent; other, 23 per cent.

A number of factors have promoted these significant increases. Since the 1990s there has been a boom in house prices and many people have used this wealth to support an increase in their consumer expenditure. A more controversial factor has been the influence of expenditure based on gambling.

Learning Activity 9.2

Here are some facts and issues concerning gambling and sport.

- Gambling is one of the largest elements of sport-related expenditure and this expenditure is larger than the amount spent playing sport and watching it (Benson, 1994).
- Government estimates that approximately 70 per cent of the adult population in the UK gambles tend to support the view that the UK is, as Horne (2006, p25) comments, a 'nation of gamblers'.
- In the Gambling Act Regulatory Impact Asessment (DCMS, 2005) it was noted that in 1999 the UK had between 185,000 and 460,000 problem gamblers.
- Employment in the gambling industry is about 100,000 full-time equivalents.
- The abolition of direct tax on gambling had a significant effect on the sport economy. It considerably expanded the size of gambling within the sport market. In 2003, expenditure on sport gambling was £2,477 million.

> ### Learning Activity 9.2 continued
>
> In 2004, gambling was estimated to provide almost £8.9 billion expenditure (or 0.8 per cent of the entire UK GDP), of which £1.3 billion was paid directly to the UK government in gambling-related duties (approximately 0.3 per cent of total government revenues). Since its launch in 1994, the impact of the UK National Lottery on sport has been dramatic. About £1.3 billion has been contributed from Lottery income to the support of 'good causes'. Sport was one of the major beneficiaries of this income.
>
> Given these observations, take some time to consider the following task: Based on your own behaviour and of those you know well, are we a 'nation of gamblers'? Draw on your own knowledge and experience to list the evidence 'for' and 'against'.

Sport-related employment

According to a number of recent economic reports (Sport England, 2007), sport-related employment is one of the fastest-growing sectors of employment in the UK. Between 1998 and 2003, employment across sport-related occupations increased by 22 per cent.

Sport-related employment is a highly diverse area that includes almost every sector of the economy. Potentially, it includes areas of retailing for selling clothes and equipment (managers and shop-assistants); manufacturing of sports products, research and design (e.g. operatives, designers, technical consultants); building companies (sports stadia, etc.); media and entertainment (sports journalists and presenters); professional sportsmen and women (athletes, coaches, managers); and health-related professionals (e.g. physiotherapists). In 2003, sport-related employment was estimated to be in excess of 421,000, or 1.8 per cent of all employment in England. To put this in context, this figure is greater than the combined employment in the radio and TV and publishing sectors. The majority of sport-related jobs are within the commercial sector and account for over 77 per cent of the total sport-related employment in England. The remaining sectors are divided, with the public sector having 12 per cent and the voluntary sector 11 per cent.

The economic impact of major sports events

For the UK, the costs of hosting some of the world's premier sporting events are now a reality. The successful bids for the London Olympic Games in 2012 and the Commonwealth Games in Glasgow in 2014 (plus the distinct possibility of the 2018 Football World Cup) means that more and more attention is being paid to the economic significance of sport within the UK. Apart from the personal investment of individuals, this is further fuelled by the interests of various financial institutions (banks, venture capitalists and entrepreneurs), due to the vast sums of money now being generated by sports business. As we have seen over the past few years in football in particular, once our major professional sports clubs became companies quoted on the Stock Exchange, they became the focus of takeovers by international financiers looking for high value investment opportunities.

In 2005, UK Sport commissioned the Sport Industry Research Centre at Sheffield Hallam University to undertake a detailed assessment of the economic impact of the funding of major sports events. They examined six major sports events supported by the World Class Events Programme funded by the UK National Lottery. Their research identified a series of important findings that clearly evidenced that these events should create a good economic return on the investment. The average return on £2.2 million of World Class Events Programme support across the six events was £7.1 million, equivalent to £3.20 for every £1 spent.

Of all the key interest groups at major events, the report found that it is the spectators who are the major determinants of economic impact. In recognition of this fact, it argued that, from an economic perspective, planning for this group requires more emphasis in comparison to the other significant groups integral to the event – the competitors, officials and media representatives.

The 'Olympic Games Impact Study', carried out for the DCMS and the London Development Agency by PricewaterhouseCoopers, is a relevant example here. The report argues that staging the London Games can produce an array of benefits. These include the stimulation of economic and social regeneration in one of the capital's poorest areas, encouraging the creation of new businesses and jobs, boosting participation in sport and speeding up investment in facilities. Overall, its main predictions suggest that there should be around £1.9 billion of direct economic benefits and in excess of £3 billion in indirect benefits. These figures seem fairly impressive when compared to the first budget predictions for the cost of the Games. However, the initial figure of £2.4 billion was a rather serious underestimate. On 15 March 2007 the government announced that the revised budget for the Games had risen to £9.35 billion. This figure is made up of a number of costs which highlight the complexity of staging the world's most important sporting event. The cost of staging the Games is now estimated at around £5.3 billion. The new venues alone (including the Olympic Park at Stratford and the athletes' village), which are part of the 'legacy of the Games', now have an estimated cost of £3.1 billion. Other costs that will have to be met from the budget will be the regeneration of areas of East London and extra security. On top of this budget the government has also set aside an additional £2.7 billion in a contingency fund in case costs rise further.

The costs are divided among a number of stakeholders. The government will provide the majority of income (£6 billion), with other funds coming from London Council Tax payers and the National Lottery. Further income will come from the International Olympic Committee; TV and marketing deals (£560m); sponsorship and official suppliers (£450m); ticket revenues (£300m); licensing (£60m); London Development Agency (£250m) (**news.bbc.co.uk/sport1/hi/other_ sports/olympics**).

Given the earlier observations regarding the vital importance of spectators, the scale of expected spectators for the 2012 Olympics is impressive. The LOCOG (London Organising Committee of the Olympic Games) have suggested that across the Olympics and the Paralympics there will be approximately 9.6 million tickets for sale – 8 million for the Olympics and 1.6 million for the Paralympics.

Considering the staggering costs, particularly in the context of the current problematic economic circumstances dominating the global and British economy, many are sceptical about the actual benefits of hosting major sports events, or the impact of new stadia, or having successful teams and individuals. Not surprisingly, LOCOG stress that the legacy of the Games is as much cultural as it is economic:

the Olympic Games and Paralympic Games will leave a powerful cultural legacy across the UK. The Cultural Olympiad will create a buzz around the UK that will last long after the Flame is extinguished at the Closing Ceremony of the Paralympic Games. The benefits that the Cultural Olympiad will hope to bring are:

- *a new awareness of cultural activity around the whole of the UK;*
- *new ways to get involved, new projects to get involved in; more people taking part in cultural activity within their local community;*
- *new partnerships in the cultural sector and around the world.*

(**www.london2012.com/plans/culture/legacy**)

Most of these benefits come in forms of social benefit that are hard to estimate and quantify (e.g. cultural activity). From a sociological perspective, it may well be that it is these other social and cultural factors that need to be emphasised rather than the simple sets of economic factors that so often become the focus of governmental and sports governing body assessments. We will explore some of these important issues in more detail in our final chapter.

Professional sport

Sport economists have established a number of resilient measures of the factors that influence the salaries of professional athletes. In all countries that are members of the European Union, one of the most important employment factors has been the establishment of individuals' 'rights' as workers under European law. Prior to the now famous Bosman case, which changed the nature of player transfers in Europe, football clubs had considerable employment control over their players who were registered with their club. The club owned this registration which was transferred between clubs when a player was sold by one club to another club. Following the 'Bosman ruling' the rights of players as employees was established. This has resulted in the free movement of footballers between clubs within and between EU countries, with no fee payable when players' contracts have expired. The ruling also meant that players and their agents or business managers could negotiate their own deals with a new club when their previous contract expired or was coming close to ending. For professional football in the UK, the end results of this free-market process have been varied and were not always foreseen.

The following are some of the main consequences of this change in market dynamics for football, arguably the sport most dramatically influenced by the Bosman ruling: many of the top players are now in very powerful positions within their clubs as their value to the club (often in the tens of millions) effectively ends once their contracts run out; a large proportion of TV income in football goes into paying for the enormous increases in players' salaries; the free market in players has encouraged a huge influx of foreign players at all levels of the English game. There has also been a recent debate suggesting that the poor performances by the England national football team are due in part to the way this free market of players operates.

In recognition of some of these problems, for a number of years FIFA has been discussing with the EU whether sport should be treated as an exception. However, recent evidence suggests that this and the limiting of the number of clubs' overseas players would be widely challenged through the European legal system.

Beyond the world of football there are also a number of issues within professional sport that are important to note. One factor identified by Lavoie (2000) is that there is good evidence of economic discrimination based on race. Sports such as American football and baseball were the most consistent offenders. Even in sports that had a majority of black athletes such as basketball where there was no evidence of salary discrimination, it was nonetheless clear that race had an economic impact in that *the greater the racial match between the team and its metropolitan population, the larger its average attendance* (Lavoie, 2000, p159).

Another important, but often neglected, factor relates to the issue of gender. In this case the evidence that can be used is extremely limited because of the restricted amount (when compared to men's sport) of professional women's sport. For the most part, economic surveys of professional sport such as that by Lavoie (2000) take little or no account of how the professional world of women's sport operates. Beyond a few sports such as tennis and a relatively small number of exceptional professional female athletes (e.g. Paula Radcliffe), in economic terms at least, women's sport remains marginalised and a long way behind that of men.

Understanding sport and consumption

Sport historians such as Mason (1988) have detailed how commercial interest in sport in Britain initially developed quite differently from that in the USA. In Britain, sport was much more directly impacted by class interests and the ideals of amateurism, whereas in the more pluralised society of the USA, the possibility of making a profit from sport was much more readily acceptable (Mason, 1988). These influences were to be long lasting and significant. In drawing extensively on the ideals of British amateur sports such as athletics, de Coubertin developed a vision of the Olympic Movement separated from the pressures of commercial interests. Yet these were also, inevitably, central to the growth of global sporting competitions as elite sport became hugely attractive to the media, advertising and other commercial interests. These contradictions were not to be resolved (if indeed they were) until the 1980s, when all amateur sport and the Olympic Movement succumbed to the allure of commercial possibilities.

Despite the ideals of amateurism, from the late nineteenth century sport had become established as a distinctive part of the British economy. Since then it has continued to expand and diversify its products. One of the most important changes to impact on sport and its commercial potential was the way in which it developed a symbiotic relationship with the new technologies of mass media. Together they have transformed each other.

From a commercial perspective, this relationship, in Britain at least, was somewhat problematic. While newspapers and magazines could exploit sport to boost their sales in respect of radio and then later television, the BBC had an effective monopoly on all broadcasting. Unlike in the USA, the new media of mass communication were given a 'public service' remit, the main elements of which can still be found in the BBC's latest charter.

The following extracts from the BBC Charter (DCMS, 2006) highlight what is meant by public service broadcasting:

The BBC's public nature and its objects

(1)   The BBC exists to serve the public interest.

(2)   The BBC's main object is the promotion of its Public Purposes . . .

The Public Purposes of the BBC are as follows–

(a)   sustaining citizenship and civil society;

(b)   promoting education and learning;

(c)   stimulating creativity and cultural excellence;

(d)   representing the UK, its nations, regions and communities;

(e)   bringing the UK to the world and the world to the UK;

(f)   in promoting its other purposes, helping to deliver to the public the benefit of emerging communications technologies and services and, in addition, taking a leading role in the switchover to digital television.

It was not until 1955 that Britain had its first commercial broadcast stations. ITV and its various franchises quickly established themselves and soon began to dispute the BBC's broadcasting monopoly and exploit the commercial potential of the unholy alliance between sport and the commercial media (Whannel, 1986). At the heart of this transformation was the changing economic environment produced by the spread of television, consumer culture and advertising, and the growth of sport sponsorship. One of the outcomes has been that sport can no longer ignore the needs of the TV companies. Whether your sport is netball or surfing, all sport organisations, large and small, now need to consider the media when planning their strategies (Whannel, 1986, 2000). Consider how television-friendly tennis is compared to squash – both racket sports, but with very different popular coverage and exposure.

This process was not the same in the USA, due to the fact that commercial media companies had existed from the outset. From the 1930s onward, there was an intensification of the relationship between various companies that wanted a more effective way to advertise their products to the male consumer (Horne, 2006). The success of this relationship quickly transformed from one of interdependence to one of dependence. As the work of Burstyn (1999) details, driven by the need of the USA's rapidly expanding commercial mass media (radio and then television) to attract advertising revenue, and the ability of sport to effectively connect men to the ever expanding range of male consumer products (especially non-sporting products), professional and elite sport relatively quickly became dependent on media revenue to run their sports.

An indirect but none the less powerful consequence of this process was that it made women largely invisible in the world of professional sport as it was a world in which a male-dominated media talked to a world of male advertising executives interested in marketing a range of male consumer products, and collectively they talked to the world of male professional and elite sport (Burstyn, 1999).

Since the 1970s significant economic, cultural and technological changes have all had a transformative impact on sport consumption (Horne, 2006). In relation to sport the most important of these have come from the developments in communication technologies. The development of satellite television opened up the broadcasting of sport in a number of different ways. In the UK the arrival of new forms of media broke the longstanding cartel between the BBC and ITV, and after pressure from the sports bodies the government had to relax its own rules and permit the new satellite and cable companies to bid for the broadcasting rights for 'nationally' important sport occasions (for example, the FA Cup Final, Wimbledon, the Boat Race, Six Nations Rugby and the Grand National).

The very significant expansion of global broadcasting networks opened up new and potentially very lucrative markets. However, it did pose one significant problem – the lack of original content with which to fill them. Channels offering endless re-runs of old soaps may be of interest to some, but they do not command the large audiences that advertisers are looking for. For these broadcasters, sport has two major advantages. The first is that sporting action is a highly mobile form of entertainment. Most of the major sports are well understood by a global audience and even when they are not, it is a fairly easy process to overdub the visual content with a commentary in the language of the receiving nation (Whannel, 2000; Miller et al., 2007). Sports programmes such as *TransWorld Sport* which operate a magazine format are prime examples of this. The second is that when compared to the costs of producing other entertainment formats (e.g. drama) sport is relatively inexpensive.

In the USA, as ever an indicator of future trends in the rest of the developed world – including the UK – the cost of broadcasting rights for sport have reached staggering proportions: in 2005 the rights for the NFL (National Football League) commanded £10.75 billion (Horne, 2006, p50). In recent times, BSkyB paid the FA £1.1 billion for the rights to broadcast football. It is estimated by industry observers that BSkyB is able to earn £150 million to £180 million a year from pub and club subscriptions to its premium sports channels. From this it is estimated that within the UK market Sky can recover almost two-thirds of the amount it paid for the rights with the revenue from pubs and clubs. Fears over a lack of competition in the broadcasting of sport have meant that the European Commission has agreed a reduction in the amount of Premiership football that Sky can broadcast. This has permitted other digitally based broadcasters to come into the market. One of the most recent of these was the Irish broadcasting company Setanta. For the seasons 2007–10, the two paid the following for broadcasting rights: BSkyB £1,314 million; Setanta £392 million. For the clubs this represents an approximate yearly payment of £18 million to each Premier League club (**www.footballeconomy.com/stats/**). For this the two broadcasters got the rights outlined in the table on p174.

Recently, an improved Football League deal was negotiated partly by allowing an increase from 60 to 70 live matches to be shown by Sky Sports, 55 of which were from the Coca-Cola Championship. Although an annual total of about £37 million is distributed to the 72 Football League clubs, a total figure about ten times higher is handed out to the 20 Premiership clubs.

With such high levels of expenditure on broadcast rights, economic viability is a major concern even for the largest global media companies. As has now become all too clear to Setanta these costs only make sense if there are other very lucrative forms of income other than subscriptions to their sports channels. The most significant of these is advertising revenue, which is itself linked to the

Sky	23 first-choice matches shown on Sundays.
Sky	23 second-choice matches shown on Sundays.
Setanta	23 third-choice matches shown on Mondays.
Setanta	8 second-choice matches + 15 fourth-choice matches shown on Saturdays.
Sky	5 first-choice matches shown + 9 third-choice matches + 9 fourth choice matches shown on Saturdays.
Sky	10 first-choice matches + 7 second-choice matches + 6 third-choice matches in mid-week and bank holidays, Saturdays and Sundays.

amounts of subscribers the company could sign up. For Setanta this proved to be too great a challenge and Setanta ceased trading in England, Scotland and Wales in mid-2009.

While full of the inflated claims of advertising, embedded in the following statement are a number of discourses that highlight the powerful relationship between sport and advertising. This is what a leading sport advertising company has to say about the relationship:

> We use the creative energy of sport to inspire winning market solutions for the world's number one brands, athletes and teams . . . The winner's mindset . . . starts with benchmarking and goal setting. We help set your ambition – and create a culture where your teams can perform flawlessly as individuals, fluidly as a team – and ultimately win convincingly over formidable components.

(Branded Sport Group 2010: **www.thebsg.eu**)

As we can see from this statement, it is a set of beliefs about the character and inherent values within sport that have endeared it to advertisers. Their desire to have their products and, more importantly, their brands associated with sport and sport stars is grounded in the way the sport's or the sport star's achievements and public image can be used to endorse the products they wish to sell or the brands they wish to develop. However, as the recent problems of the supposedly most highly paid sport star of all time, Tiger Woods, evidences even those who seem to be completely unassailable within this lucrative arrangement can all too quickly fall from grace if they fail to retain a positive image in the eye of the consuming public. This is an issue that we will explore in more detail in Chapter 11 when, as part of our examination of the globalisation of sport, we will explore the power of celebrity culture.

Learning Activity 9.3

Make a list of what you perceive to be the character and values associated with sport generally and sport stars specifically.

Once you have done this, look at a couple of non-sport magazines to see if you can spot how advertisers use these images to sell their products or enhance their brands.

As the twentieth century progressed and the processes of technological innovation and mass production (mostly driven by the profit motive of capitalism) produced ever more extensive ranges of consumer items, advertisers realised that the satisfaction of need was only one element of consumption (Sulkunen, 1997). There was another, possibly even more important, element motivating people to consume – desire. The benefit that desire brought to advertisers is that, unlike need, it is potentially open-ended. As soon as you have something you desire, the desire ends – thus, for advertisers the trick is to constantly conjure up new desires. Advertisers therefore create this year's model, this year's design, this year's colours or this year's new sport star. An example is that each new football season now starts with Premiership clubs promoting a subtly different club strip, instantly making last season's obsolete. The triumph of this form of consumption is its sensuality and pleasure. In the modern era consumption for the general public makes a crucial transition from a matter of need to a matter of pleasure (Bauman, 2001). It is an affirmation of the right of the individual to seek happiness, albeit a happiness based on one's ability to be an active participant in the process of consumption.

Learning Activity 9.4

1. Take a few moments to see if you can identify some of the ways in which you act as a consumer of sport. Make a list dividing them into two groups: those directly related to being an active participant and those that reflect a more passive consumption of sport.

Some questions/issues to consider:

- Which list is larger?
- What are its major components?
- What does this tell you about how you consume sport?

> ## Learning Activity 9.4 continued
>
> Through talking to your friends and family, see if you can recognise variations:
>
> a) based on the type of sport you are most interested in and b) based on how men or women engage with this process.
>
> 2. Practical task: go to a major high-street sports shop and walk around, carefully noting the following:
>
> - What sports goods dominate the layout of the store?
> - How much of what is being sold is directly relevant to the performance of sport and how much is clearly intended to be sold as sport fashion?
>
> Check some of the manufacturer's labels and make a list of the countries that are producing the sports goods. Some questions/issues to consider:
>
> - Are the sports goods mostly directed towards people who are active in sport or are they more fashion and lifestyle orientated?
> - Are the countries where the goods were manufactured the same as the countries of origin for the brand name under which they are being sold?

The consumption of sporting commodities may have started as a utilitarian process (buying the products necessary for the performance of the sport) or as an affirming process designed to confirm an affiliation with a team, a specific sport or a social group.

However, today it is far more than this. It has become a process of exploration (lifestyle) and the validation of identity.

Research Focus

John Horne's *Sport in Consumer Society* (2006).

While sociology has taken the ideas of consumption, lifestyle and consumer society seriously for a number of years (Featherstone, 1987, 2007; Bauman, 1998; Baudrillard, 1998; Liechty, 2002) a growing number of sport sociologists have also started to highlight the importance of the relationships between sport and processes of consumption (Rowe, 1996, 2003; Crawford, 2003; Jarvie, 2007). However, Horne's (2006) work is distinctive in that his sociological analysis of sport takes consumer culture, consumer society and consumption as its central themes. This work carefully explores problematic questions faced by sport sociologists (and sociologists more generally) in regard to how to grasp the complex relationship that exists between modern society and the growth of consumer culture.

He starts his introduction by posing the question that has challenged many of the classic sociological analyses of consumption: should we as consumers (of sport) be regarded as *dupes, victims, rational actors or heroic communicators in consumer society?* (Aldridge, 2003 cited in Horne, 2006, p1). In attempting to answer this question, Horne's exploration of the relationship between sport and consumer society establishes the need to place culture, the growth of consumer culture, and the transformative processes impacting modern society (such as globalisation) at the centre of the analysis.

To achieve this the text is divided into three sections. The first explores some of the major themes evident in this chapter – globalisation, consumerisation and the role of the mass media. The second section extends the book's critical sociological perspective and many of the debates and issues highlighted in the first section through its discussion of the intersecting processes of commodification, regulation and power-relations. The final section then turns its attention to a series of important questions regarding how individuals (rather than abstract social groupings such as class, gender or ethnicity) have experienced and in some cases radically used sport and consumption to resist social divisions and establish lifestyles and meaningful identities.

Through his detailed discussions of these themes, Horne convincingly establishes that contemporary sport is fundamentally shaped by three intersecting and interdependent forces: globalised de-regulated market capitalism, the seemingly incessant processes of commodification, and the inevitable power relations and lifestyle divisions that the inherent inequalities contained within these systems create. Whether we like it or not the first two of these processes have come to dominate sport in that the global sport-media complex allied to the corporate sponsorship of sport now finances a vast swath of the sports we regularly consume as spectators or as consumers of mass media. Because of this, one of his conclusions is that the hegemony of neo-liberal economics has created and in part relied on the 'consumerisation' of everyday life. For Horne the process of consumerisation is being driven by the powerful set of social and cultural processes (identified above) that consciously strive to produce and reproduce people who for the most part uncritically define themselves and their lifestyles through their capacity to be constant consumers. As he identifies in this concluding discussion, one of the important challenges for sport sociologists is to establish a sustained and detailed critique that demonstrates the paradoxical nature of contemporary sport. On the one hand sport has now become a means through which many people attempt to shape up *to the requirements of life in the 21st century* and *a preparation for living flexibly in a competitive capitalist world* (p165). On the other, for many it also remains *a great source of friendship/community involvement which enables people to escape (if only momentarily) from that world* (p165). Sport understood in this way has the capacity to be both a creative, expressive and meaningful engagement in physical activity and a process of disengagement, alienation and exploitation.

While this may seem to be a damning indictment of the state of contemporary sport, for Horne there are also important signs of hope in the rise of consumer activism. Especially in the age of the Internet, groups of concerned consumers now have the capacity to resist the more extreme cases of exploitation through sport consumption. Transnational companies such as Sky or Nike are hugely protective of the image of their brands and in this they are vulnerable to the concerns of the very people they make vast sums of money from. In the information age consumer activists within sport have access to a new and potent form of political power. Through their use of the Internet and social networking sites activists can now easily and publicly demonstrate their concerns about social justice and economic exploitation of the vulnerable that sports companies and organisations cannot easily ignore.

Learning Activity 9.5

Review of learning objectives

After reading this chapter and having done the various learning activities, you should be able to answer the following:

1. Why is sport such a vital part of the British (and/or global) economy?
2. How do you understand the term consumer society and should sport now be primarily understood as essentially no different from any other consumer product?
3. Are professional athletes merely workers within an entertainment business?
4. Who are your favourite sport celebrities and what positive or negative images do you think they convey through the media?
5. Could sport today survive without the media and who do you think benefits more from the relationship – sport or the media?

Chapter Review

Sportsmen and women as well as images of sporting activity are constantly used to sell us consumer goods – historical circumstances have prevailed to create a consumer society. This capital exchange equation is more easily understood as a process of commodification. Sport, especially professional sport, has become dependent on its connections with companies that make and sell consumer products that have little or no direct relevance to the world of sport. Although some sociologists have claimed that the commercialisation of sport has led to its degradation (Lasch, 1979), there is no doubt that the commercial relationships between professional elite sport, the mass media and advertising are understood by all parties to be one that they can use to develop and exploit new markets. United together, the commercial reach and influence of all three is no longer just national – despite the huge benefits to the British economy – but global.

Sport is no longer just something that is done on a playing field, track or in a sports hall. It is something that is a very visible and important part of our modern consumer society.

The habitual actions that combine to create and define our lifestyle (and our sport choices) are important because they help us to develop our own distinctive identities and because the bodies of meaning that we normally ascribe to these activities are part of the cultural knowledge that enables us to understand the world and to make predictions about it. The fact that we develop fairly effective ways of 'understanding' our social world also means that we can choose to challenge and experiment with these meanings. This is particularly so in respect of popular culture, because its transitory nature means that we do not directly challenge the institutionalised power base (e.g. you might choose to experiment with some exotic hairstyle when going out to a night club, but you remain conventional when preparing your hair for sport). This said, these challenges also have the potential to have a pronounced and conflictual impact on the existing social order/power base.

Even a simple look at our world today (and its vast and ever changing array of consumer goods) demonstrates that change is now endemic. Within sport new consumer products and practices are constantly emerging. There is a never-ending procession of fashion and technological changes that are always clamouring for our attention. The rise of our consumer society has had a profound impact on sport and sport is an integral element in its production. However, evidence is also emerging of some serious disquiet about the structures, waste and inequalities that are inherent within it. As we move into the twenty-first century new directions and challenges are beginning to confront sport and our consumer society (e.g. the anti-capitalist, anti-globalisation and environmental movements). How sport decides to deal with these challenges will be vitally important to its future.

Further Reading

Until relatively recently the sociological exploration of sport and consumer society was a relatively limited area of analysis. However, in recent years this has begun to significantly change. One of the best recent texts to read on this is Horne, J (2006) *Sport in Consumer Society*, London: Palgrave, discussed above.

There are now a variety of excellent texts that provide a comprehensive exploration of sport and the media:
Whannel, G (2000) Sport and the media, in Coakley, J and Dunning, E (eds) *Handbook of Sports Studies*. London: Sage.
Rowe, D (2004) *Sport, Culture and the Media*. 2nd edition. Maidenhead: Open University Press.

To extend your understanding of sport stars and their celebrity status read:
Whannel, G (2002) *Media Sport Stars: Masculinities and Moralities*. London: Routledge.
Cashmore, E (2002) *Beckham*. Cambridge: Polity Press.
Smart, B (2005) *The Sport Star: Modern Sport and the Cultural Economy of Sporting Celebrity*. London: Sage.

Chapter 10
Sport and the media

Ping Wu

The previous chapter explained the emergence of our consumer society and the important contribution that sport has made and is making to this emergent dimension of the modern world. The book this far has introduced a whole range of sociological concepts, theories and ideas that position sport as a key component of society. Through our understanding of ideology, discourse and hegemony in particular we have learnt that sport is much more than pleasurable physical activity. Of the many themes running through this book, the relationship between 'doing' sport and the agendas of power, control and influence has been prominent. In these complex relationships it is the media – that is, all forms of 'screen' channelling (television, computers, mobile telephones and hybrids of all three) and all forms of written word and picture channelling (advertising hoardings, magazines, newspapers, books and journals) along with digitalised commentaries of radio – that have been crucial to this positioning of sport. It is the media that have provided the possibilities for both the reinforcement of residual forms of sport – that is, sport as we have traditionally come to understand it, team games, racket sports, athletics and other existing and recognised forms – and the possibilities for new sports, or at least new forms of old sports, to emerge.

The media provide, it could be argued, the battleground for sport in the twenty-first century as ideological positions are both entrenched and resisted. This chapter suggests that sport, true to the traditions of modernity, is an 'industry' and therefore concerned with production and profit. To achieve this productivity, sport has to capture the public's imagination with something achieved through a combination of extensive high profile coverage (at least of the more powerful sports such as football) and an emphasis, through the mediation of sport, on drama. Capturing the popular imagination is not new – Riffenburgh (1993) has shown how the 'races' to reach the North and South Poles around the cusp of the nineteenth and twentieth centuries were brought into the public domain by the dramatic coverage emerging in the printed media, especially newspapers. Since that time the sophistication of the media has improved immeasurably through technical innovation, with the Internet being the latest example of the globalising propensity of sport (see Chapter 11). There is, however, ongoing evidence that the two key ideas of saturation coverage and drama remain the essence of the media's success in shaping sport in the twenty-first century. This chapter will help you to understand these processes, and in particular how the media sustain discursive agendas of gender and nationalism, for example, as well as enabling you to develop a more sophisticated understanding of media representation of sport – our understanding of sport is constructed, and the media play a key role.

This chapter is the centre-piece of a trilogy of chapters (Sport and consumer society previously and Sport and globalisation to follow) which apply the theoretical ideas of the early chapters to an understanding of sport in the twenty-first century.

On completing this chapter you should be able to explain:

- the interdependence between the media and sport industries;
- the features of mediated sports production;
- how sport is dramatised by the media;
- how mediated sport texts reinforce dominant discourses of gender relation and national identity;
- the collective characteristics of the targeted audiences of mediated sport and their experience of watching and reading mediated sport.

Introduction

Let's start our adventure from two names: Wayne Rooney and Beth Tweddle. You may not be fanatical about football, but it will still be very unlikely that you have no idea who Wayne Rooney is. Actually, it is not difficult for most of us to tell some anecdotes about the famous footballer: for example, the earnest 'once a blue, always a blue' slogan that unexpectedly made him a laughing stock, as his 'devotion' to Everton FC that nurtured him as a schoolboy prodigy was compromised by his multimillion pound move to Manchester United. Girls who rarely watch football know who his wife is and show great interest in what she wears. Then, who is Beth Tweddle and what sport does she play? Even those who call themselves hard-core sports fans may have to look for help from the likes of Google before they can give an answer. You may argue that she might not have great sporting achievements; therefore, you do not know her well. She is, indeed, not as well-known as Wayne Rooney. However, that does not mean that she has achieved less in her sport than he has in football. Wayne Rooney is, arguably, the best striker at present in the UK and one of the best in the world, but Beth Tweddle, who won gold at uneven bars in the 2006 World Championships and won gold at floor in the 2009 World Championships, is the first and only gymnastic world champion in the UK and therefore, without any doubt, *the* best gymnast this nation has ever had.

However, the footballer who is neither world champion nor European champion is far more famous than our gymnastic world champion. Very few of us have ever met Wayne Rooney or Beth Tweddle in the flesh. We owe what we know about them and the stark contrast between our knowledge of them to the mass media. It is the media that control our 'knowing' so that we 'know' so much about Wayne Rooney and so little about Beth Tweddle.

Naturally, a number of other questions follow. Why do the mass media report Wayne Rooney extensively and pay little attention to Beth Tweddle? Is that because of Wayne Rooney's personal charisma or the particular sport, football, he plays? Is that because he is male and she is female?

How far is the media portrayal of Wayne Rooney from the real person? Why is this young footballer who is barely able to prevent himself from swearing on the pitch, very often portrayed as a hero and a role-model? Relevant questions can make a rather long list. Because the mass media play such an important role in constructing our knowledge and understanding of sport, media representation of sport has become a major attraction of scholarly attention since the 1980s (Wenner, 1989).

Sport sociologists and media scholars aim to answer questions arising around mediated sport – that is media representation of sport that people watch and read – from different perspectives. There are three substantive groups that can be identified and an exploration of each of these will form the framework for this chapter. The three are:

- analysis of the **production** of mediated sport;
- analysis of mediated sport **messages**;
- analysis of **audience interpretation**.

Some theorists are centrally concerned with the production of mediated sport. They analyse the wider political, economic and cultural structure within which mediated sport production is organised. They also examine how mediated sport is produced inside media organisations. The key questions at the core of their investigation are: who has the power to affect mediated sports content and in which ways is this power exercised? Other scholars show more interest in mediated sports messages. Through analysing texts – words and images are defined as 'texts' in discourse analysis employed in these forms of socio-cultural studies – they aim to find out how the mass media intertwine discourses of gender, race, ideology and identity with sport. The subject of the third approach is the audience of mediated sport. The central concerns here are the collective characteristics of the audiences and how the audiences interpret mediated sport messages.

Let's take Wayne Rooney as an example to illustrate the above research approaches.

In order to get a good understanding of the media treatment of Wayne Rooney, we could break the investigation into three main areas. First, why do the mass media report him extensively? To answer this question, we need to know why football matters for the media and why Wayne Rooney matters for the media. Second, how do the mass media portray Wayne Rooney? To answer this question, we need to analyse reports and features about him. Third, what do the audiences think about Wayne Rooney? To answer this question, we need to know who reads and/or watches the media portrayal of him regularly and their interpretations of the media portrayal.

The production of mediated sport

Scholarly investigation of mediated sports production is at three different levels: macro, organisational and individual. At the macro level, the complex relationship between sport and the media, two major social institutions, is the main concern. At the organisational level, the institutional arrangements of mediated sports production within media organisations are under scrutiny. At the individual level, the collective characteristics and professional roles of social actors directly involved in mediated sports production, such as producers and journalists, the pressure they work under day in day out and the dilemmas they often have to face are all subjects for investigation.

Interdependence between sport and the media

A consensus regarding the relationship between the sports industry and the media has been broadly reached among sports sociologists and media scholars today. Although expressing their points of view in different words, most of the scholars agree that there is interdependence between sport and the media (Claeys and Van Pelt, 1986; Jhally, 1989; Boyle and Haynes, 2000; and Bernstein and Blain, 2003). Contemporary sports, especially spectacular professional sports such as Association Football and major North American sports will not be able to operate and survive without the huge sum of money poured in by television organisations (Dunnavant, 2004 and Smith, 2001). At the same time, the mass media are heavily dependent on sport to deliver lucrative audiences to advertisers (Boyle and Haynes, 2000 and Rowe, 2004a). The relationship is therefore symbiotic. In essence, mediated sport is a kind of commodity produced through co-operation between the sports industry and the media in order to pursue mutual interests.

The media are crucially important for sport. Since sport finished its giant and decisive leap of codification in public schools and universities in England in the late nineteenth century, mass production of sports matches as a commodity has become possible. Modern sport was introduced into many other parts of the world through the expansion of the British Empire, but it is the revolutionary developments in the technologies of transportation and communication in the 1960s that finally made sport a truly important part of popular culture on a worldwide scale (Whannel, 1992 and Real, 1998). Cheap air flights between continents made regular international competitions possible and satellite television disseminated live scenes of international competitions to people all over the world. Watching competitive sport has become a globally and frequently shared human experience and has inevitably drawn the attention of transnational corporations that target global consumers (Whitson, 1998).

In the affair between sport and commercial sponsorship, the media are not just a go-between. Instead, the media are an inseparable part of the golden triangle. The sports industry produces competitions and delivers them to sponsors, television organisations and on-site spectators. The media, including television organisations and newspapers, then deliver media representations of sports competitions to viewers, readers and, more importantly, deliver these viewers and readers to advertisers, many of whom are at the same time major commercial sponsors of sports competitions. What sponsors and advertisers are really interested in is not a real sports competition that will take place in a particular stadium and be watched by a particular number of on-site spectators; rather, it is the mediated version of the sports competition which will be read or watched by millions of people staying outside the stadium. Nowadays, how much sponsorship a sport organisation can attract directly depends on how much media coverage it can guarantee (Gratton and Taylor, 2000).

Therefore, the media, especially television organisations, have become a business partner whom sports organisations have to please. Sports organisations' thirst for television coverage of their competitions has actually accorded television organisations the power to decide when, where and how sports competitions should take place (Boyle and Haynes, 2000). Football is a good example. Football matches were traditionally held on Saturday afternoons in England, but now, football can be played and, more importantly, broadcast on television on any day of the week, as shown in the example below.

Televised football fixtures between 24 and 30 November 2007

Saturday (24 November)	Premier League (Sky and Setanta)
Sunday (25 November)	Premier League (Sky and Setanta)
Monday (26 November)	Championship (Sky)
Tuesday (27 November)	UEFA Champions League (ITV)
Wednesday (28 November)	UEFA Champions League (Sky)
Thursday (29 November)	UEFA Cup matches (ITV)
Friday (30 November)	FA Cup second-round matches (Sky)

It is noteworthy that football, as the most popular and sought-after sport, actually enjoys an advantageous position in its deal with television. The lucrative broadcasting right fees and the massive media coverage that King Football receives have made many so-called minor sports cast envious glances. In fact, it is these unpopular sports that are much bolder and more determined in reforming themselves to attract media and sponsorship interests.

Reflection Point 10.1
BBC Sports Personality of the Year, 2007

An interesting outcome of the 'achievement' of the England rugby team in coming second in the 2007 World Cup was that they were 'voted' BBC television's Team of the Year at the Annual BBC Sports Personality of the Year awards for 2007. It speaks volumes for the power and standing of team games such as rugby in our national sporting lexicon that the British cycle team – that had won seven gold medals in the 2007 World Championships – only gained a brief mention in dispatches while the team that came second in their World Cup won the award. Of further interest at the same awards ceremony is that Victoria Pendleton – triple gold medal winner at the Cycling World Championships – was not even among the ten athletes short-listed for the main award of Sports Personality of the Year. As with the example of Beth Tweddle, if the public do not get to 'know' about these achievements, the profile of the sports they represent remains subservient to those with greater media coverage.

Case Study
Volleyball's media-friendly reformation

In the late 1980s, the Fédération Internationale de Volleyball (FIVB) realised that the great difficulty in making their sport attractive to television was its side-out scoring system. Back then, it was very difficult to predict how long a volleyball match would last, and that was something television organisations resented, because air schedules needed to be strictly arranged and fixed in advance. If the duration of a match is not fixed or highly predictable, then it is simply not suitable for live broadcast. After nearly a decade of efforts, the FIVB finally dumped the old side-out system and introduced the rally-point system to all sets of a match in 1998. Now, a team will win a point if they win a rally, no matter which side serves.

*In fact, the FIVB has been an avant-garde reformer among the international governing bodies of various sports and has introduced more media-friendly changes. For example, a coloured ball was first used in volleyball; many other ball sports including football then followed volleyball's colourful 'new wave'. In November 2007, Dr Rubén Acosta, the former FIVB President who believes that the basic rule of progress is change, announced that a new softer ball which was designed to affect positively not only the appeal of volleyball, but also the ball control by players would be used in the Beijing Olympic Games (*www.fivb.org press release*). Moreover, at the Tokyo World Championships in November 1998, the FIVB started its dress revolution: all the athletes were ordered to wear newly designed, provocative, skintight uniforms. Those who refused or failed to do this were fined by the FIVB. Although at the beginning the FIVB's fashion taste was ridiculed and questioned by many teams, President Rubén Acosta was determined to make volleyball sexier to catch television and sponsor interests.*

*He said: Sports that don't have the favour of television will fade away – that is a fact, that is the reality (*www.iht.com/articles/1998/11/30/volley.t.php?page=1*). Today, leggy volleyball players, both male and female, already feel no embarrassment at all to expose their super-model-like body build in colourful and skinny outfits. In 2004, the FIVB also became the first international sports organisation that allowed journalists to join their board and congress. During the 2004 Athens Olympic Games, indoor volleyball and beach volleyball attracted more than 3.5 billion TV viewers and the FIVB expected the figure would reach 4 billion in Beijing in 2008 (*www.fivb.org*).*

On the other side of the coin, sport is of great importance for the mass media. Among the mass media, television, radio, newspapers and the Internet are the major players in the production of mediated sport, with television being the most powerful.

The media coverage that sports organisations desperately seek for is largely television coverage. However, that does not mean that television organisations do not need to worry about the supply of sports competitions that could fill in airtime. In fact, the fight for broadcasting rights to mega sporting events such as the Olympic Games and the men's football World Cup has become fiercer since the 1980s. Professional leagues of popular sport such as football have also witnessed broadcasting rights fees soaring in recent years. In the 2006–2007 season, BSkyB paid £2.5 million per match to screen the Premier League live. In the 2007–2008 season, it had to pay £4.8 million per match (*Daily Telegraph*, 6 May 2006). In February 2009, the Premier League netted £1.782 billion by selling the 2010–2013 broadcasting right and enjoyed an £80 million increase against the deal of 2007–2010 (*Daily Telegraph*, 6 February 2009).

Case Study
The Rugby World Cup, 2007

In Britain ITV purchased the exclusive TV rights for this tournament. Although the series of group stage and knock-out matches was spread over nearly six weeks, and guaranteed extensive advertising revenue for ITV, the purchase was still considered an economic gamble. In order to break even on their investment, ITV needed England (where the most sizeable viewing audiences were to be found) to at least make the quarter-finals. The logic was that if England, or any of the home nations (Scotland, Ireland and Wales), were knocked out early on, viewing figures in Britain would drop, and thereby negatively affect advertising revenue. Against the odds, given the team's group stage performances (minutely scrutinised – and criticised – by sports journalists eager for stories), England made it to the final and, despite losing this match, their achievement was enough for ITV to return a profit on their investment.

The introduction of pay-per-view sports dedicated channels caused further profound changes to the sports broadcasting marketplace. On the one hand, television organisations now deliver televised sports competitions as commodities directly to viewers who have paid for the service. This means, besides advertising revenue generated from sports broadcasting, television organisations now have another revenue stream from the sale of subscription to their sports channels. On the other hand, these 24-hour channels created 'extra' airtime to be filled (Gerrard, 2004 and Rowe, 2004a). Therefore, the need to guarantee a stable and sufficient supply of sports competitions for broadcasting has become crucial for television organisations. However, the expansion of sports coverage on television not only results in heated fights for broadcasting rights to major competitions of popular sports, but also means that minor sports now have more chances to be televised than before.

Reflection Point 10.2

Ricky Hatton's epic fight against Floyd Mayweather

On 9 December 2007, English boxer Ricky Hatton lost to defending pound-for-pound champion Floyd Mayweather in Las Vegas. However, Ricky Hatton was hardly regarded as a loser after having claimed £10 million from the contest. In a pre-match report, the *Daily Telegraph* predicted that this showdown could gross close to £60 million. More than £40 million was expected to be brought in through pay-per-view buys in the United States and £6 million from viewers in Britain.

Newspaper sports coverage has also expanded significantly since the 1990s and, as an indicator of its power, at least half of newspaper sports coverage is devoted to football. Not only are the back pages of tabloids such as the *Sun* and the *Mirror* full of football stories, quality broadsheet newspapers such as the *Daily Telegraph* and *The Times* are also obsessed with football in such a way that they are criticised by nostalgic scholars and readers as typical examples of 'dumbing down' (Boyle, 2006). You may wonder why television organisations and newspapers *have* to cover football. Is it only because we, the viewers and readers, love football? The love of our 'national game' is one reason, but the media are not simply satisfying our needs. The ultimate goal of the media, most of which are in the private sector of the market, is to make a profit. That people like football means, if football is broadcast and reported, a huge number of people are likely to watch and read regularly. The sheer size of the audience attracted by football coverage is very pleasing to advertisers and therefore, the mass media can guarantee lucrative advertising revenues by covering football. The same rationale works for sport in general. As Lafayette points out, *sport is the last frontier of reality on television . . . the only thing that can guarantee an audience* (1996, p145).

The interdependence between sport and the media may deepen in the foreseeable future because of the fast development in cross-ownerships within the media industry and between the two industries that result in vertical integration (Bellamy, 1998 and Gerrard, 2004). The uncertainty that television organisations have to face in the sports broadcasting marketplace propels the increasing invasion of the mass media in the sports industry. In the major professional leagues in the United States, that the mass media are important shareholders of many clubs is nothing new. In the UK, the high-profile but finally denied bid made by Rupert Murdoch to control Manchester United Football Club highlighted the anxiety of television organisations to guarantee their hold on broadcasting rights in a market where competition is becoming tougher and tougher.

However, the interest of the media to own major sport teams depends on how the broadcasting right is sold. If the broadcasting right is negotiated and sold collectively by the league union – the way that the Premier League operates – then individual clubs do not really have control over the broadcasting rights to their own competitions. Although the collective deal with television did cause complaints from bigger and richer clubs, the smaller and relatively poorer clubs have significantly benefited from it (Gratton and Taylor, 2000). In the long run, a sports league will benefit more from collective ownership of broadcasting rights and the then shared television money because, unlike most other industries, the generation of profit in the sports industry depends on competitiveness among all the clubs. A relatively balanced wealth distribution is more likely to guarantee the uncertainty of competition, which is the key factor to keep the audience's desire for consuming sport high. Thus, the prediction that Tiger Woods would win all four golf majors in 2008 – an unprecedented achievement – was an immensely attractive idea to 'float'; yet the probability was that he wouldn't (as, indeed, events bore out). It is this uncertainty that fuels the drama of the game and gives the media coverage of the events extra attraction.

Mediated sports production

At the organisational level, sociologists analyse how mediated sport is produced to understand why sport is represented in certain ways (Lowes, 1997; Silk et al., 2004 and Stoddart, 2006). Sports broadcasting and sports reporting are both highly institutionalised and routinised processes. In the former, the number of cameras, the camera angles, the changes between a close portrait of a particular player and a distance shot of the audience as background, replays, live commentaries and post-match quick interviews all follow certain rules rather than personal fondness or whim: this is mediated sports production. These rules, whether they are explicit or implicit, are gradually established on previous practices in numerous matches, believed to be successful, and therefore will be followed in most subsequent matches.

Learning Activity 10.1

Mediated sport, it has been suggested above, is 'reality' put through a filter so that what we actually read or watch is a collage or simulation of what actually happened or is happening.

1. Explain what is meant by the term 'rules' in the context of mediated sport.
2. List what you think these rules are, and give examples where you can from your own consumption of sport.
3. Use this information to develop a class discussion based on Boyle's (2006) suggestion that mediated sport is 'dumbing down' our knowledge and understanding of sport – in other words, aim to articulate the positive and negative consequences for us of the way sports are represented in the media.

Sports broadcasting and reporting also repeats itself cyclically. A cycle of sports news production can be a competition season (e.g. every Premier League football season starts in August and ends in May), a calendar year (e.g. the tennis or golf 'majors'), or a four-year Olympic cycle. News stories that were produced in the last cycle are usually similar either in content or pattern to those being produced in the current cycle. For example, before each round of the Premier League, there are always plenty of pre-match stories to hype up the atmosphere, and the topics are rarely beyond line-up, injury, debut, return from injury or suspension, history between the two sides that will clash, star players' ambition, managers' confidence and teams' morale. Then, on the next days following completion of a round, there are match reports and, again, the topics are very familiar: who scored, who missed, who made an unforgivable mistake, who was sent off, and what comments the managers made after the matches (Anderson, DA, 1983; Koppett, 1994 and Andrews, 2005). Comparing the stories about each round of the Premier League, you will find that the only difference is actually the names: the names of the clubs or the names of the players. Match after match, season after season, year after year and cycle after cycle, similar sports news stories are reproduced regularly. Different from most events whose news values would and could be judged only after they occur, sport competitions are presumed to be newsworthy before they take place (Koppett, 1994; Rowe, 2004a and Boyle, 2006). Not only do the media know that a particular competition will take place at a particular time months or even years before, but so too do the audiences. Therefore, sports reporting is normally planned in advance. No matter whether a football match is exciting or not, the reporter will be sent there and have to produce a story to fill in the page, space or air time allotted to his/her story in advance.

There are two important consequences of this cycle of production combined with this process of scheduled planning – and both relate to what might (following Bourdieu, 1984) be thought of as a sports media 'habitus' – that is, the unconscious patterning of everyday behaviour. First, when media production is regular, cyclical and pre-planned by the originators of sports 'texts', the encoded messages about race, gender, ethnicity, the body, consumption, commodification, and so forth are reinforced. Second, this means that a sufficient and predictable supply of news materials is crucial in sports news production, and those sports that can guarantee such a supply will be reported more extensively than those that can't. Professional football leagues in Europe and major North American leagues cover most days of the year and provide enough competitions as raw materials that the media can process to produce news stories on an almost continuous basis. This is another reason why a small number of major sports dominate sports coverage (Lowes, 1997).

Sports journalists

At the individual level, sociologists examine the unique collective features of social actors involved in mediated sports production (Garrison and Salwen, 1989, 1994; Henningham, 1995; Boyle, 2006 and Lange et al., 2007). The investigations conducted in the UK, USA and Australia all show that sports journalism is an overwhelmingly 'masculine' profession. In the UK, females account for less than one-tenth of all the sports journalists who work for national daily newspapers. More women are involved in sports broadcasting, but it is their camera-friendly faces rather than their journalistic skills and knowledge of sport that are valued. This serious gender imbalance inevitably affects the way that sport, especially gender relationship in sport, is portrayed and contributes directly to the under-representation of women's sport in the media (Rowe, 2004a and Boyle, 2006).

Another feature for which sports journalists are often criticised by their peers working in other areas of journalism is their lack of professional credibility. The sports department in a newspaper has long been ridiculed as the 'toy department' and sports journalists are very unlikely to transfer to other departments. Within the media hierarchy, sports journalists occupy a bottom position in the pecking order and are often teased as 'fans with a typewriter'. Investigative journalism is rarely employed in sports coverage and the tone of sports reporting is often sycophantic (Rowe, 2004a). The 'beat system', which is widely employed in sports coverage all over the world and effectively links individual journalists to specific sports or even specific clubs, confines sports journalists to a very small number of sports and makes them heavily dependent on limited news sources (Smith and Valeriote, 1983; Telander, 1984; Bourgeois, 1995; Lowes, 1997; Boyle and Haynes, 2000; Anderson, 2001; Brookes, 2002 and Wu, 2007). It is not unusual for a sports journalist to cover a beat (e.g. a football club) for decades or for his entire journalistic career. Lack of distance from their news sources, who are very often subjects being reported on, means that sports journalists are reluctant to risk their good relationship with the sports organisations or sportspeople, which may have cost them years of effort to establish, by reporting negatively and critically.

Textual analysis of mediated sport

Most research on the media's representation of sport examines the meanings of mediated sports texts rather than how mediated sports texts are produced. Such a focus on textual analysis, on the one hand, reflects the richness of mediated sports content; on the other hand, it reveals the difficulty in getting access to data regarding media production. Although ignoring or neglecting the mechanism of mediated sports production is an obvious flaw of many textual analyses, sociologists still get some thought-provoking findings through decoding mediated sport messages.

Dramatising sporting events

'Drama' is a natural feature of all types of television entertainment, including sports broadcasting. It also distinguishes sports journalism from other types of journalism or journalism in general. In a drama, normally there are conflicts, good guys and bad guys. This formula has been successfully transplanted in sporting coverage. Competitions between two teams are often represented as confrontation between particular players.

Victory and defeat are often interpreted as a result of a star athlete's personality rather than his/her sporting ability. The rivalry between two teams or athletes is hyped up in a series of reports that could span weeks, months or even years, in a way similar to how conflicts are built up in soap operas. Sociologists argue that, through dramatisation and personalisation, the media have created images of sports heroes and villains which are, in fact, very different from the real sportspeople in the flesh (Sparks, 2000; Lines, 2002 and Whannel, 2002). However, dramatisation and personalisation should not be regarded simplistically as a writing style fancied by sports journalists. In this television era, most of the readers already know the result, or have even watched a live broadcast of a match before they read the sports pages in a newspaper. Rather than inform the readers what happened, newspaper sports journalists need to interpret the meaning of the match and make it still sound newsworthy. In order to hold the attention of someone whose aim of reading is not necessarily the search for hard facts, sports journalists have to resort to a more colourful, larger-than-life way of story-telling.

Case Study

The 'war' between Wazza and Winker

England's football team was defeated by Portugal in the quarter-final of the 2006 Football World Cup on 30 June 2006. In this match, Wayne Rooney, who was dubbed 'Wazza' by his team-mates, was shown a red card by the referee. His Manchester United team-mate, Portuguese Cristiano Ronaldo, was seen encouraging the referee to dismiss Rooney and then winking at the Portugal bench after Rooney was sent off. This match called a halt to England's journey in Germany, but marked the starting point of a tabloid-driven hatred campaign against Ronaldo, who was titled 'Winker' afterwards. The aftermath of the match was much more dramatic than the match itself. The media, especially the tabloids, portrayed Wazza as a victim of a conspiracy, and Ronaldo the Winker as a villain who had disgustingly framed his good friend and team-mate at Manchester United.

The 'Wazza vs Winker' scenario was hyped up by the media with great passion and many slack days between the end of the World Cup and the beginning of the Premier League were filled with rumours and gossip about the two Ws. One day we were told that Wazza wanted to split Winker in two; another day we were told that Winker feared for his safety in England. Then, Ronaldo returned to play for Manchester United and stepped into a wall of hate as he faced the England fans for the first time since the World Cup. Finally, Wazza showed publicly that he had forgiven Winker by hugging him in the match between Manchester United and Fulham. From the nasty plot to the redemption, the 'winking' incident, which might have physically lasted less than half a second, was successfully made into a quasi-soap opera, which lasted for almost two months, with a typical Hollywood-style happy ending.

(Source: *The Sun*, 3 July, 13 July, 9 August and 21 August 2006)

Trivialising women's sport

The relationship between sport and gender is a hot topic in the sociology of sport (see Chapter 7). The way the media reproduce this relationship has also drawn massive interest from scholars. There is a large body of relevant literature and it is not an exaggeration to say that the media's representation of gender in sports coverage is one of the best-investigated themes relating to mediated sport (Kinkema and Harris, 1992; Creedon, 1994; Shifflett and Revelle, 1994; Trujillo, 1995; Messner et al., 2000; Dworkin and Wachs, 2000; Lines, 2002; Stempel, 2006; Crolley and Teso, 2007; Markula, 2009). The findings from this body of empirical research are similar. Through comparing newspaper page space and air time devoted to men's and women's sport, it has been found that under-representation of women's sport is a worldwide phenomenon. Although significant progress has been made in women's participation in sports during the past two decades, this progress has not been reflected in media coverage. Picking up any national daily in the UK, you will find that men's sport in general, and men's football in particular, has unchallengeable dominance on the back pages and women's sport is rarely reported.

Learning Activity 10.2

With reference to one tabloid newspaper (such as the *Sun* or the *Mirror)* and one broadsheet newspaper (such as the *Guardian* or *The Times*), select a period of time (for example, one week) and undertake your own content analysis of gender portrayal – you can find methodological guidance for this in any of the recommended texts listed at the end of the chapter.

- Do your findings support the balance suggested by other research outlined above?
- To what extent do the sports reported on in the newspapers reflect the gender stereotypes outlined above?

Through analysing mediated sports texts, sociologists also try to decode how the media reconstruct or replicate masculinity and femininity in sports coverage. Their findings show that the media intentionally stereotype male and female athletes and the media's aesthetic criteria are underpinned by hegemonic masculinity. Male athletes, especially those who play traditional men's sports such as football, rugby and boxing, are portrayed as being physically strong and mentally tough with real 'manly' manners. Their sporting talents are highlighted as the reporting focus. By contrast, female athletes, even those who play traditional men's sports, are portrayed as emotional and dependent on the support of their family and male coaches. Very often, the focus of the media's portrayal of female athletes is neither their sporting talents nor their sporting achievements. Rather, their beauty, sexiness and femininity are commonly highlighted and emphasised. Sociologists argue that the rationale underlying such media treatment of female athletes is that, although these female athletes have 'invaded' the traditional men's domain, they are still 'normal' women who are heterosexual, feminine and vulnerable. While the media are eagerly creating sports 'supermen', they try to confine contemporary female athletes to the traditional image of a good wife and mother who always gives domestic duty the top priority. Thus, the mass media are criticised by sociologists for intentionally trivialising women's sport.

Learning Activity 10.3

Identify one male-dominated sport that females play (e.g. football, rugby or cricket) and one female-dominated sport that men are involved in (e.g. gymnastics). Using an Internet search

---

Learning Activity 10.3 continued

engine, locate pictures of performers (you will find website links are useful) of both genders in your selected sports and describe the characteristics of each gender that are displayed.

1. How do you explain these characteristics?
2. To what extent do they conform to the gender stereotypes discussed in this chapter and elsewhere in this book?
3. To what extent, if any, does your evidence suggest that these gender stereotypes are being challenged?

Creating nationalistic fervour

The mass media play a very important role in constructing and reinforcing national identity and this could not be revealed better than in media coverage of international sport competitions, especially mega sporting events such as the Olympic Games and the men's football World Cup (Clarke and Clarke, 1982; Hargreaves, 1986b; Rowe and Lawrence, 1986; Tomlinson, 1989; Wenner, 1994; Bairner, 2001; Bernstein and Blain, 2003 and Hogan, 2003). The Olympic ideals advocate internationalism and aim at establishing harmonious relationships between different nations. Ironically, in practice, the Olympic Games have been changed into a hot bed of narrow nationalism where different nations compete against each other to showcase their superiority over others – an agenda enhanced and supported by the mass media. Even the journalists of the BBC, who won worldwide respect from their peers in other media organisations for their objectivity, are allowed some leeway to use 'we' and 'us' when they report British athletes' performance in the Olympic Games. As for the press, tabloid newspapers have never been shy to express and appeal for banal nationalistic fervour when England or Great Britain competes against other nations. Images of fans holding national flags and wearing national colours have become an inseparable part of media portrayals of international competitions. War metaphors are often used to hype up an unhealthy or even hostile atmosphere, and the results are always connected to an enhancement or diminishing of national pride.

Reflection Point 10.3

England failed to qualify for the finals of Euro 2008

On 21 November 2007, the England football team was defeated 3–2 by Croatia at Wembley Stadium (the multi-million pound showcase of the Football Association) and therefore failed to qualify for the final stages of the 2008 European Men's Football Championship.

The Sun reported the reactions of England fans under the headline *We Stink. It's All Over: Outraged Fans Blast Flops* (22 November 2007, p4). In the story, one of the England fans expressed his feelings as '*I was ashamed to be English after such a pathetic performance*'; and by contrast, the reaction of Croatian fans reported was: '*There are only four million people in Croatia – half as many as London. We are very proud of the way we played.*'

Understanding the audience of mediated sport

How the media intend to represent sport is one thing; how the audiences interpret media representation of sport is another. As receivers of media messages, the audiences of mediated sport also draw attention from sociologists. However, compared with textual analysis of mediated sport, research on audiences of mediated sport proves to be a difficult task. Although some investigations were conducted (Marles, 1984; Wenner and Gantz, 1989; Barnett, 1990; Crabbe, 2003 and Redhead, 2007), the findings have not shown a clear picture.

The mass media are keen to understand who watches and reads their products and what the audiences want. What concerns the media is *the size, habits and demographic profiles of audiences* (Whannel, 1998, p222). Although human beings' viewing and reading practices, and motivations and reasons for such practices are too complicated to be coded or decoded with simplistic models, it is generally accepted that mediated sports are more viewed and read by men than by women all over the world, and men enjoy aggressive narratives of sport much more than women (Sullivan, 1991 and Wenner and Gantz, 1989). No matter how significant gender difference in mediated sports audiences might be, the mass media are convinced that the majority of their viewers and readers are men and therefore their representation of sport has a strong and overt male-orientated appeal.

Here, let's rethink media treatment of women's sport and female athletes. As the media presume that the targeted audiences of their sports coverage are men who appear to prefer fast-paced confrontational sport and expect aggression and violence, which women's sport is thought to lack, the little media coverage that women's sport receives can be understood as a choice based on business strategy as well as the hegemonic ideology of gender relationship. Sexualisation of female athletes could be understood as an attempt to satisfy male audiences' desire rather than banal gender bias against females, because the sexualised media representation of female athletes is actually encouraged by the male audiences who absorb these texts actively through reading and watching sport, which has become part of their habitual patterns of leisure.

Another important feature of the audiences who watch sports broadcasting most regularly makes them very attractive to advertisers. The dominant viewing audience for sports programmes is young professional males who are not necessarily easy to reach via other advertising possibilities, yet who often have a considerable disposable income. This demographic group rarely watch other types of television programmes, but their sports interest leaves them as the likeliest group to buy into the specialist satellite and cable television sports channels. It is ongoing market research that both identifies such social groups and then 'packages' its sports production to satisfy the consumption needs.

However, media representation of sport, which is intentionally produced to cater to the audiences' taste, in turn affects the audiences' choice and experience of watching and reading sport. *While the media did not appear to have fabulous powers to determine what people thought, it did however appear to have a power to determine what people thought about* (Whannel, 1998, p225). On the one hand, satellite television and, more recently, the Internet have transcended limits of time and space, and revolutionised and extended our experience of viewing sport. On the other hand, the price we pay for watching live sports broadcasting on television or online in the comfort of our homes (or the camaraderie of the pub) is that we give up our own authority of observing to a considerable degree and only see what the media allow us to see. In fact, what we have watched on the screen is, very often, far from what really happened on-site. Some contemporary sports theorists argue that nowadays sports coverage is full of hyper-realities that are 'realer than real' (Giulianotti, 2005). For example, the replays of a goal from different angles are something that the on-site audience could not watch without the help of big screens (a growing characteristic of modern stadia so that, by extension, even being at a match does not guarantee a 'live' and 'real' viewing).

These 'realer than real scenes' give the audience new watching experiences that are otherwise impossible, but at the same time they also create a hype and pastiche atmosphere that does not exist in reality. Sociologists are concerned with how much the audiences of mediated sport are exposed to distorted versions of reality and how well they are aware of the media manipulation made possible by the sophisticated technologies available to those companies that specialise in mediated sports production.

Research Focus

If, so far, you have become interested in mediated sport through reading this chapter and want to understand the sociology of mediated sport more profoundly, then reading Raymond Boyle and Richard Haynes' book *Power Play: Sport, the Media and Popular Culture* (2000) will be a good starting point. This book is especially suitable for those who intend to gain a comprehensive knowledge of mediated sport as a foundation for their own further and more specialised research into any of the three aforementioned sub-areas of mediated sport.

Boyle and Haynes argue that *a broader range of vision beyond simply focusing on the mediated discourses of sport circulated by the media* (2000, p15) is needed when we try to understand the relationship between sport and the media, and this 'broader range of vision' is clearly reflected in their study on mediated sport. In *Power Play: Sport, the Media and Popular Culture*, Boyle and Haynes examine the historical developments of mediated sport, the political economy of mediated sport, the role that mediated sport plays in identity-formations and the consumption of mediated sport. Throughout their analysis the complexities of issues regarding mediated sport are acutely investigated. For example, when discussing the increasingly intertwined relationship between sport, the media and sponsorship, Boyle and Haynes point out:

Television's treatment of sport as an activity that occurs in some apolitical vacuum is increasingly being challenged by the very process it has helped facilitate. As links between the 'world' of

> *business and the 'world' of sport become more overt, so the separation of these worlds becomes more difficult to sustain. Rather than being an arena free from the economic structures that dictate our working environment, sport is also seen as being subject to these self-same influences.*
>
> (Boyle and Haynes, 2000, p64)

When analysing how the media deal with sports scandals, Boyle and Haynes articulate not only the rule of 'objectivity' that the media strive to abide by, but also the dilemma that the media, especially television organisations, often have to face.

> *This was most pronounced in television sport programmes, where a tension arose between the sports pundits' peripheral role of passing comment on the violation of the sporting order and their promotion of the sport as a televisual spectacle . . . Television's protection of the culture of sport serves to maintain the hegemonic position it enjoys with sport, for it knows that it must not kill the goose that lays the golden eggs.*
>
> (Boyle and Haynes, 2000, p107)

It is such consistent awareness of the political economy of contemporary mediated sport and its determining impact on the production of mediated sport messages that distinguishes Boyle and Haynes' study from some textual analyses in which scholarly attention is too narrowly and, to some extent, rather naïvely placed only on words and images used by the media to represent sport.

In their analysis of how mediated sport helps to reproduce and reinforce hegemonic masculinity, the multi-perspective approach is employed again. First, Boyle and Haynes examine the media portrayal of male sports stars and suggest that:

> *Lack of ability in sport can, where male familial and peer pressure exists, lead to low self-esteem and a sense of failure. Similarly, if determination to succeed in sport is found wanting, athletes may be criticized in the media for not showing enough grit and courage to achieve their goal.*
>
> (Boyle and Haynes, 2000, p135)

Later, they lay critical eyes on how hegemonic masculinity is reinforced through the consumption of mediated sport by conducting an empirical study on men's experience of viewing boxing on television.

> *Gay men in the study equated contact and team sports with dominant hegemonic masculinities that exemplified the macho, often violent, ideology displayed through sport by a large proportion of the male population . . . the way different masculine identities are constructed do have a significant bearing on the experiences and interpretative strategies of viewing violent sports on television.*
>
> (Boyle and Haynes, 2000, p194)

In a nutshell, Boyle and Haynes' *Power Play: Sport, the Media and Popular Culture* is not only a rich source of knowledge of mediated sport, but also a good exemplification of how to develop sound and rounded sociological argument.

Raymond Boyle is a professor at the Centre for Cultural Policy Research in the University of Glasgow. He is one of the prominent scholars in the development of research on mediated sport. For example, his 2006 book *Sports Journalism: Context and Issues* employs a sophisticated approach to analysis of mediated sport, examining the complexities of sports journalism within the historical, political, economic and cultural contexts.

Richard Haynes is a senior lecturer in the University of Stirling. His research interest in the relationship between sport and the media has resulted in a number of publications, including another book with Raymond Boyle: *Football in the New Media Age* (2004).

Chapter Review

Today, the most common way in which people consume sport is watching it on a screen, although newspapers have proved remarkably resilient as sites for the construction of our knowledge about sport in modern society. The way that we understand sport is, to a great extent, gained from these key media and, thereafter, shaped by the social, political and economic agendas supported by those media. As a student who tries to understand the role that sport plays in today's society, you cannot bypass or ignore the role that the media play in promoting sport's profile and highlighting sport's central position in popular culture and social practice. However, our everyday life is so media-saturated that we often simply take media representation of sport for granted and accept it as a true reflection of reality without questioning. In fact, mediated sport is not only underpinned by hegemonic ideologies and dominant discourses of gender, race and identity, but also produced through a complicated and often routinised process where media organisations and sports organisations co-operate and contest at the same time.

Reading between the lines to understand the deeper meaning of mediated sports texts is important, but it is far from enough to get a comprehensive vision of the whole picture. As Wenner (1998, p9) points out, macro-level political-economic analyses of sports and media organisations form the backbone of mediated sports studies. Sport and the media need each other and operate to mutually support the other's agenda. By presenting sport as a social drama, sports stories can be 'given legs' – that is, extended over time – to capture and retain our interest in the athletes and their antics. The emergence of sports celebrities in an age of mediated sport is far from coincidental.

At the end of this chapter, let's rethink one of the questions proposed at the beginning: why do the media report Wayne Rooney extensively? Now, you should know that it is not simply because 'we love him!'

Further Reading

Any of the references cited in this chapter will offer detailed insights into the world of mediated sport, and these are listed at the end of the book. The following books, however, are of particular interest because they provide a more extensive overview of the key learning points from the chapter.

Wenner, LA (ed) (1998) *MediaSport.* London and New York: Routledge.

Rowe, D (ed) (2004) *Critical Readings: Sport, Culture and the Media.* Maidenhead: Open University Press.

Boyle, R and Haynes, R (2000) *Power Play: Sport, the Media and Popular Culture.* Essex: Pearson Education.

Markula, P (ed) (2009) *Olympic Women and the Media: International Perspectives.* Basingstoke and New York: Palgrave Macmillan.

Chapter 11
Sport in a global world

Peter Craig

This chapter, the third in the trilogy of chapters aimed at extending your understanding of sport in the twenty-first century, is a logical extension of the discussions of consumption and sport media that have led us to this point. By recognising that many aspects of sport are an integral element of our consumer culture, and that the ways we understand sport are often mediated in ways consistent with powerful social, political and economic forces, we have identified how sport is a contributing element in the formation of our modern world. Though the global economy that drives and benefits from this consumer culture is all too evidently subject to problematic variations, booms and busts, and despite the troubling fact that many aspects of consumer society seem at odds with the challenges of climate change (Giddens, 2009) there is as yet limited direct evidence that these processes are about to radically change.

Sport, as we have already seen, is far from immune to capitalism – rather, it is deeply infiltrated by the ideas of competition, status, commodification and consumption – so it is hardly surprising that sport can be seen as a vehicle for the promotion of its vested interests on a global scale. The discussion that follows aims to develop these ideas and asks the obvious questions that arise from these observations: How is sport embedded in the globalised world? What are the costs and benefits for sport emerging out of these globalising processes? Does sport offer ways of resisting processes of globalisation and can sport offer alternative perspectives to some of the dominant conceptualisations of globalisation?

In addressing these questions the chapter will not attempt to provide you with definitive answers to these questions as they are based on complex, fluid and dynamic processes. Rather, in this brief exploration the chapter aims to help you encounter some of the processes as a way of further understanding sport in the twenty-first century.

Learning Objectives

On completing this chapter you should be able to:

- explain the role that sport plays in globalisation;
- provide an overview of the major themes within a sociological analysis of globalisation;
- explain what is meant by 'network society';
- explain how some aspects of the globalisation of sport are being resisted and used to create alternative understandings of globalisation.

Introduction

One of the sociological arguments that has been a recurrent theme within the preceding chapters is that the development of a sociological analysis of sport must proceed from an understanding of the modern world as a complex and changing structure. The 'realities' of this modern world emerge out of an interaction between individuals (us!), the impact of social institutions and the bodies of knowledge through which we understand and give meaning to that world. While our actions as sportsmen and women can be routine, habitual and conforming, they can also be potentially critical and transformative.

As the twenty-first century proceeds, it is clear that we are living in a world that is changing rapidly and that seems to be becoming more unpredictable, disordered and sometimes threatening (Giddens, 2009). Many of the patterns of everyday life that seemed to be an accepted part of that world are now less certain. One of the terms that you have probably heard in reference to some of these changes is 'globalisation'.

In its most typical guise, globalisation is more often than not represented as an economic process. On a daily basis, the media constantly remind us of the interconnections between the world's financial markets and the importance of huge transnational corporations such as Microsoft whose commercial operations seem to stretch uninterrupted across all national boundaries. However, as numerous social theorists (e.g. Appadurai, 1996; Giddens, 2001) have stressed, globalisation cannot be simplistically reduced to an economic process and its reach extends into the routine and familiar aspects of everyday life such as sport:

Although economic forces are an integral part of globalisation, it would be wrong to suggest that they alone produce it. Globalisation is created by the coming together of political, social, cultural and economic factors. In recent times it has been driven forward by the development of the information and communication technologies that have intensified the speed and scope of interaction between people all over the world.

(Giddens, 2001, p52)

During global sporting 'mega-events' (Roche, 2000) such as the World Cup and the Olympics it is not unusual for billions of people across the world to watch these sporting events live and in their own homes. Delivered into every home with a television set and/or other screen-based channels, modern sport has come to be seen, even by sociologists whose work normally takes little direct interest in sport, to epitomise our increasingly globalised world. The physicality, the drama and the secular nature of modern sport enables it to cross boundaries of language, religion and culture. As we have discussed in some detail in Chapter 10, sport's universal appeal means that it is a powerful tool aiding the construction of global markets, and for the assignment of status within those markets.

The impact of sport on the processes of globalisation and the impact of globalisation on sport are, however, somewhat of an enigma. When we attend, either as participants, officials or spectators, the world's major sporting events such as the Olympics or any of sport's world championships, or when we watch these events live on our screens, the world seems to be a small and fairly familiar place. Yet, for most of us, the reality of our actual physical involvement in sport is much more likely to be locally, county or regionally based. What it means to live and play sport in this global–local context, how it is being transformed and how these transforming processes can be understood have become questions that cannot be easily ignored.

In analysing how we have come to see the world as closely interconnected, it is important to recognise that globalisation is not a recent social phenomenon (Giddens, 2002; MacGillivary, 2006) nor a recent sporting one (Keys, 2006; Tomlinson and Young, 2006). Indeed, it could be argued that pre-history and the migration of the human race across all the continents of the world is its primary source. However, there is also no doubt that in modern times the process has gained a dramatic momentum. The underlying reasons for this include:

- the emergence of a range of modern technologies that enable people, goods, money, images, ideas and cultures to rapidly (even instantaneously) move around the world;
- the impact of colonisation by powerful Western countries;
- the development of global capitalism and systems of production;
- the emergence of social movements that are global in their scope and interests.

For theorists such as Giddens (1991) and Castells (1996), the impact of technology has led to a series of profound changes. The new computer-mediated technologies in particular have facilitated the *compression of time and space* (Giddens, 1991, 2001).

People all around the world can now have a sense of sharing and experiencing events such as the Olympic 100 metres final in 'real time', even though the physical action may be occurring on the other side of the planet. What's more, the timing and experience of the competition is further collapsed or even displaced as it can be replayed and shown from different camera angles and at slow motion. In a real sense, the event is taking place not only in the Olympic stadium (i.e. at a particular time and in a particular place), but simultaneously in every place where a television set is tuned into it. With these ideas in mind, we can now begin to suggest a more formal definition of globalisation.

Definition: globalisation

Globalisation can thus be defined as the intensification of worldwide social relations which link distant localities in such a way that local happenings are shaped by events occurring many miles away.

(Giddens, 1990, p64)

Globalisation refers to the processes of 'global compression' through which people increasingly regard the world as one place.

(Robertson, 1992)

Before we engage in a detailed sociological exploration of sport and its connections to globalisation, a good starting point is for you to briefly examine some of your own assumptions about globalisation.

Learning Activity 11.1

Based on the issues briefly highlighted by the introduction, take a few moments to write down your own understanding of globalisation and how you perceive it as directly affecting your own life. Some questions to consider:

- If asked, could you describe and explain globalisation?
- How does globalisation impact you and your life?
- Do you have a positive or negative attitude towards globalisation and its impacts?
- How strongly do you consider yourself to be defined by being a citizen of a nation with a distinctive and autonomous culture?
- How does globalisation impact on your experience of sport?

Based on your answers to these questions, see if you can categorise your own experience and understanding and concerns about globalisation. Jarvie (2006) has four broad categories that you could use to categorise your answers:

- political globalisation;
- social globalisation;
- cultural globalisation;
- economic globalisation.

If this exercise seems difficult, don't worry. The purpose of the activity is to help you realise that globalisation is not only a process happening 'out there' and transforming how your world operates, it is also something that is happening 'in here' in your own life and within your experience of sport. When you have completed the chapter, you might like to repeat the exercise to see if the results are significantly different.

Creating the global imagination: the role of popular culture

In writing about how we come to understand ourselves as members of a nation with a shared sense of traditions and values, Benedict Anderson (1983) develops the idea of the 'imagined community'. The main thrust of Anderson's argument is that in the reality of modern life we can never meet more than a tiny fraction of the multitude of people with whom we share a sense of national identity. For this to happen, we need to develop a range of social and cultural activities that routinely create the sense that we all share a common community.

The key to this was the development of media technologies that enable this 'imagined' world of the nation to be presented to us on a daily basis (Edensor, 2002). Through the media's constant reminders, the idea that we belong to and share a national space and culture becomes rooted in our consciousness (Rowe and Stevenson, 2006; Tomlinson and Young, 2006). This same process of 'imagining' is also essential to the understanding of ourselves as members of a global community. One way to consider this is to think about how science and technology are constantly transforming our perceptions of the world. Although this may seem to you to be a now distant historical event, it is less than fifty years since the space programme produced a unique view of the planet – the view of Earth from space. This enabled our perspective to change – to see ourselves sharing a world floating in space. Today, the debates about climate change and what we should do about it continue to dramatically reinforce this idea of a shared 'global space' (Giddens, 2009).

Many who hold powerful positions in our cultural, economic and political institutions often refer to globalisation as a given reality of everyday life. This does not of course mean that everybody has a positive or uncritical view of it (MacGillivary, 2006; Harvey, Horne, and Safai, 2009). From a sociological perspective, this naturalising of globalisation into our everyday language and speech habits needs to be understood as a 'discourse'. As you should recall from the discussion in Chapter 7, sociologists use the term 'discourse' to explain that our understandings of particular aspects of our social world (in this case, sport and globalisation) occur within a framework of interconnected ideas that act together in ways that tend to fix how we typically understand our social world. For instance, today wherever in the world you might be, there is a fairly well-established interpretation of elite sport. If asked, most people would assume that it involves professional attitudes within sport, that the economic power of the globalised network of professional sport means that athletes are often very well paid, that global sport relies on its media presence and that in most instances it has remained dominated by masculine and Western interests.

When we talk about globalisation, we therefore need to be careful that we do not use the term simplistically. The fact that sport appears to have developed a global presence does not mean that this occurred due to some natural or inevitable condition of the modern world. As we shall see in the next section, globalisation theorists are deeply divided as to its causes, benefits and problems.

Sport and globalisation: an overview of competing theories

As with other difficult and challenging social processes, the complex nature of globalisation has meant that in its attempt to explain it, sociology has developed a number of competing theories. Even the way sociologists use the term shows just how contested the theoretical field is. For some, globalisation refers to 'real' historical processes largely beyond the scope of individuals and even nations to control. For others, it is more of a conceptual tool whose purpose is the critical development of ideas and ways of thinking about the processes inherent within it.

Equally, like many of the sociological concepts we have introduced you to (class, gender and modernity are examples), the term itself is not neutral. For those who are concerned with the way that capitalism has created global structures of inequality, globalisation is often perceived as a controversial and at times a harmful process. Others perceive it more favourably and focus on its potential to extend the processes of modernisation that have drawn the people of the world closer together (Giddens, 2002).

A number of commentators have tried to classify the various theories. Maguire (1999, 2000) identifies a number of broad schools: world-system theory, world polity theory and world culture theory. However, Held et al. (1999) and Giddens (2001) suggest a different typology that some influential sport theorists such as John Hargreaves (2002) have drawn on in their analysis of sport and globalisation. This typology has three elements:

- the sceptics;
- the hyperglobalisers;
- the transformationalists.

The sceptics

This is the least prominent of the three perspectives and therefore we will only deal with it briefly. The main thrust of the 'sceptical' view is that globalisation is not a new phenomenon. There are a number of points within this analysis worth noting as they provide a set of critical questions that you should bear in mind as we explore the two other categories.

First, the process of global economic integration was already well established by the nineteenth century. Second, the vast majority of 'global trade' is actually regionalised and based within three regional groups – Europe, Asia-Pacific and North America. Third, it is pointed out that the suggested decline in the importance of the nation-state is a gross over-representation of the facts. If anything, it is argued, the integrity of the nation-state is being enhanced rather than diminished by globalisation. National governments (Giddens, 2001) and national organisations such as our national governing bodies of sport remain powerful arbiters of our everyday experiences. For sociologists such as Giddens (2002) the position of those who were sceptical about the existence of globalisation is now largely discredited.

The hyperglobalisers

Not surprisingly, those theorists who might be termed 'hyperglobalisers' take almost the opposite perspective to that of the sceptics. From their analysis, globalisation is a very concrete reality whose consequences are profound and will impact on nearly every part of the world. Globalisation is seen as an unstoppable flood sweeping across national borders, making the power of national governments to exercise control over their economy, cultural life and their citizens relatively ineffectual. They suggest that as people realise how ineffectual nationally focused organisations actually are, they will create an upward pressure that will require all nations to work internationally and transnationally. The inevitable outcome will be the emergence of a global society (Hargreaves, JE, 2002) and the formation of a global system of governance. This system of governance, however, will be less hierarchical than that usually associated with the nation-state. The plurality of interests within this new global political order will mean that no single institution, organisation or individual can define or impose its own ideology or definitions of what is valuable. Within our contemporary world two prominent examples of how nations are agreeing to work co-operatively in this new global reality are the United Nations and the European Union.

Organisations such as those governing sport also require the ability to make policy decisions that address the international and global dimensions of the sport. While the formal term for this sort of organisation – an 'international non-governmental organisation' (INGO) – may be fairly unfamiliar, names of actual INGOs, such as the International Olympic Committee (IOC) and the International Amateur Athletic Federation (IAAF) are likely to be much more familiar.

Rather than decrease problems, it can also be argued that the existence of globalised systems of governance and culture act as a source of new conflicts. The decision of some 'Western' countries to use military intervention or economic sanctions to 'encourage' countries who do not appear to be adhering to the agreed principles of the free market or even the maintenance of appropriate levels of 'human rights' is one example. Another is the resistance of some Islamic countries to processes of global modernisation and the concurrent rise of Islamic fundamentalism. Within sport there is always the suspicion that the way the countries of the world organise their sport is always bound to fall short of the global standards laid down by the world's sporting INGOs. The fact that we seem to be constantly discovering new problems within sport (such as drug abuse and corruption) can actually be taken as a sign of the strength of the world sporting culture. In a diverse, conflictual and decentralised globalised world, the values that sport provides act as common models for thinking and acting that help create bridges and increase trust between diverse groupings (Putnam, 2007).

Another of the key architects of globalisation's inevitable progress are 'transnational corporations' (TNCs), companies that see their systems of production and their markets as operating in a more or less 'borderless' world (Ohmae, 1990). As we have discussed in our examination of sport and consumer culture, some of the world's biggest TNCs such as Microsoft, Nike, Coca-Cola, Sky and Vodaphone, are either sport based or have a deep and enduring relationship with it.

By the end of the twentieth century, a global culture had developed and penetrated all societies. Sport is one of its most prominent forms. While the origins of modern sport can be argued as emanating from the West, and Britain in particular, sport is no longer just the preserve of the West. Its globalised forms have become a common heritage, institutionalised across the globe and supported by a network of transnational organisations, INGOs and TNCs.

Allied to this perspective, but with a much more pronounced criticism of its economic basis, is world-system theory (Wallerstein, 2004). Wallerstein draws extensively from a Marxist perspective to argue that globalisation needs to be conceptualised as a historical and developmental process that was more or less completed by the end of the twentieth century. The driving force behind globalisation is capitalism's endless search for markets and profits. The economic and political power that this created inevitably favoured European and Western First World countries who were able systematically to exploit poorer and Third World countries.

As we progress further into the twenty-first century, the capitalist world economy is moving ever more into a series of crises (the most notable is that posed by climate change and our need to consume less) which suggests that the freedom of free-market capitalism to seek an almost endless accumulation of capital via the processes of commodification (Wallerstein, 2004) is starting to erode.

The transformationalists

In recent years a number of theorists (Giddens, 1990, 2002; Robertson, 1992; Held et al., 1999) have been responsible for establishing the 'transformationalist perspective' as one of the most rigorous versions of globalisation (Hargreaves, JE, 2002, p26).

Giddens's (1990) analysis of modernity provides the starting point for understanding the institutional dimensions of the global system. For Giddens (1990), the four institutional characteristics of the modern world – the international system of nation-states; the global capitalist economy; the international systems of production and its globalised division of labour; and the world's military order – are the basic components underpinning the development of globalisation.

In brief, Robertson's (1992) account takes a more historical view of globalisation. He argues that globalisation has gone through a number of distinct historical phases:

- **the germinal phase** (1400–1750) characterised by the growth of new national communities;
- **the incipient phase** (1750–1870s) characterised by the emergence of nation-states, colonialism and world trade;
- **the take-off phase** (1870s–1920s) characterised by the emergence of global communication systems and international events such as the Olympic Games;
- **the struggle for hegemony** (1920s–1960s) characterised by the struggle between states for power and leadership in the world – in sport, this was particularly evident in the way the superpowers of the USA and the USSR used international sport as an extension of the Cold War;
- **the uncertainty phase** (1960s to the present) characterised by new forms of global relationships due to technological advances and an intensification of migration – patterns of global culture emerge and are resisted through increased nationalism and an emphasis on traditional religious beliefs (adapted from Bilton et al. 1996, p59).

Although the various theorists who take a transformationalist perspective develop distinctive analyses, they share the dominant sociological understanding of globalisation, which is that globalisation should not be understood as a uniform or uni-directional process. The process of globalisation that characterises our contemporary age is the outcome of *the unprecedented conjunction of forces, institutions, organisations and infrastructures that have led to a flood of goods, services, people, images and symbols across the globe* (Hargreaves, JE, 2002, p27). Based on this account, globalisation needs to be understood as revolutionary, uncertain, and contested.

Learning Activity 11.2

Two of the major forces of globalisation are the way global communication networks such as the Internet connect people together and make available a vast array of knowledge and the power of transnational corporations to influence the lives of people around the world. The purpose of this exercise is to integrate these in order to extend your understanding of how both are interconnected and how they impact the experience of sport around the world.

Read the two following passages:

Acting responsibly in the global world

Nike responsibility – innovate for a better world

We believe in the power of sport to unleash potential. That's why we will invest a minimum of $315 million in grants, product donations and in-kind support through 2011 to give excluded youth greater access to sport.

This year, we'll help bring sport to a Somalian girl growing up as a refugee in Kenya, to a young homeless man from Scotland with a passion for football, and to kids in New Orleans who are rebuilding their communities.

We'll provide Nike products, resurface old playing fields, fund community-based programs and help young people create their own communities.

These impacts come as we've evolved how we frame, define and approach corporate responsibility. We see corporate responsibility as an integral part of how we can use the power of our brand, the energy and passion of our people, and the scale of our business to create meaningful change. So we've set aggressive business targets that embed our corporate responsibility goals into the company's long-term growth and innovation strategies, because we believe there's no better way to achieve them than to tie them directly to our business.

(www.nikebiz.com/responsibility/)

(If you wish, you can explore further Nike's representations of its evolved sense of corporate responsibility at **http://nikeresponsibility.com/**)

Living in the global world

The Sri Lankans were playing a Test match against India at the Sinhalese Sports Club in Colombo. Loitering outside the heavily guarded gates was a young boy, barefoot, his scrawny legs sticking out of dirty shorts. Unable to afford the price of a ticket, he bided his time, hoping for a glimpse of Aravinda de Silva, Chaminda Vaas or some other deity of south Asian cricket. His tattered tee shirt was hand-decorated, with the letters N-I-K-E and a big, black swoosh, the Nike symbol, carefully drawn in felt tip pen. Like so many others around the world, this boy was prepared to do for free what Michael Jordan will do only for millions of dollars. At least, unlike so many of his contemporaries, he was not

•••▶

Learning Activity 11.2 continued

paying over the odds for the privilege. Replicating corporate symbolism was as close as he could come to joining the consuming classes.

The barefoot Sri Lankan was not alone. America's tatooists report that the swoosh is their single most requested design. And if Nike is too downmarket for you, there is always the elite 'sports watch' market, in which an Alexander McQueen design gets the Colin Jackson endorsement. Because modern sport is universal and secular – crossing boundaries of language, religion, culture – it is a handy tool for the construction of global markets, and for the assignment of status within those markets.

(Marqusee, 2000; source: **www.frontlineonnet.com**)

Based on these two passages, assess how each of the three theoretical positions highlighted above would account for these different perspectives.

Sport and global culture

One of the most persistent debates within the sociological analysis of global sport is concerned with the process of cultural globalisation (Maguire, 1999, 2000; Jarvie, 2006). The emergence of a global culture with sport as one of its pre-eminent cultural products is one of its most prominent forms. This argument suggests that all cultures and societies are becoming more alike (homogenisation) and interactive (hybridisation). This process is dominated by the power of Western media interests (particularly American ones) and other forms of mass communication such as the Internet. When the socialist societies of Eastern Europe opened their borders to the global flow of consumer commodities, because of the significance of sport within their cultures, some of the very first imports were Nike and Reebok sports clothes and shoes (Bilton et al., 1996).

In the global world, the desire to be seen as modern, progressive and fashionable collapses almost without comment into 'being Western'. John Hargreaves's (2002, p32) examination of global sport makes much the same observation:

Globalised sport is, by and large, driven by the West, and since America in so many ways leads the West, it should come as no surprise to learn that globalised sport is highly Americanised.

For some sports historians, there is a causal link between colonisation, sport and the imposition of a cultural imperialism. However, this is a claim that sport by itself cannot really sustain. Apart from the interests of capital, crucial to the growing dominance of Western forms of culture are the spread of English as the 'world language' and popular forms of Western culture such as music, television programmes and films.

Definition: cultural imperialism

The aggressive promotion of Western culture based on the assumption that its value system is superior and preferable to those of non-Western cultures.

(Bilton et al., 1996, p68)

The ability of the West's cultural imperialism to impose a homogenised global (sporting) culture has been rightly questioned (Robertson, 1992; Maguire, 1999). The globalisation of culture has never been a uniform or uni-directional process. Appadurai's analysis (1995) of the decolonisation of Indian cricket details some of the interconnected forces that accommodated the adoption of cricket within Indian culture while at the same time decentring it from its English–British cultural definitions and incorporating it into its own expression of a vibrant and confident nationalism. This process has continued with the formation of the Indian Premier League, which has continued to extend India's position as one of the powerhouses of twenty-first century cricket.

At a more personal level, it is also self-evident that people do not experience their lives or their sport at the global level. Sport as an athletic performance is always experienced in 'local' contexts. In many respects, people find it difficult to fully identify with the global. Because of its diversity of history, languages and cultures, the 'global community' does not as yet really possess a collective cultural identity. As Smith (1995) describes, in most respects global culture is essentially 'memoryless'. In attempting to reflexively understand their lives, people not only seek meaning, they also do this by acting and being part of a community and a society that locates them into specific tangible places and spaces. The outcome of this process provides order and certainty to their lives and gives them identity.

What is paradoxical about our contemporary age is that, at the same time as we can see these forces of globalisation at work, it is also evident that there are strong 'countercurrents'. The sense of 'dislocation' created by the global, creates a powerful countercurrent – the need for the 'local' (to be 'located'). Globalisation, paradoxically, has caused an intensification of our awareness of the local. Its uncertainties help to create an emphasis on the importance of the 'home', the local community and the nation. However, if we wish to understand the local character of our lives and the changing nature of the places in which we live, we have to grasp both the wider global context of which we are part *and* what it is that makes us distinctly local.

In simple terms, we are part of more than one world. We live local versions of the world and in so doing we have to locate ourselves within the wider global context. This has led some to put forward an alternative conceptualisation of the process – 'glocalisation' (Horne, 2006) – which attempts to capture the fact that the global and the local are not dichotomous entities but, on the contrary, completely interdependent. There is a need to step back from some of the rhetoric of globalisation and see that sporting experiences exist in a localised world where cultural boundaries still exist and are seen to be important. None the less, this is also a world where these boundaries are also becoming increasingly permeable.

In recent years the work of numerous prominent sport sociologists – Maguire (1999, 2000), Bairner (2001), Houlihan (2003), John Hargreaves (2002), Jarvie (2006), Horne (2006) – all point to the same conclusion: that the local, and more specifically the nation, remains a vital element determining the experiences of much of our sport. Our homes are where we watch it and it is within our local communities where we mostly take part in it. These are the places and spaces where our 'friends' and relationships within sport exist. This is where we learn the significance of sport in our lives, such as playing for local teams or going to the pub to passionately cheer on the national team.

This argument suggests that, while world culture has an array of homogenised and commodified elements, people around the world have the capacity to define their experience of globalisation in their own distinct ways. Global sport even within its most powerful manifestations such as the Olympcs cannot claim a universal consensus. Regions and nations differ in their approaches to sport and different ethnic and religious groups overtly challenge some of its core notions, such as individual rights, racial and gender equity. It is clear that even with globally powerful organisations such as the IOC, FIFA or Nike influencing its globalised sporting forms, there is little indication that we are inevitably moving towards a completely homogeneous world. Nevertheless, offsetting this local focus there is clear evidence to suggest that sport is part of the broader global transformations of the twenty-first century.

The global transformation of sport

Appadurai (1990) has focused on how the interaction and interpenetration of cultures occur. He identifies five dimensions:

- ethnoscapes;
- technoscapes;
- financescapes;
- mediascapes;
- ideoscapes.

As a number of sport sociologists have recognised (Maguire, 1999; Jarvie, 2006 and Horne, 2006), these dimensions provide a useful framework for developing our understanding of sports globalisation.

Sporting ethnoscapes

These involve the migration of sports people around the world. Within professional and elite level sport there is a global demand for highly talented players, managers, coaches and sports administrators. The impact of globalisation on sport's labour force is immediately apparent to anyone watching professional sport in the UK. Whether your favourite sport is cricket, rugby or football, all the major teams now recruit much of their playing, coaching and management talent from around the world. The success of this strategy is made evident by examining the names of the world's wealthiest football clubs, which are now all based in Europe. Long-established South American clubs with massive fan bases have fallen down the list as satellite and cable cash flows into the big western European leagues which have become an irresistible lure to the best of their players. The increasing penetration of satellite and cable broadcasters into the South American market means that these European matches, filled with the best of South America's footballing talent, can be broadcast to South American homes, reinforcing the superior status of European football and thus increasing the likelihood that many of its future sporting talent will join the migrant flow.

Sporting technoscapes

These include the worldwide market in sports technology, clothes and shoes. Also included is the technological development of the sports environment. From golf course design to the building of prestigious sports stadia, there is a global transfer of specialist technologies that include track, roofing and recording technologies, and lighting systems. Expanding the consumption of sporting goods within a sport is often achieved by introducing new technologies that enhance sporting performance – a good example might be graphite framed tennis rackets.

Sporting financescapes

These are created by the global flows of capital and wealth that circulate through the way that many of our best known sports clubs are traded on the world's stock markets.

The international trade in players and coaches, which runs into millions of pounds, is clearly a part of this process. The two preceding chapters have already discussed the issues of media rights, sponsorships and endorsements that collectively offer further evidence of the working of financescapes.

Although these global market forces are an important engine driving the global expansion of sport, it is important to note that this process is not always completely beneficial. The exploitation of the poor in the global production of sport consumer goods is a serious concern and is subject to increasing resistance. Markets can also fail or go into recession. One of the most spectacular examples of this was what happened to a German company called KirchMedia (Rowe, 2004b).

In 1996 FIFA sold KirchMedia the rights to the 2002 and 2006 World Cups for a reported £2.3 billion. The cost of this investment proved to be excessive, however, and KirchMedia found it difficult to sell the broadcasting rights to other media companies. The BBC, for instance, refused to pay the massively increased fee for the 2002 World Cup which they estimated to be seventy times higher than the costs they incurred for the 1998 World Cup (BBC Sport Online, 2001). The result was that KirchMedia had to accept much lower bids for the rights and it lost massive amounts of money that led to its collapse and that of some of its major partners. One of these partners was ISL, one of the world's major marketing groups, which was forced to file for bankruptcy in May 2001. The impact on sport was profound and led to a number of sports, such as Formula One racing, having significant financial problems.

Sporting mediascapes

The issues informing the sporting mediascapes should already be familiar to you as they have been extensively covered in the preceding two chapters. They include how the sport-media complex transmits a huge diversity of sporting action to global, regional and national audiences (Horne, 2006). Their ability to broadcast live and recorded sport from practically anywhere into any home with a television or radio is a powerful example of how this technology 'collapses time and space' and brings events that are happening far away to our immediate attention. Stoddart (1997) argues that the media's involvement in the globalisation of sport needs to be understood not only in terms of the consumption of media products, but as part of a process of convergence that will give the media companies ever more power and control. Stoddart's (1997) prediction that this convergence would involve the merger of television, computer and telecommunications has proved to be accurate, as the current packages from Sky and Virginmedia all too clearly show.

Today, the media's global influence is even more pervasive and in respect of the Internet has permitted new and in some cases quite radical forms of global interconnections between sports fans and their beloved sport (e.g. official and unofficial online fanzines and the debates and reflections that are available on sites such as the BBC's sport editors blog: **www.bbc.co.uk/blogs/sporteditors/**).

Sporting ideoscapes

These are bound up with the production and reproduction of *the ideologies or philosophies expressed by, in and through sport* (Jarvie, 2006, p100). To some degree, these ideoscapes lie within the control of the various powerful organisations that exert significant levels of influence over global sport. As Hoberman (1993) details, globalisation is frequently depicted as a fateful competition among corporations, nations or regions of the world. Whether one supports, opposes or is largely unaware of how globalisation is impacting on sport will depend on the knowledge and experiential basis that one uses to assess its advantages and disadvantages.

If you take the viewpoint that the benefits of sport should be for all, then your assessment is likely to focus on how public finance can be used to help the UK sports councils and the national governing bodies deliver this aspiration for every citizen. If, however, your view is that sport is largely something done by competitive individuals acting on their own behalf, it is likely that you will have a more positive outlook on the way transnational corporate interests have colonised and globalised sport. The ideology of free market capitalism underpins its power and expansion, and makes the concept of competition one of the defining principles of international (sporting) relations. However, as Sugden (2002, p61) suggests, the conflict between these ideological positions has not gone by uncontested but, *in the struggle among those who seek to overwhelm sport for largely corporate and/or personal gain and . . . those who want to protect sport as a popular domain of civil society . . . it is the latter who have lost out.*

The global hegemony of capitalist economic relations within a deregulated globalised market is constantly framed by the conceptualisation of competition as a natural condition of human existence. The manner in which the media, commercial interests and those of national and international governing bodies have used sport fixes this idea firmly in our popular culture. Integral to this view of competition is a neo-social Darwinism that only the strong and fittest will (indeed should) survive and prosper (and hence will generate the wealth from which 'we' will also prosper). Given, however, that competition in sport or in commerce does not start with a level playing field, it is small wonder that many countries in the developing parts of the world express deep concerns about having to accept a global economic and sporting system in which the winners and losers are for the most part already predetermined.

Sport in the (global) network society

Given the arguments so far put forward, it should now be clear to you that globalisation is a complex and multi-layered process. However, as Castells (1996, p47) persuasively argues, our globalised world needs to be understood as being now bound into a *network interconnecting all of the world's societies.* For Castells (1996, 1998) the driving force behind this network is capitalism's shaping of *social relationships over the entire planet.* The global networks that *network capitalism* have penetrated and formed include sport (Castells, 1996; Sugden, 2002). The ways in which the global flows have coalesced into the network also means that global sport has its darker side, as its diffuse nature means that corrupt and illegal practices can also flourish.

The various scandals that have impacted on global sport over the last few years (e.g. illegal betting syndicates) also evidence the dark underside of globalisation, and need to be realistically included as one of the powerful forces seeking to exploit sport's huge popular base. Within sport's global network, corporate sponsors, advertising and marketing agencies, media empires, government bureaucrats and politicians all have an investment, and all seek, fairly or unfairly, to shape it for their own ends. The questions faced by sport globally regarding match-fixing, the corrupt governance of global sport (Simpson and Jennings, 1992; Sugden and Tomlinson, 1998; Jennings and Sambrook, 2000) and about the authenticity of the spectacle are by no means confined to football, the World Cup and the Olympics. In recent times, cricket, tennis, athletics and cycling have all had major scandals that have damaged their credibility. The question that obviously arises is what can be done to help global network sport develop a greater level of transparency and accountability?

In addressing this question in respect of football, Sugden (2002, p78) makes the following critical assessment:

> In Europe, South America and Africa, football, perhaps more than any other area of popular culture, captures the collective imagination and animates the discourse of citizenship . . . football clubs and national teams carry meanings beyond the moment of consumption. They stand for things such as community, tradition, social solidarity and local and national distinctiveness . . . football still needs to be protected from the more avaricious and predatory ways of unregulated global capitalism. FIFA, as currently constituted, is patently obviously incapable of providing this protection. For this reason, they, and global sports organisations like them, should not escape the attention of those activists who are dedicated to the democratic reform of the global political economy.

We are in an age where concerns regarding the negative impact of globalisation generally and on sport specifically seem to be growing and becoming more vocal. In his assessment of this, Jarvie (2006) identifies a number of strategies that are being considered as possible ways to counterbalance globalisation's more negative outcomes.

These include:

- a reassertion of the power of national and local sports organisations;
- the return of economic, political and cultural power to localities;

- quotas on the migration of sports talent into the country;
- re-evaluation and redistribution of wealth derived from sport to alleviate poverty;
- support for campaigns such as 'Sport Relief' and pressure groups that require powerful sporting TNCs such as Nike to act in more environmentally responsible and equitable ways, and international sports federations, such as FIFA, to adopt more accountable and democratic procedures. (Adapted from Jarvie, 2006, p103)

More recently, work by Harvey, Horne and Safai (2009) has suggested that a number of global social movements have started to place much more emphasis on forms of globalisation that promote democracy, social justice and human rights allied with an ever expanding level of concern with the global environment and the threat of climate change. While for many, sport seems to be still somewhat dislocated from these movements for change, the authors present some powerful evidence that sport is and will continue to be drawn into these positive debates about the equity, fairness and sustainability of global systems (such as those impacting and transforming sport).

Sport stars, celebrities and the global culture of sport

While the development of global sport is bound up with the processes of economic and cultural transformation associated with the global diffusion of capitalist forms of consumption (Smart, 2007), by itself this does not fully explain why sport has become such an important element of global popular culture. In his analysis of this question Smart (2007) draws on a series of themes that should now be familiar to you. These are the need to understand the intersections between the development of:

- national and international sport;
- sports goods companies;
- media interest;
- sponsorship;
- consumer culture;
- and the rise of the sporting celebrity.

The power of celebrity in modern sport is not a particularly new phenomenon. In the nineteenth century even amateur sport figures such as WG Grace had huge iconic status.

Even though the profession of team games was yet to reach the heights it has today, from the early years of the twentieth century in the North of England, football sport stars were regularly feted on the streets. Although they may have had celebrity status at this time, they would have still lived in the same communities as the people who gave them their celebrity. At this time, sporting celebrity was more often associated with the recognition of heroism (Holt, 1989) than with the wealthy lifestyle of today's stars and their 'WAGS'. Today, we regard sport stars as an ever present part of sport. Since the rise of the celebrated sport star, the world of sport has been transformed by its close association with the media, sponsorships and the other commercial processes.

The global diffusion of modern sport through the sport-media matrix and its networked elements of transnational media and commercial corporations (Castells, 1996, 1998) has enabled the celebrity sport star to become an almost universal global cultural form. Association with sport events and sporting figures presented through global broadcasting, sponsorship and endorsement arrangements offers commercial corporations unique access to global consumer culture.

Today, the image and presence of these celebrity sport stars is ever present. We cannot go far without encountering a celebrity. As I go into my workplace at the university I am confronted with a life-size image of the Chelsea star Frank Lampard looking at me from the side of a telephone box, advertising a new range of sports clothing. When I go into a high street shop I am surrounded by magazines full of celebrities. When I turn on my computer, websites such as MSN have whole sections dedicated to celebrities. Much more negatively, the phenomena of 'reality television' (remember that sport was probably the first and is still the most powerful form of reality TV) has projected the image of ordinary people doing relatively ordinary things into the arena of celebrity. Celebrity has become defined by having a media presence.

Not surprisingly, a few very high profile sporting celebrities have received considerable levels of attention. Michael Jordan, Tiger Woods, Wayne Rooney and the person we will focus on here, David Beckham, lead the way.

Sporting celebrity: the case of David Beckham

Beckham is not just a person with exceptional footballing talent, he is a 'global brand' (Cashmore, 2002). Like the owners of other global sporting brands (Nike, Adidas, Reebok, Manchester United), he has gone to some lengths to make sure his brand is well managed and developed. As Cashmore (2002) and Whannel (2001, 2002) have pointed out, the power of celebrity is their ability to represent that life has 'possibility' and that our desires – the ordinary people's – can be fulfilled. Part of the success of the Beckham 'brand' was his representation that an ordinary 'working class lad', albeit with a sporting talent, through his dedication and hard work, good management and a celebrity marriage, was able to achieve global stardom.

Research Focus

Joe Maguire

As Professor Alan Klein of Northeastern University Boston acknowledges in his preface to one of Maguire's most recent contributions to the sociological study of sport and globalisation, *Power and Global Sport* (Klein, cited from Maguire, 2005, pvii), *Maguire deserves to be called the pioneering figure in the study of sport and globalization*. While this contribution extends across almost three decades and covers a range of single authored, multiple authored and edited texts and journal articles (e.g. Jarvie and Maguire, 1994; Maguire, 1988, 1993a, 1993b, 1995, 1996, 1999, 2000,

2005) this consideration of his work will focus on what is still his most detailed and substantive elaboration of the interconnection between sport and globalisation, *Global Sport: Identities, Societies, Civilisations* (Maguire, 1999).

The book is divided into two main sections. The first section (which will be the major focus of this short review) maps out the historical processes and the often complex and unresolved conceptual debates that inform the global sport process. Drawing on these debates (particularly the work of Robertson (1992)), Maguire seeks to integrate and align these concepts (many of which have already been foregrounded in the preceding chapter) with a critique of globalisation that emphasises the need for a process-sociology drawing on long-term historical and cultural processes. In the second section, his focus is on a synthesis of this figurational-process-sociological perspective with the global flows identified through the work of Appadurai (1990) to explore some of the consequences and contemporary empirical examples of globalised sport.

Based on the work of Elias and Dunning (1986) and their focus on how sport was an essential contributor to the civilising processes of modernity, Maguire emphasises that an understanding of globalisation needs to proceed from a critical examination of a number of issues: networks of power and how these create processes of mutual interdependency between social groups and nations; the ways in which Western cultures (more formally termed occidental) used cultural practices such as sport to mark out boundaries of prestige and status between the 'west and the rest'; the changing and dynamic relationships between core (insider) and peripheral (outsider) cultural groups and nations; how these relationships and the interconnections between previously autonomous societies and civilisations were practically encountered, accommodated and resisted by those who confronted them.

Maguire goes on to detail how English folk games and pastimes were transformed into many of the sports that we would be familiar with today (a process he refers to as 'sportization' p79) and which were subsequently exported around the world as an integral feature of modernity's civilising processes. He then goes on to explore in some detail how this sportization process parallels, though not exactly, the five phases of globalisation identified by Robertson (see p206 above). Maguire's analysis powerfully demonstrates how modern sport became intrinsically linked to the various phases of globalisation. Through its initial germination phase in eighteenth-century English society sport became linked to the beginning of the world-wide diffusion of modern social structures that took place between 1870 and 1914. During this time of European Empires (Hobsbawm, 1987) the cultural characteristics of sport were predominantly English and to a lesser degree European in character. One of the outcomes of the next phase of globalisation was a direct response to it as countries began to create powerful nationalist movements that were spurred on by the rise of regular large-scale sports international competitions. As the twentieth century matured, a new and distinct phase of globalisation took off as the power of American society and culture began to exert a significant impact on both sport and globalisation. As well as its growing political, economic and military power, American cultural products such as film and new American sports (baseball, basketball and volleyball) began to expand around the world along with their distinctive systems of training, management, professionalism and consumption. In the most recent phase of globalisation (but almost certainly not the last) processes of resistance to cultural homogenisation have become more evident. For Maguire there are at least five distinct global sporting processes evident here: the rise of new social movements that directly alter some of the old power structures in global sport (e.g. the women's movement, the anti-apartheid movement); the spread of new sporting forms whose origins are non-Western (e.g. Judo, Karate, Tai Quon Do, Sumo); the spread of new, more individualised forms of 'adventure sports' (e.g. surfing, BASE jumping, etc.), the 'creolisation' of sport evidenced in some of the recent changes in world football and cricket and the return to highly localised and traditional forms of sport (Shinty and Gaelic football) that help reinforce distinctive national identities.

Although written a decade ago Maguire's work provides a powerful response to many of the naïve and generalised assumptions about sport and globalisation. The global flows that impact sport are multi-dimensional and involve the complex interconnection and hybridisation of many cultures whose outcomes will continue to transform sport throughout the coming century.

Learning Activity 11.3

Review of learning objectives

Through completing the chapter, you should be able to answer the following:

1. What is it about sport that causes so many social commentators to recognise the relationship between sport and globalisation?
2. Through an application of Appadurai's (1990) five dimensions of globalisation, explain the connections between sport and the processes of globalisation.
3. How has the globalisation of sport benefited and harmed British sport?
4. What role do sports stars play in promoting globalisation?

Chapter Review

Globalisation is a complex phenomenon with a long history. In this historical dimension the emergence of global characteristics has not been a smooth curve of progression but a series of 'waves' with peaks and troughs, though with a marked acceleration towards the present time. Sport is a global phenomenon which, as the model of 'scapes' illustrates, has had a major role to play in the acceleration of these global characteristics. However, not all sports have benefited from global promotion. The unequal distribution of resources at local, regional and national level in the UK for different sports (so that, for example, football is dominant, media exposed and powerful, while table tennis is subordinate, poorly media promoted and relatively powerless by comparison) is projected to the global stage – and powerful sports extend their power.

The picture is further complicated by the paradox of globalisation, which is that destabilising global forces accentuate the 'social anchors' provided by the local contexts in which all sports are actually experienced. Additionally, beyond the evident local resistance to globalisation, there are further anti-global sentiments growing around the 'dark' side of sport such as drug use, gambling, match fixing and an enhanced alliance of global environmental issues and the physical, political, social and economic impacts of sport.

There can be no doubt that globalisation is a powerful force transforming the world and the world of sport more specifically. We live in a shrinking world of relatively cheap global travel possibilities that have helped developed a booming market in sport tourism. Paradoxically, this is happening at a time when around the world there is growing concern about climate change and some of these concerns are directed at sport tourism and its dependency on air travel with its high levels of pollution. These developments are a part of the globalised network of societies whose livelihoods and economies are irrevocably allied to the needs of capitalism and its markets aligned to the sophistication of modern communication technologies. As sport has become inexorably intertwined with consumerism, media promotion and globalisation so its position has become more significant in shaping modern globalised society. As the outcomes of these processes are very uneven, and in some cases negative, there are also some signs that around the world people involved with sport are beginning to reflexively plot a more enlightened vision of sport in a global world.

Further Reading

For a general introduction to the basic sociological issues within the analysis of globalisation read:
Chapter 3: A changing world, in Giddens, A (2006) *Sociology*. 5th edition. Cambridge: Polity Press.

For a well-balanced overview of the general sociological debates informing the connections between sport and globalisation read:
Chapter 4: Sport and globalisation, in Jarvie, G (2006) *Sport, Culture and Society: An Introduction*. London: Routledge.
Maguire, J (2000) Sport and globalisation, in Coakley, J and Dunning, E (eds) *Handbook of Sports Studies*. London: Routledge.

For a comprehensive exploration read:
Maguire, J (1999) *Global Sport*. Cambridge: Polity Press.

For an exploration of the interconnections between sport, globalisation and consumer culture read:
Chapter 2: Consumer culture and the global sports market, in Horne, J (2006) *Sport in Consumer Society*. London: Polity Press.

For an overview of how global movements are starting to impact sport and politics read:
Harvey, J, Horne, J and Safai, P (2009) Alterglobalisation, global social movements, and the possibility of political transformation through sport, *Sociology of Sport Journal* Vol 26 pp 383–403.

Part Four

New games:
emergent
and transformative
forms of sport?

Chapter 12
Sport and the body

Peter Craig and Amanda Jones

This chapter will introduce you to some of the important reasons why sport sociologists are taking an increasing interest in the body. In engaging you with this sometimes complex terrain of theories and concepts, our intentions are twofold. The first is to extend your sociological understanding and analysis of sport to an arena of our lives that we are all intimately familiar with – our bodies. The second is to challenge some common everyday assumptions about the body in sport. One of the most persistent of these regards the 'sporting body' as a 'natural' biological entity best understood by physiologists and biomechanicians whose primary aim is to help athletes and coaches enhance its performance. While this is a powerful and perfectly acceptable way of understanding the body, it also tends to distract attention from an understanding of the sporting body as a sociological issue. Quite rightly, this will take us back into some issues with which you should now be familiar: how the sporting body acts as a powerful marker of our social identity in terms of our gender, race, ethnicity, social class and physical/mental ability/disability; how social and cultural institutions such as the media influence our sporting decisions to train, discipline and at times punish or pamper our bodies; how our decisions about our sporting body are connected to our actions as consumers.

Learning Objectives

On completing this chapter you should be able to:

- explain how the sporting body needs to be understood as a biological, social and cultural construction;
- demonstrate through a critical explanation of sporting examples how these constructions have patterned class and gendered views of the 'sporting body';
- detail how sport in modern society is one of the principal means of disciplining, controlling and constraining the body;
- explain how body culture within sport has become a key marker of identities in consumer culture and lifestyle;
- outline some of the major concerns informing a feminist analysis of the sporting body.

Introduction

All forms of social behaviour, none more so than sport, require us to be, albeit at very different levels of intensity, physically active. All forms of physical activity, in turn, require us to use our bodies. On the surface these simple, common-sense observations seem to require little in the way of a sociological explanation. Yet, as soon as we begin to look more deeply into these processes, their real complexity quickly becomes evident. The body and its physical attributes of strength, skill, endurance, speed, grace, style and sexual attractiveness are constantly being monitored and evaluated (Hargreaves, JA, 2000). The body is not only the physical core of all sport, images of bodies performing sport are also some of sport's most evocative symbols.

In the twenty-first century, we live in a world that is obsessed with concerns about lifestyle and identity, and many of these are focused on body image. The briefest scan of the popular newspapers and magazines or television channels will demonstrate that there is a vast array of articles, images, advertisements and programmes that constantly bombard us with messages about bodies. As we discussed in Chapter 9, these media produce powerful discourses through which we become socially and culturally aware of how our bodies are subject to social evaluations allied to sets of social practices and behaviours (e.g fitness training, dieting, etc.). These articles, advertisements and images constantly remind us about how we (and our bodies) should 'conform' and look. If you think back to the role that sporting celebrities play in our consumer society (discussed in Chapter 10), you may quickly recognise that one of the 'taken for granted' ways of evaluating our bodies suggests that we see trim and athletic-looking people as conveying a sense of energy, discipline and organisation, and that these qualities are likely to make the individual: a) more sexually attractive and b) socially successful. Although these sport stars may have admirable (but not always) personal qualities, one of their main selling points is their 'athletic body'. This is why sport stars are such an attraction to advertising agencies and companies.

As conscious and reflexive individuals, it is clear to all of us that our bodies are much more than their biology; they are the physical manifestation of our sense of identity. They are the vehicles through which we 'present' our selves to the world around us and more often than not how the world presents itself back to us. As the arguments that occur in many households in the morning all too clearly evidence, the requirements of getting ready to go out and be 'seen' by others are far from simple. Indeed, they can be directly threatening and full of worry. Seen in this light, sport is therefore much more than a collection of competitive and physical activities. It is a way of conditioning, developing and disciplining our bodies in ways consistent with these idealistic representations. The interest of sport sociologists in the body is therefore focused on exploring and understanding this 'body culture'; the social construction of the body and how sport and the body are 'sites' for the promotion and contestation of competing views of the body; how, as the social world is changing and becoming more diverse (see Chapter 8), our views of the body in sport are also changing.

The sociology of the sporting body

Within sociology the focus of the investigations and analyses has directed attention to how our bodies are affected by a variety of social influences (Giddens, 2001). As Giddens (2001, p144) stresses, *the body isn't something we just have . . . Our bodies are deeply affected by our social experiences, as well as the norms and values of the groups to which we belong.* The intention of developing a sociological understanding of the body is to help us grasp how modern society and the processes of social change have had a dramatic impact on the body. In their examination of the body, sociologists do not imply that issues such as health, illness and injuries are unimportant or imaginary. Rather, how we encounter and experience them in our bodies are forms of social practice that can be observed, codified and understood within a variety of contexts. It is important to realise, therefore, that how we conceive the body in exercise or sport has no necessary, fixed historical or universal meaning. As we shall explore below, the ways we use and seek to physically develop our bodies are directly related to how we have learned to understand them through our locations in different cultural contexts (e.g. male or female).

Some of the clearest social and cultural 'interconnectedness' between our bodies and our social world is evidenced by how our rapidly changing world has impacted on our bodies and how we use them for work, leisure and play. You are doubtless aware that we live in an age where scientific advances mean that computer and genetic technologies are having profound moral, social and political consequences for sport and the body. Concerns about obesity are now widespread, yet the ways health professionals and politicians are addressing this problem have yet to fully come to terms with how some of our 'taken for granted' social structures are changing and having a dramatic impact on our bodies. Some of the social issues that are now recognised as important factors in the growth of obesity are how family structures are becoming transformed and diversified; the creation of a relatively sedentary existence (watching TV and playing computer games, driving cars and working at desks); the mass production and easy accessibility of relatively cheap convenience foods that are often consumed for pleasure rather than need.

Learning Activity 12.1

Over the next week keep a diary of how active you are over each 24-hour period.

For each half-hour period of the day use a simple 1–5 scale to record your level of activity (1 = very inactive (e.g. sleeping or lying down) and 5 = intense physical activity (e.g. playing a game of squash or a hard training session). Do not worry too much about being very exact – it is not a scientific investigation. However, be diligent and make sure you record the full week. Over the same week you also need to keep a diary of what you eat and drink and your reasons for consuming it. Again, you should keep this fairly simple. The food category should be either whether it was a pre-prepared food or something that was created from 'natural'

•••▶

Learning Activity 12.1 continued

food sources. The reason should be either 'hungry/thirsty' or 'other' (there are lots of possible reasons but recording these is not essential to this task, so keep it simple).

Based on your findings, take some time to reflect on the following:

- Do you have an active or sedentary lifestyle?
- Over the course of the week what was the percentage of moderate/intense physical activity (4 and 5 on the scale) compared with being very or moderately inactive (1 and 2 on the scale)?
- What are your eating habits like? Do you think you have a healthy diet?

Do you think that you are active enough to 'burn off' the calories you are consuming?

- What are the important factors that underpin this lifestyle (work, college/school, spending time socialising with family or friends, membership of sports teams or clubs, etc.)?
- Do you foresee this lifestyle substantially changing – why or why not?
- What is the impact of your lifestyle on your body and how you and others perceive it?

Many people who are involved with working with people whose bodies are 'in crisis' – for example, people who have problems with obesity, eating disorders or health problems such as heart disease – are now realising that simply telling people that they should eat less and take more exercise does not get very far. People often have lifestyles that have become full or routine, familiar, comforting or have imposed habits that may underpin the problems they are having. For instance, a single parent mother who is reliant on hourly-paid work at the minimum wage (this often results in working 50–60 hours per week) might well be told she needs to find more time for exercise and the preparation of the family meals. However, to do so means that she will need to alter substantially significant elements of her lifestyle and the power to undertake these alterations may well not easily lie within her ability or circumstances. As well as providing information about what she (as an individual) needs to do, many health professionals are realising they also need to provide the necessary social support structures that can facilitate these changes (e.g. free crèche facilities at sport and leisure centres).

In their review of the contribution of sociology to the study of the body, a number of sport sociologists (Coakley, 2003; Jarvie, 2006) have detailed how the social and cultural contexts in which our bodies are located affect the relationship between the body, identity, and society (Turner, 1984; Shilling, 2003). The body is no longer seen as a fixed biological entity but as socially and culturally differentiated. These sociologically based analyses have established a number of important ideas that are transforming our understanding of sport and the body.

- They challenge assumptions based within the medicalised view of bodies that the biology of humans is a natural condition separate from the social world.
- They question some of the ways that modern society has imposed certain social and moral views of the body as an object – something for us to train, discipline, keep healthy and monitor.
- They question the simplistic and stereotypical ways we allocate the physical attributes of the body (in terms of its reproductive organs, skin colour, hair type, levels of physical or mental impairment, etc.) to socially constructed and imposed categories of gender, race, ethnicity, age and disability.
- They question how the assumptions produced by the interaction of the above issues have led to the way that sport has been organised and developed historically.

Sport, modernity and 'healthy bodies'

In our examination of sport and disability (see Chapter 8) we pointed out that one of the most powerful models for understanding the disabled body in sport is the medical model. As we explained, health and physical ability, as well as having a rational and biological basis, are culturally and socially defined. The growth and development of medicine and the scientific analysis of the body paralleled the development of modern society, so it should not be surprising that they are deeply intertwined. As modernity developed, public concerns over the health of people within our expanding towns and cities focused attention on the rational control of two interconnected social problems. The first was disease and the second was the 'health' of social groups such as the working class who were assessed as following unhealthy lifestyles.

For the growing body of modern health professionals who sought to establish control of the health of the population, disease became viewed as an abnormal condition with objective and identifiable causes that could be overcome. Illness or malfunctioning bodies could (and should) be objectively studied by medical experts who could then identify the source of the problem and rectify it. The power of this detached and rational 'medical gaze' was that it placed those who were its subjects in a very passive position.

Definition: medical gaze
The medical gaze is the detached and value-free approach taken by medical specialists in viewing and treating a sick patient.

(Giddens, 2001, p693)

Consider what happens when you have a sports injury. You may well be taken to the Accident and Emergency Department of your local hospital where you will be seen by a doctor who will attempt to define your injury and prescribe the appropriate course of treatment. For most of us, this experience requires that we passively permit the doctors and nurses to do 'their work', even when on occasion this may well cause significant discomfort. The pay-off for our passivity towards the way these medical professionals treat our bodies is that we expect to get well as a result of their ministrations. Sociologists working within an interactionist framework have identified these processes and have defined this as the sick role (Giddens, 2001). The question this raises for sport sociologists is whether these same role definitions also pattern the relationships between coaches and their athletes.

Historically, the training of the body in sport has been informed by the application of medical knowledge whereby sports physiologists and coaches focus this knowledge on enhancing the physical capabilities of the body or aiding its effective recovery from injury. In some important ways the same role exists between the coach and athlete as between the doctor and the patient. In sport, the coach has a similar power to that of the doctor in that they can tell us what to do with our bodies in terms of physical training and the learning of skills. For the most part, our role as athletes is to passively accept the 'prescriptions' of the coach because we believe (based on our judgements of their qualifications, experience and reputation) that they are attempting to improve our sporting performances. The sociological point to be drawn from this discussion is to realise that there are clear inequalities of power within this relationship and that while in most instances this works positively, they can be used on occasion in coercive and abusive ways. Many coaches, especially in professional sports, condition their athletes to accept pain and injury as an outcome of striving to be the best (Coakley, 2003) and that injuries which lead to a permanent disabling of athletes are unfortunate but inevitable outcomes of the physical nature of some sports (e.g. boxing and rugby).

Sport, the body and social class

As we discussed in a number of the early chapters of the book, historically, the Victorian concept of athleticism had a dramatic impact on the formation of modern sport and how the body was seen in sport. As an ideology, it served to socially justify and reproduce the demarcation between social classes, and within social classes the divisions between men and women and the conceptualisation of masculinity and femininity. Through the paternalistic imposition of ideas such as 'muscular Christianity', the deployment of sport and athleticism by the Victorian middle class had the direct objective of 'improving' the moral and physical wellbeing of working-class bodies. The French sociologist Pierre Bourdieu (1984, 1993) has played a vital role in establishing how sport, the body and social class are socially interconnected. He sets out a number of key theoretical concepts that many contemporary sport sociologists (Sugden and Tomlinson, 2000; Giulianotti, 2005; Jarvie, 2006) have now adopted in their attempt to understand the body as a symbol of distinction. These are 'habitus', physical capital and social field (see Chapter 7 for a more extended discussion). Within the characteristic patterns of thought, behaviour and social practice, class habitus patterns how the various social classes understand their bodies. Bourdieu argues that the working-class body is often viewed in terms of its functionality as a productive machine and this is often central to working-class patterns of employment and social role. By contrast, *The dominant classes view the body as a project and have available resources to choose whether to place an emphasis on the intrinsic or extrinsic functioning of the body* (Jarvie, 2006, p222). The middle classes are considered to have more control over their health, which can be exercised by choosing an appropriate lifestyle. For instance, within working-class communities the realities of manual labour tend to create an emphasis on a robust, strong and physically powerful body. Among the middle class the emphasis is on bodies that are rationally controlled and improved.

Middle-class bodies tend to be judged less on their power or strength (today, some exceptions to this are now evident, one of the most obvious being the powerful bodies of professional rugby players) than on their function and ability. For Bourdieu, this 'embodiment of class' is also then reflected in the sort of sports that are enjoyed and dominated by athletes drawn from their various class communities. Examples of this are the pre-eminence of working-class players in sports such as football or boxing, and the middle-class fixation with games such as cricket and golf, where skill and technique are more important than physical size or strength.

Understood in this way, the body can be seen as constituted through and a reflection of the social structure, its material context, and its habitual social and cultural routines and tastes. Moreover, as Jarvie (2006) points out, the concept of habitus also helps us to locate the way social structures and individual actions and choices also manifest themselves with the 'performance' of the sport. Thought of in this way, playing a sport well requires us to become *a competent social actor . . . having mastery over social practices that involves a feel for the game* (Jarvie, 2006, p222).

Case Study

Let's briefly consider the game of basketball, which in terms of the classifications suggested above highlights how other cultural factors such as race and ethnicity can also have a significant impact on how sports develop stereotypic assumptions about their 'embodied' character. At one level, basketball is a sport that, like all others, we have socially to learn in respect of its rules, regulations, skills and strategies. On another level, as we become more experienced and proficient, our playing and how we use our bodies to play become more integrated. When athletes get 'in the zone' the boundaries between their skilled use of their bodies and their physical engagement with the sport become blurred.

As all the great exponents of the game, such as Michael Jordan, evidence, when your playing of sport becomes 'embodied' in this way, the athlete and their body appear to be able to play instinctively and achieve sporting actions that amaze and stun the audience. When he was at the height of his career, Jordan's phenomenal ability on the court was seen to epitomise the supreme power and potential of the African-American body. The mistake made by many commentators when viewing this sort of sporting action is then to refer to it as natural or even 'God-given'. The seemingly effortless skill of all great sports people may draw from a genetic wellspring. However, this potential is never manifest without its development through many years of coaching and repetitive practice.

Learning Activity 12.2

This task involves a game of people-watching, your powers of observation and interpretation. Start watching by examining the size and shape of individuals who might pass you by in your college canteen or other large area where people gather. From looking at them, can you categorise them in terms of:

- having lifestyles that are physically active;
- the main sports they might play?

If possible, do this as a group, compare your answers and then discuss what clues you each used to categorise the people you observed. Although it is not necessary to do so, if possible approach the individual and ask them to confirm whether you were correct.

Some questions for you to consider:

- What did you observe?
- How easy or difficult did you and the others in your group find the task?
- How much of an influence was the shape of the body and how much were the styles of clothes, shoes and hair styles, etc.?
- If you did manage to talk to any of those you observed, how accurate was your labelling of them?
- What were the things you got right and what did you get wrong?
- What do you think a sport sociologist would conclude from your findings?

Because of the way different sports require different forms of physical engagement (consider the embodied difference between a darts player being 'in the zone' and a scrum half in rugby), Bourdieu argues that bodies are involved in the creation and reproduction of social difference that is displayed through accent (e.g. the sometimes restricted vocabulary of football players), poise (e.g. the refined and balanced stance of the trained gymnast) and movement (e.g. the bouncing gait of many basketball players). Over time, the sporting body tends to adopt the imprint of the social class with which the sport is most closely associated. There are three main factors which sociologists have recognised as crucial to this formation: an individual's social location, including their material circumstances of daily life; the particular social characteristics underlying the formation of their class habitus; and the development of their cultural tastes, likes and dislikes (Jarvie, 2006, p222). However, not all bodies have the same shape or develop the same habits and capacities. The sporting habitus that certain people occupy through their class is also importantly impacted by gender and racial power relations that can create distinctive patterns of social relations that cannot be simplistically reduced to the influence of social class.

Sport, gender and the body

Not surprisingly, given the powerful social interest in gender, much of the research into the body has often focused on how the body becomes the focal point for discourses about masculinity, femininity and sexuality. The increasing participation of women in sports that have been the traditional domain of men and their representations of the interconnectedness between the physicality of sport and masculinity (e.g. the sculpted and muscled body builder or the aggressive and sometimes violent physical contest of rugby) have opened up debates that have challenged some of these dominant discourses and the assumptions about the gendered and sexualised body. What these debates evidence is that our notions about sport, gender and the body change over time. As the growing body of sport sociology identifies (Hargreaves, JA, 1994; Birrell, 2000; Scraton and Flintoff, 2002), the gendered body in sport involves a variety of social and cultural processes that demonstrate that:

- the bodies of men and women cannot be regarded as homogeneous;
- our views of the gendered body are deeply influenced by the prevailing social and cultural circumstances;
- the increasing social and cultural diversity (in terms of race and ethnicity) of most Western societies have created new and sometimes challenging representations of gender and sexuality;
- the gendered and sexualised bodies of athletes are both facilitated and constrained by these circumstances;
- sport can act as both an arena where new identities based on the physicality and sexuality of the body can be explored or made subject to threats of repression, violence and abuse;
- the media have a powerful influence in the ways that the sporting body is displayed as a site of appropriate or inappropriate gender behaviour and sexuality.

The work of a number of feminist writers on the body (Butler, 1990; Bordo, 1993) exemplifies some of the most important dimensions of these processes. They have established how medical discourses about the body, such as those discussed above, have historically acted in ways that have constrained women (and men) in sport. By imposing its versions of language, knowledge and truth, the medical establishment has tended to normalise and regulate the functions of women's bodies and hence their gendered sense of identity. The result has been that within our society the bodies of women are often subject to powerful discourses that serve, even today, to culturally position them in terms of their capacity to bear and nurture children. This view stresses the importance of the 'female' body's reproductive capacity as natural and socially desirable, while other physical body states such as those created by the dedicated female athlete who devotes her life to training her body for sporting achievement are seen as potentially dysfunctional or unnatural (Hargreaves, JA, 1994; Birrell, 2000).

Twenty-first century sporting heroines such as Ellen MacArthur, Paula Radcliffe and Dame Kelly Holmes bear witness to these processes. As their autobiographies detail, women use their bodies for all sorts of things other than child-bearing and do not necessarily consider their sporting bodies as either abnormal or dysfunctional. They are 'real women' who consider sporting endeavour as 'normal'. While some such as Paula Radcliffe may combine sport and motherhood, for others mothering may not be for them a priority or a necessity.

What we can learn from a sociological reading of these texts is that the sporting bodies of these women are constantly being evaluated. As elite sportswomen, their bodies are expected to deliver world-class sporting performances and this often necessarily engages them with medical and scientific models of the 'female body'. However, unlike men, the public and, as the autobiographies also demonstrate, private evaluations of women's sporting bodies do not end with a rational assessment of the body's ability to deliver a sporting performance. Rather, because their bodies are also expected to conform to social norms regarding their gender, they are also constantly being evaluated through discourses of femininity and sexuality.

Definition: femininity
The culturally prescribed norm of a 'feminine' body.

Definition: masculinity
The culturally prescribed norm of the 'masculine' body.

Definition: discourse of attractiveness
In Western contemporary culture this would be a body that is slim, toned, attractive and sexy.

Under the surveillance and disciplinary power of coaches and physiologists, the bodies of athletes are regularly hooked up to machines to be tested for various components of fitness or biomechanical efficiency. Even in our more liberal age, many successful sports people find themselves under a veil of suspicion that questions their performances and sexuality. An example of how some of these scientific and medical discourses, articulated through the media, have attempted to constrain the sportswoman's body is illustrated in the case study below:

Case Study

In the Guardian, *13 February 1998, a headline read:* Breasts, PMT and the Pill Bar Women from Boxing . . . *women should not be licensed to box professionally because pre-menstrual tension makes them unstable.*

This article, and the many similar ones that appeared in the media at the time, examined the struggle between Jane Couch, Britain's then World Welterweight Champion, and the British Boxing Board of Control (BBBC). It was a case that highlights how the popular media can act in ways that reproduce traditional constructions of femininity. The articles tended to mirror the social discomfort of women choosing sporting careers, such as professional boxing, which were deemed appropriate for men but not for women because they demanded physical aggression. The entire BBBC defence was based on the woman's reproductive body, citing 'problems' such as water retention, lumps in her breasts, pregnancy, contraception and heavy periods. Once again, 'biological' arguments were overtly being applied to women's bodies in order to control their sporting behaviour.

Jane Couch, alias 'the Fleetville assassin', finally won her case on 30 March 1998. Sporting history was made as the court ruled that the BBBC was discriminating against sportswomen. The outcome was that on 14 August 1998 Jane Couch became the first woman to be granted a professional boxing licence in Britain.

Learning Activity 12.3

Carry out a Google search on the Jane Couch story. Read the archive newspaper articles. In the light of the issues identified above, look carefully at the use of language to see if you can identify the gendered power relations within their discussion of the case. Make a list of the actual arguments and the evidence being put forward by both sides.

   Some questions for you to consider:

1. If you had been the judge, what decision would you have made and why?
2. Can you think of any arguments like this about men's bodies?
3. What is your assessment of the role played by the media in reporting the case?

Sport, the body and power

In recent years the work of Michel Foucault (1976, 1980) has had a major influence on the sociological understanding of power relations and the social construction of the body. While it could be argued that we have agency in creating our own identities (for example, 'a student', a 'hockey player'), as we have shown throughout the text there are a large number of social and cultural practices that normalise (Foucault, 1976) how we as men and women come to understand and assess what sports we should be involved with, our bodies and their sports performances.

   Foucault's analysis of the body shows how the body is the basis on which our individual identities, and our senses of autonomy, power and freedom or social inequality are built. These power relations are central to the social construction of 'other' bodies (the racialised body, the ethnic body, the gay body, the disabled body) and their experience of sport. In respect of gendered bodies, Foucault's work suggests that historically, changing social conditions have invested them with various and changing forms of power. The diversity of views of the body that confront us in our contemporary society causes our understanding of them to become fractured, shifting and unstable. If Foucault is right, the outcome is that establishing our gendered body involves us with complex socially guided activities that reinforce particular sporting pursuits as expressions of masculine and feminine 'natures'. What is most important to draw from this work is the way in which we as individuals become our own 'body police', charging our own consciousness with assessing our body and its shape, and, when required, deciding to discipline it through exercise regimes and diets. More often than not, we do not require the voice or the disapproving gaze of others to feel guilty about our lack of exercise or our expanding waistline – our own are more adequate.

Thought of in this way, the sporting body becomes a text to be read and interpreted. As we hope you found out through doing learning activity 12.2, we all have developed the capacity to read and interpret bodies, although as always in human affairs some are much better at it than others. How we interpret the text of the body is based on the messages that we get from looking at a body; the assumptions we have learned to make about it. For example, in our contemporary society the images that the media constantly present to us suggest quite explicitly that the aesthetic ideal of a body is that of the slim, toned, athletic body. These images teach us to worry about fat, to treat it with distaste, to marginalise the larger body and often attach assumptions of laziness and unhealthy lifestyles to it. This is, of course, an image of the body that other cultures actively question and resist. From a sociological perspective, the assumed connections between the 'athletic body' as a 'healthy body' and the fat body as an 'unhealthy body' need to be questioned. In understanding the body within sport it is important once more to emphasise that the dominant conceptualisations of modern sport are grounded in discourses that emphasise performance and celebrate the attributes of power, speed and strength, all of which have historically been seen as symbols of masculinity (Hargreaves, JA, 1994). Through this construction our image of sport is often permeated by implicit assumptions about men's superiority and women's inferiority. The questions that this observation inevitably invokes are whether there are other ways to envision sport and what would be the outcome if we did change our views? The disputes that would inevitably be created would probably revolve around what we consider the essence of sport and its defining characteristics (competition, aggression, speed, and strength). It is not the purpose of this book to speculate on what the outcome may be, but to observe that, as we become more socially diverse, there will almost inevitably be challenges to what we consider to be the quintessential nature of sport (Hall, 1996). If people are to feel empowered in sport, then those of us involved in sport need to be aware that if sport does not consciously attempt to address the issues of equity and fairness raised by the above analysis, then some alienated groups may well feel they have no other recourse but to create alternative forms of sport organised according to their own agendas.

Learning Activity 12.4

To close this section of the chapter, take a few moments to reflect carefully on your own childhood experiences in respect of how you became aware of:

- your body's 'gender';
- the sort of behaviours you were expected to take part in that demonstrated you knew how to behave in gender-appropriate ways;
- the sanctions that might occur if you acted in gender-inappropriate ways;
- the role played by sport in assigning and confirming gender.

Learning Activity 12.4 continued

One of the things that this exercise might have made you aware of is how you or others have both accepted and accommodated aspects of the social and cultural ascription of gender, and rejected and resisted aspects of it. As with the previous tasks, having completed this activity you should also try to reflect on what your experiences mean so that we can develop a sociological analysis of the gendered body in sport.

Sport, exercise and the consumption of the body

The significance of the emergence of a consumer society on sport was discussed in Chapter 9. Based on the discussion presented in that chapter, it is now possible to connect the ideas of sport, consumption and the body. This section explores the socio-cultural dimensions that explain how the sporting body secures consumers.

Jennifer Hargreaves (1987) analyses the relationship between sporting bodies, desire, consumer culture and consumers. She argues that the bodies in advertisements can be read by consumers and that this 'reading' evokes desires to adopt the values and identities of this idealistic and simulated sporty, happy, successful, slim and popular body. The commodification of bodies in the world of advertising incites participation in fitness practices and encourages consumers to 'discipline' themselves by adopting behaviours to achieve their desire for a positively evaluated body and identity. Sport, together with fashion, eating and drinking, cooking, dieting, advertising and a wide range of aids to sexual attractiveness, are deployed in a constantly elaborating programme of mediated representations whose objective is to confirm the belief that the consumption of these products and activities is vital to our achievement of a positive self-identity. As we suggested in the above discussion of the work of Michel Foucault, the maintenance of the body is not something that is easy to ignore in our image-conscious age. The body is one of the prime obsessions of consumer culture and its discourses of health and fitness, exercise, dieting and beauty.

In examining these interconnected themes and how they are constructed through the intersection of social structures and the reflexive actions of individuals seeking to construct meaningful lives, sociologists have drawn on the concept of lifestyle (Chaney, 1996). If the vast array of lifestyle programmes on our televisions are anything to go by, it seems that today we have a national and individual preoccupation with 'healthy bodies' and 'healthy lifestyle'. In typifying this, Howell (1991, pp266–267) argues that the *workout yuppie* is a symptom of *a consumerist definition of the quality of life* that *encompasses a self preservationist conception of the body*. At the heart of this process is an interplay between the conceptualisation of the fit body, and the notion of character, morality and responsibility. Here, we can once again observe that fundamental to this conceptualisation are the scientific and medical discourses that encourage us to manage our bodies in ways that avoid illness and physical degeneration. In creating our 'lean and active' lifestyle, we are encouraged to accept without question that in acting in this way we are providing our bodies with a sense of betterment, pleasure, freedom, success and positive self-esteem.

Within the expansion of middle-class leisure and 'lifestyle' consumption, health, fitness and exercise have become the answers to our desire for the body beautiful. One constantly hears the slogan 'Exercise makes you feel good and look good.' Images of bodies behaving in a 'fun-loving' way with the ethos of 'life is too short' evidence discourses of the importance of 'staying young'. The thin active body in consumer culture often infers a promise of youthful health, happiness, success and sociability (Gruneau, 1993).

Learning Activity 12.5

As you watch television over the course of about a week take some time to identify and, if possible, record some of the television advertisements that use the sporting or exercised body to secure our attention as consumers. Some issues you should consider:

1. What products are they selling and what messages are the marketing companies giving to the viewer?
2. What is the role of the body in the stories?
3. When sporting images are used, what images of the 'fit body' do they convey and do the products they advertise have anything to do with sport?
4. If they do not, why do you think the company and their advertising agency have decided to use sporting bodies and sports stars to market their products?

One of the issues you may have identified in completing the previous activity was the importance of how we clothe and adorn our bodies. From a sociological perspective, rather than as a fashion statement, 'workout' clothing can be understood as being made from specialist textile technologies that we consume because they accentuate the shape of the active body. Being able to display a fit and athletic body shape can in turn be seen as a process of empowerment, especially when it is displayed in places that celebrate it (the health and fitness club, the sports field). Tight-fitting sports clothing and fashion can be seen to perpetuate discourses of hegemonic masculinity and femininity and, specifically, the discourse of the sexualised body. However, while clothing can be seen both as a function of hegemonic power, it can also be used as a way of empowering the self and resisting the imposition of dominant norms. For example, many men and women are conscious of how our consumer society imposes unachievable and sometimes unhealthy images of the body and therefore choose to wear baggy clothes to resist such discourses.

The formation of 'body dilemmas' are central in consumer culture, and the concerns they produce are partly responsible for the contemporary boom in the fitness industry. However, it is also important to recognise that this boom, while to some degree cutting across all sections of the population, is primarily an element of middle-class consumption and lifestyle. In her discussion of these issues, Maguire (2002) has usefully discussed two further ways of examining the sporting body – the 'calculating body' and the 'motivating body'.

Calculating bodies

One of the inevitable realities of our consumer culture and its attachment to the body is that the body has become a site for consumer investment. This, according to Maguire (2002, p456), has created bodies that are deemed to *be accountable, predictable and calculable*. Once again, this perspective places the body in the realms of science in order that it can be measured, weighed and objectively evaluated. The outcome is that it has become the responsibility of the individual to control their body and to measure and monitor its features – for example, fitness magazines teach consumers how to measure the fat content of their bodies (Body Mass Index; BMI), and how to analyse their food consumed in terms of input and output of calories.

Learning Activity 12.6

How do you 'calculate' your body? Think over your daily habits and what you do to control and manage your body. You may give examples from other people in your life.

Some everyday processes you might want to reflect on:

- Why do you feel that other people or you have to make calculations about your body?
- Do you use bathroom scales? Why do you think people 'hide' them away in the privacy of their bathrooms?
- Do you discuss their 'calculation' of your weight with others? Do you have a body weight that you think of as ideal and desirable? What would you do to achieve this ideal?
- Have you dieted in order to change the shape of your body (gain weight or lose weight)? Did people make any comments on the change of your body shape and what did you feel about their evaluations?

The suggestion made by Maguire (2002) is that there is a link between the sporting and active body seen in advertising and our elevated preoccupation with health. Through her analysis of fitness magazines, she argues that *Health is not only a benefit of exercise, but a quantifiable, predictable profit* (Maguire, 2002, p456). From this she suggests that our conceptualisations of the fit body have come to equate exercise with control over health. Today, many medical, government and media reports aggressively promote exercise as a positive and necessary element in the establishment of a healthy lifestyle. There may be many different ways to define what it is to be healthy, but they all have other discourses attached to them. The discourse of 'exercise is good for you' is starting to be seen as no longer a personal choice but a response to general concerns about health and a necessary means of improving the physical, social and psychological health of the population. The medical benefits cited are numerous and include the reduced risks of cardiovascular disease, stress, obesity and a preventative measure against osteoporosis.

These sorts of rational calculations about the body are fuelled by a range of discourses (such as the 'risks' of not having a healthy body), the outcome of which can be anxiety and an overreaction to exercise that may be detrimental to health. Athletes often drive themselves to believe that they can overcome all physical obstacles and that they thrive on pushing their bodies to new limits. Consciously, many sports people are moving their (calculable) goals to make their bodies go faster for longer. This is evidenced in the development of sporting events such as the Ironman triathlon that are designed to test the body almost to destruction. However, such behaviour and associated ritualistic training practices also convey ways in which the athlete is subjected to sporting formations that may have little to do with health, and indeed may well have a damaging and crippling impact on the body. In their selling of fitness, some sports and the fitness industry can be more generally argued as promoting discourses that encourage the person to rationalise unhealthy and irrational behaviour as a sacrifice for the ultimate goal of achieving evermore greater levels of fitness.

Motivating bodies

One of the problems faced by those desiring to get fit – and also those professionals whose livelihoods are dependent on helping us get fit – is the difficult transition from thinking or reading about fitness to the actual 'doing' of fitness and the subjugation of our bodies to its routines, physical demands and discomforts. As Maguire (2002, pp458–459) points out, managing the body and achieving the calculated rewards we identified in the previous section face three basic obstacles:

First, the physiological inertia of the body means that change is slow and must be kept up. The body is not only slow to change, but also prone to lose ground through ageing, injury and inactivity. Second, the . . . increase in sedentary forms of work means that exercise is an increasingly uncommon everyday habit; becoming fit requires overcoming the resilience of behavioural patterns of inactivity. Third, exercise involves a lot of work if the participant is to see results, which poses a challenge to an industry that sells fitness as leisure. Exercise competes with other (less strenuous and sweaty) leisure activities.

Maguire (2002) argues that, in their attempt to convince us of the benefits of exercise, the fitness industry and fitness magazines specifically seek to establish a number of discourses that provide a range of motives that can be used to inform and encourage our desire for fit and healthy bodies. These discourses not only educate the consumers of fitness about the practical physical requirements of developing fit bodies, but more importantly about the production of positive lifestyle habits (deemed to be essential for success) that need to be developed through discipline. Akin to the rational demands of the founding fathers of mass production (such as Henry Ford, the American car maker) consumers are encouraged to produce habitual rational behaviours such as time management, exercise and self-scrutiny. In reward, they are promised the production of an ideal body that is admired and thus can become their ticket to social success.

Presented in this way, the fit body and the sporting body more generally become fully integral to, and an essential component of, a well-balanced and successful lifestyle. This clearly reinforces the analysis of Foucault (1976) in that discipline and critical self-reflection become established as the crucial foundations of the successful individual (Foucault, 1976) and a healthy, fit and attractive/desirable body. Moreover, it also brings our attention back to many of the same modernist assumptions that underpinned the formation and codification of modern sport: the need for constant improvement and learning; the importance of predictable routines and physical practices; the ability of critical self-assessment through detailed record-keeping; and the habitual benefits of moral virtues such as industry, chastity, temperance and cleanliness. In how it markets itself the fitness industry may seem to be an arena of consumer lifestyle choices, but once we begin systematically to analyse its construction from a sociological perspective, it quickly becomes evident that its roots remain firmly located in the same social and cultural ground that facilitated the growth of modern sport and the formation of the sporting body.

Research Focus

Dawn Penney

Penney, D (2002) (ed) *Gender and Physical Education; Contemporary Issues and Future Directions.* London: Routledge

As this chapter has discussed, the body is seen by many sport sociologists (Penney, 2002; Scraton, 1998; Hargreaves, JA, 2000) as a contested terrain on which power and resistance are fought out. Sociological research that focuses on bodies underpinned by pedagogy, has become a significant area within the field as it questions how young people learn about their bodies and develop embodied identities through different physical cultures such as schools. As the work of Penney and Evans (2002) details, the body is central to physical education (PE) and the key vehicle for the expression of subject knowledge; it is continually exposed to the gaze of others. Penney's critical analysis of the curricular process helps us to understand how young people experience their bodies (not just in sport or PE), the themes of the body that emerge, and the curricular processes and strategies that successfully support this critique. Traditionally the body has been schooled along restricted and prescribed gender regimes (example: Rich, 2001). Penney's research (Penney, 2002; Evans and Penney, 2008) shows evidence of how both the content and pedagogical practices of PE are constructed (and reproduced) through narrow discourses of femininity and heterosexuality. Accordingly, young men and women learn to use their bodies to perform the required 'feminine' and 'masculine' codes for acceptance within PE and schooling more generally (Clarke, 2002, p42*).* In *Gender and Physical Education* (2002) Penney offers a wide-ranging critical sociological analysis and comprehensive commentary on issues relating to gender and young bodies in the context of the National Curriculum PE. In its presentation of a wealth of original research, it delivers a comprehensive (and long overdue) overview of the progress and shortcomings of contemporary policies and practice in PE as they relate to gender, and reflects on the similarities and differences between developments in the UK, US and Australia.

In far more detail than has been possible to provide in this chapter, Penney's contribution to sports sociology challenges existing perceptions of gender, equity and identities of boys' and girls' bodies in PE. Penney (2002) draws upon the extensive research to provide an analysis, description and critique of the direct and indirect influences of central government, local education authorities, schools, departments and teachers in the development of policy and practice in PE. The highly political nature of policy developments in education, and PE in particular, is demonstrated clearly throughout.

Penney's work considers why professionals of PE should be concerned with gender issues and *draw attention to longstanding inequalities in the policies and practices of physical education in schools, and address the roles that teachers, teacher educators and researchers can play in either reinforcing or challenging sexism and inequality in Physical Education* (Penney and Evans, 2002, p4). The authors answer crucial questions such as 'why do we need a gender agenda?' by outlining how historically PE has developed in explicitly gendered ways. Using the example and context of PE, Penney's work (2002) provides a particularly vivid and comprehensive illustration of the processes involved in the development of the National Curriculum for Physical Education in England and Wales between 1988 and 1995.

Penney and Evans (2002) critically analyse policies and practices and conclude that over the last 20 years *there has been little surface level, let alone deep structural change . . . and a paucity of gender related innovation evident in physical education* (p3) that is due to an absence of positive policies from the government. Evans and Penney (2002, 2008) not only demonstrate the undeniable need for a gender agenda in contemporary policy, curriculum development and everyday pedagogical practice in PE, but also inform the development of that agenda and in particular, extend what we regard as longstanding and now outdated 'discursive boundaries' or the ways of thinking and acting in physical education and sport (p4). Penney contributes to the sociology of sport by offering a new framework for research, policy and practice with a view to advancing gender equity, and addresses the roles that teachers, educators and policy makers can play in challenging existing inequalities.

As this brief overview demonstrates, Penney's contribution to a critical analysis of current research that focuses on young *Bodies in Pedagogy* has been significant. A valuable contribution to existing literature, Penney (2002; Evans and Penney, 2008) helps students and researchers piece together the last ten years of policy-making in education and offers a new perspective on the future of physical education in the United Kingdom. Penney's focus on issues of young bodies in PE and the National Curriculum makes a significant contribution to the field of sport sociology. There is a need for more inquiry-based research on Physical Education that focuses on pupils' questions and concerns about the body – or 'body as curriculum'.

Learning Activity 12.7

Review of learning objectives

When reflecting on what you have learnt through this chapter, consider how you might respond to the questions and statements outlined below:

1. Drawing on your own experience of sport and exercise, clearly outline how the body can be sociologically understood as a biological organism that can be subjected to rationalised forms of physical training.
2. Taking football or boxing as an example, explain how social class can impact on our experience of sport and the production of recognisable body habits and styles.
3. What are the arguments that a feminist analysis of sport might put forward to justify the claim that even today many women feel their bodies are subjected to coercive forms of social control though sport?
4. Are men's bodies subjected to the same levels of social control and discipline and is there any evidence that this is starting to change?
5. Why is it important for our society that people are encouraged to become self-disciplined in terms of how they 'work' and exercise their bodies?
6. Are fat people merely lazy individuals who should be more responsible in terms of their exercising and eating habits?
7. Can you show through examples drawn from your own experience how body culture and processes of consumption are important dimensions of your social identity and lifestyle?

Chapter Review

This chapter was designed to act as a useful starting point for your further work on the sociology of sport and the body. As one of its major themes we have considered some of the important sociological arguments that suggest that sport in modern society is one of the principal means of disciplining, controlling and constraining the body. In doing this, we have detailed how sport, the body and society need to be understood as interconnected social and cultural constructions. Thought of in this way, the body is much more than a mere biological organism. Our bodies are social and cultural projects, a 'work in progress', that, as with the rest of life, require decisions and the investment of time and capital in all its forms. Central to this analysis is the concept of lifestyle. Our bodies and sport are allied to aspirations about our lifestyle and concerns over health. In examining these issues, the discussion also highlighted how our sporting bodies are probed, measured, evaluated and monitored all with the intention of aspiring towards an idealised body shape that is socially constructed to reflect images of the consuming body, the calculating body and the medicalised body.

The habitual actions that combine to create and define our lifestyle and, hence, our sport are not only important because they help to socially differentiate us from others, but also because they normatively attach powerful domains of meaning through which we understand our bodies. This awareness of our bodies is impacted by social and cultural structures such as class and gender. Situated within these habitual patterns of thought and behaviour we learn to ascribe specific forms of cultural knowledge that enable us to understand the realities of our specific social context and to make predictions about how we and our bodies should act within it.

A central theme within the sociology of the body is the cultural construction of a consumer who is equipped with an informed awareness of the problems of social status and consumer lifestyle. The expanding fitness industry promotes lifestyle as the basis for social identity and mobility. Sport and exercise are marketed as 'good for you' in that they produce health improvements, empowerment and increased popularity through the production of attractive bodies. However, as the critical assessment of sport sociologists identifies, access is commodified and subject to market forces. This inevitably means that many are unable to afford either the time or money to develop the bodies or healthy lifestyles that are constantly promoted to them.

Further Reading

For a general introduction to sociology of the body read:

Giddens, A (2006) Chapter 6: Sociology of the body: health, illness and aging, in *Sociology*. 5th edition. Cambridge: Polity Press.

For an excellent but more challenging and extended exploration of the social and cultural construction of the body read:

Shilling, C (2003) *The Body and Social Theory*. 2nd edition. London: Sage.

To extend your understanding of the social construction of bodies in sport read:

Cole, C (2002) Body studies in the sociology of sport, in Coakley, J and Dunning, E (eds) *Handbook of Sports Studies*. London: Sage.

Scraton, S and Flintoff, A (eds) (2002) *Gender and Sports: A Reader*. London: Routledge.

Jarvie, G (2006) Chapter 10: Sport, body and society, in *Sport, Culture and Society: An Introduction*. London: Routledge.

To extend your understanding of how our bodies are integral to the formation of lifestyle and consumer culture read:

Horne, (2006) Chapter 6: Sport, identities and lifestyles in consumer culture in sport, in *Consumer Culture*. London: Palgrave.

Chapter 13
Sport and adventure

Paul Beedie

Adventure is a term used in different ways in modern society. Depending on which definition is followed, it broadly refers to 'uncertainty of outcome'. Such uncertainty, as in not knowing what is around the next corner in a physical sense and/or not knowing what the future holds for a person in the social sense, is always with us so that 'adventures' are an ongoing possibility in all of our lives. Because a defining characteristic of modernity is change, in one sense 'adventure' – as in not knowing what the future holds – is with us all the time. It is, however, the alignment of adventure and exploration, and physical pursuits such as climbing, sailing, canoeing, caving, snowboarding, surfing, orienteering, trekking and mountain biking – in other words, the doing of adventure activities – that is the focus of this chapter. Collectively known as 'risk pursuits', investigation of these activities represents an opportunity to extend the discussion of the book into new territory and, as we shall see, the ways these activities are integrated into social life tell us a great deal about the tensions and contradictions of contemporary times.

Learning Objectives

On completing this chapter you should be able to understand:

- that adventure has helped shape the modern world;
- how various theoretical ideas and models help to explain the socio-cultural relationship between sport and adventure;
- that traditional or mainstream sport is both 'resistant' and 'emergent' in relation to adventure;
- that adventure can take three main forms (education, recreation/tourism and sport) and that each makes a contribution to modern society.

Introduction

Adventure pursuits make physical demands – they require active participation and engage with risk. We can think of 'traditional' adventure pursuits that have a long-standing heritage and operate in wild places (e.g. mountaineering) and 'new' adventure pursuits – typically those that locate to built-up urban areas and are predicated upon technological innovation (e.g. skateboarding). Traditional pursuits have emerged from a historical context that has its origins in exploration – Columbus, Drake and Cook sailed and mapped across the globe; the early fur trappers in Canada paddled across the wilderness establishing routes and outposts as they went; upper-class English gentlemen explored the Alps in the nineteenth century before Eric Shipton and Harold Tilman and many others undertook comparable explorations in the bigger and wilder Greater Himalaya in the twentieth century. Additionally, overland journeys on foot have been documented throughout history and include early migrations from Asia into North America via the Bering Strait, the travels of Marco Polo and those in Africa of Dr Livingstone. These exploratory journeys could not have happened without engaging with risk.

In the preface to his book *Risk*, Adam (1995) says that no one wants an accident, but everyone wants to be free to take risks. We live in a culture that both glorifies risk and employs an army of bureaucrats to reduce it. Here he encapsulates the essence of the structure–agency debate: it is generally recognised that modernity requires 'progress' and that this takes many forms, but in a broad interpretation this requires 'exploration' of the world. This is why we have always revered the achievements of famous explorers. As Riffenburgh (1993) has shown, modern society has a hunger for news about the latest discoveries and the dramas that commonly accompany these – a good example is the 'race for the South Pole' in 1912, as is the ascent of Everest in 1953. However, at the same time the interests of society must be served in terms of stability, rationalisation and control, establishing comfort zones rather than pushing beyond boundaries. As this chapter will show, adventure sports strive to 'explore' new physical and social territory, but must do so within a framework of the structuring dimensions of modernity.

Adventure exploration

Adventure exploration is especially important in modernity because exploring achieved a number of important outcomes. It gave the explorer (and by extension the authority or country sponsoring or supporting the explorer) knowledge of new places and thereby an opportunity to take from those places raw materials and goods to benefit the sponsoring country's economy. It also created the opportunity to extend power and control beyond the home nation so that the 'discovered' places were likely to absorb, or have imposed on them, the cultural standards and operating systems of the explorer's country. This is how empires have always been built. For example, the industrial revolution began in Britain. This gave unprecedented power first to Britain and then to Western nations more generally (including the USA and Canada). It is the framework of modernity generated by these unprecedented social and economic developments that continued to follow explorers into all 'unknown' places in the world. These places were only unknown to Western people, nevertheless the mythology surrounding exploration embedded itself in Western thinking, and, because we are still driven by the same ideas and ambitions as those that defined the emergence of the modern world, adventure has remained an integral part of our culture today.

Contemporary forms of adventure

This historical legacy, together with the persuasive ideology of capitalism, remains and continues to shape three contemporary forms of adventure. To a large extent these forms all reinforce the place of adventure in Western thinking. In adventure *education*, outdoor pursuits such as climbing, camping, canoeing, compass sports and sailing continue to dominate the activity programmes. Adventure education is essentially concerned with people's personal growth and advancement of self-knowledge. In this respect, the adventure activities, which might be thought of as 'traditional' adventure pursuits, become a means to an end – part of the learning process in which the target is to learn in the broadest understanding of the term. The learning process might be thought of as the acquisition of educational capital, and the introduction to activities can promote a life-long interest as adventure *recreation*. Such traditional activities are also a significant foundation for adventure *tourism*, although here the rationale for participation has arguably more to do with gaining social capital. Adventure tourism represents a commercial development of adventure that uses the same pursuits as adventure education but, because it is primarily concerned with adventure as business, it is always looking for new places and new adventure activities to attract paying clientele. These usually wild places have a particular attraction and represent symbolic capital to be acquired through journeys 'off the beaten track'. A combination of technical developments in adventure equipment, some lateral thinking and a competitive market has led to the development of adventure pursuits that are less traditional: bungy jumping is a good example, but there are others such as white water rafting. These activities represent a distillation of adventure into relatively short but intense adventure experiences, often 'packaged' with videos, t-shirts, photographs and other merchandise that might be thought of as 'evidence' of the experience and therefore operate as social capital to the benefit of the participants back in their everyday lives.

Definition: adventure education
Personal growth and the acquisition of knowledge through participation in activities that encompass risk.

Definition: adventure pursuits
Adventure activities such as climbing, sailing, hillwalking, caving, mountaineering and canoeing – that is, activities that encompass risk.

Definition: adventure tourism
The alignment of travel packages and adventure pursuits consistent with commodity exchange.

Lastly, there is a form of adventure that brings together the ideas of risk and uncertainty integral to adventure with the overtly competitive dimension of *sport*.

Adventure sports therefore nudge into the territory of conventional athleticism and draw on many of the characteristics familiar to people who play sport. These include training regimes, diet scrutiny and a systematic approach to regular competitions. The traditional adventure pursuits are not immune to the encroachment of sporting characteristics, so we have, for example, climbing competitions, canoeing and sailing regattas, and mountain marathons for walkers and fell runners. Training regimes are about the acquisition of physical capital, although this is transferable into other forms of capital, particularly social capital (by becoming a star performer) and economic capital (through prize money and sponsorship deals).

Although this framework suggests three different forms of adventure, there is considerable blurring of the boundaries. Adventure education, for example, may use less traditional pursuits such as mountain biking and abseiling as young people pick up on media images of adventure as excitement. Adventure tourism packages may include participation in or the spectating of adventure sports. Star performers in climbing competitions may work in adventure education and therefore understand the personal growth potential that adventure offers. These ideas are developed in the sections below.

Definition: outdoor education
Structured learning outside the conventions of the classroom.

Definition: adventure recreation
Engaging with adventure pursuits (indoors or outdoors, in 'natural' or artificial settings) as leisure choices.

Definition: adventure sport
New and traditional adventure pursuits that have taken on characteristics consistent with sporting competitions.

The sociology of adventure

Three social theorists have made a significant contribution to explaining the sociology of adventure: Georg Simmel (Frisby and Featherstone, 1997), Ulrich Beck (1992) and Anthony Giddens (1990, 1991). Simmel was developing his theoretical orientation over 100 years ago, yet his ideas remain relevant today. Simmel was broadly concerned with how individual behaviour is shaped by social forces, particularly those relevant to the human propensity for gregariousness (the formation of groups), but at the same time we exist as individuals with an 'inner life' of our own. Simmel's social-psychological position sees social life as a kind of battleground in which we engage with conflicting ideas: we need to be both an individual and stand out from the crowd, but to do so risks social alienation from 'normal' society. This explains Simmel's concerns with fashion because dress codes and other elements of consumption provide a way of establishing who we are in a social context – that is, a sense of identity. Following this line of reasoning it could be argued that adventure today is a fashion. As youngsters, we may be introduced to adventure via outdoor education, we may choose to pursue certain adventure activities as recreation and, money and circumstances permitting, we may buy adventure tourism packages.

Here, Simmel explains the relationship between adventure and ordinary life:

An adventure is certainly a part of our existence, directly contiguous with other parts that precede and follow it; at the same time, however, in its deeper meaning, it occurs outside the usual continuity of this life. Nevertheless, it is distinct from all that is accidental and alien, merely touching life's outer shell . . . it is a foreign body in our existence which is yet somehow connected to the centre; the outside, if only by a long and unfamiliar detour, is formally an aspect of the inside.

(Simmel, 1911, in Frisby and Featherstone, 1997, p222)

Simmel's foundational contribution to the sociology of adventure is threefold. He recognises the need for adventure as an assertion of individuality amid the structures of state control. At the same time, he recognises how all social activity moves towards the 'centre' in a way that diminishes the extraordinariness of an adventure through the necessity of social continuity. Lastly, he acknowledges that capitalism has the potential to shape social activities to its own ends. This analysis is complex, but sets out a position that adventure is an 'outer' experience, an attempt to transcend the rational by, for example, actively engaging risk. The problem is that if adventures stand alone beyond the social, they become ahistorical and are of the moment with no past or future. How do we know we are having an adventure if there is no social reference point? If an adventure is a denial of the present as structure – that is, it is based on distance and alienation – we have no measurement of our adventure experience. Simmel suggests that a number of reference points are necessary for people to make sense of their adventure experiences: words and images are embedded in Western cultural ideas of the 'adventure'.

In many respects Simmel's relationship between inner and outer is similar to the broader social discussions about structure and agency. Given that social conditions are constantly changing, and that change is destabilising, this creates what Ulrich Beck (1992) has called 'risk society'. The social world we live in has been made by historical change and transformation, but we are not simply the product of our current circumstances as we can construct our own sense of identity. However, we can only do this within the social rules that set out the broader context. Modernity and its components of industrialisation, capitalism, surveillance and weaponry is defined by a scientific rationalism, the ambition of which is control of the physical world. It has been argued *that risk is the negative consequence of such sentiments and possibly the price to pay for humanity naïvely thinking that such control was possible in the first place* (Miles, 2001, p124).

Taking a modernist view of the world, Beck (1992) argues that a combination of technologies and human ambition for control have created a world where, although the evident risks of everyday life (such as builders falling off scaffolding, aircraft crashing and food poisoning) have been controlled through sophisticated Health and Safety Executive (HSE) driven risk-management strategies, the 'risks' that exist today and impact on all our lives are both greater than ever and less visible. Examples are terrorism attacks or fall-out from nuclear power generation, or infectious diseases such as AIDS, or 'super-bugs' resistant to antibiotics. In his argument for a 'risk society', Beck emphasises structural changes in modernisation as the catalyst for a risk society. Today, we appear to be less constrained by structure (e.g. there is more access to university, it is acceptable to 'come out' about sexual orientation and to have single sex marriages) but more constrained by a private fear of the risks generated by this changing society (e.g. Internet chat rooms, nuclear power, BSE). This has led, according to Furedi (1997), to a 'culture of fear' whereby we increasingly cocoon ourselves in layers of physical and social protection, cutting ourselves off from the real world while simultaneously relying on 'experts' to guide us through the complexities. Even this dependence is suspect because of the sometimes conflicting views presented by the scientific community. Moreover, although real risks may not be any greater than in previous generations, the communication of tragedy through a proliferation of media outlets may make it appear so. This is certainly the case with adventure activities that are clearly directly linked to risk.

Reflection Point 13.1

When two schoolgirls were swept to their deaths stream walking in Stainforth Beck (Beedie and Bourne, 2005), media coverage amplified the profile of the incident to imply that this type of tragedy could occur at any time to your children. The adventure education lobby's counter argument was that many lives are lost through obesity-related diseases such as strokes, heart attacks and diabetes resulting from inactive lifestyles (Bailie, 2004), but this was never adequately offered as a balanced argument. So, we are left with the impression that adventure activities are dangerous and that these risks should be avoided.

While the principle of a risk society defining our contemporary world is generally accepted by sociologists, not all subscribe to the environmental–structural argument presented by Beck. Giddens (1990, 1991), for example, through his theory of structuration (first introduced here in Chapter 4) develops insights to the relationship between risk and identity that emphasises 'reflexivity' – that is, as individuals we think consciously about our social circumstances and develop patterns of behaviour that may avoid risk, but equally might choose to engage with risk. More so than Beck, therefore, Giddens emphasises the proactive potential of engaging risk in so far as we all have the capacity to shape the structuring dimensions of life through individual actions. Despite most definitions of risk being 'the potential to lose something of value', it is possible to engage with risk in ways that are positive – that is, the potential to gain something of value (e.g. intrinsic satisfaction, physical capital, status or an affirmation of accumulated skill). It is in this spirit that adventure in society remains vibrant today, although, as we shall see in the discussion of the three forms of adventure below, the structure–agency framework remains a useful way of understanding adventure as a social phenomenon.

Types of risk and the management of risk

So, the control, reduction and potentially the elimination of risk is a central concern of the modern world. We are in, however, a society full of complexity, ambivalence and paradox: risk is a key example. In many ways we celebrate the idea of risk-taking as famous adventurers and their deeds are promoted in the media. There is a human fascination with adventure as the popularity of stories such as *Touching the Void* demonstrate. A further example is the way images of adventure sports are used in brochures to promote activity holidays, and, increasingly, as a positive attraction for schools operating in a competitive education market. A central paradox exists, however: this is that risk-based activities must be safe, particularly when school children are involved. It is this latter dimension of contemporary society that has led logically to the circumstance whereby risk assessment – that is, the prediction, calculation and quantification of risk – has become an essential part of everyday life.

Risk assessment as promoted by the HSE favours a cognitive position based on a set of assumptions that see the world governed by 'laws' that, once understood, lead to (complete) control of an environment. In this way of thinking, risk is objective and can be identified and positioned in the context of these laws. An alternative position, the one promoted through the sociological stance essential to this book, does exist however, which sees the world as socially constructed. The basic assumption here is that nothing is a risk or everything is a risk depending on the 'meaning' that we allocate to a particular circumstance, so that risk is subjective. The fact that both these positions exist demonstrates the complexity of modern society. Government-sponsored authorities such as AALA (the Adventure Activities Licensing Authority) have a difficult job to do because they must support and implement a bureaucratic system of control (objective) within adventure activity providers based upon a framework of risk assessment, but at the same time deal with an ongoing manipulation of the idea of risk in society based on emotional (subjective) responses to isolated 'news-worthy' incidents such as Stainforth Beck. Nevertheless, it is difficult to argue against a systematic organisation of adventure forms (such as adventure education) based on assessment of risk – the management of risk (and its implicit agenda of control over the natural world) has always been a part of adventure in all its forms.

Although risk can be both objective and subjective, all risk in adventure activities must be managed. When adventure meets sport it is the structural aspects of sport that contribute to managing adventure situations. Haddock (1993) identifies three types of risk: absolute risk (the uppermost limit of risk inherent in a situation with no safety controls), real risk (the amount of risk that exists at a point in time, that is, absolute risk adjusted by safety controls) and perceived risk (an individual's subjective assessment of the real risk present at any time). It has been suggested that people's perceptions of risk are influenced by a number of factors. These include: confidence level, leader, equipment familiarity, venue, experience level, mood, degree of tiredness, psychological make-up, awareness of limitations, knowledge of the situation and fear of the unknown. It can be argued that perceptions of risk are influenced by so many variables that 'risk' becomes a relative term because many of these components can be managed.

All adventure activities are managed to a greater or lesser extent. This is evidenced by the ubiquity of RAMS (Haddock, 1993), referring to 'risk analysis and management systems'. These are both formal (bureaucracy) and informal (social pressure to conform) so that today, for example, a round-the-world sailor would not be allowed to leave port without adequate navigation and safety equipment on board. RAMS change real risk to perceived risk by degrees but with the swing towards perception, the question is raised: what is *real* adventure? The logical culmination of a slide into adventure control is a mediated world (de Zengotita, 2005) where virtual adventure becomes more real than 'real' adventure. Such a circumstance is already identifiable with the technologies used to create indoor climbing walls – some of these (see the Living-Stone section of the Foundry in

Sheffield, for example) are 'as good as' proper rock climbing. Varley (2006) refers to such developments as 'post adventure' by which he means that the uncertainty of outcome which is the essence of adventure is controlled, rationalised and managed away leaving us with 'adventure flavoured' activities which are a far remove from the original notion of an adventure. The problem becomes how to acknowledge the point at which adventure is 'managed away' from the activity – as Simmel recognised, the 'centre' retains control.

Hard and soft adventure

Attempts to categorise, and thus manage adventure activities have some variations, but essentially all see 'hard' adventure as physically demanding, dangerous and exploratory. Examples would include high altitude mountaineering, cave diving, polar journeys, sailing in the Southern Ocean, white water kayak descents and other activities that generally require specialist competence, a substantial degree of independent decision making, physical fitness and an ability to extend comfort zones. Hard adventures are commonly undertaken in wild environments. Conversely 'soft' adventure is physical (i.e. active) but not demanding. It is controlled or managed, contained and recreational. Examples would include nature trail-type walking, off-road cycling on waymarked paths, pony trekking, piste skiing and other activities that make light demands on specialist skills, require average levels of fitness and generally operate in places that are neither remote nor wild environments.

Learning Activity 13.1

Martin Lyster's book *The Strange Adventures of the Dangerous Sports Club* (1997) explains, among other things, the first British-based bungy jumping 'trials' on Bristol Suspension Bridge above the Avon Gorge. Using the book and/or other sources, and drawing on ideas of risk management outlined in this chapter, explain how bungy jumping has become popular and how it fits into the framework of subjective and objective risk.

Peter Varley (2006) has taken this basic 'hard–soft' model and developed it into what he calls 'the Adventure Commodification Continuum'. This model, he argues, provides a basic framework for understanding adventure 'consumption'. The model has a vertical axis which moves from little or no risk management by experts to complete management, and a horizontal axis which at its intersection with the vertical axis has complete rationalisation, standardisation and marketing control, but by moving across acknowledges increasing natural and uncontrollable risk. Different adventure activities reside on different points of the continuum. At the left ('comfort and convenience') end of the continuum are staged events, balloon rides, bungy jumps and safari tours for example – engagement is considered to be 'shallow'. To the right (the 'chaos and death') end of the continuum are solo mountaineering ascents, open sea kayak crossings and accidental survival situations – engagement here is considered to be 'deep' and much closer to the original concept of adventure as exploration. The model is useful because it recognises that not all adventures are the same and that risk management is a key variable in determining the 'adventurousness' of the experience. The model is however constructed with an understanding of commodification exchange as its foundational premise and therefore, rather like all models taking a Marxist perspective, reduces the benefits of an adventure experience to a measurable exchange equation that takes little heed of other potential benefits gained by engaging with adventure activities – empowerment, fitness, self esteem and confidence for example. Nevertheless, it becomes clear that managing risk is a common element of all three forms of adventure outlined below.

Managing risk

Whether as an individual or as part of a group, when we become active in adventure pursuits we have to think through the extent and the type of risk that is integral to our chosen activity. There are four possibilities:

- **retain the risk** as the frequency and severity is low (e.g. valley walks, supervised educational 'pond dipping' trips);
- **reduce the risk** by using strategies such as planning from guidebooks, weather forecasts and training regimes (e.g. Duke of Edinburgh Award expeditions with valley-based campsites and 'distance supervision' of the walkers);
- **avoid the risk** in situations when management will not work (e.g. avoiding avalanche slopes, portaging difficult white water rapids, calling off a planned caving expedition because rain is forecast);
- **transfer the risk** by bringing in 'experts' such as mountain guides or by buying a 'package' from a reputable adventure tourism company (e.g. climbing on an indoor climbing wall). Thus, it becomes clear that adventure, risk and the management of risk are interrelated and form the foundational understanding for all forms of adventure.

The way that adventure is defined is continually being modified by the complex of social, political and economic forces operating today so that any definitions are actually 'works in progress' because, in the social world, circumstances are rarely located in clearly defined boundaries. It is important to understand that although 'education' and 'recreation' may have some common ground (e.g. to take up rock climbing involves learning about the sustainability of the climbing environment, the political circumstances of access and how to use climbing equipment), the ambition of each is subtly different. Similarly, there is common ground between 'adventure tourism' and 'adventure sports' (e.g. guided ski mountaineering in the Alps might operate alongside more conventional skiing). Moreover, it is hard to argue that an adventure package tour that takes people to other countries and involves enjoying alternative cultures has no educational value. Nevertheless, for the purposes of understanding adventure in society it is useful to use the three categories suggested. Assuming the sociological framework outlined above concerning a risk society, adventure can be seen as developmental (adventure education), escape (adventure recreation), commercial opportunity (adventure tourism) and competition (adventure sport). The following introduces a few of the key issues in each of these areas.

Adventure education

The use of wild places for enlightenment, education and personal development has a history that can be traced back to ancient times when ideas of 'rites of passage' and transformative points of growing up emerged across a range of cultures around the world – an example is the aboriginal 'walkabout'. These cultural phenomena along with documented innate drivers for exploration (variously known as the Ulysses factor) have contributed to a sense of adventure in humans that has been linked with cultural progress, power and domination and/or control of the known world and its extension to the unknown world. Thus, a link between adventure, exploration and education has always existed.

Colin Mortlock (1984) is arguably the foremost British adventure education theorist (see 'Research focus' section in this chapter). His theoretical ideas have two main elements. First, there is the notion of holistic development. Mortlock argues that conventional education overemphasises cognitive development at the expense of other areas of development. In a curriculum driven by classroom-based learning, there is little room for physical development and almost no room for emotional education. These latter two elements are balanced in his concept of holistic development as he argues that adventure-based learning not only engages the mind, but also requires physical action and, because of the risks inherent in the activities, is likely to generate apprehension and thus emotional engagement – there are real consequences with adventure activities.

Second, Mortlock recognised that adventure is not fixed but varies from person to person and from place to place, and even from time to time. His demonstration of this is the model of stages of adventure. This model sets risk on one axis against competence on the other. Mortlock recognises four 'stages' of adventure and suggests that 'adventure' is the best stage for learning. 'Frontier adventure' is the aspirational point for maximum satisfaction as a person's comfort zone is stretched, but the person just about remains in control of the circumstances.

Mortlock's (1984) model of adventure participation

- Stage 1 **Play** – this is physical activity with no real or perceived risk. Fear is absent.
- Stage 2 **Adventure** – this is activity that presents a challenge because there are real consequences of getting things wrong (a capsize in a kayak, for example). Here, competence is generally greater than the risks. Fear is buried.
- Stage 3 **Frontier adventure** – this level is finely balanced as the competence to deal with the challenge is tested to its limits. This is the level of maximal arousal where the intensity of the experience determines the positive outcomes. When things go well, it is at this level where there is a propensity to experience 'flow'. Fear is just about kept under control.
- Stage 4 **Misadventure** – here the scales tip the wrong way and, as the risks are greater than the participant's ability to deal with them, the outcome is likely to be physical and/or mental and emotional harm. Fear becomes panic.

The concentration required when active at one's 'frontier' promotes the potential for 'flow' experiences (Foley et al., 2003). Flow is an experience that is *engrossing, intrinsically rewarding and outside the parameters of worry and boredom* (Csikszentmihalyi and Csikszentmihalyi, 1999, p153). It is a transcendent state that offers a holistic personalised experience that, although possible in all walks of life, has most commonly been linked to adventure experiences.

The flow experience in adventure pursuits

- Activity requires skill and a challenge in a demanding environment.
- There is total immersion in the activity – participants do not see themselves as separate from what they are doing.
- Actions develop with a clear goal orientation such as getting to the top.
- Concentration is enhanced and 'disagreeable' parts of one's life are put to one side.
- There is a feeling of control as skill and challenge are matched.
- A sense of transcendentalism is emergent – an awareness of detail and a 'oneness' with the immediate surroundings.
- The sense of time is transformed – living for the moment through complete absorption.

Mortlock has made a strong case for adventure education through the application of his model, with activities mostly pitched at level two (adventure) so that maximum learning can happen because fear is buried. Nevertheless, there is still a tension between self exploration in 'dangerous' places while undertaking overtly risk-based activities and the idea of adventure as uncertainty of outcome, a tension neatly captured by Tom Price (1978, p651) in his essay 'Adventure by numbers':

> The idea of adventure is now widely accepted in education, yet when one comes to think of it, it is extraordinary that something that is by its very nature so fortuitous and uncertain of outcome should be harnessed and brought into the service of educational programmes . . . What is so valuable and formative in an adventure is the commitment it invariably calls for . . . The real core of the business is the enrichment through exposure to experiences and through various feasts of the senses . . . You cannot plan adventures. The best one can do is to let them happen.

Thus, a significant result of using adventure as a form of education is that it requires careful management of risk, perhaps to the elimination of uncertainty of outcome. This fundamental tension is also evident in adventure recreation and adventure tourism.

Adventure recreation and adventure tourism

Adventure tourism suggests activity, engaging risk and exploration. Moreover, exploration suggests some kind of boundary or frontier. The proximity of a frontier generates excitement in all sectors of tourism (defined by temporary spatial displacement) but is particularly important to adventure tourists as in this sector there is an expectation of considerable excitement. For example, Douglas (2007, p11) captures the appeal of the 'towering Matterhorn' to tourists in Zermatt in the Swiss Alps:

> *Most of us, however, are content to admire it from the town square or from a chair lift. Climbing the Matterhorn is a risky enterprise requiring experience and fitness, even if you hire a mountain guide. But if you're a fit walker and want to experience some of the thrill of Alpine climbing without taking on the Matterhorn, then Zermatt is an ideal place to have a go.*

Here the excitement is generated by the *brilliant world of dazzling snow and ice and cobalt skies beyond* and by feeling *wonderfully invigorated by the cold sharp air* (Douglas, 2007, p11). It is this physical and sensory attraction that appeals to tourists who aspire to climb mountains, but it is also the iconic status of certain mountains, a circumstance sustained by discursive agendas drawing on dramatic exploratory events such as the 1865 Matterhorn tragic success of the first ascent, that add to this excitement.

When adventure appears to offer an escape opportunity, the balance between structure and agency is apparent. According to Tejada-Flores (1978), choosing to do adventure activities is a 'game' that we choose to play (or not). These games are bounded by socially defined 'rules'. With adventure as recreation we choose to operate through our own decision making; when choosing to 'play' is part of an adventure tourism package, we are more likely to place our faith in the expertise of others. The model provided by H Brown (2000) provides a useful scale for discussing this idea. Brown's model moves from *Passenger to Participant to Partner to Practitioner* (Brown, H, 2000, p37) with a commensurate change in the level of personal responsibility. The 'passenger' is least involved in the decision-making experience, the 'participant' more so, while the 'partner' shares responsibility and the 'practitioner' has the skills, knowledge and expertise to operate more independently of a guide or instructor.

Applying this model to a package adventure tourism 'frame' seems useful in locating tourists at different levels of ability and influence. For example, thrill-seeking voyagers at the 'passenger' end of the continuum demand experiences *where it is expected that providers carry all the responsibility* (Brown, H, 2000, p37). The majority of adventure tourists may arguably come from a position where they *understand some of the risks in the situation, they accept that they need to act responsibly, pay attention and put into practice what they are told* (Brown, H, 2000, p37). These people can be thought of as 'participants', but all participants have the potential for self empowerment through the activities they undertake, even when these might be thought of as 'shallow' adventure as defined by Varley (2006). There are clearly commonalities here with the Brown model and the Varley (2006) continuum outlined above. Indeed, the potential to move across the continuum as experience, skill and judgment in adventure activities develop in a person – in the way that Brown (2000) suggests is an outcome of an active engagement in adventure activities – is a further critique of Varley. We are complicated beings operating in a world that is constantly in flux. For example, an observable trend in adventure tourism is the collapse of the difference between adventure guides and their clients. Increasingly, the most dedicated adventure tourists with an accumulation of experience undertake tours to participate in, for example, mountain biking, kayaking and off-piste skiing (with the latter offering helicopter-facilitated expeditionary trips). Due to the long-term nature of their involvement in the activity, time, money and physical investments are high with an accordant coalescence with their guides' characteristics. These individuals are operating in the role of 'partner' who *recognises that they need to take responsibility for assessing situations, understanding causes of problems and working-out in depth solutions and strategies, however they know that the instructor is still there to support them* (Brown, H, 2000, p38).

This progressive skill attainment of participants is a rational response to the risks that are integral to adventure activities. The very 'doing' of adventure brings with it a learning experience predicated on the acquisition of skill and experience that repositions the participant on the continuum. This process is supported by empirical evidence. An ethnographic study of kayakers notes: *the relationship between the participants and the guides was an involved two-way relationship, with participants both seeking and providing knowledge* (Kane and Zink, 2004, p336). At the most advanced end of the continuum the 'practitioner' (Brown, H, 2000, p38), has a completely independent ability to partake in adventure activities. Indeed, many such individuals can be noted to be driving the demand for an increasing amount of skills courses in various adventure activity disciplines. Information about provision from two premier adventure tourism companies – **www.adventure.co.nz** and **www.jagged-globe.co.uk** – shows a drift towards this kind of participant, so that, as with more conventional sports, people who undertake adventure pursuits, either as recreation or as adventure tourism, might be thought of as establishing an adventure-focused 'career'.

Swarbrooke et al. (2003) suggests that adventure tourists follow 'career' paths in that skill and experience lead to a demand for greater challenges. At Jagged Globe, for example, the mountain ascents advertised are given a code that reflects a combination of altitude, technical difficulty, remoteness and the physical stamina and skill required to make the ascent. Having successfully completed a 2C, for example, a client may plan for a 3A ascent for the following year. Literature from Jagged Globe suggests that 60 per cent of its clients return for further mountain ascents with them. Returning clients are more experienced and are likely to have progressed across the scale of Brown's model. Mountaineering appears to make demands on its participants because of the timescale of engagement in climbing and the 'seriousness' of the high mountain environment as hard adventure.

Climbing is not an 'homogenous sport' but a series of related activities, each with its own terrain, problems, satisfactions and rules (Tejada-Flores, 1978). These are a series of 'games': *the decision to start playing is just as gratuitous and unnecessary as the decision to start a game of chess.* The games are:

- The Bouldering Game;
- The Crag Climbing Game;
- The Continuous Rock-Climbing Game;
- The Big Wall Game;
- The Alpine Climbing Game;
- The Super-Alpine Game;
- The Expedition Game.

Ethical climbing then becomes the correct application of the socially derived rules. Moving through the framework reduces the rules so that to climb Everest ladders is permissible, but to use a ladder to climb a boulder is to miss the obvious point of experiential challenge. The rules of a lower order game can be applied to a higher order game but not vice-versa. This is an example of how social groups, in this case climbers, can control and define the parameters for the way adventure activities operate. The 'governing bodies' of climbing may exist, but in much less formalised ways than those of conventional sports.

Adventure sports

The boundaries between adventure as recreation and adventure as sport are not clearly defined. Broadly stated, the differences relate to the purpose of the activity, and in particular the degree of overt competition involved. Thus, many activities that might be thought of as recreational (e.g. surfing) do have a competitive arm (as in surf competitions – see **www.britsurf.co.uk**). Competitive urges vary with age, gender and situation so that even an activity demonstrably uncompetitive could become so (e.g. a Duke of Edinburgh expedition). Many of these competitive urges may come from more broadly based ideological positions (e.g. capitalism) and as such link more directly to issues of social status and distinction. Given the prominence of sport in our society, it would seem logical to suggest that adventure as sport is likely to grow. This is certainly the case in the USA where Jarvie has shown (2006, p270) that, whereas mainstream sports such as golf, ice hockey and soccer have shown modest growth (around 15 per cent), other mainstream sports such as tennis and baseball have seen dramatic declines in participation. Overall, the growth in mainstream sports is less than 2 per cent. Alternative sports conversely have grown by 245 per cent. Many of these alternative sports are what Wheaton (2004) calls 'lifestyle sports'. Many of these are adventure based and include kayaking, surfing, wakeboarding and indoor climbing. The biggest growth is seen in sports such as mountain biking and snowboarding at 420 per cent and 238 per cent respectively. This percentage change shows a rise in individual adventure sports and a decline in team-based sports.

Learning Activity 13.2

Parkour is a relatively new adventure activity which featured in the starting sequence to the 2006 James Bond film *Casino Royale*. Using web-based research, note its main features and explain where it originated. You should then make an assessment of how popular it has become with whom, and finally note where parkour takes place today. Summarise these points to contribute to a class-based discussion on where to position parkour in the framework of adventure (education, recreation/tourism, sport) set out in this chapter.

Drawing on ideas first set out by the cultural theorist Raymond Williams, Wheaton (2004) identifies the need to move beyond the simplistic categories of traditional/mainstream sport set against alternative/lifestyle sport. In particular, she identifies 'residual' and 'emergent' elements of sport culture: the suggestion here is that, rather than assume two categories, sports that 'emerge' as resistant to the dominant culture (for example, snowboarding on ski slopes) actually contain 'residual' evidence of mainstream sport. For example, snowboarding may be organised in zones within a ski-resort and may also develop racing categories, such as slalom, and rules not dissimilar to conventional skiing. Snowboarding is now also an Olympic sport. So, to think about adventure as sport requires incorporation of such ideas. When Wheaton (2004) discusses lifestyle sports, she identifies a number of characteristics that support Jarvie's (2006) suggestion that participation in alternative sports is growing and that many of these 'alternatives' are adventure based. Wheaton's list of lifestyle sport characteristics is included in the following (Wheaton, 2004, pp11–12).

Lifestyle sport characteristics

- Historically, a recent phenomenon with many 'new' sports such as wind surfing and snowboarding, or of re-emerging 'residual' sports such as surfing.
- Grass-roots participation rather than spectating, as with the X-Games, for example.
- Sports based on the consumption of new objects such as boards and bikes.
- Commitment in time and/or money to 'forms of collective expression', i.e. social identity.
- Participation as fun, hedonism, involvement, self-actualisation and 'flow', which is resistant to institutionalisation, regulation and commercialisation.
- Considerable emphasis on creative, aesthetic and performative expressions of sport.
- Predominantly white and middle class, but much more than just 'youth' participation. In some cases there is much less gender differentiation than in traditional sports.
- Predominantly individualistic in form.
- Predominantly non-aggressive activities that do not involve bodily contact.
- The places used are 'liminal' zones, usually without created or fixed boundaries.

Rural and wild places (such as beaches, hills, moors and woodlands) are popular because they feed a nostalgic desire for the simplicity and perceived authenticity of the past. However, urban places do feature with important growth sports such as parkour and the more specialist sports such as BASE jumping.

What this analysis tells us is twofold. First, that adventure as sport is a growing area attracting academic investigation that combines data collection and theoretical exploration. Second, that adventure sports are very broadly defined with a range from adventure as sport (for example, indoor climbing competitions) through to adventure as lifestyle choices (for example, being part of the social scene of surfing).

There are many examples of adventure as sport where mainstream sport frameworks of rules, regulations and competition are becoming evident. Some have existed for many years; an example here would be kayaking, which has long been an Olympic sport as flat water racing and as white water slalom since the Munich Olympics in 1972 (which marked this sport's arrival on the world stage by building one of the first artificial white water slalom courses). Others are much more recent, often because of residual pressures from those prominent in that sport. Climbing is a good example of this because historically the 'competition' was understood to be internal (with the 'demons' in one's head) or with the challenges consistent with wild nature – not with other climbers! However, after many years of vociferous debate, a compromise was reached in Britain whereby climbing competitions were allowed, but only on artificial walls, not natural crags (this is not necessarily the case in other countries). This circumstance also allowed the standardisation of routes climbed in competition and for variations in categories for males and females, children and adults, bouldering (unroped climbing above large mats) and roped lead climbing (where the roped climber must clip the rope into bolts placed at stages up the climb).

In both these examples, the sports people participating are usually following conventional participation patterns that include regular training regimes, diet controls, weight training and technique performance training – just like conventional sports people – to a level consistent with their ability and aspirations. Adventure sports of this kind enhance the profile of the 'star' performers. An interesting development has been the arrival of the 'adventure celebrity' – usually young, dynamic and very media literate, as a quick search through relevant websites will evidence (try *YouTube* for video clips of the professional climber Chris Sharma in action).

However, there are also examples of people who take up adventure sports as lifestyle choices at the other end of the range set out above. For many of these people the 'sport' becomes a way of escaping the strictures of everyday life – the attraction is that there appear to be few rules, regulations and competition. In this respect, the sport choices we make from the huge array of possibilities around us today are important determinants of our sense of identity: adventure becomes a consumer choice. The indications are that the processes of individualisation evident in contemporary Western societies are suited to adventure sports that are mostly about the person and the challenge rather than the team confrontation of many mainstream sports.

Learning Activity 13.3

You need to research and present information about a well-known person from adventure. Sources might include biographical and autobiographical accounts, obituaries, magazine contributions, websites, documentation from administrative perspectives such as editorials and club journals. For example, if you choose Alison Hargreaves you might use her book *A Hard Day's Summer* (1995) and the article by Douglas 'The mother of all climbs' (2007), and then refer to other media accounts of her achievements and Jim Ballard's own (1996) book about his life with Alison. Depending on who you select to research, you are likely to find both similarities and differences between what might be thought of as the old generation (e.g. Chris Bonington) and the new generation (e.g. Chris Sharma).

Research Focus

Colin Mortlock

My introduction to Colin Mortlock began when I was undertaking a PGCE in outdoor education in Bangor and the 'great man' came to deliver a guest lecture. He was quiet and unassuming, extraordinarily well informed and arguably, because of a series of publications throughout the 1970s (and thereafter), the most important 'adventure' theorist in the UK. At a time when 'adventure theory' did not really exist he forged important academic precedents and in doing so made the case for adventure education a coherent and rational cause. Colin Mortlock was a historian graduate of Keble College Oxford who went on to take a teaching award in physical education (PE) from Loughborough. His early teaching career in PE included outdoor pursuits and his growing expertise and knowledge led him to a position of Head of the Woodlands Outdoor Centre in the Wye valley in 1965. The formative years he spent there led to a series of short but focused publications which encapsulated his central thesis concerning the transformative potential of outdoor adventure journeys. In *Adventure Education and Outdoor Pursuits* (1973), which was published by the PE Association, he began formulating his ideas about holistic education. He argued that conventional secondary education over emphasised cognitive learning (in classrooms using standard pedagogical methods) at the expense of physical education (more of which was required to balance the cognitive) and yet both these areas in turn paid lip-service to emotional development. It is the latter component of holistic development that adventure education can facilitate, as well as encompassing elements of cognitive learning – albeit outside the classroom – and, by definition physical education through engaging with active pursuits.

Mortlock's emergence as a teacher was formative in developing his thinking – it was what he felt passionate about – and this background had a logic that aligned PE and 'adventure' from the 1970s in ways that anticipated the 'Outdoor and Adventurous Activities' integrated into the PE National Curriculum as it emerged in the 1980s. I picked up the story in 1978 with his publication *Adventure Education*, a 44-page monograph that struck me as impressive for two main reasons; first it was published by the author himself and second, the clarity and succinctness of its case. Precision and clear thinking has been a hallmark of Mortlock's publications. This is evident in arguably his most famous and influential book *The Adventure Alternative* (1984). Although much of the substance of this book had arrived in his 1970s publications (which included a rock climbing guide to the Pembrokeshire sea cliffs), *The Adventure Alternative* is the text that is most widely cited by adventure theorists the world over. Mortlock's conceptualisation of holistic development, his sensitising to environmental degradation and other issues of journeying outdoors (which anticipated our contemporary 'green' agendas by at least a decade) and his four stage model of adventure (set out in the chapter above) have proved enduring and resilient as adventure theory has emerged. In his next book *Beyond Adventure* (2001) he moves on to explore journeys in wild places as the building blocks of an inner journey that can reveal profound truths about our self and our place in the world. I completed my own Mortlockian journey of sorts when I heard him speak again in 2003. Older and perhaps 'wiser' myself, I asked him what had happened to his thinking about adventure education for young people today, and his reply was guarded. It is possible that, like many of us that take an interest in adventure and how it discursively influences society, he recognises the immense complexity of the relationship between risk, adventure and opportunity: to paraphrase what Bear Grylls said on a BBC Radio Two interview (17 October 2009): young people today don't lack for ambition and adventure, what they lack in the tightly regulated and constrained modern world is opportunity. While Mortlock's interests might have moved on into the deep reflective world of immersion in wild nature – a world of shrinking wilderness and increasing commodification, as the chapter above outlines – there are many people like myself whose lives have been transformed by his inspirational thinking.

Chapter Review

Developing Mortlock's argument that adventure is located in the person undertaking the activity, it has been suggested that people will have different adventure thresholds, and that different activities and different places will contribute to the difficulties of standardising the adventure experience in relation to education, recreation, tourism or sport. However, two important points can be made. First, following Beck, we do live in a risk society, a paradoxical outcome of human desire to control the modern world. Second, following Simmel, we strive for individuality in a world where multiple choices about what we might do are omnipresent. If those choices involve adventure activities, we feel the 'pull of the centre' – invisible but powerful forces that shape our behaviour towards conformity, even as we strive for individuality. Such forces have been heavily determined by commercial interests (such as determinants of 'fashion'), suggesting that capitalist ideologies continue to operate. So, adventure does still exist, and we are free agents in the way we choose to engage with such activities, but we are also operating in a social world that retains structural controls over our ambitions. Modernity was built on exploration and the 'adventure' of risk-taking entrepreneurs. Adventure is a malleable term, but here the focus has been on adventure as sport – that is, physical activities that engage with risk. Most of the theoretical models explained in this chapter represent a scale or a continuum. We can think of adventure sports as a continuum. On the left side of such a continuum there are educational, recreational and/or touristic forms where skills and personal qualities are developed and tested across a range of activities and in different places. Additionally, these sports may be to the right of a continuum where structuring dimensions of sport (such as competitions, rules, regulations, league tables and training regimes) position the activities more obviously in the realm of conventional sports. Many activities span the continuum with positions to the left and right. Climbing is an example, found both as exploratory efforts in wild places demanding survival skills as well as climbing skills (to the left), yet also as indoor climbing competitions with referees and media coverage that encourages sponsorship and other commercial activity (to the right).

Adventure sports therefore offer the potential for people to be 'sporty' in ways that are less structured and more individualised than in the mainstream sports explored elsewhere in this book. In this respect adventure sports might be seen as 'emergent' in that they can challenge conventional ways of doing sport – a good example is parkour, an alternative interpretation of using an urban environment for physical enjoyment through imaginative challenge. When sports choices merge with lifestyle choices, conventional standards of socialisation and stratification may be redefined – for example, 'new' adventure sports may have less gender differentiation than more traditional sports. Surfing is not strictly speaking a new sport, but as a lifestyle choice it has attractions for both genders as participants. However, many sports offer evidence of 'residual' characteristics that operate to transform this emergent energy into something much closer to conventional sport formats. It is often the power of commercial and business interests that determine this resistance to change, and with the emergence of professional adventurers the ongoing battlegrounds of structure versus agency and the individual versus society evidenced elsewhere in this book remain.

Further Reading

Barnes, P and Sharp, R (2004) *Outdoor Education*. Lyme Regis: Russell House Publishing.
Short chapters covering a full range of adventure education issues. Many of these, such as gender, risk management and professionalism are useful as they cover issues relevant to the understanding of sport and adventure.

Rinehart, R and Sydnor, S (eds) (2003*) To the Extreme: Alternative Sports Inside and Out*. Albany: SUNY Press.
A well-organised book that offers a collection of paired essays about a whole range of adventure sports. The essays complement each other as one is written by an academic and one is written by a practitioner from that sport. Sports covered include sky-dancing, surfing, mountain biking, snowboarding and climbing.

Swarbrooke, J, Beard, C, Leckie, S, and Pomfret, G (2003) *Adventure Tourism: The New Frontier*. Oxford: Butterworth-Heinemann.
This is a textbook about adventure tourism. It draws on a theoretical framework derived from tourism studies rather than sociology, but it does have some interesting observations about the relationship between adventure and tourism.

Macfarlane, R (2003) *Mountains of the Mind*. London: Granta.
This very readable book is the best explanation of the social construction of mountains I have read. The text mixes accessible theoretical ideas of social and cultural context with accounts by the author of his own mountaineering experiences.

Wheaton, B (ed) (2004) *Understanding Lifestyle Sports*. London: Routledge.
Similar to the Rinehart and Sydnor book in that the adventure sport focus determines the structure of the book (chapters on climbing, windsurfing, snowboarding, etc.). This book, however, is more directly concerned with the relationship between doing these sports and the resulting sense of social identity.

Browne, D (2004) *Amped: How Big Air, Big Dollars and a New Generation Took Sports to the Extreme*. London: Bloomsbury.

Ethnographic data combines with informed argument to show that commercial interests are powerfully deterministic of how the 'buzz' sports (skateboarding and snowboarding in particular) have developed.

Curran, J (1999) *High Achiever: The Life and Times of Chris Bonington*. London: Constable.

One of the great 'significant others' in the sport of mountaineering and he's still alive and active!

MacArthur, E (2002) *Taking on the World*. London: Penguin.

At one level this book tells the story of MacArthur's race to break the solo round-the-world sailing record – and it is a gripping account, especially the crossing of the Southern Ocean. The book offers many additional insights if one applies a sociological 'lens': particularly useful are themes of risk management, the influence of technology and the modernist desire to set and break records. MacArthur is a sailing professional, dependent on sponsorship to supply her boats, but symbolically representative of a female achieving fame in an adventure setting largely dominated by men. Lastly, the book suggests that our oceans may well constitute the last great wilderness on our planet – that adventurers (male or female) who journey in such places can still be hailed as heroes or heroines suggests that residual forms of adventure still have considerable popular appeal.

Useful websites

- www.adventure.co.nz
- www.jagged-globe.co.uk
- www.britsurf.co.uk

Chapter 14
Sport and community

Peter Craig, Paul Beedie and Gordon Mellor

Issues of identity and values are intrinsically difficult and controversial. They raise questions which go to the very heart of what we mean when we talk about concepts of citizenship, community and civil society.

(Denham Report, 2001, p12)

We miss community because we miss security, a quality crucial to a happy life, but one which the world we inhabit is ever less able to offer . . .

(Bauman, 2001, p144)

Sporting and cultural opportunities can play an important part in re-engaging disaffected sections of the community, building shared social capital and grass roots leadership through improved cross-cultural interaction.

(Denham Report, 2001, p28)

This chapter has two main aims. The first is to suggest ways in which sociology seeks to understand sport and its relationship to community. The second is to contextualise the major themes of this book. Our objectives are to:

- introduce you to some of the sociological theories and concepts that help explain the relationships between modern society, community and sport;
- help you explore some of the ways sport is used to address issues of cultural diversity;
- help you critically evaluate the relationship between major sports events and the possibilities for community sport.

Learning Objectives

By the end of the chapter you should be able to:

- give sociological explanations of the following terms:
  - civil society;
  - community;
  - communitarianism;
  - social capital;

- explain how sport is connected to these social structures and processes;
- describe why a community sport legacy is seen to be essential in the planning and organisation of major sports events such as the 2012 Olympics;
- provide an evaluation of the 'power of sport' to help reverse social fragmentation and the loss of community;
- explain why sport is regarded as an important activity in the development of social capital.

Introduction: sport and community – the power of sport?

This book has set out how modern sport is connected to processes of social and cultural differentiation and how these are influenced by unequal power relations. We have shown that the way people have access (or not) to various forms of capital is particularly important. The world is rapidly transforming and sport is an important agent of change.

Through your exploration of these debates you should now be convinced that sport in the UK and Ireland is much more than an enjoyable set of competitive physical activities. Sport is rooted into the very fabric of the social world in ways we often take for granted. Given its social, cultural and economic significance it is not surprising that governments and sport sociologists such as Sugden and Tomlinson (2002) now openly talk about the '*power of sport*'. A report by the Institute for Community Cohesion (ICoCo) uses this very term. In its introduction it claims that:

> The power of sport is huge. It can transform people's lives in so many ways. It can improve personal health, build teamwork and even turn the most disaffected of young people into disciplined athletes . . . Sport can also change communities. Sport can unite communities – and the country as a whole – in common cause.
>
> (ICoCo, 2006, p1)

This belief in the power of sport to positively impact people's lives will be explored in what follows with a view to critically evaluating the relationship between policy, sport and community. The complexity of the social, economic and cultural issues that inform this discussion are summed up by the following two quotations as the government's ambition is set alongside the applied perspective offered by the ICoCo.

> We need to promote sporting activity across racial and religious boundaries. Sport should be a great unifier . . . over the next six years we should be aiming to reduce to zero the number of people who play only with and against people of their own race and religion. Get it right and the legacy from the Olympics will not just be medals, or sporting infrastructure, or regeneration in East London, or a positive image of Britain abroad, but vital bridges between communities who have used sport to promote tolerance and understanding.
>
> (David Miliband MP, Scarman Memorial Lecture, 31 January 2006)

. . . sport can also just reflect society's divisions too. All of our inequalities are reflected on the
sports field and, all too often, sports activities are completely divided failing to grasp the
opportunity to build bridges between communities.

(ICoCo, 2006, p1)

Today within Britain and Ireland the problems of poverty, social inequality and poor social
mobility are combining with a number of processes that are rapidly transforming both countries.
One of the most potent is the human impact of globalisation in terms of the unprecedented global
flows of vast numbers of people and how this has increased levels of cultural diversity. For many, this
rapid increase in racial and ethnic diversity is a major cause of concern (Wetherell, 2007) that needs
to be addressed by creative policies that can help increase social cohesion.

However, these problems are not new. Stretching back many generations Britain and Ireland have
seen numerous and at times violent confrontations between their diverse communities. While the
problems of Northern Ireland's divided society have been thoroughly examined (Darby, 1983;
Keogh and Haltzel, 1993; Dunn, 1995) the causes and ramifications of the more recent levels of
civic violence have become closely associated with increasing ethnic and cultural diversity (Denham,
2001). For many of those living in places directly impacted by these changes, this has created
understandable feelings of dislocation and fear (Denham, 2001). These feelings have in turn
produced a number of problematic social outcomes. One has been the increasing development of
segregated communities within which different ethnic groups are effectively leading 'parallel lives'
(Wetherell, 2007). Another has been the rise in radical right wing political groups such as the British
National Party and the English Defence League and the rising threat of violent confrontation.

More positively, another outcome is that many people in Britain (Maxwell, 2009) and Ireland
(Scheibner and Morrison, 2009) are recognising the urgent need to understand how and why
community cohesion is under threat. There are, however, practical issues such as how to create and
sustain community projects – many of which are sport based – which celebrate diversity while helping
to build and sustain the levels of trust and social engagement. Clearly both are required to build the sort
of progressive, community-based, solidarity that our societies now need (ICoCo, 2006; Tam, 2007).

Modern society, community and sport

Sociological perspectives of community

In their attempts to understand the structural and interpersonal realities of modernity sociologists
have often assumed that there is an essential distinction between the parts of social life dominated
by the institutions of the 'modern state' and the residues of traditional life characterised by the desire
for and the benefits of a shared communal life (Bauman, 2001; Delanty, 2003). Although somewhat
of a simplification, many of the classic sociologists such as Weber tended to view modern communal
life as the ever shrinking part of a social world that had yet to be fully rationalised, organised and
controlled by the forces of modernity and its 'iron cage' of modern state bureaucracy (Wagner,
1994). One of the prevailing sociological perspectives common to much of this work was that
modern society seemed to have an insatiable appetite to colonise and administer all aspects of

human affairs (Wagner, 1994). For many on the left of the political spectrum who viewed the power of capitalism and liberal individualism to be socially divisive, this was something to be welcomed; for those on the right these were processes that had to be resisted.

These debates have been associated with two interlinked terms: civil society and community.

Definition: civil society

An arena between the spheres of the state, on the one hand, and domestic and interpersonal relations on the other.

(Jarvie, 2003b, p141)

Definition: community

A mode of belonging that is symbolic and communicative rather than an actual institutional arrangement, and that is variable, capable of sustaining modern and radical social relationships as well as traditional ones.

(Delanty, 2003, p31)

As a counterpoint to an ever expanding impersonal and rationalised modern world, early sociological analyses of community were increasingly orientated towards two connected but distinctive debates. One is focused on perceptions of loss, absence and nostalgia for more communal ways of living (Bauman, 2001). The other emphasises that within the lived realities of everyday modern life people have a need for cultural activities and communal spaces to establish shared meaning and interpretations that underpin a sense of shared reality. This reality is in turn allied to the development of a sense of belonging whose connections stretch from the local across social divisions to the imagined perceptions of a shared national community (Anderson, B, 1983; Preston, 1997; Edensor, 2002). Essential to this construction of community are the ways different cultural groups share familiar and accessible social spaces. Within urban Britain and Ireland these would typically be the neighbourhood and its streets, parks, local schools, pubs, shops, churches and sport clubs.

Bauman (2001) argues that the political and public discourses surrounding the use of the term community have a contemporary resonance as they present images of security and social solidarity making powerful and emotive desires for identity and belonging seem attainable. However, for Bauman (2001, p9) there is a problem in that for many this 'imagined' reality of community remains a *dream impossible to realise*. Hence, though these understandings of community continue to retain a very powerful appeal, there is also no doubt that they have also become problematic and possibly unsustainable.

Delanty (2003), in one of the most detailed contemporary sociological examinations of the concept of community, suggests that in its contemporary form we need to accept that most of the community settings people now live in are no longer bounded by traditional modern representations of identity and belonging based on relatively stable perceptions of ethnicity, religion, gender or class. He argues that we now need to understand community as *an expression of a highly fluid communitas – a mode of belonging that is symbolic and communicative rather than an actual institutional arrangement, and that it is variable, capable of sustaining modern and radical social relationships as well as traditional ones* (p31).

Community is, therefore, far more than a 'place' or some abstract manifestation of shared cultural practices that might form the basis of our communication and interactions with others (Johnson, 2007). The social realities of communal living create a tension between our ability to act autonomously and the 'responsibilities' of modern life – its rules and regulations – that invariably 'discipline' our capacity to act (Bourdieu, 1984; Giddens, 1991; Foucault, 1976). Being a member of a community demands that we participate in activities that demonstrate to others our faith, loyalty, solidarity and commitment (Rogaly and Taylor, 2007; Alexander, 2007). It is these sentiments and the processes that underpin their production and reproduction that have formed the basis of much sociological debate about the political dimensions of community and those who are deemed to be its 'citizens'. In the context of contemporary concerns about social fragmentation (Wetherell, 2007), the political stance in the quotes cited at the start of the chapter, can be seen to be rooted in a pragmatic as well as an ideological desire for a reinvigorated sense of solidarity (Giddens, 1994), rather than the failed policies of multiculturalism (Phillips, 2005) and the liberal individualism of the market and consumerism (Speth, 2008; Cable, 2009).

Definition: communitarianism
A political philosophy stressing the importance of community and shared values for social order and stability.

(Bilton et al., 1996, p504)

Communitarianism is a highly contested political concept which evokes a variety of theoretical debates that attempt to focus attention on the tensions between the freedoms and rights of the individual and the responsibilities of citizenship.

(Delanty, 2003)

The 'communitarian turn' may well reflect the desire in many to address some of the excesses, inequalities and insecurities of our 'individualised society' (Bauman, 2001). Its recognition of the need for civic renewal and the concomitant development of a range of community-based projects can be argued as offering the possibility of empowerment (Tam, 2007). However, there also tends to be an inherent conservatism in many aspects of these policies that stresses the need for *small government, small groups, voluntarism and patriotism* (Delanty, 2003, p91). The conflicts around recourses, identity and belonging that exist in these communities are socially constructed and institutionally systemic. The idea (however appealing) that a renewed sense of citizenship and social integration can be promoted through the work of local community groups using activities such as sport has, not surprisingly, been the subject of critical and somewhat sceptical sociological analyses (Long and Sanderson, 2001).

Reflection Point 14.1

The Labour government (2009) has put forward an action plan for civil renewal called 'Together we can' (**http://togetherwecan.direct.gov.uk/**). This policy commits many of the government departments, including the Department of Culture, Media and Sport to a wide ranging set of action points that are intended to systematically extend how people perceive their citizenship. Its aim is to give local people and local communities more influence and power to improve their lives. Although this plan came into being some time after Delanty (2003, p90) put forward his assessment of what he terms 'governmental communitarianism', it reflects many of the ways the discourse of community has continued to be absorbed into official policy-making.

These debates emphasise political ideologies which impact on sport organisations and their implicit values. For example, individual sports such as athletics and tennis reflect an emphasis on competition, hard work and success. The rules governing these sports are focused on the fairness of the system and the rights of the individual inside a self-chosen and autonomous desire to competitively test oneself against another. Team sports on the other hand emphasise the need for the individual to subjugate their own interests to the needs of the group or team.

Learning Activity 14.1

Based on the debates and issues raised above, here are some questions to consider:

- Can you describe and explain your understanding of the characteristics of community?
- What, if anything, makes you care about community?
- How far do you agree that Bauman (2001) is right to claim that today 'community is an impossible dream to realise'?
- How strongly do you consider yourself to be defined by the 'place' you grew up in?
- What role has your participation in sport played in developing your sense of community?

Community, citizenship and sport

Communitarian debates about citizenship are about the 'politics of recognition' in our transition to a 'multicultural society'. This explains policy emphasis on equality and the production of a system of sport organisations that are legally bound to celebrate the rights of *all* individuals whatever their gender, race, religion, disability or sexual orientation. This is a vision of sport that takes on a global dimension through the work of the IOC who proudly state that the Olympic mission is: *To bring the peoples of the world together, the Olympic Movement develops programmes that provide concrete responses to social inequality* (IOC Values, 2009).

Though most of the discussion so far has focused on issues relating to diversity and multiculturalism, it is important to recognise that other groups are connected to these processes and policy frameworks. As we have detailed in previous chapters, it is often women who have taken the lead in arguing for more equity within society and more specifically within sport. This is a point emphasised by the Women's

Sports and Fitness Foundation (WSFF, 2009: **www.wsff.org.uk/about/**) who advocate a society of active women and see sport as fundamentally important to achieving this aim.

The assumption evident in this and many of the policy documents put out by UK government departments such as the Department for Culture, Media and Sport, 'think tanks' such as the Institute for Community Cohesion and by the national governing bodies of sport and Sport England, is that sport has a proven capacity to contribute to the development of citizenship, integration and social cohesion (Jarvie, 2006). However, this assumption seems to gloss over the capacity of groups to use sport as a marker of their own exclusive identity. At some levels this is not seen as particularly problematic as it is an accepted part of our sporting culture that rival fans gather at sport stadia to urge on 'their' team, to berate the opposition with songs and chants with the expected culmination of the celebration of the sporting demise of their rivals. Sport has always had traditions that promote rivalries that are strongly connected to national, local, ethnic, class and gender identities. As Craig and Rees (1994) in their analysis of sport in South Africa and Craig and Reid (1999) have argued in their analysis of Celtic culture, sport has as much capacity to divide and create conflict as it does to unify and provide valuable bridges that cross the many divides that fracture our local and national communities.

Over the past two decades the sociological analysis of sport in the Northern Irish, Irish and Scottish contexts (Sugden and Bairner, 1993; Jarvie, 2003b; Bradley, 2007) highlights that, if sporting practices become aligned to political, social and economic practices that systematically marginalise or threaten what people hold to be legitimate identities, then far from being a force for solidarity, sport is one of the contributing factors reinforcing social and cultural divisions and conflict. In his more recent discussion of this issue, Jarvie (2006, p71) provides an important commentary detailing that sport has the ability to contribute to *strong forms of cultural identity* that may help *foster forms of fundamentalism that might take little recognition of the ways in which it might contribute to human rights violations, or as a spectacle help to conceal forms of injustice, or poverty, or mal-distribution of wealth*. Moreover, as Jarvie (2006) also argues, the 'feel good factor' aligned to sport generally and massive sports events such as the 2012 London Olympics specifically, tends to displace critical and questioning voices.

Learning Activity 14.2

If you think about how you might have heard various views on the 'power of sport' from parents, teachers, coaches, politicians and the media, you should be able to recognise that it is relatively easy for politicians, civic leaders, the media and sport organisations to slip into uncritical (if we were to use a more formal sociological term here it might be communitarian) representations of sport, that for those who harbour strong feelings of displacement, social disadvantage and discrimination merely reinforces their scepticism and enhances further their feelings of marginalisation.

●●● ▶

Learning Activity 14.2 continued

1. Take some time to ask your family, friends, coaches and team-mates to tell you what they think about the positive role sport can play in our society. Listen carefully to their responses and see if they reflect some of the ideas detailed above. If possible, and always being sure to be very sensitive to the person's feelings, see if you can ask them to provide evidence to support their views.
2. Start paying close attention to the way sport, particularly international events like the FIFA World Cup and the Olympic Games is discussed by politicians, civic leaders, sport organisations and those responsible for staging these events. Try and identify if these views represent some of the themes identified above.

Having done these two tasks you should consider both the sources of these opinions and whether any evidence was presented to support them.

Sport and social capital

In recent years the work of French social theorist Pierre Bourdieu (1986), has increased both academic and political interest in how sport (Giullianotti, 2004; Jarvie, 2006) can help generate different forms of capital – notably economic, cultural, social and physical capital.

Definition: economic capital

For Bourdieu (1986), economic capital is not merely defined by objective economic wealth. Economic capital needs to be understood as the ability to control and direct the use of economic resources such as financial wealth or physical assets so as to benefit one's own interests (or those of your group), and the extent of the wealth and resources that can be used in this way.

Definition: cultural capital

For Bourdieu (1986), cultural capital is defined by access to cultural processes and products. These include the ways by which educational, social and intellectual knowledge can be used to advantage the social and economic position of a particular individual or group.

Definition: social capital

For Bourdieu and Wacquant (1992, p119), social capital refers to the sum of the resources, actual or virtual, that accrue to an individual or group by virtue of possessing a durable network of more or less institutionalised relationships of mutual acquaintance and recognition.

For Putnam (2000, p19), social capital refers to connections among individuals – social networks and the norms of reciprocity and trustworthiness that arise from them.

Definition: bonding social capital

For Putnam (2007), bonding social capital refers to ways that social capital and its associated networks and social practices help produce and reproduce distinct homogeneous groups of people. Within sport the ways in which fanship operates is an example of bonding social capital in that connections between fans and their club are often directed at producing exclusive identities based on loyalty for the particular team while at the same time defining most other teams as rivals.

Definition: bridging social capital

For Putnam (2007), sport also has the capacity to produce bridging social capital in that sport necessarily creates social networks between socially heterogeneous groups. In other words sport relies on groups forming leagues, competitions and governing organisations that have a high degree of mutual interdependence.

Much of Bourdieu's (1986) work was directed at understanding how social distinctions, particularly in respect to social class, are socially produced and reproduced. For Bourdieu (1986), capital and therefore class power has at least three dimensions: economic, cultural and social capital. Bourdieu's concept of social capital emphasises how class power and conflict is directed by the ability of an individual or group to advance vested interests. The benefits of social capital stem from the capacity of a group's social networks to create supportive relationships and 'mutual' obligations and how these are then used to enhance the social standing of the group and its members. Social capital therefore acts as a vital resource in the social struggles between groups. For instance, for the middle classes, membership of golf or tennis clubs provide them with a range of mutual benefits that go far beyond the playing of the sports. Business and social contacts can all be enhanced through the membership of these clubs that not only advantage their members but also reinforce their distinctiveness from other classes. In this sense social capital does not act as a way of bringing diverse groups together but does the reverse – it acts to keep them socially separated.

More recently, the work of Robert Putnam (2007) and his rather different conceptualisation of social capital has become very influential. For Putnam (2007), what matters most is not the ways social capital can create conflict between its diverse groups but how within communities cultural organisations and traditions help promote values of trust, commitment and solidarity. According to Lin (2001), the extent that people are engaged in voluntary organisations such as those that typify most community sport, is a reflection of the social capital available. If Putnam is correct, then community-based organisations are vital in counteracting the divisive effects of cultural diversity and building the bridging mechanisms necessary for social cohesion (Jarvie, 2006). For these reasons, Putnam (2007) argues that social capital has two very different forms: bonding social capital and bridging social capital.

Sport, bonding and bridging social capital

The Olympic Games and other global sports events offer the potential to both reflect in the glory of elite athletic success and build a community sport legacy on the communal momentum achieved by these significant others. When people view the nation's athletes successfully competing and proudly representing their country, the images that are beamed into our homes, pubs and clubs of our sporting heroes wrapped in the national flag can have a profound impact. Looking across most of our major sports it is evident that the diversity of the nation is represented. Many of these new heroes are from black and minority ethnic backgrounds, they may be disabled or able-bodied, their sexuality is largely seen as irrelevant. Viewing these athletes wearing their national colours or standing proudly as the national anthem is played, serves to remind us that we live in a society increasingly characterised by its diversity not by its sameness. In that sense international sport provides us with an image of Britain or Ireland that connects people to the nation's sporting history and heritage, while at the same time serving to define a sense of national identity, connecting people to the present and its own transforming realities. Understood in this way sport produces a social process that helps bond and unify society.

Another major interest for Putman is how voluntary associations have a positive influence on the social interactions and levels of co-operation between individuals and groups (Putnam, 2007). He suggests they improve the flow of information about the trustworthiness of individuals and allow for the reputations of individuals (and groups such as sports clubs) to be transmitted and refined. They also create a social framework within which past successful collaborations between individuals and groups can be remembered and act as a 'template for future collaboration' (Putnam, 1993, pp173–174). This is the process that lies at the heart of what Putnam terms *bridging social capital*.

Understood in this way, participation in sporting activities and membership of sports clubs and organisations create a range of benefits for individuals, groups and the wider community. Supporting this perspective, Burnett's (2006) analysis of the development of 'active community clubs' in South Africa suggests that even in the highly fractured, impoverished and violent urban contexts of post-apartheid South Africa, structured sport programmes have the capacity to generate social capital opportunities for young people.

Sport, multicultural communities and identity

In the modern, globalised and networked world, most people now have the capacity to develop new forms of community and create new and sometimes radical views of belonging and solidarity based on religion, ethnicity, gender, disability and lifestyle choices. These in turn are transforming the world of sport and the roles that sport plays within that world. Elsewhere we have discussed the 'running phenomenon', which illustrates the point about change: running communities traditionally formed around athletic and road running clubs but now people who are unable to commit to conventional club membership can join a virtual running club (**www.uknetrunner.co.uk**) to collate information about races and share their experiences with other members via blogs and other postings. This breaking down of conventional social boundaries is connected to the rise of multiculturalism.

Sport and multicultural communities

Social, cultural and political transformations have been created by rapid inward flows of people into countries whose cultures and traditions are often quite distinct from those of the (im)migrant. As Bourne (2007, p1) details, there is today little need to debate the reality of 'multiculturalism' because it is self-evident in the UK as ethnic groups have settled and their customs, traditions and diversity have merged into the mainstream. Thus, Delanty (2003, p92) is able to state: *No discussion of community can avoid the question of multiculturalism.*

In much of the work of the founding fathers of sociology there was little concern regarding this matter as the cultural identity of a society was uncontroversial. When it was deemed to be an issue it was mostly seen as a structural problem relating to the need to develop more effective mechanisms of assimilation. The inevitable failure of this process has had a number of outcomes. Some of the initial populist reactions to the changing demographic characteristics of British society, such as racism, which often characterised these reactions, would today be seen by most as inappropriate and illegal. In its more formal responses governmental and legislative accommodations to this increasing cultural diversity were largely dealt with through social policies of integration and equality legislation.

In the recent past, segregation, discrimination and racist attitudes were commonplace in many sports, whereas now all of these would be deemed unacceptable. The question faced by sports organisations today is not how can sport be an exclusive domain for one particular racial or ethnic group, but how sport might remove barriers to participation and how can it act as a mechanism to build trust and solidarity between diverse communities.

Definition: assimilation
The 'absorption' of ethnic minority and immigrant population cultures into the cultures and practices of the host society.

Definition: integration
The processes whereby a minority group adapts itself to a majority society and is accorded equality of rights and treatment.

(Henry, 2005, p4; Amara et al., 2004, p5)

The discourses within liberal multiculturalism assumed that once people had equal rights then the dynamics of a democratic political system, allied to market forces, consumer culture and individual lifestyle preferences, would intercede (Delanty, 2003). The expectation was that the emerging multicultural society would be transformed into a 'melting pot' characterised by the new social and cultural formations enabling integration to take place and an overarching shared identity to be established. Twenty years on, these utopian visions seem rather naïve. The reality for the UK and more recently Ireland, has been the largely unfulfilled aspiration for co-operation and respectful co-existence (Henry, 2005; Scheibner and Morrison, 2009; Maxwell, 2009). For many, particularly in the often highly fragmented and decaying housing estates that characterise many cities, the predominant experience has been one of increasing social fragmentation, insecurity and hostility. One reaction to these outcomes has been that this view of multiculturalism has started to be radically reassessed (Bourne, 2007) with the failures of multiculturalism potentially leading to a danger of Britain *sleep-walking into segregation* (Phillips, 2005).

Sport and emergent forms of identity

One of the social theorists whose work has been of great significance in understanding some of the far-reaching and profound changes that have been impacting the modern world is Manuel Castells (1997, 1998). Castells' work has helped chart the way that new forms of technology and flows of information have impacted the structural characteristics of modern societies. In our increasingly 'networked' and individualised world, Castells (1998) argues that a new politics of difference has emerged that is reasserting the power and attraction of communal identity. This has permitted numerous diasporas to revive the commitment to their original cultures and national communities. In recent times Britain and Ireland's membership of the European Union (EU) has meant that both countries have become powerful magnets for economic migrants from the poorer countries of the EU. While Britain's colonial past has meant that migration into the UK has been a long-standing problematic process, in the case of Ireland, the impact of inward migration and the problems of racism and ethnic tension are a relatively new social concern.

The problem is balancing the economic benefits of this migrant labour force with the identity issues created by the arrival of many thousands of migrants into Britain and Ireland's towns and cities. Both countries face the need to create community-based social structures that can help people safely explore the often very sensitive boundaries between identities that are seen as legitimate and reflecting the country's historic traditions and those seen as alien and which are often associated with marginalised migrant or ethnic groupings. On the positive side of this transformation, Castells suggests that 'project identities' are beginning to emerge that are attempting to connect people in new forms of identification that are more closely allied to the current times.

In the case of Ireland, in a little over three decades and underpinned by its membership of the EU, Irish society has been transformed. While the national self-confidence that developed with the emergence in the 1990s of the 'Celtic Tiger' economy has recently been dented, the successful global branding of its cultural activities (music, dance, and sport) remains robust. One of the main beneficiaries of the globalisation of Ireland's culture industries has been Ireland's global diaspora. Until recently, Ireland's main export was its people. For many dispersed Irish their identity relies on an 'imagined' sense of ethnicity that was and still is based on memories and traditions rather than on any concrete experience of life in Ireland. For example, though it has had little impact on the rest of the world, the Gaelic Athletic Association's sporting traditions of football and hurley have regularly reappeared within the various Irish communities around the world.

Sport, community and social cohesion

The inevitable impact of increasing cultural diversity in most Western societies requires a sustained set of responses if these communities (national and local) are to begin to re-establish their social cohesion. In Putnam's (2000) analysis, a cohesive community can only emerge where there is a societal commitment to sustain sufficient levels of community organisations (such as sport, but also including other cultural activities such as dance and the arts) that can provide the civic glue needed to produce extensive, secure and valued contacts between the different cultural groupings. As the quotations cited at the beginning of the chapter indicate, sport is often conveniently presented and singled out, sometimes very naïvely (Coalter, 2007, 2008; Jarvie, 2006), by politicians and civic leaders as the vehicle for the development of the common vision and sense of belonging that characterise a cohesive community.

Case Study
Queen's Park, Bedford

Jonathan Long and Ian Sanderson (2001) developed a research project to find evidence of the discursive claims for the social benefits of sport. Government policies based on the principle that sport provides social benefits have been largely uncontested and, for Long and Sanderson (2001), largely untested. Their critical investigation of community sport points out that, when deconstructed, the discourse actually appears to support two different political agendas – liberal ideas about social democracy (e.g. equity and breaking down barriers) and the more right field concerns with regulation and social control.

Their methodology drew a list of commonly held benefits of sport from the extant literature: this included enhanced self-confidence, empowerment, crime reductions, social integration and co-operation, community pride, economic generation and improved employability as well as improved health and positive environmental change. They subsequently conducted a postal survey of directors of leisure services, the results of which appeared to support their assertion that the evidence to support the commonly held beliefs about community sport was not only difficult to quantify but in many instances distinctly lacking. They followed this up by interviewing workers in the sport and leisure industry (such as sport development officers) and again found ambivalence and inconsistency in their search for evidence.

The authors concede that just because they cannot find a great deal of evidence to support the case for community sport as beneficial to all people, this is not to suggest that benefits don't accrue – their qualitative data in particular shows that there is a clear perception and belief that, for example, sport does reduce crime – a perception that is important in generating a positive sense of community with people more accepting of and at ease with the members of that community.

The main conclusion they draw from their research is that there are benefits from sport and leisure initiatives but the details of what these are and how they might operate need to be more fully understood – for example, changes through sport might be considerable for the individual but small in the bigger picture of developing community cohesion.

Thus, the power of sport remains self evident as these findings show, and community-based significant others continue to develop sport and leisure initiatives in the genuine belief that sport can simultaneously address issues of equity and inclusion at the same time as incorporating aspects of social control and regulation.

This situation is well illustrated by the work of the Reverend Jay MacLeod and the Queen's Park Basketball Club in Bedford. The Anglican church that Jay MacLeod was appointed to in 2003 sits in a central location in the ethnically diverse Queen's Park on the west side of Bedford and is within a few hundred metres of an Islamic mosque and a huge Sikh temple. Recognising that there are 'communities within communities' in this area, Jay and his team of multi-faith based workers introduced basketball to youngsters who, for a whole range of economic, social and cultural reasons – such as religious boundaries (and implicit constraints for certain groups of people) – lacked sporting opportunities outside those provided by the local schools. The basketball initiative has been hugely successful and has ongoing momentum through partnerships with bodies such as Sport England and the University of Bedfordshire (and its BA Sport and Community Leadership students in particular). The club operates across social and religious boundaries and caters for different age groups by broadly delivering 'fun' sessions for the youngest members, 'training' sessions with opportunities to compete in local leagues and tournaments for the teenagers and 'street-ball' sessions for the older teenagers and young adults who are more concerned with playing but not via the more formal coaching activities which structure the sessions for the younger players.

Here, then, is evidence of the power of sport to contribute to community cohesion. But the case also highlights the ongoing complexity of the relationship sport has with community – the Queen's Park Basketball Club is a commendable model but there are clearly still many community groups it does not reach and it is dependent upon volunteers to organise and coach whose efforts may not be sustainable. Moreover, the religious heterogeneity of some of the teams leads to complications when basketball tournaments are scheduled during religious festivals and/or on Sundays, for example. Thus community sport remains an evolving and adapting entity, difficult to pin down but an important component of many aspects of social change.

As this chapter has detailed, the hoped-for community sport legacy of the 2012 London Olympiad, should be welcomed. However, if sport is to play an active role in the development of a sustainable process of change with Britain and Ireland's diverse communities, some of the claims advanced for the capacity of sport to achieve social cohesion need critical evaluation and a more nuanced understanding of the gaps which can often exist between authority-based policy and understanding, and the realities of the social dynamics of the communities they are designed to impact on. For example, Coalter (2007, 2008) has observed that the expectations people have of sport as a means to 'solve' social problems are often unrealistic. Moreover, recent sociological research suggests that the evidence supporting this view is at best limited (Spaaij, 2009, p248; Long and Sanderson, 2001). Further evidence of a simplistic connection between investment in Olympic sports facilities and the capacity of these to enhance a sense of community via a 'legacy of access' is provided by Beedie and Mellor (2009) and Weed and Ladkin (2009), who suggest:

The Olympic and Paralympic Games do not inspire everyone in the same way – in fact, what inspires some may have the opposite effect on others. In particular, evidence suggests that elite sport rarely motivates physical activity take-up among non-participants and the least active. For these groups, the 2012 Olympic and Paralympic Games should be promoted as a four year festival of community participation events rather than an elite sport competition.

(www.canterbury.ac.uk/News/)

Sport and community conflict

Denham's (2001) report into the civic violence that erupted in many of Britain's towns at the start of this decade suggests geographical segregation can work against community dialogue, entrench more serious concerns such as fear of racist attacks and work against equality of choice because of unequal distribution of resources.

The reality of the persistent and enduring social divisions evident in many communities is that deep mistrust and hurt, often incorporated within cultural traditions, have become an ingrained element of the tensions between groups (national, local, class, ethnic, racial, gender or sexual). Although sometimes more ideological than factual the view that sport, particularly in the context of large scale sporting events such as the Olympics, can be a neutral and safe meeting point for diverse and alienated groups has an enduring power and relevance. Whether it is the 'ping-pong' diplomacy that took place between the USA and China during the 'Cold War'; or the ability of rugby to bring together Afrikaners and blacks in South Africa or Irish nationalists and Unionists in Ireland; or the capacity of local football, cricket or basketball clubs to cross the ethnic divisions, sport has the undoubted capacity to build bridges and act as a catalyst for positive encounters.

The case of the 2012 Games and their community sport legacy

The legacy statement makes a commitment that the 2012 Games will:

- make the UK a world-leading sporting nation;
- transform the heart of East London;
- inspire a generation of young people to take part in local volunteering, cultural and physical activity;
- make the Olympic Park a blueprint for sustainable living;
- demonstrate the UK is a creative, inclusive and welcoming place to live in, visit and for business.

(DCMS, 2008a)

In respect of all these commitments, the government has also developed a series of specific policy initiatives. Given the focus of this chapter, it is the third of these commitments with which our main interest lies. This inspiration of young people through sport has been given a series of 'headline ambitions' that evidence how 2012 might impact levels of civic engagement:

Giving time and expanding horizons: tens of thousands more young people giving time to their local communities as a result of the 2012 Games.

New cultural activities: tens of thousands of young people participating in cultural activities as a result of the 2012 Games.

Engaging and learning: thousands of schools, colleges, universities and other learning providers inspiring young people through the Olympic and Paralympic values.

Going global: three million young people overseas accessing quality physical education and sport, and at least one million participating in these regularly by 2010 (DCMS, 2008a).

The successes of the 2012 Games will be assessed by a broad range of measures. The manner in which community sport is developed, enhanced and how diverse populations are encouraged to become active remains but one, albeit a very important one. To date we have seen an inevitable emphasis on Olympic sports rather than a community informed approach. This is understandable yet it reveals a somewhat limited train of thought. Legacy planning seems to have been 'bolted on' to the demands of staging the Olympic Games (Sadd, 2009), again understandable but constrained. It seems that we also see a lack of joined-up thinking across government about what the legacy is, what it can deliver, and what opportunities it offers. For example, government departments such as the Department of Health (DH) want active lifestyles while the Department for Media, Culture and Sport (DMCS) emphasises sporting success.

Government departments are target driven and the problem is that these are measurement specific (e.g. non-elite or community sport is assessed by participation rates, and healthy activity by the threshold of achievement – adults require thirty minutes of raised heart-rate, five times a week). These measurements, however laudable, reduce quality to quantity. We also see mixed messages in the media and health discourse about ideal body shape and size. This ignores the fact that despite the rhetoric, one can be fat and fit, or thin and unfit. Furthermore, lazy is not the same as sedentary, the latter being created by the social environment. The environmental dominance of the car is still unrivalled even though the use of taxes as a disincentive is well established (Beedie and Mellor, 2009).

Yet sport and its funding remain threshold and target driven and underpinned by a health rationale (Beedie and Mellor, 2009). The Department of Health calculate that the direct cost of inactivity in Britain is £8.3 billion per year; only 40 per cent of males reach the activity threshold and only 28 per cent of females do so; male and female activity declines with age and activity rates are significantly lower in certain ethnic, regional and socio-economic groups; indeed it is estimated that over seven million adults are not active enough to meet the Chief Medical Officer's (CMO) recommendations (ibid). This brief critique of the Olympic legacy ambition reminds us that perspectives about community sport are multi-dimensional and operate a whole range of agendas meaning that, despite ambitions for 'joined-up thinking' about health, activity, sport and lifestyle, the balance is very often skewed by the socio-cultural and economic conditions of that moment in time: we are therefore reminded that nothing is fixed in sport and that a sociological view of this important component of the modern world remains an essential framework for understanding how the world of sport operates as a reflection of the world that it has helped construct.

Overview

This chapter should have enabled you to understand the complex, problematic but enduring relationship that sport has with the idea of community. As the opening sections of the chapter detailed, modernity has often created a real sense of insecurity, the counterpoint of which has been a restless search for community (Bauman, 2001). For many there is a persistent desire to find a personal sense of meaning through the maintenance of close relationships with others which are rooted in the contradictory conditions of life in the twenty-first century. For theorists such as Delanty (2003), the contemporary focus of this process has been based in a communicative process which has emphasised a discursive rather than a bounded sense of community and a fixed set of institutions that pattern and structure the experience.

While there is some merit in this argument, the position put forward here is that the physical realities of the localities in which people live – the organised and institutional structures, the physical spaces and places and the social activities we take part in within these spaces – have a powerful and enduring impact on routine patterns of daily life and the sense of identity and belonging these sustain.

Because of its capacity to reach across the class, racial and ethnic divides that also characterise these localities, sport has the potential to bring people together in a shared sense of belonging which we can think of as community. However, the extent to which sport alone can fulfil this ambition has been challenged by the complexity of the political agendas 'using' sport (that is for both liberal ambitions of equity, and the more directive agendas of the use of sport as a means of social control and the designation of active lifestyles for all) and by the difficulties of quantifying the evidence to support the broadly held beliefs about the benefits of sport.

Though elaborated somewhat differently to the conclusions reached by Jarvie (2006, pp336–37), this chapter has highlighted a number of important propositions regarding the relationship between sport and community.

Some of the positive aspects identified are:

- Modern sport, from the time of its major development and rationalisation in the nineteenth century (see Chapter 2), has had powerful identifications with local and national spaces and places (Bale, 1994, 2003). These positive identifications can provide a focus for community groups.
- Politicians and civic leaders have often co-opted sport in the construction of civic pride and nationalistic sentiments.
- Sport, particularly in the context of important media sports such as Premiership football clubs (e.g. Arsenal's Emirates Stadium) and global sports events such as the Olympics (e.g. London 2012) has become the vehicle for important urban regeneration projects whose impact and legacy stretches far beyond the confines of sport.

From a more negative perspective:

- Sport has a powerful capacity to create forms of collective identity that are nationalistic and jingoistic (e.g. when English teams play Germany or Argentina); sectarian (e.g. the relationship between Celtic and Rangers fans in Glasgow) or racist (e.g. the behaviour of some fans associated with a number of teams within the English football leagues). Moreover, in recent times the fact that a number of sportsmen and women have felt it necessary to set up sports associations and competitions that are largely composed of specific ethnic, religious or sexuality groupings, indicates that sport can still act as a powerful means of social distinction (e.g. the Jewish football league in London).

- More broadly for sport in the community, as civil society declines, the capacity for sport to exist beyond its commodified and individualised forms (in terms of leagues and the volunteerism that most 'amateur' and community/neighbourhood sport requires) also declines because those groups of people not interested in the forms sport currently takes will not be persuaded to enhance a sense of community through this medium.

In addition to these observations there are also important processes of social, cultural, economic and environmental change that are changing and will continue to change the very assumptions that up to now have often been taken for granted, but which can now be seen as increasingly problematic.

The ability of those individuals in a community who have the capacity to work together and develop positive leadership roles in the development and maintenance of cohesive communities (e.g. faith leaders, sport and community officers, coaches and business leaders) must be developed. Unless the capacity of local leadership in sports is developed, it will be difficult for sport to fulfil the difficult tasks it is being set. As Jarvie observes: *sport alone cannot sustain vibrant living communities* (2007, p337). Vibrant communities require a whole range of necessary elements that may be connected to the world of sport but which are also quite distinctive: good employment opportunities, effective schools, good housing, efficient transport, recreational spaces.

Research Focus

Grant Jarvie

The sociological study of sport and the community has until relatively recently been an underdeveloped field. As this chapter has detailed, the current changes impacting most European and North American societies in terms of increasing diversity allied to decreasing social cohesion has, however, focused the attention of policy makers to practioners and academics.

One of the few British sport sociologists to systematically examine the links between sport and the nature of twenty-first century communities is Grant Jarvie. His most recent text *Sport, Culture and Society: An Introduction,* develops some of the major themes that have informed his contribution to sport sociology over the past two decades (see Jarvie, 1997, 2000, 2003a, 2003b, 2004, 2006 and Jarvie and Maguire, 1994).

While the main concern here is to highlight his reflections on sport and community, if this text can be said to have a unifying theme, it would be his broader sociological concern to justify his premise that contemporary society and culture cannot be fully understood *without acknowledging the place of sport* (Jarvie, 2006, p2). For Jarvie, sports in the twenty-first century are influential international phenomena that have connections to the important processes of social change impacting the political and economic conditions of our contemporary world and, at a more personal level, people's concerns over identity and lifestyle.

Emerging from this, he seeks to detail how the effects of sports extend far beyond their fields of play, the athletes and officials who take them into the everyday cultural practices that characterise nations and their increasingly diverse communities. While these connections may not always be obvious, within the practical realities and struggles of everyday life, sports none the less have a real and enduring presence within national cultures and the biographies of individuals and families.

Through the various sections of the text Jarvie details how at one level sports draw people together on the basis of fun, friendship, competition or their inherent physicality and movement and how in bringing people together sports are also inevitably connected into some of the most important and often troublesome aspects of everyday life: declining civic engagement; the erosion of community within the context of liberal individualism and consumer culture; the allied problems of poverty and unhealthy lifestyles (Jarvie, 2003b, 2006). The evident contemporary concerns that community within Britain (and in most advanced Western societies) has progressively weakened have therefore created a 'live agenda' directed at community-building (Jarvie, 2003b, p139) seeking to establish the re-energising of positive, meaningful and sustainable civic engagement.

One of the strengths of Jarvie's (2006) work is his desire to move beyond theoretical reflections into a grounded and critical exploration (through practical examples drawn from around the world) of the capacity of sport to have a positive influence on social change. In doing so Jarvie challenges what he clearly sees as the naïve notion that sports are always open and inclusive. All sports can be, and often are, annexed by groups seeking to foreground their own particular identity. Whether this is done in the name of the nation, region, community or specific cultural group it always creates rivalry and the risk that others are to be excluded or marginalised. In his critical examination of community sport, this lack of diversified engagement concerns Jarvie because it fails to realistically deal with the problems of diversity and all the cultural differences or representations that can be presented through sport (Jarvie, 2006, p 383).

On the positive side, Jarvie also charts how across the world public protests and campaigns by athletes and community activists have not only successfully established awareness of various marginalised groups but successfully harnessed the power of sport to initiate and sustain movements for change. These examples range from the Black civil rights movement in America, to the anti-apartheid movement, to the rights of 'first-nation' peoples such as the Aborigines in Australia to contemporary concerns about climate change.

Jarvie's focus on international examples, allied to his earlier work on Scottish sport (2003), develops the relationship between sport, community and social change and is a substantive and useful contribution to the field. His concerns that some of the expectations of sport are too ambitious and at times a little naïve are also important to note. The diversity of sport's social, cultural and physical activities have some capacity to help address a range of pressing social problems but this can only be successfully sustained if policies proceed from a critical understanding of the complex social, cultural and economic processes that underpin them. As Jarvie has previously noted: *There is an urgent need within the sociology of sport . . . to develop new accounts of recognition that can accommodate a fuller complexity of social identities rather than being limited to analysing uniform facets of sporting identity (class, race, gender, nationality) that promote reification and separatism* (2004, p581).

Chapter Review

This chapter has used the idea of community, and the connections between sport and community in particular, to illustrate one focus for the theoretical and conceptual materials covered in this book. It has been shown, for example, that far from being isolated categories of stratification the social structures of gender, age, class, ethnicity and race operate simultaneously to define our social worlds in general and our sense of community identity in particular. Social capital has been shown to be a crucial concept in understanding how ideas of community are generated and sustained, and in particular the concepts of bonding and bridging capital neatly encapsulate the enduring tensions and ambivalence that exists in the ideas of networking implicit in the use of this concept. The key terms of civil society, community and communitarianism have been shown to have a political dimension that illustrates our more general theme about power and the distribution of resources – for example it is significant that new sporting developments in the community tend to attract people who already engage with sport rather than those groups currently disengaged.

Thus we have shown how sport has great potential to act as a positive force for community development but that this process is not exclusive to sport as a mechanism, and where sport is used the cohesion generated is just as likely to be offset with more negative consequences. Nevertheless, while ideas of community continue to be prominent in government thinking, official policy and the resultant discursive agendas, sport will continue to be seen as a powerful agent of social and political change, most immediately evidenced, as we have shown throughout this book, by the way that global sporting events such as the Olympic Games continue to have significant impacts upon the social conditions of our times.

References

Abercrombie, N and Warde, A (1998) Inequality and selection in education, in Giddens, A (ed) *Sociology: Introductory Readings*. Cambridge: Polity Press, pp323–329.

Adam, J (1995) *Risk*. London: UCL Press.

Adorno, T and Horkheimer, M (1977) The culture industry: enlightenment as mass deception, in Curran, J, Gurevitch, M and Woollacott, J (eds) *Mass Communication and Society*. London: Arnold.

Alexander, C (2007) Cohesive identities: the distance between meaning and understanding, in Wetherell, M, Lafleche, M and Berkeley, R (eds) *Identity, Ethnic Diversity and Community Cohesion*. London: Sage, pp115–125.

Amara, M, Aquilina, D, Henry, I, and Taylor, M (2004) *Sport and Multiculturalism*. Brussels: European Commission: DG Education and Culture.

Anderson, B (1983) *Imagined Communities*. London: Arnold.

Anderson, DA (1983) Sports coverage in daily newspapers, *Journalism Quarterly*, Autumn, 60: 497–500.

Anderson, WB (2001) Does the cheerleading ever stop? Major league baseball and sports journalism, *Journalism and Mass Communication Quarterly*, Summer, 78/2: 355–382.

Andrew, J (2003) *Life and Limb: A True Story of Tragedy and Survival Against the Odds*. London: Portrait.

Andrews, D (2000) Posting up: French post-structuralism and the critical analysis of contemporary sporting culture, in Coakley, J and Dunning, E (eds) *Handbook of Sports Studies*. London: Sage.

Andrews, D (2004) Speaking the 'universal language of entertainment': News Corporation, culture and the global sport media economy, in Rowe, D (ed) *Critical Readings: Sport, Culture and the Media*. Maidenhead: Open University Press.

Andrews, P (2005) *Sports Journalism: A Practical Introduction*. London: Sage.

Appadurai, A (1990) Disjuncture and difference in the global and cultural economy, *Theory, Culture and Society*, 7: 207–236.

Appadurai, A (1995) Playing with modernity: the decolonization of Indian cricket, in Breckenridge, C (ed) *Consuming Modernity: Public Culture in a South Asian World*. Minneapolis: University of Minnesota Press.

Appadurai, A (1996) *Modernity at Large: Cultural Dimensions of Globalization: Public Worlds Volume 1*. Minneapolis: University of Minnesota Press.

Armytage, WHG (1955) Thomas Arnold's views on physical education, *Physical Education*, 47.

Arnold, T (1869) *Culture and Anarchy*. London.

Audit Commission (2006) *Public Sports and Recreation Services: Making Them Fit for the Future.* Audit Commission for Local Authorities and the National Health Service in England. London.

Bailie, M (2004) Rewards from risk: the case for adventure activity, in Barnes, P and Sharp, B (eds) *Outdoor Education.* Lyme Regis: Russell House Publishing.

Bairner, A (2001) *Sport, Nationalism and Globalisation: European and North American Perspectives.* Albany: State University of New York Press.

Bale, J (1994) *Landscapes of Modern Sport.* London: Leicester University Press.

Bale, J (2001) *Sport, Space, and the City.* London: Routledge.

Bale, J (2003) *Sports Geography,* 2nd edition. London: Routledge.

Ballard, J (1996) *One and Two Halves to K2: The Journey of Alison Hargreaves' Family to K2.* London: BBC Books.

Barnes, P and Sharp, R (2004) *Outdoor Education.* Lyme Regis: Russell House Publishing.

Barnett, S (1990) *Games and Sets: The Changing Face of Sport Television.* London: British Film Industry.

Barthes, R (1973) *Mythologies.* St Albans: Paladin.

Baudrillard, J (1998) *The Consumer Society: Myths and Structures.* London: Sage.

Bauman, Z (1998) *Work, Consumerism and the New Poor.* Buckingham: Open University Press.

Bauman, Z (2000) *Liquid Modernity.* Cambridge: Polity Press.

Bauman, Z (2001) *The Individualized Society.* Cambridge: Polity Press.

BBC News (2009) Fears over child fitness levels **http://news.bbc.co.uk/go/pr/fr/-/1/hi/health/8425161.stm**

Beck, U (1992) *Risk Society: Towards a New Modernity.* London: Sage.

Beds on Sunday newspaper (2009) 'Wendy Bowled Over by Honour'.

Beedie, C and Mellor, G (2009) *The Legacy: A Community First Approach for London.* Leveraging Social, Cultural & Health Benefits from London 2012 Conference. SPEAR Christ Church University Canterbury.

Beedie, P and Bourne, G (2005) Media constructions of risk: a case study of the Stainforth Beck incident, *Journal of Risk Research*, 8(2): 331–339.

Bellamy, RV Jr (1998) The evolving television sports marketplace, in Wenner, LA (ed) *MediaSport.* London: Routledge.

Benson, AL (2000) *I Shop Therefore I Am: Compulsive Buying and the Search for Self.* Lanham, MD: Jason Aronson.

Benson, J (1994) *The Rise of Consumer Society 1880–1980.* Harlow: Longman.

Berger, P (1973) *The Social Reality of Religion.* Harmondsworth: Penguin.

Berger, P and Luckmann, M (1966) *The Social Construction of Reality.* New York: Anchor Books.

Bernstein, A and Blain, N (2003) Sport and the media: the emergence of a major research field, in Bernstein, A and Blain, N (eds) *Media, Culture: Global and Local Dimensions.* London and Portland: Frank Cass Publishers.

Bilton, T, Bonnett, K, Jones, P, Skinner, D, Stanworth, M and Webster, A (1996) *Introductory Sociology.* 3rd edition. London: Macmillan.

Bilton, T, Bonnett, K, Jones, P, Lawson, T, Skinner, D, Stanworth, M and Webster, A (2002) *Introductory Sociology.* 4th edition. London: Macmillan.

Birley, D (1993) *Sport and the Making of Britain.* Manchester: Manchester University Press.

Birrell, S (2000) Feminist theories for sport, in Coakley, J and Dunning, E (eds) *Handbook of Sports Studies.* London: Sage.

Birrell, S and Donnelly, P (2004) Reclaiming Goffman: Erving Goffman's influence on the sociology of sport, in Giulianotti, R (ed) *Sport and Modern Social Theorists.* London: Palgrave-Macmillan.

Blake, A (1996) *The Body Language: The Meaning of Modern Sport.* London: Lawrence & Wishart.

Blandon, J and Machen, S (2007) *Recent Changes in Intergenerational Social Mobility in the UK.* London: Sutton Trust.

Bocock, R (1992) Consumption and lifestyles, in Bocock, R and Thompson, K (eds) *Social and Cultural Forms of Modernity.* Milton Keynes: Open University Press and Cambridge: Polity Press.

Bordo, S (1993) *Unbearable Weight: Feminism, Western Culture and the Body.* Berkeley: University of California Press.

Bourdieu, P (1984) *Distinction.* London: Routledge.

Bourdieu, P (1986) The forms of capital, in Richardson, G (ed.) *Handbook of Theory and Research for the Sociology of Education.* New York: Greenwood Press, pp241–258.

Bourdieu, P (1993) *Sociology in Question.* London: Sage.

Bourdieu, P and Wacquant, L (1992) *An Invitation to Reflexive Sociology.* Chicago: Chicago University Press.

Bourgeois, N (1995) Sports journalists and their source of information: a conflict of interests and its resolution, *Sociology of Sport Journal,* 12: 195–203.

Bourne, J (2007) *In Defence of Multiculturalism,* Institute for Race Relations, Briefing Paper No.2.

Bourne, J (2009) *In Defence of Multiculturalism.* **www.irr.org.uk/pdf/IRR_Briefing No.2**.

Boyle, R (2006) *Sports Journalism: Context and Issues.* London: Sage.

Boyle, R and Haynes, R (2000) *Power Play: Sport, the Media and Popular Culture.* Essex: Pearson Education.

Bradley, J (2007) *The Gaelic Athletic Association and Irishness in Scotland.* Glendaruel: Argyll Publishing.

Bredemeier, BJ, Weiss, MR, Shields, D and Cooper, B (1987) The relationship between children's legitimacy judgments and their moral reasoning, aggression tendencies, and sport involvement, *Sociology of Sport Journal,* 4: 48–60.

Brittain, I (2004) Perceptions of disability and their impact upon involvement in sport for people with disabilities at all levels, *Journal of Sport and Social Issues,* 28(4): 429–452.

Brohm, JM (1978) *Sport, A Prison of Measured Time.* London: Pluto.

Brookes, R (2002) *Representing Sport.* London: Arnold.

Brown, G (2000) Emerging issues in Olympic sponsorship: implications for host cities, *Sport Management Review,* 3(1): 71–92.

Brown, H (2000) Passengers, participants, partners and practitioners: working with risk to empower groups, *Horizons,* 12: 37–39.

Browne, D (2004) *Amped: How Big Air, Big Dollars and a New Generation Took Sports to the Extreme.* London: Bloomsbury.

Burnett, C (2006) Building social capital through an 'Active Community Club', *International Review for the Sociology of Sport*, 41(3–4): 283–294.

Burstyn, V (1999) *The Rites of Men: Manhood, Politics and the Culture of Sport*. Toronto: Toronto University Press.

Butler, J (1990) *Gender Trouble, Feminism and the Subversion of Identity*. London: Routledge.

Cable, V (2009) *The Storm: The World Economic Crisis and What it Means*. London: Atlantic Books.

Cashmore, E (2002) *Beckham*. Cambridge: Polity Press.

Castells, M (1996) *The Rise of the Network Society*. Oxford: Blackwell.

Castells, M (1997) *The Power of Identity*. Oxford: Blackwell.

Castells, M (1998) *The End of the Millennium*. Oxford: Blackwell.

Chaney, D (1996) *Lifestyles*. London: Routledge.

Claeys, U and Van Pelt, H (1986) Sport and the mass media: like bacon and eggs, *International Review for the Sociology of Sport*, 21(2/3): 93–101.

Clarke, A and Clarke, J (1982) Highlights and action replays – ideology, sport and the media, in Hargreaves, JA (ed) *Sport, Culture and Ideology*. London: Routledge and Kegan Paul.

Clarke, G (2002) Outlaws in sport and education? Exploring the sporting and educational experiences of physical education teachers, in Scraton, S and Flintoff, A (eds) *A Reader in Gender and Sport*. London: Routledge.

Clarke, J and Critcher, C (1985) *The Devil Makes Work*. Basingstoke: Macmillan.

Coakley, J (2003) *Sports in Society: Issues and Controversies*. 8th edition. New York: McGraw-Hill.

Coakley, J and Donnelly, P (2004) *Sport in Society*. Toronto: McGraw-Hill.

Coakley, J and Dunning, E (eds) (2000) *Handbook of Sports Studies*. London: Sage.

Coalter, F (2007) Sports clubs, social capital and social regeneration: 'ill-defined interventions with hard to follow outcomes'? *Sport in Society*, 10(4): 537–559.

Coalter, F (2008) *A Wider Social Role for Sport: Who's Keeping the Score?* London: Routledge.

Coe, S (2009) Olympism and youth – towards a more active society, Speech to the IOC Congress, Copenhagen, 4 October 2009.

Cole, C (2002) Body studies in the sociology of sport, in Coakley, J and Dunning, E (eds) *Handbook of Sports Studies*. London: Sage.

Crabbe, T (2003) The public gets what the public wants: English football fans, 'truth' claims and mediated realities, *International Review for the Sociology of Sport*, 38/4: 413–425.

Craib, I (1984) *Modern Social Theory: From Parsons to Habermas*. New York: St Martin's Press.

Craig, PG and Rees, CR (1994) The Springbok Trials: some critical reflections on South Africa's Unity Games, in Wilcox, R (ed) *Sport in the Global Village: Comparative Perspectives*. Morgantown: Fitness Information Technology.

Craig, PG and Reid, I (1999) Reconstructing nationalism on the Celtic Frontier, in Nathul, N and Brehony, M (eds) *Nationalisms: Old and New*. London: Macmillan.

Crawford, G (2003) The career of the sport supporter: the case of the Manchester storm, *Sociology*, 37(2): 219–237.

Creedon, P (ed) (1994) *Women, Media and Sport: Challenging Gender Values*. London: Sage.

Crocker, T and Davies, B (2009) Caster Semenaya. One of the world's most highly talented sporting teenage athletes. Or is she a cheat?, *Masters Athletics*, Autumn, 89: 24–25.

Crolley, L and Teso, E (2007) Gendered narrative in Spain: the representation of female athletes in Marca and El Pais, *International Review for the Sociology of Sport*, 42/2: 149–166.

Csikszentmihalyi, M and Csikszentmihalyi, I (1999) Adventure and the flow experience, in Miles, J and Priest, S (eds) (1999) *Adventure Programming*. State College Pennsylvania: Venture Publishing.

Curran, J (1999) *High Achiever: The Life and Times of Chris Bonington*. London: Constable.

Darby, J (1983) *Northern Ireland: The Background to the Conflict*. Belfast: Appletree Press.

DCMS (2005) Gambling Act Regulatory Impact Assessment, **www.culture.gov.uk/images/publications/GamblingAct2005RIA210405.pdf**

DCMS (2006) BROADCASTING: Copy of Royal Charter for the Continuance of the British Broadcasting Corporation. HMSO: Norwich.

DCMS (2008a) *Before, During and After: Making the Most of the London 2012 Games*, **www.culture.gov.uk**

DCMS (2008b) *London 2012 Legacy Research, Wave 2 Quantitative Report*, London: DCMS, **www.culture.gov.uk**

Delanty, G (2003) *Community*. London: Routledge.

Denham, J (2001) *Building Cohesive Communities: A Report of the Ministerial Group on Public Order and Community Cohesion*. Home Office.

de Zengotita, T (2005) *Mediated: How the Media Shape Your World*. London: Bloomsbury.

Donald, J and Rattansi, A (eds) (1992) *Race, Culture and Difference*. London: Sage.

Douglas, E (2007) The mother of all climbs, *The Observer*, 26 August 2007.

Dunn, S (1995) *Facets of the Conflict in Northern Ireland*. Basingstoke: Palgrave Macmillan.

Dunnavant, K (2004) *The Fifty-Year Seduction: How Television Manipulated College Football, From The Birth of the Modern NCAA to the Creation of the BCS*. New York: Thomas Dunne Books.

Dworkin, SL and Wachs, FL (2000) The morality/manhood paradox: masculinity, sport and the media, in Mckay, J, Messner, MA and Sabo, D (eds) *Masculinities, Gender Relationships and Sport*. Thousand Oaks, CA: Sage.

Edensor, T (2002) *National Identity, Popular Culture and Everyday Life*. Oxford: Berg.

Eitzen, DS (2000) Social control and sport, in Coakley, J and Dunning, E (eds) *Handbook of Sports Studies*. London: Sage.

Elias, N and Dunning, E (1986) *Quest for Excitement: Sport and Leisure in the Civilising Process*. Oxford: Blackwell.

Engstrom, LM (2008) Who is physically active? Cultural capital and sports participation from adolescence to middle age – a 38 year follow up study, *Physical Education and Sports Pedagogy*, 13(4): 319–343.

Evans, J and Penney, D (2008) Levels on the playing field: the social construction of physical 'ability' in the physical education curriculum, *Physical Education and Sport Pedagogy*, 13(1): 31–47.

Featherstone, M (1987) Lifestyle and consumer culture, *Theory Culture and Society*, 4: 55–70.

Featherstone, M (1991) *Consumer Culture and Postmodernism*. London, Sage.

Featherstone, M (2007) *Consumer Culture and Postmodernism,* 2nd edition. London: Sage.

Fiske, J (1989) *Understanding Popular Culture.* London: Unwin Hyman.

Fleming, S (1994) Sport and South Asian youth: The perils of 'false universalism' and stereotyping, *Leisure Studies,* 13: 159–177.

Foley, M, Frew, M and McGillivray, D (2003) Rough comfort: consuming adventure on the edge, in Humberstone, B, Brown, H and Richards, K (2003) *Whose Journeys? The Outdoors and Adventure as Social and Cultural Phenomena.* Penrith: IOL.

Foucault, M (1976) *Discipline and Punish.* London: Allen Lane.

Foucault, M (1980) Truth and power, in Gordon, C and Foucault, M (eds) *Power/Knowledge: Selected Interviews and Other Writing 1972–1977.* London: Pantheon Books.

Foucault, M (1981) *The History of Sexuality: An Introduction.* Harmondsworth: Penguin.

Foucault, M (1990) *Politics, Philosophy, Culture: Interviews and Other Writings, 1977–1984.* New York: Routledge.

Frisby, D and Featherstone, M (1997) *Simmel on Culture.* London: Sage.

Furedi, F (1997) *Culture of Fear.* London: Cassell.

Game Plan: A Strategy for Delivering Government's Sport and Physical Activity Objectives (2002), Cabinet Office Strategic Unit, London, **www.cabinetoffice.gov.uk/media/cabinetoffice/ strategy/assets/game_plan_report.pdf**

Garrison, B and Salwen, MB (1989) Newspaper sports journalists: a profile of the 'profession', *Journal of Sport and Social Issues,* 13/2: 57–68.

Garrison, B and Salwen, MB (1994) Sports journalists assess their work: their place in the profession, *Newspaper Research Journal,* 15/2: 37–49

Gellner, E (1974) *Legitimation of Belief.* Cambridge: Cambridge University Press.

Gellner, E (1992) *Postmodernism, Reason and Belief.* London: Routledge.

Gerrard, B (2004) Media ownership of teams: the latest stage in the commercialisation of team sports, in Slack, T (ed) *The Commercialisation of Sport.* London and New York: Routledge.

Giddens, A (1984) *The Constitution of Society: Outline of the Theory of Structuration.* Cambridge: Polity Press.

Giddens, A (1989) *Sociology: A Brief but Critical Introduction.* Cambridge: Cambridge University Press.

Giddens, A (1990) *The Consequences of Modernity.* Cambridge: Polity Press.

Giddens, A (1991) *Modernity and Self Identity.* Cambridge: Polity Press.

Giddens, A (1994) *Beyond Left and Right: The Future of Radical Politics.* Cambridge: Polity Press.

Giddens, A (2001) *Sociology.* 4th edition. Cambridge: Polity Press.

Giddens, A (2002) *Runaway World.* London: Profile Books.

Giddens, A (2006) *Sociology.* 5th edition. Cambridge: Polity Press.

Giddens, A (2009) *The Politics of Climate Change.* Cambridge: Polity Press.

Giulianotti, R (ed) (2004) *Sport and Modern Social Theorists.* Basingstoke: Palgrave-Macmillan.

Giulianotti, R (2005) *Sport: A Critical Sociology.* Cambridge: Polity Press.

Goffman, E (1959) *The Presentation of Self in Everyday Life.* Harmondsworth: Penguin.

Goffman, E (1997) Civil inattention and face engagements in social interaction, in Giddens, A (ed) *Sociology: Introductory Readings.* Cambridge: Polity Press, pp26–31.

Goldlust, J (1987) *Playing for Keeps: Sport, the Media and Society.* Cheshire: Longman.

Goldthorpe, J, Lockwood, D, Bechhofer, F and Platt, J (1968–9) *The Affluent Worker in the Class Structure.* Cambridge: Cambridge University Press.

Gratton, C and Taylor, P (2000) *Economics of Sport and Recreation.* London and New York: E & FN Spon.

Green, M and Houlihan, B (2005) *Elite Sport Development: Policy Learning and Political Priorities.* London: Routledge.

Greendorfer, S (1981) Female socialization into sport: childhood influences. Paper presented at the National Convention of the American Alliance for Health, Physical Education, Recreation and Dance (Boston, MA, April 13–17).

Gruneau, R (1983) *Class, Sports and Social Development.* Amherst: University of Massachusetts Press.

Gruneau, R (1993) The critique of sport in modernity: theorising power, culture and the politics of the body, in Dunning, EG, Maguire, JA, and Pearson, RE (eds) *The Sport Process: A Comparative and Developmental Approach.* Champaign, IL: Human Kinetics.

Guardian (1999) Breasts, PMT and the pill bar women from boxing, 13 February.

Guttmann, A (1978) *From Ritual to Record.* New York: Columbia University Press.

Guttmann, A (2000) The development of modern sports, in Coakley, J and Dunning, E (eds) *Handbook of Sports Studies.* London: Sage.

Guttmann, A (2002) *The Olympics: A History of the Modern Games.* Urbana: University of Illinois Press.

Guttmann, A (2003) Sport, politics and the engaged historian, *Journal of Contemporary History,* 38(3): 363–375.

Haddock, C (1993) *Managing Risks in Outdoor Activities.* Wellington: NZMSC.

Hahn, H (1984) Sports and the political movement of disabled persons: examining non disabled social values, *Arena Review,* 8/1: 1–15.

Hall, MA (1996) *Feminism and Sporting Bodies.* Champaign, IL: Human Kinetics.

Hall, S (1992) New ethnicities, in Donald, J and Rattansi, A (eds) *Race, Culture and Difference.* London: Sage.

Hamilton, P and Thompson, K (eds) (2002) *The Uses of Sociology.* Oxford: Blackwell Publishers.

Hargreaves, A (1995) *A Hard Day's Summer: Six Classic North Faces Solo.* London: Hodder & Stoughton.

Hargreaves, JA (ed) (1982) *Sport, Culture and Ideology.* London: Routledge and Kegan Paul.

Hargreaves, JA (1986) Where's the virtue? Where's the grace? A discussion of the social production of gender relations in and through sport, *Theory, Culture & Society,* 3: 109–121.

Hargreaves, JA (1987) The body, sport and power relations, in Horne, J, Jary, D and Tomlinson, A (eds) *Sport, Leisure and Social Relations.* London: Routledge & Kegan Paul.

Hargreaves, JA (1994) *Sporting Females: Critical Issues in the History and Sociology of Women's Sports.* London: Routledge.

Hargreaves, JA (2000) *Heroines of Sport: The Politics of Difference and Identity.* London: Routledge.

Hargreaves, JA (2004) Querying sport feminism: personal or political?, in Giulianotti, R (ed) *Sport and Modern Social Theorists*. London: Palgrave.

Hargreaves, JA and McDonald, I (2000) Cultural studies and the sociology of sport, in Coakley, J and Dunning, E (eds) *Handbook of Sport Studies*. London: Sage.

Hargreaves, JA and Vertinsky, PA (2007) *Physical Culture, Power and the Body*. London: Routledge.

Hargreaves, JE (1982) Sport, culture and ideology, in Hargreaves, JA (ed) *Sport, Culture and Ideology*. London: Routledge and Kegan Paul.

Hargreaves, JE (1986a) Constructing media sport, in Tomlinson, A (ed) (2007) *The Sport Studies Reader*. London: Routledge.

Hargreaves, JE (1986b) *Sport, Power and Culture: A Social and Historical Analysis of Popular Sports in Britain*. Cambridge: Polity Press.

Hargreaves, JE (2002) Globalisation: sport, nations and nationalism, in Sugden, J and Tomlinson, A (eds) *Power Games: A Critical Sociology of Sport*. London: Routledge.

Harvey, J, Horne, J and Safai, P (2009) Alterglobalisation, global social movements, and the possibility of political transformation through sport, *Sociology of Sport Journal*, 26: 383–403.

Held, D, McGrew, A, Goldplatt, J and Perraton, J (1999) *Global Transformations: Politics, Economics and Culture*. Cambridge: Polity Press.

Henningham, J (1995) A profile of Australian sports journalists, *The ACHPER Healthy Lifestyles Journal*, 42/3: 13–17.

Henry, I (1993) *The Politics of Leisure Policy*. Basingstoke: Macmillan.

Henry, I (2005) Sport and multiculturalism: a European perspective [online article]. Barcelona: Centre d'Estudis Olimpics UAB. [Consulted 11/11/09] **http://olympicstudies.uab.es/pdf/wp102_eng.pdf**.

Henry, I and Theodoraki, E (2000) Management organizations and theory in the governance of sport, in Coakley, J and Dunning, E (eds) *Handbook of Sports Studies*. London: Sage.

Hoberman, J (1984) *Sport and Political Ideology*. London: Heinemann Education.

Hoberman, JM (1986) *The Olympic Crisis: Sport, Politics and the Moral Order*. New Rochele, NY: AD Caratzas.

Hoberman, J (1993) Sportive nationalism, in Allison, L (ed) *The Changing Politics of Sport*. Manchester: Manchester University Press.

Hobsbawm, E (1987) *The Age of Empires*. London: Weidenfeld and Nicolson.

Hogan, J (2003) Staging the nation: gendered and ethnicised discourses of national identity in Olympic opening ceremonies, *Journal of Sport and Social Issues*, 27/2: 100–123.

Holt, R (1989) *Sport and the British: A Modern History*. Oxford: Clarendon Press.

Hong, F (1998) The Olympic Movement in China: ideals, realities and ambitions, *Culture, Sport and Society*, 1(1): 149–168.

Horne, J (2006) *Sport in Consumer Society*. London: Palgrave.

Horne, J and Jary, D (1987) The figurational sociology of sport and leisure of Elias and Dunning: an exposition and a critique, in Horne, J, Jary, D, and Tomlinson, A (eds) *Sport, Leisure and Social Relations*. London: Routledge & Kegan Paul.

Houlihan, B (1991) *The Government and Politics of Sport*. London: Routledge.

Houlihan, B (1997) *Sport, Policy and Politics: A Comparative Analysis*. London: Routledge.

Houlihan, B (2000) Politics and sport, in Coakley, J and Dunning, E (eds) *Handbook of Sports Studies.* London: Sage.

Houlihan, B (ed) (2003) *Sport and Society: A Student Introduction.* London: Sage.

Houlihan, B and Green, M (2006) The changing status of school sport and physical education: explaining policy change, *Journal of Sport, Education and Society,* 11(1): 73–92.

Houlihan, B and White, A (2002) *The Politics of Sports Development: Development of Sport or Development through Sport?* London: Routledge.

Howe, J (2003) Drawing lines – a report from the extreme world, in Rinehart, R and Sydnor, S (eds) *To the Extreme: Alternative Sports Inside and Out.* Albany: State University of New York Press.

Howell, J (1991) A revolution in motion: advertising and the politics of nostalgia, *Sociology of Sport Journal,* 8: 258–271.

Hughes, R and Coakley, J (1991) Positive deviance amongst athletes: the implications of overconformity to the sport ethic, *Sociology of Sport Journal,* 8(4): 307–325.

Hughes, T (1858 and later editions) *Tom Brown's School Days.* London: Macmillan & Co.

Institute for Community Cohesion (2006) *The Power of Sport, Practice: Sport and Cohesion,* online document, **www.cohesioninstitute.org.uk**

IOC Values (2009), **http://www.olympic.org/en/content/Olympism-in-Action/**

Jarvie, G (1997) Sport and social problems in unprincipled societies, in Nardis, P, Mussino, A and Porro, N (eds) *Sport, Social Problems, Social Movement.* Milan: Edizioni Seam.

Jarvie, G (2000) Sport, racism and ethnicity, in Coakley, J and Dunning, E (eds) *Handbook of Sports Studies.* London: Sage.

Jarvie, G (2003a) Internationalism and sport in the making of nations, *Identities,* 10(4): 537–551.

Jarvie, G (2003b) Communitarianism, sport and social capital: neighbourly insights into Scottish sport, *International Review for the Sociology of Sport,* 38(2): 139–153.

Jarvie, G (2004) Sport in changing times and places, *British Journal of Sociology,* 55(4): 579–587.

Jarvie, G (2006) *Sport, Culture and Society: An Introduction.* London: Routledge.

Jarvie, G (2007) Sport, social change and the public intellectual. *International Review for the Sociology of Sport,* 42(4): 411–424.

Jarvie, G and Maguire, J (1994) *Sport and Leisure in Social Thought.* London: Routledge.

Jennings, A (1996*) The New Lords of the Rings: Olympic Corruption and How to Buy Gold Medals.* London: Pocket Books/Simon and Schuster.

Jennings, A and Sambrook, C (2000) *The Great Olympic Swindle: When the World Wanted its Games Back.* London: Simon and Schuster.

Jhally, S (1989) Cultural studies and the sports/media complex, in Wenner, LA (ed) *Media, Sports, and Society.* London: Sage.

Johnson, N (2007) Building an integrated society, in Wetherell, M, Lafleche, M and Berkeley, R (eds) *Identity, Ethnic Diversity and Community Cohesion.* London: Sage, pp24–33.

Kane, M and Zink, R (2004) Package adventure tours: markers in serious leisure careers, *Leisure Studies,* 23/4: 329–345.

Keogh, D and Haltzel, MH (1993) *Northern Ireland and the Politics of Reconciliation.* Cambridge: Cambridge University Press.

Keogh, V (2002) *Multicultural Sport: Sustaining a Level Playing Field.* Melbourne: Centre for Multicultural Youth Issues.

Keys, B (2006) *Globalizing Sport: National Rivalry and International Community in the 1930s.* London: Harvard University Press.

Kidd, W (2002) *Culture and Identity.* London: Palgrave.

Kinkema, KM and Harris, JC (1992) Sport and the mass media, *Exercise and Sport Science Reviews,* 20: 127–159.

Kirk D (2003) Sport, physical education and schools, in Houlihan, B (ed) *Sport and Society.* London: Sage.

Koppett, L (1994) *Sports Illusion, Sports Reality.* Urbana and Chicago: University of Illinois Press.

Lafayette, J (1996) Twelve to watch in 1996: Fox Sports' popularity soars with fans, *Electronic Media,* 22 January: 126 and 145.

Lange, KM, Nicholson, M and Hess, R (2007) A new breed apart? Work practices of Australian internet sports journalists, *Sport in Society,* 10/4: 662–679.

Lasch, C (1979) The degradation of sport, in Tomlinson, A (ed) (2007) *The Sport Studies Reader.* London: Routledge.

Lavoie, M (2000) Economics of sport, in Coakley, J and Dunning, E (eds) *Handbook of Sports Studies.* London: Sage.

Liecthy, M (2002) *Suitably Modern: Making Middle-Class Culture in a New Consumer Society,* 3rd edition. Princeton: Princeton University Press.

Lin, N (2001) *Social Capital. A Theory of Social Structure and Action.* Cambridge: Cambridge University Press.

Lines, G (2002) The sports stars in the media: the gendered construction and youthful consumption of sports personalities, in Sugden, J and Tomlinson, A (eds) *Power Games: A Critical Sociology of Sport.* London and New York: Routledge.

Loland, S (1995) Coubertin's ideology of Olympism from the perspective of the history of ideas, *Olympika: The International Journal of Olympic Studies,* 4: 49–78.

Long, J and Sanderson, I (2001) The social benefits of sport: where's the proof?, in Gratton, C and Henry, I (eds) *Sport in the City: the Role of Sport in Economic and Social Regeneration.* London: Routledge.

Lowes, MD (1997) Sports page: a case study in the manufacture of sports news for the daily press, *Sociology of Sport Journal,* 14: 143–159.

Loy, J and Booth, D (2000) Functionalism, sport and society, in Coakley, J and Dunning, E (eds) *Handbook of Sports Studies.* London: Sage.

Loy, J and Booth, D (2002) Functionalism, sport and society, in Coakley, J and Dunning, E (eds) *Handbook of Sports Studies.* London: Sage.

Lucas, JA (2009) *John Apostal Lucas: Teacher, Sport Historian, and One Who Lived His Life Earnestly. A Collection of Articles and Essays with an Autobiographical Sketch.* Lemont Berlin: Eifrig Publishing.

Luschen, G (1981) The system of sport – problems of methodology, conflict and social stratification, in Luschen, G and Sage, G (eds) *Handbook of Social Science of Sport.* IL: Stipes, Champaign.

Lyster, M (1997) *The Strange Adventures of the Dangerous Sports Club*. London: The Do-Not Press.

MacArthur, E (2002) *Taking on the World*. London: Penguin.

Macfarlane, R (2003) *Mountains of the Mind*. London: Granta.

MacGillivary, A (2006) *A Brief History of Globalisation: The Untold Story of Our Incredible Shrinking Planet*. London: Robinson Publishing.

Machiavelli, N (trans Donno, D, 1981) *The Prince*. Bantam.

MacLaren, A (1895) *Physical Education*. Oxford.

Maguire, J (1988) The commercialization of elite English basketball 1972–1988 – a figurational perspective, *International Review for the Sociology of* Sport, 23(4): 305–323.

Maguire, J (1993a) Bodies, sportcultures and societies: a critical review of some theories in the sociology of sport, *International Review for the Sociology of Sport*, 28(1): 33–52.

Maguire, J (1993b) Globalisation, sport and national identities: The Empire Strikes Back?, *Society and Leisure*, 16(2).

Maguire, J (1995) Common ground? Links between sports history, sports geography and the sociology of sport, *Sporting Traditions, The Journal of the Australian Society for Sports History*, 12(1): 3–25.

Maguire, J (1996) Far pavilions? Cricket migrants, foreign sojourns and contested identities, *International Review for the Sociology of Sport*, 31(1): 1–23.

Maguire, J (1999) *Global Sport*. Cambridge: Polity Press.

Maguire, J (2000) Sport and globalization, in Coakley, J and Dunning, E (eds) *Handbook of Sports Studies*. Sage, London.

Maguire, J (2005) Power and global sport: zones of prestige, emulation and resistance. London: Routledge.

Maguire, J, Jarvie, G, Mansfield, L and Bradley, J (2002) *Sport Worlds: A Sociological Perspective*. Leeds: Human Kinetics.

Maguire, JS (2002) Body lessons: fitness publishing and the cultural production of the fitness consumer, *International Review for the Sociology of Sport*, 37(3/4): 449–464.

Marcuse, H (1964) *One Dimensional Man*. London: Routledge.

Markula, P (ed) (2009) *Olympic Women and the Media: International Perspectives*. Basingstoke and New York: Palgrave Macmillan.

Marles, V (1984) The public and sport, in *BBC Broadcast Research Findings*. London: BBC.

Marqusee, M (2000) Sports as apocalypse: why global sport is in crisis, *Frontline*, 17, Issue 16 (web publication: **www.frontlineonnet.com**).

Mason, T (1988) *Sport in Britain*. Cambridge: Cambridge University Press.

Maxwell, R (2009) Caribbean and South Asian identification with British society: the importance of perceived discrimination, *Ethnic and Racial Studies*, 32(8): 1449–1469.

McIntosh, PC, Dixon, JG, Munrow, AD and Willetts, RF (1957) *Landmarks in the History of Physical Education*. London: Routledge and Kegan Paul.

Messner, MA, Dunbar, M and Hunt, D (2000) The televised sports manhood formula, *Journal of Sport and Social Issues*, 24: 380–394.

Miles, S (2001) *Social Theory in the Real World*. London: Sage.

Miller, D (1995a) Consumption as the vanguard of history: a polemic by way of introduction, in Miller, D (ed) *Acknowledging Consumption: A Review of New Studies*. London: Routledge.

Miller, D (ed) (1995b) *Acknowledging Consumption: A Review of New Studies*. London: Routledge.

Miller, D (2003) *Athens to Athens: The Official History of the Olympic Games and the IOC, 1894–2004*. Edinburgh: Mainstream.

Miller, T, Lawrence, G, McKay, J and Rowe, D (2001) Global sport media, in Tomlinson, A (ed) (2007) *The Sport Studies Reader*. London: Routledge.

Morgan, WJ (1994) *Leftist Theories of Sport: A Critique and Reconstruction*. Chicago: University of Illinois Press.

Mortlock, C (1978) *Adventure Education*. Milnthorpe: privately published.

Mortlock, C (1984) *The Adventure Alternative*. Milnthorpe: Cicerone Press.

Mortlock, C (2001) *Beyond Adventure*. Milnthorpe: Cicerone Press.

Murray, B (1992) Berlin in 1936: old and new work on the Nazi Olympics, *The International Journal of the History of Sport*, 9(1): 29–49.

Nixon, H and Frey, J (1996) *A Sociology of Sport*. Albany: Wadsworth.

Ohmae, K (1990) *The Borderless World: Power and Strategy in the Industrial Economy*. London: Collins.

Olympic Charter, **www.olympics.org**

Penney, D (2000) Physical education: in what and whose interests? in Jones, R and Armour, K (eds) *Sociology of Sport: Theory and Practice*. Edinburgh: Pearson Education, pp58–66.

Penney, D (ed) (2002) *Gender and Physical Education: Contemporary Issues and Future Directions*. London: Routledge

Penney, D and Evans, J (2002) Talking gender, in Penney, D (ed) *Gender and Physical Education: Contemporary Issues and Future Directions*. London: Routledge.

Phillips, T (2005) After 7/7: sleepwalking back to segregation, 22 September, http://www.cre.gov.uk.

Preston, R (1997) *Political and Cultural Identity: Citizens and Nations in a Global Era*. London: Sage.

Price, T (1978) Adventure by numbers, in Wilson, K (ed) *The Games Climbers Play*. London: Diadem.

Putnam, R (2000) *Bowling Alone: the Collapse and Revival of American Community*. London: Simon and Schuster.

Putnam, R (2007) *E pluribus unum*: diversity and community in the twenty-first century. The 2006 Johan Skytte Prize Lecture, *Scandinavian Political Studies*, 30(2): 137–174.

Putnam, RD (1993) *Making Democracy Work. Civic Traditions in Modern Italy*. Princeton: Princeton University Press.

Real, MR (1998) MediaSport: technology and the commodification of postmodern sport, in Wenner, LA (ed) *MediaSport*. London and New York: Routledge.

Redhead, S (2007) Those absent from the stadium are always right: accelerated culture, sport media, and theory at the speed of light, *Journal of Sport and Social Issues*, 31/3: 226–241.

Rees, R and Miracle, A (2000) Education and sport, in Coakley, J and Dunning, E (eds) *Handbook of Sports Studies*. London: Sage.

Rich, E (2001) Strong words, tough minds, trained bodies: a life history narrative analysis of female student teachers of physical education. Unpublished PhD thesis, Loughborough University.

Riffenburgh, B (1993) *The Myth of the Explorer: The Press, Sensationalism and Geographical Discovery.* London: Belhaven.

Rigaur, B (2000) Marxist theories, in Coakley, J and Dunning, E (eds) *Handbook of Sports Studies.* London: Sage.

Rinehart, R and Sydnor, S (eds) (2003) *To the Extreme: Alternative Sports Inside and Out.* Albany: SUNY Press.

Robertson, R (1992) *Globalisation: Social Theory and Global Culture.* London: Sage.

Roche, M (2000) *Mega-events and Modernity: Olympics and Expos in the Growth of Global Culture.* London: Routledge.

Rogaly, B and Taylor, B (2007) Welcome to 'Monkey Island': identity and community in three Norwich housing estates, in Wetherell, M, Lafleche, M and Berkeley, R (eds) *Ethnic Diversity and Community Cohesion.* London: Sage.

Rojek, C (2000) *Leisure and Culture.* Basingstoke: Macmillan.

Rojek, C (2001) *Celebrity.* London: Reaktion Books.

Rowe, D (1996) The global love-match: sport and television, *Media Culture and Society*, 18: 565–82.

Rowe, D (2003) *Sport, Culture and the Media: The Unholy Trinity.* Milton Keynes: Open University Press.

Rowe, D (2004a) *Sport, Culture and the Media.* 2nd edition. Maidenhead: Open University Press.

Rowe, D (ed) (2004b) *Critical Readings: Sport, Culture and the Media.* Maidenhead: Open University Press.

Rowe, D and Lawrence, G (1986) Saluting the state: nationalism and the Olympics, in Lawrence, G and Rowe, D (eds) *Power Play: Essays in the Sociology of Australian Sport.* Sydney: Hale and Iremonger.

Rowe, D and Stevenson, D (2006) Sidney 2000: sociality and spatiality in global media events, in Tomlinson, A and Young, C (eds) *National Identity and Global Sports Events.* New York: State University of New York Press.

Sadd, D (2009) *London's Elusive Social Legacy: Leveraging Social, Cultural & Health Benefits from London 2012.* Conference. Christ Church University Canterbury: SPEAR.

Sage, G (1990) *Power and Ideology in American Sport: A Critical Perspective.* Champaign, IL: Human Kinetics Books.

Schaffer, K and Smith, S (2000) *The Olympics at the Millennium: Power, Politics and the Games.* New Brunswick, NJ: Rutgers University Press.

Scheibner, GB and Morrison, TG (2009) Attitudes towards Polish immigrants to the Republic of Ireland: an integrated threat analysis, *Ethnic and Racial Studies*, 32(2): 1431–1448.

Scraton, S (1998) *Shaping Up to Womanhood: Gender and Girls' Physical Education.* London: Open University Press.

Scraton, S and Flintoff, A (2002) Sport feminism: the contribution of feminist thought to our understandings of gender and sport, in Scraton, S and Flintoff, A (eds) *Gender and Sports: A Reader.* London: Routledge.

Scruton, J (1998) *Stoke Mandeville: Road to the Paralympics.* Aylesbury: Peterhouse Press.

Shifflette, B and Revelle, R (1994) Gender equity in sports media coverage: a review of the NCAA News, *Journal of Sport and Social Issues*, 18/2: 144–150.

Shilling, C (2003) *The Body and Social Theory*. London: Sage.

Silk, M, Slack, T and Amis, J (2004) Bread, butter and gravy: an institutional approach to televised sport production, in Rowe, D (ed) *Critical Readings: Sport, Culture and the Media*. Maidenhead: Open University Press.

Simmel, G (1911/1997) The adventure/the alpine journey, in Frisby, D and Featherstone, M (eds) (1997) *Simmel on Culture*. London: Sage.

Simpson, V and Jennings, A (1992) *The Lords of the Rings: Power, Money and Drugs in the Modern Olympics*. London: Simon and Schuster.

Smart, B (2003) *Economy, Culture and Society*. Maidenhead: Open University Press.

Smart, B (2005) *The Sport Star: Modern Sport and the Cultural Economy of Sporting Celebrity*. London: Sage.

Smart, B (2007) Not playing around: global capitalism, modern sport and consumer culture, *Global Networks: A Journal of Transnational Affairs*, 7/2: 113–134.

Smith, A (1995) *Nations and Nationalism in a Global Era*. Cambridge: Polity Press.

Smith, GJ and Valeriote, TA (1983) Ethics in sport journalism, *Arena Review* 7/2: 7–14.

Smith, ML (2004) *Olympics in Athens 1896. The Invention of the Modern Olympic Games*. London: Profile Books.

Smith, RA (2001) *Play-by-Play: Radio, Television and Big-Time College Sport*. Baltimore, MD: The Johns Hopkins University Press.

Spaaij, R (2009) Sport as a vehicle for social mobility and regulation of disadvantaged urban youth: lessons from Rotterdam, *International Review for the Sociology of Sport*, 44(2–3): 247–264.

Sparks, C (2000) Introduction: the panic over tabloid news, in Sparks, C and Tulloch, J (eds) *Tabloid Tales: Global Debates Over Media Standards*. Oxford: Rowman and Littlefield.

Speth, J (2008) *Bridge at the Edge of the World: Capitalism, the Environment, and Crossing from Crisis to Sustainability*. Yale: Yale University Press.

Sport England (2005) *The Active People Survey 2005/6*. London: Sport England.

Sport England (2007) *The Economic Importance of Sport in England 1985–2005: Summary Report*, Sports Industry Research Centre: Sheffield Hallam University.

Sport Northern Ireland (2007) *Community Sport Programme: End of Year Report Year 2 (of 3) 2006/7*. Belfast: Sport Northern Ireland.

Sports Council (Great Britain) (1993) *Sport for People with Disabilities: Guidelines for Governing Bodies of Sport*. London: Sports Council.

Stempel, C (2006) Televised sport, masculinist moral capital, and support for the US invasion of Iraq, *Journal of Sport and Social Issues*, 30/1: 79–106.

Stoddart, B (1997) Convergence: sport on the information superhighway, *Journal of Sport and Social Issues*, 21/1: 93–102.

Stoddart, B (2006) Sport, television, interpretation and practice reconsidered: televised golf and analytical orthodoxies, *Sport in Society*, 9/5: 865–878.

Storey, J (1993) *An Introductory Guide to Cultural Theory and Popular Culture.* London: Harvester Wheatsheaf.

Strinati, D (1995) *An Introduction to Theories of Popular Culture.* London: Routledge.

Struna, NL (2000) Social history and sport, in Coakley, J and Dunning, E (eds) *Handbook of Sports Studies.* London: Sage.

Sugden, J (2002) Network football, in Sugden, J and Tomlinson, A (eds) *Power Games: A Critical Sociology of Sport.* London: Routledge.

Sugden, J and Bairner, A (1993) *Sport, Sectarianism and Society in a Divided Ireland.* London, Leicester University Press.

Sugden, J and Tomlinson, A (1998) *FIFA and the Contest for World Football: Who Rules the People's Game?* Cambridge: Polity Press.

Sugden, J and Tomlinson, A (2000) Theorizing sport, social class and status, in Coakley, J and Dunning, E (eds) *Handbook of Sports Studies.* London: Sage.

Sugden, J and Tomlinson, A (eds) (2002) *Power Games: A Critical Sociology of Sport.* London: Routledge.

Sulkunen, P (1997) Introduction: the new consumer society – rethinking the social bond, in Sulkunen, P, Holmwod, J, Radner, H and Schulze, G (eds) *Constructing the New Consumer Society.* London: Macmillan.

Sullivan, DB (1991) Commentary and viewer perception of player hostility: adding punch to televised sport, *Journal of Broadcasting and Electronic Media,* 35/4: 487–504.

Swarbrooke, J, Beard, C, Leckie, S, and Pomfret, G (2003) *Adventure Tourism: The New Frontier.* Oxford: Butterworth-Heinemann.

Tam, H (2007) The case for progressive solidarity, in Wetherell, M, Lafleche, M and Berkeley, R (eds) *Identity, Ethnic Diversity and Community Cohesion.* London: Sage, pp17–23.

Tejada-Flores, L (1978) The games climbers play, in Wilson, K (ed) *The Games Climbers Play.* London: Diadem.

Telander, R (1984) The written word: player–press relationships in American sports, *Sociology of Sport Journal,* 1: 3–14.

The Gambling Act Impact Regulatory Assessment (2005) **www.culture.gov.uk/images/publications/ GamblingAct2005RIA210405.pdf**

Thomas, N (2004) Sport and disability, in Houlihan, B (ed) *Sport and Society.* London: Sage.

Thwaites, T, Davis, L and Mules, W (1994) *Tools for Cultural Studies: An Introduction.* Melbourne: Macmillan.

Tomlinson, A (1989) Representation, ideology and the Olympic Games: a reading of the opening and closing ceremonies of the 1984 Los Angeles Olympic Games, in Jackson, R (ed) *The Olympic Movement and the Mass Media: Past, Present and Future Issues.* Calgary: Hurford Enterprises.

Tomlinson, A (2004) *The Sports Studies Reader.* London: Routledge.

Tomlinson, A and Young, C (2006) Culture, politics, and spectacle in the global sports event: an introduction, in Tomlinson, A and Young, C (eds) *National Identity and Global Sports Events.* New York: State University of New York Press.

Toohey, K and Veal, AJ (2000) *The Olympic Games: A Social Science Perspective.* Oxford: Oxford University Press.

Trujillo, N (1995) Machines, missiles and men: images of the male body on ABC's Monday Night Football, *Sociology of Sport Journal*, 12: 403–423.

Turner, BS (1984) *The Body and Society.* Oxford: Basil Blackwell.

UK Sport (2006) *The Economic Impact of Six Major Sports Events Supported by the World Class Events Programme in 2005 and 2006: Overview of Findings.* UK Sport/Sheffield Hallam University.

UK Sport (2009) Disability Equality Scheme 2007–2009. [Consulted 15/11/09] **www.uksport.gov.uk/pages/current_equity_programmes**.

Varley, P (2006) Confecting adventure and playing with meaning: the adventure commodification continuum, *Journal of Sport and Tourism*, 11(2): 173–194.

Veblen, T (1953) *The Theory of the Leisure Class.* New York: Mentor.

Wagner, P (1994) *A Sociology of Modernity: Liberty and Discipline.* London: Routledge.

Walford, G (1998) Education and private schools, in Giddens, A (ed) *Sociology: Introductory Readings.* Cambridge: Polity Press, pp329–336.

Wallerstein, I (2004) *World-Systems Analysis: An Introduction.* New York: Duke University Press.

Warde, A (2002) Setting the scene: changing conceptions of consumption, in Miles, S, Anderson, A and Meethan, K (eds) *The Changing Consumer: Markets and Meanings.* London: Routledge.

Weed, M and Ladkin, A (2009) *Tourism Flows, Sport, Health and Community Well-being* (a report on the ESRC regional research to date). Leveraging Social, Cultural & Health Benefits from London 2012 Conference. SPEAR Christ Church University Canterbury.

Wenner, LA (1989) Media, sports, and society: the research agenda, in Wenner, LA (ed) *Media, Sports, and Society.* London: Sage.

Wenner, LA (1994) The dream team, communicative dirt, and the marketing of synergy: USA basketball and cross-merchandising in television commercials, *Journal of Sport and Social Issues*, 18/1: 27–47.

Wenner, LA (1998) Playing the MediaSport game, in Wenner LA (ed) *MediaSport.* London: Routledge.

Wenner, LA and Gantz, W (1989) The audience experience with sports on television, in Wenner, LA (ed) *Media, Sports, and Society.* London: Sage.

Wetherell, M (2007) Community cohesion and identity dynamics: dilemmas and challenges, in Wetherell, M, Lafleche, M and Berkeley, R (eds) *Identity, Ethnic Diversity and Community Cohesion.* London: Sage.

Whannel, G (1986) 'The unholy alliance': notes on television and the re-making of British Sport 1965–1985, *Leisure Studies*, 5/1: 22–37.

Whannel, G (1992) *Fields in Vision: Television Sport and Cultural Transformation.* London: Routledge.

Whannel, G (1998) Reading the sports media audience, in Wenner, LA (ed) *MediaSport.* London and New York: Routledge.

Whannel, G (2000) Sport and the media, in Coakley, J and Dunning, E (eds) *Handbook of Sports Studies.* London: Sage.

Whannel, G (2001) Punishment, redemption and celebration in the popular press: the case of David Beckham, in Andrews, D and Jackson, S (eds) *Sport Stars*. London: Routledge.

Whannel, G (2002) *Media Sport Stars: Masculinities and Moralities*. London: Routledge.

Wheaton, B (ed) (2004) *Understanding Lifestyle Sports*. London: Routledge.

Whitson, D (1998) Circuits of promotion: media, marketing and the globalization of sport, in Wenner, LA (ed) *Media, Sports, and Society*. London: Sage.

Willis, P (1998) Dossing, blagging and wagging: countercultural groups in the school environment, in Giddens, A (ed) *Sociology: Introductory Readings*. Cambridge: Polity Press, pp337–343.

Wilson, T (2002) The paradox of social class and sports involvement, *International Review for the Sociology of Sport*, 37(1): 5–16.

Women's Sports and Fitness Foundation (2009), **www.wsff.org.uk/**

Wright Mills, C (2002) *The Sociological Imagination*. Harmondsworth: Penguin.

Wu, P (2007) Co-operation, confrontation and conflict: an investigation of the relationship between the news media and sports administrative organisations in contemporary China, unpublished PhD thesis, accessible in the library at De Montfort University.

Young, DC (1996) *The Modern Olympics: A Struggle for Revival*. Baltimore: Johns Hopkins University Press.

Young, DC (2004) *A Brief History of the Olympic Games*. Malden, MA: Blackwell Publishers.

Websites

www.adventure.co.nz

www.bbc.co.uk/blogs/sporteditors

www.britsurf.co.uk

www.cabinetoffice.gov.uk/media/cabinetoffice/strategy/assets/game_plan_report.pdf

www.canterbury.ac.uk/News

www.ccpr.org.uk

www.culture.gov.uk

www.culture.gov.uk/images/publications/2012LegacyActionPlan.pdf

www.culture.gov.uk/images/publications/GamblingAct2005RIA210405.pdf

www.diversity.toolkit.org.uk

www.efds.net

www.eis2win.co.uk

www.fdso.co.uk

www.fifa.com/aboutfifa/federation/mission.html

www.fivb.org

www.fivb.org press release

www.footballeconomy.com/stats

www.frontlineonnet.com

www.homeoffice.gov.uk

www.iht.com/articles/1998/11/30/volley.t.php?page=1

www.irr.org.uk/pdf/IRR_Briefing No.2
www.jagged-globe.co.uk
www.london2012.com
www.london2012.com/en/ourvision
www.london2012.com/plans/culture/legacy
www.london2012.org
www.londonsportsforum.org.uk
www.nbcsports.com/olympics
www.nikebiz.com/responsibility
www.olympic.org
www.olympics.org.uk
www.olympic.org/uk/index_uk.asp
www.perseus.tufts.edu/olympics
www.sportdevelopment.org.uk/html/ethnicity2000
www.sportengland.org
www.sportengland.org/sport_england_the_magazine__annual_review_2005
www.sportni.net
www.sportscotland.org.uk
www.sports-council-wales.org.uk
www.statistics.gov.uk
www.thebsg.eu
www.uknetrunner.co.uk
www.uksport.gov.uk
www.uksport.gov.uk/pages/current_equity_programmes
www.uksport.gov.uk/pages/drug_free_sport
www.wsff.org.uk/about

Index

05542061